Study Guide
Psychology
Fifth Edition

LIBRARY
NORTHBROOK COLLEGE
BROADWATER ROAD
WORTHING
WEST SUSSEX
BN14 8HJ
TEL: 01903 606451

KT-471-444

£12.95

C616132

Study Guide

GLEITMAN, FRIDLUND, REISBERG
Psychology
Fifth Edition

JOHN JONIDES
UNIVERSITY OF MICHIGAN

PAUL ROZIN
UNIVERSITY OF PENNSYLVANIA

W · W · NORTON & COMPANY · NEW YORK · LONDON

NORTHBROOK COLLEGE DESIGN + TECHNOLOGY		
616132	Class No 150	
MACAULAY	26 Aug 1999	
Location.	WE	

Copyright © 1999, 1995, 1991, 1986, 1981 by W. W. Norton & Company, Inc.

All rights reserved
Printed in the United States of America

Cover illustrations: (*Left*) Michelangelo Buonarroti, *David*, detail of head in profile. Accademia, Florence, Italy. Photograph courtesy Scala/Art Resource, NY. (*Right*) Michelangelo Buonarroti, *Studies for the Libyan Sybil* (copy). Uffizi Gallery, Florence, Italy.

Permission and credits appear on page 285, which constitutes an extension of the copyright page.

ISBN 0-393-97366-2 (pbk.)

W. W. Norton & Company, Inc., 500 Fifth Avenue, New York, NY 10110
   http://www.wwnorton.com

W. W. Norton & Company Ltd., 10 Coptic Street, London WC1A 1PU

1 2 3 4 5 6 7 8 9 0

CONTENTS

ACKNOWLEDGMENTS

The authors would like to thank Caroline Arnold, Jason Fabozzi, Elizabeth Gross, Georgia Larounis, Jennifer Lerner, Laura Lowery, Maureen Markwith, Linda Millman, Deborah Reyher, Nathan Witthoft, and Barbara Zeeff for their contributions and valuable suggestions.

In the course of developing the sections entitled "Investigating Psychological Phenomena" for each chapter, we have had occasion to seek the advice of colleagues and students who have particular expertise in the areas in question. We would like to acknowledge the help of Lyn Abramson, Henry Gleitman, Aaron Katcher, Charles G. Morris, Lorraine Nadelman, Harriet Oster, Christopher Peterson, Martin E. P. Seligman, W. John Smith, Marjorie Speers, and Edward Stricker. We also thank Walter Love and Jeannie Morrow for special assistance in field testing a number of the activities that we have included.

Finally, we thank Cathy Wick for her encouragement and advice throughout the development of the text in prior editions, and April Lange, the editor for this edition, for her good judgment, help, and encouragement at all stages. We also thank Christa Grenawalt for help with page references and Gale Miller, our copyeditor.

The authors of this guide are listed in alphabetical order on the title page.

TO THE STUDENT

This study guide is designed to help you to understand and apply the material presented in *Psychology*, Fifth Edition, by Henry Gleitman, Alan Fridlund, and Daniel Reisberg. Each chapter in the study guide corresponds to one in the textbook. There are four sections in each study guide chapter: Learning Objectives, Programmed Exercises, Self Test, and Investigating Psychological Phenomena. The first three sections will help you determine the essential ideas of the chapter, as well as give you experience with possible test questions. The fourth section, Investigating Psychological Phenomena, allows you to extend your knowledge of some issues raised in the text. This section will also give you a feeling for how the data used by psychologists are collected, and how theories are tested in psychology. Let us briefly review the function of each of these sections.

LEARNING OBJECTIVES

We have provided an outline of the key issues discussed in each chapter. Each entry in the outline refers to a basic fact, theory, or relationship that you should have learned from the chapter. These entries are listed in order of occurrence in the chapter and are arranged under the same headings used in the chapter. It may be useful to read the learning objectives before reading the chapter, as well as after. They will help to orient you to the major issues, or the "big picture," of the chapter.

PROGRAMMED EXERCISES

For each chapter of the text, we have provided fill-in-the-blank questions. These questions test your basic knowledge of the key words and concepts of the chapter. These questions are very straightforward and can be looked up and verified in the text. So that you will know whether you are correct, the answer has been provided on the right side of the page. Be sure to cover that side of the page with your hand or a piece of paper as you do the exercises.

To facilitate locating the answers in the text, the programmed exercises are also arranged under the major headings of the textbook, and they follow the order of presentation in the text. This allows you to see which fact or theory pertains to which major point of the chapter.

SELF TEST

For each chapter in the text, we have prepared a self test composed of multiple-choice questions. They also follow the order of the text. In general, these questions are more difficult than the fill-ins, though both types of questions cover the range of materials presented in the text. The multiple choices sometimes highlight subtle distinctions, ask for some amount of integration, or test your ability to apply some of the material in the text.

Since multiple-choice questions are commonly used in examinations, and since they can also be very instructive, we will spend some time in this section discussing how to answer them. We will also describe and illustrate some different types of multiple-choice questions used in this study guide.

First, some basic strategies. Most multiple-choice questions on examinations, and in this study guide, have four or five choices. On most examinations there is a penalty of $-1/3$ point for wrong answers of four-choice questions, and $-1/4$ point for wrong answers on five-choice questions. This would mean that wild guessing should net a score of zero. But if you can eliminate even one choice, it pays to guess among the remaining alternatives.

Read each question carefully. Try to understand the *point* of the question. Read through the alternatives. The answer may be obvious to you. If not, try to eliminate some of the choices. You may be able to eliminate choices on the following grounds:

1. The choice is inherently inconsistent, illogical, or actual nonsense (e.g., word salad: a bunch of usually relevant terms combined in a meaningless way).

2. The choice makes sense and may even be true, but it is not an *answer* to the question.

3. On the basis of your knowledge, the choice is just the wrong answer to the question.

Get used to sorting out sense from nonsense and relevant from irrelevant answers. These skills will stand you in good stead in many of your activities outside of this course. Work with the remaining choices (if more than one choice remains), and do the best you can to determine the best fit between the question and the answer.

We will illustrate a number of different types of multiple-choice questions, all represented in this study guide. For each example we will indicate the correct answer and add comments on some of the incorrect choices.

Straight factual questions. Many multiple-choice questions simply ask for your knowledge of facts: names, definitions, and basic concepts.

1. The Prime Minister of Great Britain at the end of World War II was:
   a. Neville Chamberlain
   b. Winston Churchill
   c. Harold Wilson
   d. Sir D. Winter
   e. Anthony Eden

Comment: This is a very straightforward question. You know it or you don't. The answer is *b*, Winston Churchill. The other names were selected to make the question somewhat difficult: Three of the other choices were prime ministers of Great Britain at the beginning or after the war, and one, Sir D. Winter, is a fictitious name.

2. The best way to describe inflation is:
    a. increase in the gross national product not accompanied by increased unemployment
    b. a general increase in prices
    c. a decrease in the money supply
    d. a decrease in the value of the monetary system, when associated with a gross national product
    e. another form of recession

Comment: This question is more difficult than 1. This is in part because the choices are more difficult. The correct answer is *b*. Answers *a*, *c*, and *e* are just wrong. Though *a* is consistent with inflation, it does not define it. Item *d* is inherently wrong; that is, it is sort of nonsense. What does it mean to decrease the value of the monetary *system* as opposed to money? And everything is associated with some gross national product. Keep your eyes open for nonsense. There is a lot of it in the world.

Evaluating evidence for a theory. In this type of question you are asked to judge whether particular results (real or hypothetical) support a particular theory (or which theory would be supported or opposed by a particular result). The theory and/or results may have been presented in the text, or they may be introduced in the question. The question tests both your knowledge of the materials, and your progress in understanding how to evaluate evidence. This type of question is often formulated in the negative—"Which of the following would be evidence against theory X?"—simply because it is usually easier to come up with results supporting major theories than results opposing them. We will assume, for the next sample question, that you have read in some text or other that Yentzel claimed that the crime rate increases as population mass and density increase. (Yentzel is a fictitious name.)

3. Which of the following would be evidence against Yentzel's theory? (Note: We assume that New York is larger than Philadelphia, which is larger than Tucson.)
    a. Philadelphia has a crime rate higher than Tucson.
    b. A few cities with increasing population also have increasing crime rates.
    c. A few cities with decreasing population have an increase in crime rate.
    d. Philadelphia has a lower crime rate than New York.
    e. The ratio of murder to robberies is lower in New York than in Tucson.

Comment: The correct answer is *c*, because this result is opposite to what would be predicted by Yentzel's theory. Answers *a*, *b*, and *c* are supporting evidence for the theory. Answer *e* is irrelevant: The theory says nothing about the types of crime, and *e* says nothing about the overall crime rate. (Note another clue to the right answer: *b* and *c* are opposites, so it is likely that one is evidence against the theory. However, clever exam writers know about this and sometimes put in opposites that are irrelevant to the question, to keep you on your toes.)

Extending a principle or theory to a new situation. This type of question tests your understanding of a principle, theory, or concept by asking you to apply it to a situation other than those presented in the text.

4. If the saying "a stitch in time saves nine" were applied to medicine, one would recommend:
    a. reducing the amount of sewing in surgery
    b. increasing the cost of medical insurance
    c. increasing the frequency of checkups
    d. increasing the number of physicians
    e. making prescription drugs available over the counter

Comments: The correct answer is *c*. To answer the question, one must understand the saying and translate it into medical terms. This translation would be something like: Medical precautions can lead to avoidance of major illnesses. Alternative *a* is irrelevant to the *real* meaning of the saying and simply follows the *literal* meaning. Answer *b* would not lead, in any direct way, to avoidance of illness. But *b* is a sort of correct answer, since one might assume that increasing the cost of medical insurance would lead to increased coverage. The answer says increasing the cost, not the amount of insurance. Answer *c* relates directly to the saying: More checkups should lead to early discovery of illnesses that might prove harmful if allowed to develop. While *d* might well cut down the rate of illnesses, it is not a direct way of arriving at prevention. Lastly, *e* is irrelevant to the issue raised in the saying.

Relating different ideas or facts, or integrating materials. This type of question often involves materials from different sections of a chapter, or perhaps from different chapters (we have refrained from the latter, since we don't know the order in which you will be reading the chapters in the book).

5. The President of the United States is related to the electoral college as a U.S. Senator is related to:*
    a. his or her own college faculty
    b. the voters of his or her state
    c. the members of the House of Representatives
    d. the state of his or her electors
    e. the state of his or her voters

Comment: The correct answer is *b*. The electoral college is the group of people who actually elect the president. The voters of a senator's state are the people who elect the senator. Item *a* is totally wrong and simply a play on the word college. Item *c* is factually wrong. Item *d* is wrong and doesn't make too much sense, and item *e* is a reversal of the correct answer and has no relation to the question.

INVESTIGATING PSYCHOLOGICAL PHENOMENA

For each chapter of the text, we have presented one or two activities or experiments. These activities build upon concepts or theories presented in the chapter and extend and deepen your knowledge and understanding of these concepts or theories.

---

*This type of relation is often stated as "President of the U.S.: electoral college::U.S. Senator: _____"

The activities give you an opportunity to understand something about the progress of psychology as a science. While the text emphasizes our current understanding of psychology, the activities emphasize the process through which we arrive at this understanding. How is the theory tested? How do psychologists get data to describe basic relations or test theories? How do they analyze the data? We hope to give you a feeling for how progress is made, while at the same time indicating the problems and difficulties associated with the serious study of something as complex as the human mind.

We have attempted to provide you with a variety of activities. Some emphasize the generation or testing of theories, others data collection or analysis. We have tried to cover the major methods of data collection used by psychologists: Among all the activities are included examples of the experiment, the questionnaire, direct observation, and the interview. In many cases we provide data from studies we have done with introductory psychology students as a base for comparison with the data you collect. In each activity in which you collect data, we guide you through some analysis of the data and get you to try to interpret the data and relate it to issues raised in the text. If your instructor wishes to include the activities as part of the course, he or she may ask you to tear out the report (data) sheet pages, and hand them in. These sheets are duplicated at the end of the book in Appendix 3. Otherwise, you may consider these activities as a less formal extension of your education in psychology.

We have tried out all of these activities on undergraduate students like yourselves. We have only included studies that work out for the great majority of students. Of course, with people as variable as they are, all the studies that you do on one of a few students will not show the same results. But we expect that most of you will get most of the predicted results.

Many of the most important phenomena in psychology cannot be included in these activities because they must be measured under controlled conditions, which you could not easily arrange. Some involve expensive equipment, like timers that can time thousandths of a second, or panels of lights and switches. Some important relations are not striking enough to be seen in one or a few participants. We have tried to find, for each chapter, at least one activity that can be appreciated within the limits that you will be working under. We require no equipment other than pencil, paper, some sort of second indicator (stopwatch, digital watch with second indicator, or a watch with a second hand), and materials presented within this study guide. We have limited the time demands on you for any activity to less than one hour. In all but a few cases, we have limited the number of participants to a very few. At the beginning of each activity, we indicate the equipment involved and the time demands it will make on you and the participants.

These activities are designed to be both educational and entertaining. We hope that you find that they meet these goals.

Study Guide
Psychology
Fifth Edition

CHAPTER 1

Introduction

Learning Objectives

THE SCOPE OF PSYCHOLOGY

1. What is psychology?

Electrically triggered images
2. What do experiments on electrical stimulation of the brain tell us about the relationship between psychology and physiology?

Ambiguous sights and sounds
3. What determines the interpretation of an ambiguous stimulus?

The perceptual world of infants
4. How does the study of infants suggest that some abilities may be innate?

Displays and the evolution of communication
5. How is social interaction in animals mediated by displays? How do displays differ from one animal to another? Give examples.

Complex social behavior in humans
6. How are humans more complex in their social behavior than other animals?

A SCIENCE OF MANY FACES

7. Discuss the range of phenomena studied by psychologists.

Dreams as mental experiences
8. How are private mental experiences, like dreams, studied by psychologists?
9 What does anecdotal evidence tell us about the makeup of dream content?

Dreams as behavior
10. What behaviors are indicative of dreams? How are rapid eye movements related to dreaming?
11. How does the EEG help us to study dreaming?

Dreams as cognition
12. What is meant by "cognition" and how is it related to dreaming?
13. What factors make for better dream recall?

Dreams and natural selection
14. Define the comparative approach and give an example of how it might apply to a behavior characteristic of dreaming.

Dreams and social behavior
15. How are dreams social?

Dreams and culture
16. How are dreams treated differently by different cultures?

Dreams and internal conflict
17. Understand the elements of Freud's theory of dreams.

Dreams and human development
18. Trace the development of the concept of a "dream" in children. How do children think of dreams?

Dreams and individual differences
19. What evidence tells us that differences in personalities are reflected in dreams?

Perspectives on psychology
20. What fields have contributed to the development of psychology? What are psychology's approaches to the study of the individual?

THE TASK OF PSYCHOLOGY

21. What is, and what is not, the main purpose of psychology? How does it contrast with literature?

Programmed Exercises

THE SCOPE OF PSYCHOLOGY

1. Psychology involves not only the study of the mind, but also the study of _____.   behavior

2. Electrical stimulation of the brain sometimes results in reports of _____.   sensations

3. _____ is an important determinant of how we perceive an ambiguous figure.   Context

4. The study of perceptual skills in infants using the visual cliff shows us that some skills are _____ while others are _____.
   learned, innate (built-in)

5. In animals, social interactions depend largely on _____ forms of communication.
   innate

6. Many types of animal communication are based on signals called _____.
   displays

7. The behavior of panicky crowds is determined not only by each individual, but also by individuals' _____ interactions.
   social (group)

A SCIENCE OF MANY FACES

8. According to Aristotle, dreams are mental _____ of events that occurred during the dreamer's waking life.
   evocations

9. A waking experience is most likely to appear in a dream if the experience was highly _____.
   emotional

10. The stage of sleep that is characterized by dreaming and rapid movement of the eyes is termed _____ sleep.
    REM

11. An important tool to study dreaming is the _____, which measures brain activity.
    EEG or electroencephalogram

12. When different species of animals are surveyed to gain insights about evolutionary change in behavior, this is called the _____ approach.
    comparative

13. According to Freud, dreams represent the individual's inner _____ between inner urges and societal constraints.
    conflict

14. Children have a hard time distinguishing _____ from _____ events.
    subjective, objective

15. _____ people often report dreams that are far more bizarre than those of other people.
    Schizophrenic

THE TASK OF PSYCHOLOGY

16. Psychology, like other sciences, seeks _____ principles to explain its phenomena, rather than concentrating on individual events.
    general

Self Test

1. Psychology is the:
   a. science of the mind
   b. science of behavior
   c. both of the above
   d. none of the above

2. When the brain is stimulated electrically:
   a. visual experience may occur
   b. previous memories may be blocked
   c. new memories are blocked
   d. none of the above

3. If we are first shown a picture of a rat and then the ambiguous figure below, we will most likely see:

   a. the man
   b. the rat

4. The visual cliff results suggest that:
   a. perceptual skills are learned
   b. perceptual skills are innate
   c. perceptual skills could be innate
   d. none of the above

5. According to Aristotle, dreams:
   a. are outlets for creative energies
   b. are manifestations of physical discomfort during sleep
   c. are of telepathic origin
   d. are reoccurrences of events in the real world

6. Outside stimuli:
   a. always find their way into dreams
   b. never find their way into dreams
   c. sometimes find their way into dreams
   d. are all that dreams are made of

7. Dreams occur during:
   a. all types of sleep
   b. slow-wave sleep
   c. the end of the night only
   d. REM sleep

8. The comparative approach to the study of dreaming might involve:
   a. studying the EEG patterns of various animals while they are sleeping

c. the rat or the man, depending on other factors
d. neither the rat nor the man

b. studying the cycles of REM sleep in various animals
c. comparing humans and monkeys in how often they have slow-wave versus REM sleep during the night
d. all of the above

9. Culture:
   a. has influence only on dream content
   b. determines only how people interpret dreams
   c. influences both dream content and interpretation
   d. may or may not influence our dreams at all depending on the particular culture

10. In Freud's view, dreams:
    a. are a result of physical discomfort during sleep
    b. represent a compromise between biological urges and societal constraints
    c. serve as reminders of the events of the day
    d. pertain mostly to current events in real life

11. Young children think of dreams as:
    a. physical objects
    b. a special reality sent from outside
    c. purely subjective experiences
    d. both a and b

12. The dreams of schizophrenic individuals are often:
    a. more sedate than those of others
    b. more exciting than those of others
    c. more bizarre than those of others
    d. not substantially different from those of others

13. Psychology consists of the study of
    a. mental experiences
    b. cognition
    c. social processes
    d. all of the above

Answer Key for Self Test

1. c p. 1	8. d p. 7
2. a p. 1	9. c p. 8
3. b p. 2	10. b p. 8
4. c p. 3	11. a p. 9
5. d p. 5	12. c p. 10
6. c p. 5	13. d p. 10
7. d p. 6	

Investigating Psychological Phenomena

THE CONSISTENCY OF DREAMS

Equipment: None
Number of participants: One, yourself
Time per participant: Ten or twenty minutes
Time for experimenter: Ten to twenty minutes

Although Chapter 1 is meant as a general introduction to psychology, it also provides us with an opportunity to illustrate how a particular phenomenon can be studied scientifically. The text outlines various approaches that have been used to study the phenomenon of dreams. These approaches entail different kinds of experimentation to study dreaming. Let us illustrate one kind of experimental approach that is useful. The technique used in this approach involves collecting ratings or categorizations of various stimuli. Here are the specifics:

One of the fundamental issues in dream research concerns the extent to which dreams represent the realization of basic problems, wishes, needs, or areas of concern to the dreamer. Freud's theory of dreams, for example, claims that the content of dreams is determined primarily by these factors. This suggests that the dreams of any one dreamer ought to be identifiably more similar to one another than the dreams of several dreamers. The question then arises: Is there consistency in a dreamer's dreams?

To test this idea, nine dream reports have been transcribed below. These reports were collected from three individuals, with three reports collected per individual. Your task is to select which three dreams were produced by each of the three individuals who were sampled.

There are several criteria that you could use to classify the dreams. One caution: You might think to use the language characteristics, that is, the use of certain consistent phrases, but don't be led astray by such a strategy. Language characteristics would not be appropriate criteria, since the purpose is to assess whether there is evidence of consistency in dream *content*. So you should concentrate on the content of the dreams as a basis for classification.

DREAM 1

A girl and I were being chased through a woods. We entered a log cabin. We were hiding when two people came in after us. One of the men who entered was tall with a thick dark beard. He looked like a typical backwoodsman. His assistant, by contrast, was short and fat. I decided to outsmart them. I crawled into a back room and began to make some noise. I stood on a box holding a milk bottle in my hand. The man entered, I hit him over the head several times, but the bottle did not break and he only laughed. The next thing I knew, the man was pointing a two-barrelled shotgun at me. I noticed that the ends of the barrels seemed magnified. He shot me in the lower right stomach. I looked down at the hole, saw the blood, and felt very weak. Then I was driving in my car by some railroad tracks. The wheels of my car became stuck on the tracks; my car would only move backward. I saw a train approaching rapidly and somehow managed to move off the tracks. I watched a huge train go past. My car continued moving in reverse. I had to keep the car moving perfectly straight, which was a very difficult task, and the train only missed me by inches. As I sped backward, I noticed a fence alongside the tracks, I saw a spot where the fence had been pushed down. I got out, picked up my car, and climbed over the fence. As I did this, I noticed two wounds, the one from the shotgun and a similar mark on the other side of my body, I began to look for a girl, not sure if I was looking for the one who had been with me in the cabin. I searched through a series of backyards, hiding behind bushes. I felt guilty about something. I found the girl I was looking for; she helped me attempt an escape. She led me back over to the fence, which was on a hill above the tracks. I started to climb the fence, which resembled a baseball backstop, but I was too weak from my wounds to be successful. The girl climbed on ahead and offered to hold my shirt as I climbed. Suddenly, two men on the railroad tracks below caught my eye. They were shooting at me with a bow and arrow. I told the girl not to worry; I thought I would be safe because the wind would deflect the arrows. Three or four of the arrows missed, but I was finally hit on my left front pocket. Luckily, the arrow had pierced my wallet instead of going into my leg. (In real life I keep my wallet in another pocket.)

DREAM 2

New York was being attacked by Germans. My mother told me not to worry. She told me that the last time the Germans attacked, only three persons who were in a cemetery had been killed. I went to warn my grandmother, who was at my uncle's basement apartment. My aunt was standing outside of the building. She also told me not to worry; she said she would wait outside for me. I walked down two flights of stairs. Strangely, the walls were made of dirt. I saw several of my relatives. Suddenly, I heard a loud noise. Water poured out of one of the walls. My uncle and cousin were covered with dirt. I dug them out just before they would have suffocated. I left with my grandmother. Then, things changed to a cemetery; I saw people walking behind a coffin. I was looking down from an aerial view. (I have had this kind of dream once before, several years ago.)

DREAM 3

I was with a group of people in the church I attended as a child. I knew most of the people there. I saw Paul Newman among the group. Guns appeared from somewhere; everyone grabbed one. Two groups formed; shooting started. I watched Newman fight a burly man. It seemed I became Newman—I could hear and feel everything he felt and heard. We threw "ourself" out into the open to try for a clear shot, but had no time to shoot before we were shot by the burly man. We felt the searing pain; I was sure death was imminent. Suddenly, the pain cleared. We shot the burly man, killing him. The fighting ended. We went inside, once again having our own identities. I saw Newman shaking his head, saying that it was only supposed to have been a game.

DREAM 4

I was on a highway, walking instead of driving. There were no cars, and everyone was walking, but I felt as if I were in a car. I saw someone I knew; we started talking. I got off at the exit to the beach. I walked up a circular ramp. The end of the ramp resembled a manhole. I had a bathing suit on under my clothes, but I had no towel. I started looking for one. I found two that looked as if they did not belong to anyone, so I took them. A woman approached me while I was lying on the sand. She said they were her towels. I told her I had taken them by mistake; she said she was going to call the police. I stayed; the police never came.

DREAM 5

I was in a restaurant or a cafeteria. I picked up some food. I thought it was a dessert and expected it to be sweet and delicious. Instead, I found that it tasted terrible. I thought someone had substituted salt for sugar in the recipe. I felt as though the salty taste grew and grew; I was now alone in a vast, dry wasteland with no relief in sight. (I woke up with the taste of salt still parching my mouth.)

DREAM 6

First, I was seated on the top bunk of my bed. I was with some friends. Then I found myself walking around piles of boards. My house had been destroyed—either it had collapsed or burned down—and my belongings were covered with rubble. Then I was outside the house digging a ditch longer than it was deep. Building materials lay nearby. While I dug, I got dirt in my hair. I wanted a hat, so I went to the part of the house where the boards were. After finding a hat, I started out of the rubble. Some of the boards fell out of place; they knocked my father's car, our dog, and a chair over a steep cliff. I did not look over the cliff. I could hear my father's car smash into pieces. Then I saw a large field below the cliff. The dog and the chair also broke into pieces. The pieces began moving end over end to the other side of the field. When they stopped rolling, they were reassembled. I felt very unhappy about all this. I returned to the ditch and saw my father. I told him not to worry as he would soon be getting a company car. Then things changed and I was driving in my convertible with three friends. We had a case of beer with us. The road was covered with snow, although it was only snowing lightly at that moment. We stopped at a house where I walked around to the yard. It was twenty-three minutes to six, and I had to be home at five, but I felt that I could not tell my friends this. I saw my roommate swinging on a pole in the backyard. He said he wanted to swing up onto a window ledge. I offered to help; he refused my offer. Eventually we both got up on the ledge. I looked in through the window. A lady was in the kitchen. By now it was almost six, so I jumped down from the ledge, saying I had to go. I was alone.

DREAM 7

I was in a room I am familiar with but cannot now identify. A girl I work with was also there. The room made me think of Patricia Hearst; perhaps she had lived there. I thought she might be close by. I searched for clues. I wanted to find the clue that would solve the kidnapping case. I found something small lying on the floor; it was thin and cylindrical with screwlike threads at one end. I felt that this might be the clue to the kidnapping that I was looking for, but when I showed it to the girl she said it was something of hers. She took it.

DREAM 8

My brother and I were standing on a patio waiting for something. Four or five large jet planes passed the yard. The planes were a few feet above the ground. As my brother went to get a better look, another plane came by and snatched him up. He was strapped into a seat like a baby's car seat. Next, I was inside a house. I was handed a tube about a foot long. The tube was clear; it had white caps at either end. Something was inside—something red and jellylike. It reminded me of lobster. I was shocked when they told me it was my brother. I wanted to let him out of the tube; I was also afraid of what might happen. The organism was fighting violently; it was my brother. A strange-looking person entered the room then. He said he was my brother. I thought the person was wearing a disguise. I grabbed him; we started to fight. Somehow I was convinced it was my brother. I said, "I hate to do this, but it's for your own good." Next I found myself walking with two friends towards a building. I had books in my hand. I then noticed that all of the lights in the town were off, so that there was no sense in continuing to go where I had intended. I crossed the bridge and left my friends, telling them I was going back for something. I returned to the patio. People were coming towards me. My brother was standing beside me. A group of girls I knew walked out of the building; I then recognized it to be a movie theater. I walked over to one of the girls, who said that she had seen an "awfully strange movie." I was very relieved that everything that had just happened to me was only a movie, and that my brother was safe beside me.

DREAM 9

I was going to school in Paris. I did not feel that I was really in Paris, however. I received a letter from a friend. He had just spent two weeks in Lorraine. He thought I should also travel. I decided to go to Geneva.

Write your answers in the spaces below:

Dreamer A _____ _____ _____

Dreamer B _____ _____ _____

Dreamer C _____ _____ _____

After you have made your judgments, check the correct answers on the bottom of this page. How correct were you? Based on your results, what would you conclude about the consistency of people's dreams? What is the implication of these conclusions for a theory of dreams?

ANSWERS TO DREAM EXPERIMENT

Dreamer A _____ 8,6,1

Dreamer B _____ 9,4,2

Dreamer C _____ 7,5,3

PART ONE
ACTION

CHAPTER 2

Biological Bases of Behavior

Learning Objectives

1. Offer two answers to the question: Why should psychologists be interested in the nervous system?

THE ORGANISM AS A MACHINE

2. Be familiar with Descartes' conception of the reflex, and how, in part, it still forms the basis of animal and human action.

HOW THE NERVOUS SYSTEM IS STUDIED

3. What is a neuron, and approximately how many are in the human brain?

Clinical observation

4. Indicate the advantages and disadvantages of studying the human brain by clinical observations of patients with brain damage.

Invasive techniques

5. Describe the advantages and ethical limitations of using invasive techniques to study the human brain.
6. Contrast activation and inactivation techniques for studying brain function, indicating the nature of ablation, lesioning, transection, intracranial recording, intracranial stimulation, and chemical stimulation through cannulas.

Neuroimaging techniques

7. Understand the mode of operation of the neuroimaging instruments that reveal brain anatomy: CT (CAT) scan and MRI.
8. Understand how neuroimaging instruments can measure brain activity or function by using EEG, PET scan, and fMRI.
9. Be aware of the advantages and disadvantages of each of the neuroimaging and other techniques for exploring the brain. Evaluate ease of obtaining information, invasiveness, ethical concerns, and type of information (activity, structure) obtained.

THE ARCHITECTURE OF THE NERVOUS SYSTEM

The evolution of nervous systems

10. Describe the tendency toward increasing centralization in the evolution of the nervous system.

The developing nervous system

11. Explain how the neural tube develops into the hindbrain, midbrain, and forebrain.

The major structures of the central nervous system

12. Describe the basic anatomy of the brain: What functions do the hindbrain, midbrain, and forebrain serve? Indicate the capacities and limitations of animals transected between hindbrain and midbrain (low-decerebrate animal), between midbrain and forebrain (high-decerebrate animal), and between cortex and the rest of the forebrain.
13. Describe the subcortical structures in the forebrain, and their function.

The central nervous system's connections with the body

14. Be able to distinguish the peripheral and the central nervous system, and the somatic and autonomic nervous system.

THE CORTEX

15. Explain the nature and functions of the convolutions of the cortex.
16. Know the structure of the cerebral cortex, including the four lobes.

Localization of function in the cortex

17. Explain localization of function, and phrenology as an early, crude attempt to establish it.

Projection areas

18. Describe the function of projection areas of the brain, and indicate what determines how much space in these areas is devoted to different parts of the body.
19. What are nonprimary (association) areas?
20. What are apraxia, agnosia, and prosopagnosia?
21. What are the symptoms of the neglect syndrome and the Gerstmann syndrome, and what brain damage causes each?
22. Distinguish fluent and nonfluent aphasias in terms of site of brain damage and type of symptoms.
23. Describe some of the symptoms of prefrontal lobe damage.

ONE BRAIN OR TWO?

24. Explain the meaning of lateralization, and how the brain organization of left-handers differs from that of right-handers.

Evidence from split brains

25. What are split brain patients, and what is the function of the corpus callosum?
26. What does research on people with split brains tell us about the differences between the cerebral hemispheres?

Hemispheric lateralization in normal participants

27. Be able to explain how PET scans and measures of response time indicate which hemisphere of normal people is more activated.

Two modes of mental functioning

28. What are the two modes of mental functioning that some believe are associated with the right and left hemispheres? How has this notion been distorted in the process of popularization?

BRAIN FUNCTIONS AND NEURAL HIERARCHIES

Hierarchies in small neural circuits

29. Indicate what it means to say that the nervous system is organized hierarchically.

Disinhibition

30. What is disinhibition, and how does it relate to hierarchies?

Who is in charge?

31. In what sense is the central nervous system organized in a "loose" hierarchy?

The neuron

32. What is a neuron? What are dendrites, the axon, the myelin sheath, and the nodes of Ranvier?
33. What purposes do the sensory neurons, motoneurons, and interneurons serve?

Glial cells: Unsung heroes of the nervous system

34. Describe the nature and function of glial cells.

How the nervous system makes its own circuitry

35. Appreciate the magnitude of the problem of ensuring appropriate connections of nerve cells in the brain during development, and indicate some of the processes that bring this about.

The electrical activity of the neuron

36. Be able to describe the electrical activity of the neuron: Know the difference between resting potential and action potential.
37. Describe the events involved in the reversal of membrane polarization.
38. How is the nerve impulse propagated? What is the role of myelin?
39. What is the all-or-none law?
40. What effect does stimulus intensity have on the number of neurons stimulated and on the frequency of impulses?

INTERACTION AMONG NERVE CELLS

Inferring the synapse

41. How did Sherrington infer the existence of the synapse?
42. Describe spatial and temporal summation, and inhibition, in simpler neural systems (e.g., the spinal animal).

The synaptic mechanism

43. Describe Loewi's classic demonstration of the existence of neurotransmitters.
44. Know the anatomy of the synapse (pre- and postsynaptic neurons and membranes, synaptic gaps, synaptic vesicles, and neurotransmitters), and the way that neural excitation (the nerve impulse) is transmitted across the synapse.
45. Be able to explain how inhibition and excitation occur at synapses, and how the postsynaptic neuron integrates the various inhibitory and excitatory effects on it.
46. What are the basic differences between action potentials and synaptic transmission?
47. What is a neurotransmitter? Give some examples.
48. What is the lock-and-key model?
49. Distinguish primary and secondary messengers in neural function.
50. What are drugs called agonists and antagonists, and what are the different ways in which they can exert their effects?
51. What are the effects of some major neurotransmitters (acetylcholine, serotonin, dopamine, and norepinephrine)? How are these effects modified by (respectively) curare, prozac, chlorpromazine, and amphetamines?
52. Indicate the opposing ways in which dopamine has been proposed to be involved in schizophrenia and Parkinson's disease.

INTERACTIONS THROUGH THE BLOODSTREAM

Blood circulation

53. Describe the circulation of blood to the brain, and the blood–brain barrier.

The endocrine system

54. Explain the mode of action of the endocrine system, and know the similarities and differences among the types of interaction and transmission in the nervous and endocrine systems.

RECOVERY FROM BRAIN INJURY

Repair from within

55. Describe how recovery of damaged neurons, collateral sprouting, and substitution of function allow for recovery from the loss of nerve cells in cerebral lesions.

Repair from without

56. Describe the process of brain grafts in rats, and its promise for the treatment of Parkinson's disease and Alzheimer's disease.

Rehabilitation

57. Know the differences among three modes of recovery from cerebral damage: self-repair, transplantation, and rehabilitation.

SOME FINAL COMMENTS

58. Discuss the differences between psychological and physiological explanation, and when each is appropriate.

Programmed Exercises

THE ORGANISM AS A MACHINE

1. The conception of organisms as machines can be traced to the great French philosopher _____.

   Descartes

2. According to Descartes, excitation from the senses leads to muscle contraction in what we now call a _____.

   reflex

HOW THE NERVOUS SYSTEM IS STUDIED

3. The individual nerve cells that collectively comprise the nervous system are called _____.

   neurons

4. In the method of _____ _____, the symptoms of individual patients with brain damage are assessed.

   clinical observation

5. _____ techniques involve stimulating or inactivating parts of the nervous system.

   Invasive

6. Nervous tissue is damaged in a local area with the three techniques of _____, _____, and _____.

   ablation, lesioning transection

7. Brain activity can be measured by intracranial _____, and activated by intracranial _____.

   recording stimulation

8. Chemicals can be introduced into local brain areas with the use of _____.

   cannulas

9. The two principal ways of imaging the structure (anatomy) of the human brain are _____ _____ and _____.

   CT (CAT) scan, MRI

10. Brain electrical activity is measured directly with the _____. The electrical response of the brain to stimulation is measured with (electroencephalography) _____-_____ _____.

    EEG event-related potentials

11. Brain activity can be measured by rate of uptake of different brain areas of a radioactive substance using the _____ scan. A less invasive technique measures metabolic activity in the brain revealed by exposing the brain to a varying strong magnetic field. This technique is called _____.

    PET

    fMRI

THE ARCHITECTURE OF THE NERVOUS SYSTEM

12. Early in evolutionary history, the cell bodies of many interneurons began to clump together to form _____. This is an early stage in the evolution of _____ control.

    ganglia, central

13. The development of the vertebrate nervous system proceeds from neural _____ to neural _____, and then to the three thickenings that form the _____, _____, and _____.

    plate
    tube, hindbrain, midbrain forebrain

14. The brain and spinal cord together comprise the _____ _____ _____.

    central nervous system

15. The portion of the hindbrain concerned with controlling some critical body processes, such as respiration and heartbeat, is called the _____.

    medulla

16. The portion of the hindbrain that controls bodily balance and motor coordination is called the _____.

    cerebellum

17. In the brain anatomy, and in the hierarchical organization of action, the part of the brain that comes between the hindbrain and forebrain is called the _____.

    midbrain

18. The _____ is a part of the forebrain involved in the control of behavior patterns that stem from basic biological urges such as feeding.

    hypothalamus

19. An older portion of the cerebral hemispheres with particular importance in the mediation of emotional and motivational activities is called the _____ _____.

    limbic system

20. The _____ _____ are subcortical structures involved in movement regulation. Movement disorders such as tremors or jerky movements follow damage to this area, as in _____ diseases.

    basal ganglia

    Parkinson's (or Huntington's)

THE CORTEX

21. Label the four major lobes of the human cerebral cortex.

A. _____   C. _____

B. _____   D. _____

A. frontal

B. parietal

C. occipital

D. temporal

22. The structure labeled E is the _____ _____.

E. lateral fissure

23. Label the following structures on the sketch of the human brain.

A. _____

B. _____

C. _____ _____

D. _____ _____

A. hindbrain (medulla)

B. cerebellum

C. cerebral cortex

D. corpus callosum

24. The idea and demonstration that different parts of the brain have different functions is called _____ of function.

localization

25. An early form of this, based on individual differences in the size of bumps in the skull under the scalp, was called _____.

phrenology

26. Excitation of the left _____ _____ _____ will lead to movements of the right side of the body. This illustrates _____ control.

motor projection area (motor homunculus), contralateral

27. In humans, the greatest amount of cortical space for motor functions is assigned to the _____ and the _____.

fingers, tongue

28. Each portion of the body surface is represented in the sensory homunculus, located in the _____ area, or the _____ _____ projection area.

somatosensory, primary sensory

29. The portion of the cerebral cortex that is part of neither the primary motor nor the primary sensory areas is described as the _____ or _____ area.

nonprimary, association

30. _____ is a serious disturbance in the organization of voluntary action.

Apraxia

31. A disorganization of aspects of the sensory world, without loss of basic sensory capacities, is termed _____. When this type of disorder primarily involves a deficit in face recognition, it is called _____.

agnosia
prosopagnosia

32. A disorder of attention in which a patient ignores one side of his or her world and body is called the _____ _____. It usually results from damage to the _____ _____ lobe.

neglect syndrome, right parietal

33. The _____ syndrome usually involves damage to the _____ _____ lobe, and includes symptoms such as calculation problems, left–right confusions, and finger agnosia.

Gerstmann, left parietal

34. A patient with a primary disorder in the expression of speech can be described as suffering from language apraxia, or a _____ _____. This disorder is commonly caused by lesions in _____ area, in the _____ _____ lobe.

nonfluent aphasia
Broca's, left frontal

35. In right-handed persons, aphasia usually results from lesions in the _____ hemisphere.

left

36. A language defect reflected primarily by an inability to comprehend language, or a language agnosia, is described as a _____ _____. The lesions responsible for this disorder commonly occur in _____ area, located in the _____ _____ lobe.

fluent aphasia
Wernicke's, left temporal

37. Difficulty in applying strategies, lack of spontaneity, and deficits in response inhibition characterize patients with damage in the _____ area.

prefrontal

ONE BRAIN OR TWO?

38. The asymmetry of function in the human cerebral cortex is described as _____.

lateralization

39. In terms of differences in function between left and right cerebral hemispheres, left-handers are generally less _____ than right-handers are.

lateralized

40. A right-hander who, following a stroke, has great difficulty with spatial representation, maps, and interpretation of complex drawings, probably has a lesion in the _____ hemisphere.

right

41. A split-brain patient is someone whose _____ _____ has been surgically severed.

corpus callosum

42. A right-handed split-brain patient would probably not be able to name a common object placed in his or her _____ hand.

left

43. Lateralization can be demonstrated in normal individuals by demonstrating that right-handers show a longer _____ _____ to name objects flashed to their left visual field as opposed to their right visual field.

response time

44. Many psychologists believe that _____ and _____ processes represent radically different modes of thought, which reflect different clusters of intellectual functioning. To right-handers they assign _____ processes to the left hemisphere and _____ processes to the right hemisphere.

verbal, spatial

verbal, spatial

45. Some psychologists believe that the left hemisphere is specialized for the organization of _____, since such a function would be relevant to both _____ and _____ skills. They believe that the right hemisphere motor is specialized for the organization of _____.

time, language, manual

space

BRAIN FUNCTIONS AND NEURAL HIERARCHIES

46. Command roles at lower levels of the central nervous system are often assumed by small circuits, which often produce rhythmic cycles of activity, called _____ _____ generators.

central pattern

47. The nervous system is organized in layers of control, such that higher centers control those centers below them. This pattern of organization is called _____.

hierarchical

48. An increase in the strength of a reflex when higher brain centers are removed is called _____.

disinhibition

BUILDING BLOCKS OF THE NERVOUS SYSTEM: NEURONS AND NERVE IMPULSES

49. The basic building block of the nervous system is the nerve cell, or _____.

neuron

50. The basic unit of nervous function is the _____ _____.

nerve impulse

51. Label the following diagram of the neuron.

A. _____   dendrites

B. _____   cell body

C. _____   axon

D. _____ _____   myelin sheath

E. _____ _____ _____   nodes of Ranvier

52. Receptor cells _____ stimulus energy into nerve impulses.   transduce

53. The axons of _____ _____ terminate in effector cells and activate the _____ _____.   motor neurons, skeletal musculature (muscles)

54. In complex organisms, the vast majority of neurons are neither sensory nor motor, but rather _____. Their connections form the _____ of the central nervous system.   interneurons, microcircuitry

55. The very numerous nervous system cells that form a scaffold for the system, and constitute the _____ sheath, are called _____ cells.   myelin, glial

56. The parts of the brain containing many myelinated axons are called _____ matter. The rest is called _____ matter.   white / grey

57. The fine wire or tube that allows investigators to record electrical activity in neurons is called a(n) _____.   microelectrode

58. The _____ _____ of the neuron is about –70 millivolts.   resting potential

59. The reversal of polarization that passes along a nerve fiber when it is stimulated is called the _____ _____.   action potential

60. When the nerve cell membrane is depolarized past its _____ _____ by an _____ stimulus, a(n) _____ _____ results.   excitation threshold / adequate, action potential

61. Ion _____ and ion _____ maintain the resting potential. The opening of the ion _____ is responsible for the sharp voltage change called the action potential.   pumps, channels / channels

62. The _____ speed of the nerve impulse would be relatively slow, except that _____ wrapped around the neuron allows the impulse to jump form one _____ _____ _____ to another.

propagation, myelin
node of
Ranvier

63. The disease _____ _____ involves deterioration of the myelin surrounding neurons.

multiple sclerosis

64. The _____-_____-_____ law states that the size of the action potential and its speed are independent of the intensity of the stimulus, provided the stimulus is above threshold intensity.

all-or-none

65. The above-mentioned law does not apply to the stimulation of nerves since there is much variation in the _____ of the neurons in the nerve.

thresholds

66. Stimulus _____ is conveyed by both increases in the number of neurons firing and by increases in individual neurons' _____ of firing.

intensity
frequency

INTERACTION AMONG NERVE CELLS

67. The gap between the axon terminals of one neuron and the dendritic processes of another is called the _____.

synapse

68. The existence of the synapse was inferred from evidence at the level of _____ by the great English physiologist _____.

behavior
(Sir Charles) Sherrington

69. Sherrington studied simple _____ in the _____ animal.

reflexes, spinal

70. Subthreshold stimulation at two adjacent points, when applied simultaneously, may lead to a response. This illustrates the phenomenon of _____ _____.

spatial summation

71. Subthreshold stimulation, when applied a few times in rapid succession, may lead to a response. This illustrates the phenomenon of _____ _____.

temporal summation

72. According to Sherrington, temporal summation occurs because of integration at the _____, which is accomplished by "storage" of excitation from previous stimulation.

synapse

73. Sherrington observed that when a flexor muscle contracts, the corresponding extensor relaxes. This is an example of _____ _____.

reciprocal inhibition

74. Whether a neuron fires or not is determined by the net result of its integration of _____ and _____ stimulation.

excitatory
inhibitory

75. Loewi's classic experiment showed that stimulation of the vagus nerve to the heart caused release of a _____, which we now call _____.

neurotransmitter,
acetylcholine

76. Electrical activity is transmitted across the synapse by neurotransmitters, from the _____ neuron to the _____ neuron.

presynaptic, postsynaptic

77. The synaptic vesicles contain chemical substances called _____.

neurotransmitters

78. Label this diagram of a synapse.

A. presynaptic
   membrane
B. postsynaptic
   membrane
C. synaptic vesicle
D. neurotransmitter
E. synaptic gap (or
   synapse)

79. The activity of the postsynaptic neuron results from the summation of _____ and _____ postsynaptic potentials. These are produced by _____ liberated by firing of the presynaptic neuron.

inhibitory
excitatory,
neurotransmitters

80. While action potentials are all-or-none, synaptic potentials are _____.   graded

81. Inhibitory neurotransmitters _____ the nerve's resting potential, while excitatory neurotransmitters _____ it.   increase / decrease

82. Excitatory neurotransmitters open _____ channels in the postsynaptic membrane.   ion (sodium)

83. Neurotransmitters are eventually removed from the synaptic gap by deactivation or by _____ _____.   synaptic uptake

84. The idea that neurotransmitters only affect the postsynaptic membrane if their shape fits the shape of certain receptor sites on that membrane is called the _____-_____-_____ model.   lock-and-key

85. Acetylcholine, dopamine, serotonin, and norepinephrine are all _____.   neurotransmitters

86. Neurotransmitters secreted by the presynaptic cell are called _____ messengers. Chemical processes in the postsynaptic cell that regulate its sensitivity are called _____ messengers.   primary / secondary

87. Drugs that enhance a transmitter's activity are called _____. Drugs that impede a transmitter's activity are called _____.   agonists / antagonists

88. Some drugs enhance synaptic function by interfering with _____ by the presynaptic cell. Some drugs act by altering the levels of substances called _____, which are required for the synthesis of particular neurotransmitters.   reuptake / precursors

89. Curare, chlorpromazine, and amphetamines are _____ that affect synaptic transmission.   drugs

90. The action of the neurotransmitter _____, which causes muscles to contract, is blocked by the drug _____.   acetylcholine / curare

91. The _____ _____ _____ _____, such as prozac, enhance the effect of _____, and are used therapeutically to treat depression and obsessive-compulsive disorder.   selective serotonin reuptake inhibitors (SSRIs), serotonin

92. The arousing effects of the neurotransmitter _____ are enhanced by the group of drugs called _____.   norepinephrine / amphetamines

93. The arousing effects of the neurotransmitter _____ are blocked by the drug _____, which is used to treat the major mental disorder _____.   dopamine, thorazine / schizophrenia

94. _____ and _____ disease may be "opposites" in the sense that the former may result from dopamine excess and the latter from dopamine deficiency.   Schizophrenia, Parkinson's

INTERACTIONS THROUGH THE BLOODSTREAM

95. The brain gets special protection from potential toxins in the blood through the action of the _____-_____ _____.   blood–brain barrier

96. The _____ glands secrete _____ into the bloodstream.   endocrine, hormones

97. _____ are chemical messengers that are distributed indiscriminately throughout the body, while _____ exert their effects in a very limited area.   Hormones / neurotransmitters

RECOVERY FROM BRAIN INJURY

98. Recovery, within the nervous system, from loss of cerebral nerve cells can occur by the processes of recovery of _____ _____, _____ _____, and _____ _____ _____.   damaged neurons, collateral sprouting substitution of function

99. The brain's capacity to recover, generally greater in younger people, is called its _____.   plasticity

SOME FINAL COMMENTS

100. Brain _____ involving fetal brain tissue of rats have had some success, and hold the promise to replace dopamine-secreting cells lost in _____ disease and acetylcholine-secreting cells lost in _____ disease.

transplants
Parkinson's
Alzheimer's

101. Three modes of recovery from cerebral brain damage are _____, _____, and _____.

self-repair,
transplantation,
rehabilitation

102. For explanations of certain types of events, such as why a particular person opposes legalization of drugs, a _____ level of explanation is more appropriate than a _____ level.

psychological,
physiological

Self Test

1. Which of the following commonly observed characteristics of human or animal behavior goes counter to Descartes' reflex notion?
   a. the withdrawal response upon touching a hot object
   b. the appearance of a behavior (e.g., running) in the absence of any obvious stimulus
   c. the existence of nerves connecting receptors and effectors to the brain
   d. the repeatability of reflexes
   e. none of the above

2. By viewing animal behavior as the result of a machine's responding to external stimuli, Descartes made the claim that:
   a. animal behavior is governed by physical laws and is therefore predictable
   b. animal behavior can only be understood in terms of the hierarchical organization of the nervous system
   c. animals must have rich mental lives
   d. neither humans nor animals have free will
   e. introductory psychology is *the* fundamental science

3. Clinical observation has the following advantage(s) over other techniques for investigating the human brain:
   a. it is replicable
   b. it can measure the activity of the brain
   c. it can control precisely the area of the brain that is damaged
   d. it allows for detailed analysis of symptoms produced by specific brain damage in an individual
   e. it is more invasive

4. Which of the following brain exploration techniques can be described as inactivating?
   a. ablation
   b. intracranial stimulation
   c. MRI
   d. EEG
   e. CT (CAT) scan

5. Following are lists of three brain exploration techniques. Which of the lists presents the techniques in this order: stimulates brain tissue, has no or minimal effect on brain tissue, destroys brain tissue?
   a. intracranial stimulation, intracranial recording, MRI
   b. chemical introduction with cannulas, EEG, lesioning
   c. CAT scan, MRI, PET scan
   d. EEG, MRI, ablation
   e. fMRI, transection, MRI

6. In terms of providing information about structure versus activity, EEG is to CAT scan as:
   a. PET scan is to fMRI
   b. intracranial stimulation is to PET scan
   c. ablation is to MRI
   d. transection is to PET scan
   e. fMRI is to MRI

7. Which of the following procedures would you most prefer to experience, assuming your brain was normal and your aim was to keep it that way?
   a. ablation
   b. lesioning
   c. EEG
   d. PET scan
   e. c or d

8. Assume a patient is suspected of having brain seizures (uncontrollable activity in some part of the brain). Which brain exploration technique(s) would be most likely to reveal the affected brain area?
   a. EEG
   b. CAT scan
   c. fMRI
   d. a and b
   e. a and c

9. Neuron is to ganglion as
   a. brain is to hierarchical organization
   b. ganglion is to brain
   c. excitation is to inhibition
   d. synapse is to neurotransmitter
   e. dentist is to pain

10. Match the structure on the left with its associated function on the right
    i. medulla   a. respiration and heartbeat
    ii. cerebellum   b. basic biological urges
    iii. hypothalamus   c. balance and motor coordination

    i. _____

    ii. _____

    iii. _____

11. Which of the following statements is *not* true of the limbic system?
    a. it is a subcortical structure
    b. it is anatomically associated with the hypothalamus
    c. it is present on both sides of the brain
    d. it is involved in the control of emotional and motivational activities
    e. it integrates the functions of the cerebral hemispheres

12. In which of the following sequences are the main divisions of the central nervous system arranged in ascending order?
    a. peripheral, somatic, autonomic
    b. cerebellum, integration centers, transmission tracts
    c. spinal cord, autonomic system, brain
    d. spinal cord, basal ganglia, hypothalamus
    e. spinal cord, brain stem, cerebral hemispheres

13. The lobes of the cerebral hemisphere are:
    a. frontal, parietal, occipital, temporal
    b. hindbrain, midbrain, forebrain
    c. limbic system, corpus callosum, cerebral cortex
    d. each cerebral hemisphere is a single lobe of the cerebral cortex
    e. none of the above

14. What part of an elephant might you expect to have a particularly large representation in the motor homunculus?
    a. the ears
    b. the front legs
    c. the back legs
    d. the trunk
    e. the eyes

15. Following a stroke, a patient shows grossly diminishing sensitivity to touch and other stimulation in the right hand and arm. The probable site of the lesion is:
    a. the motor homunculus
    b. the left somatosensory area
    c. the right somatosensory area
    d. the left frontal area
    e. the right frontal area

16. A disorder in the organization of voluntary movement is called:
    a. agnosia
    b. aphasia
    c. apraxia
    d. amenorrhea
    e. none of the above

17. A person exhibiting an inability to coordinate the separate details of the visual world into a whole suffers from:
    a. visual agnosia
    b. receptive aphasia
    c. a lesion in Broca's area
    d. a lesion in Wernicke's area
    e. visual apraxia

18. A patient with the neglect syndrome and damage to her right parietal area looks straight at the X in the figure below. She is asked how many dots she sees. The answer we would expect is:

    • • X • ⋮

    a. 1
    b. 2
    c. 3
    d. 4
    e. 5

19. Just as a fluent aphasia can be described as a language agnosia, a nonfluent aphasia can be described as:
    a. a fluent dyslexia
    b. a language neglect
    c. a language apraxia
    d. a language deficit
    e. none of the above

20. Apraxia, neglect syndrome, and nonfluent and fluent aphasia have in common:
    a. lesions in the same brain area
    b. basic sensory and motor functions are intact
    c. some deficit in voluntary motor function
    d. a and b
    e. a and c

21. Damage in a left-handed person in the language center often has less drastic consequences than in a right-handed person because:
    a. left-handers are slower to develop language functions
    b. recovery is more rapid in the left hemisphere in left-handers
    c. the hemispheres are not as functionally lateralized in left-handers
    d. highly developed visual-spatial abilities compensate for language loss
    e. a and d

22. Afferent input from the right hand projects primarily to the left hemisphere while the left hand projects primarily to the right hemisphere. In an average right-handed, split-brain patient, which hand would the patient have to use to handle an unseen object in order to name it?
    a. the left hand
    b. the right hand
    c. neither hand could do it
    d. both hands could do it equally well
    e. a split-brian patient cannot name any objects

23. A right-handed person has lost the entire projection area of his left occipital cortex, as shown below, but is otherwise normal. Which of the following deficits would you expect?

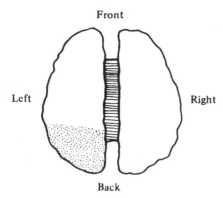

Front

Left   Right

Back

   a. loss of the right side of his visual field
   b. loss of the left side of his visual field
   c. inability to produce speech despite ability to understand it
   d. inability to understand speech despite the ability to produce it
   e. inability to read

24. The same person referred to in the previous question suffers an additional defect: His corpus callosum is completely cut. What is the extent of his deficit?
   a. inability to produce or understand speech
   b. inability to produce speech despite understanding it
   c. inability to understand speech despite the ability to produce it
   d. inability to read
   e. visual agnosia

25. For a normal right-handed person, which of the following findings would be expected?
   a. a shorter response time to respond to a spatial problem presented in the left visual field
   b. better vision in right visual field
   c. longer response time to respond to a verbal problem presented in the right visual field
   d. all of the above
   e. b and c

26. In which of the following tasks would you expect superior performance from the left hemisphere of a right-hander?
   a. matching paint colors
   b. recognizing faces
   c. remembering a series of movements to be performed in a specific order
   d. drawing the floor plan of a familiar house
   e. all of the above

27. Theories of lateralization hold that, for right-handers, the left hemisphere is more involved with _____, and the right hemisphere is more involved with _____.
   a. spatial material, verbal material
   b. organization in time, organization in space
   c. PET scans, CAT scans
   d. visual perception, auditory perception
   e. a and d

28. Disinhibition and central pattern generators both illustrate the principle of:
   a. inhibition
   b. arousal
   c. lateralization
   d. hierarchical organization
   e. a and d

29. The phenomenon of disinhibition:
   a. exists only in insects
   b. depends on reflex interaction, especially in the spinal cord
   c. reveals the presence of inhibition
   d. takes place entirely within a single neuron
   e. all of the above

30. Seriously apraxic patients can sometimes perform actions as part of automatic routines in the face of an inability to perform these acts on command. This suggests:
   a. hierarchical organization of motor function
   b. a disorganization of the sensory world
   c. a lesion in Broca's area
   d. a disorder in function of the brain stem
   e. agnosia

31. A rat with its brain transected above the hindbrain (low-decerebrate animal) will chew food placed in its mouth, but this chewing is not affected by its state of food deprivation. If the transection is made above the hypothalamus, this acceptance of food will depend on its state of deprivation, but unlike a fully intact rat, it will not search for food. This is an example of:
   a. the projection areas
   b. disinhibition
   c. inhibition
   d. hierarchical organization
   e. none of the above

32. Which of the following is *not* part of an individual neuron?
   a. axon
   b. myelin sheath
   c. synapse
   d. dendrite
   e. cell body

33. Receptor cells:
    a. are always a specialized part of sensory neurons
    b. transduce physical stimuli into neural impulses
    c. are responsible for the conduction of optic stimuli
    d. a and b
    e. b and c

34. Which of the following properties are characteristic of interneurons?
    a. they usually show much branching of dendrites
    b. they form the microcircuitry of the central nervous system
    c. they comprise the majority of neurons
    d. all of the above
    e. none of the above

35. When graphed over time, the complex electrical event known as the action potential looks something like:

A

B

C

D

    e. none of the above

36. The all-or-none law states that
    a. the threshold of a single neuron is a property that alternates between two extreme values but never has any of the values in between
    b. reflexes cannot involve just the spinal cord; the entire nervous system must respond by generating a central excitatory state
    c. an axon terminal releases a chemical substance, called a neurotransmitter, when an action potential arrives
    d. the frequency of spikes in an individual nerve fiber increases with the number of action potentials per unit time
    e. once a stimulus exceeds the threshold of an individual neuron, further increases in stimulation intensity make no difference in the height and form of the action potential generated

37. The all-or-none action potential is:
    a. accompanied by depolarization of the nerve membrane
    b. accompanied by opening of the sodium channels in the membrane
    c. propagated from one part of the membrane to another
    d. all of the above
    e. none of the above

38. How can the nervous system represent increase in the intensity of a *stimulus*?
    a. by an increase in the size of the action potential in every neuron fired by the stimulus
    b. by an increase in the number of neurons being fired by the stimulus
    c. by an increase in the frequency of firing in the neurons fired by the stimulus
    d. b and c
    e. a and c

39. Sherrington used a spinal animal in order to:
    a. eliminate inhibition
    b. simplify the system he was studying
    c. take advantage of brain modulation in neural activity in the spinal cord
    d. study the irreversibility of conduction
    e. cut expenses

40. From his observations of temporal and spatial summation in reflexes, Sherrington inferred the existence of:
    a. receptors
    b. inhibition
    c. the synapse
    d. disinhibition
    e. the simple reflex

41. Consider this example: Brief strong stimulation of a receptor produces no movement, but a longer period of stimulation causes a particular muscle to stop contracting. These results could most easily be explained by the principles of:
    a. excitation and inhibition
    b. inhibition and spatial summation
    c. all-or-none law and inhibition
    d. temporal summation, spatial summation, and the all-or-none law
    e. inhibition and temporal summation

42. Sherrington reported that the time (reflex latency) between stimulation of a reflex and the reflex response was much longer than the time it would take for an action potential to go from the receptor to the muscle. This "delay" could be accounted for in terms of:
    a. inhibition
    b. excitation
    c. spatial summation
    d. the time for depolarization of the axon membrane
    e. the time for the neurotransmitter to cross the synaptic gap and stimulate the postsynaptic neuron

43. Axon conduction resembles synaptic transmission in that:
    a. both involve neurotransmitters
    b. both are about the same speed
    c. both are all-or-none
    d. all of the above
    e. none of the above

44. Many neurons fire action potentials at a moderate rate even when they are not receiving synaptic excitation from presynaptic neurons. This is called spontaneous activity. Which plot indicates what would happen to the firing rate of such a neuron if it was first exposed to synaptic inhibition and then synaptic excitation?

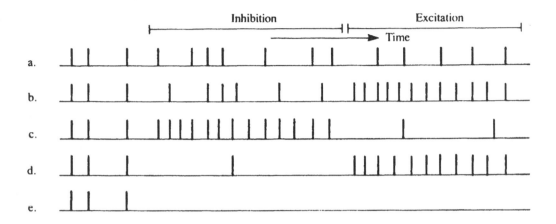

45. Both excitatory neurotransmitters and above-threshold depolarization of axons:
    a. open ion channels
    b. produce synaptic delay
    c. explain temporal summation
    d. all of the above
    e. none of the above

46. The lock-and-key model accounts for:
    a. the existence of neurotransmitters
    b. the summation of excitation and inhibition in postsynaptic neurons
    c. the fact that specific neurotransmitters stimulate specific postsynaptic neurons
    d. the release of neurotransmitters from synaptic vesicles
    e. the all-or-none law

47. Thorazine and curare have in common the fact that they:
    a. block the action of specific neurotransmitters
    b. enhance the action of specific neurotransmitters
    c. produce postsynaptic inhibition
    d. produce postsynaptic excitation
    e. relieve the symptoms of schizophrenia

48. Many researchers now believe that in at least some cases of depression, the cause is low levels of dopamine or norepinephrine in the brain. If this were true, then we would expect chlorpromazine to _____ depression, and amphetamines to _____ depression.
    a. increase, decrease
    b. decrease, increase

    c. increase, increase
    d. decrease, decrease
    e. have no effect on, have no effect on

49. A new drug is found to increase arousal. All but one of the following are possible modes of action of that drug. Which is *not*?
    a. blocks reuptake of dopamine
    b. increases availability of norepinephrine
    c. blocks the enzyme that breaks down dopamine at the synapse
    d. mimics the effect of norepinephrine
    e. blocks the postsynaptic receptor for norepinephrine

50. Hormones and neurotransmitters are both:
    a. secreted only by endocrine glands
    b. secreted into the bloodstream
    c. chemical messengers
    d. all of the above
    e. none of the above

51. Recovery from cerebral damage occurs in a number of ways. Which of the following actually involves addition of new nerve cells to the damaged brain?
    a. transplantation of fetal nerve tissue
    b. rehabilitation
    c. collateral sprouting
    d. substitution of function
    e. all of the above

Answer Key for Self Test

Investigating Psychological Phenomena

SPEED OF THE NERVE IMPULSE: THE USE OF REACTION TIME IN THE MEASUREMENT OF A PSYCHOLOGICAL PROCESS

Equipment: A stopwatch that indicates seconds
Number of participants: Five
Time per participant: Fifteen minutes (all participants are involved at the same time)
Time for experimenter: Twenty-five minutes

One of the great stumbling blocks to advances in theory about psychological processes was the belief that thought, and hence nervous impulses, occurred instantaneously or nearly so. In fact, the German physiologist Johannes P. Müller (1801–1858) once estimated that the speed of the nerve impulse was eleven million miles per second. Naturally, this claim that nerve impulses travel at an immeasurably fast rate discouraged scientific research on the physiology of the nervous system and encouraged mystical or dualistic interpretations of mind. It also discouraged study of the speed of various mental activities, research that is today an important cornerstone of the field of cognitive psychology.

In 1850, Herman Ludwig Ferdinand von Helmholtz (1821–1894) succeeded in measuring the speed of the nerve impulse and found it to be much slower than previously believed, between fifty and one hundred meters per second in humans. This finding was followed by intensive investigation of the nervous system within the framework of the physical and biological sciences. It also opened the door to the use of reaction time as a tool in the study of thought processes. This experiment is an attempt to familiarize you with the general logic used by a psy-

chologist who is interested in measuring the speed of a psychological event that cannot be directly observed. To accomplish this, you must first understand the experiment that Helmholtz performed and also how his experimental technique can be applied to the measurement of the speed of the nerve impulse in humans.

Helmholtz's technique was quite simple. He first dissected out a muscle and an attached nerve fiber from a frog's leg. The experiment then consisted of stimulating the nerve at various distances from the muscle and measuring the length of time between nerve stimulation and muscle contraction. First, he electrically stimulated the nerve close to the point at which it was attached to the muscle, then he stimulated the nerve farther from this point of attachment. He found that the second reaction time (i.e., the time between stimulation and contraction) was longer than the first. To obtain an estimate of nerve impulse speed, he used a simple bit of reasoning: The difference in time between the two measurements must correspond to the time it takes the impulse to travel the distance between the two points of stimulation (see figure). Hence, the distance between the points of stimulation divided by the time *difference* between the conditions of stimulating close to the muscle versus stimulating farther away should yield an estimate of nerve impulse speed. This is how he obtained his estimate of fifty to one hundred meters per second. Let A and B be two points of stimulation, M be the point at which the nerve connects to the muscle, t_A be the time to contraction from stimulation at A, and t_B, the time to contraction from stimulation at B.

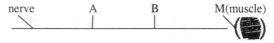

Then $\dfrac{(A \text{ to } M) - (B \text{ to } M)}{t_A - t_B}$ = speed of nerve impulse.

Happily, Helmholtz's estimate can be demonstrated in humans without resorting to dissection. You might suppose that the simplest way to do this would be to perform the following sort of experiment: Stimulate someone on the ankle (e.g., by pinching) and have the participant respond by pushing a button as soon as he or she feels the stimulation. With a good timer, you could then measure the time between stimulation and depression of the button. To estimate nerve conduction time, you would then measure the total distance between ankle and brain, and between brain and finger, add the two together, and divide this number by the participant's reaction time. But there are complications that make this procedure unsuitable. Part of the reaction time, for example, would be due to the length of time it took the participant to decide to press the button, a figure that is obviously more than simply nerve impulse time. From the point of view of processes in the nervous system, the reaction time includes the time to cross synapses as well as axon conduction time. In short, total reaction time is a confounded measure.

Thus, the experiment must be made more complicated. Using Helmholtz's logic, one could measure not only the time between ankle stimulation and response, but also between, say, upper arm stimulation and response. The ankle condition should result in a longer reaction time than the upper arm condition. The difference between these reaction times corresponds to the time it takes for the nerve impulse to travel a distance equal to the difference between the ankle and the finger, and the upper arm and the finger. Notice that this difference excludes any time due to such things as decision-making processes. So the nerve conduction time can be estimated by subtracting the distance of the upper arm to the brain from the distance of the ankle to the brain (the distance from the brain to the finger is constant) and dividing by the reaction time difference.

In practice, the reaction time for either stimulating the ankle or stimulating the upper arm is quite small, and hence a clock that measures time in hundredths of a second would be needed to measure it. This problem can be solved by adding together the reaction time of several people; after obtaining the total time, simply dividing this by the number of people would give the average individual time. This general mass reaction time technique will be used to measure the speed of the nerve impulse. Perform the nerve impulse speed experiment in the following way:

Get five people to participate. Have them form a circle with each person very loosely clasping the ankle of his or her neighbor to the right. Tell everyone to squeeze the ankle they are holding when they feel their ankle squeezed. Be sure the participants' eyes are closed during all trials. You can then start the experiment by squeezing one person's ankle and simultaneously noting the time on a second hand of a watch. Now watch the ankle that you squeezed. When you see it squeezed for the fifth time (excluding your initial squeeze) note the time that elapsed. Repeat this procedure for a total of five times, each time recording the time in the spaces provided in Part I of the answer sheet (record results to an accuracy of .1 second).

Next have everyone in the circle release the ankle they are holding and grasp the upper arm, *just below the shoulder* of the person to their right. You run another five trials exactly as you did for the ankle trials, each time recording the time in Part II of the answer sheet.

You will probably note that the total reaction time dropped within each set of five trials. Why? Hopefully, the last two to three trials yielded about the same values.

These ten trials serve as practice: The group of five participants and the measurer "learn" in some general way, to do this task efficiently. Having completed practice, you are now ready to begin the measurement of the speed of the nerve impulse. Run four more trials as before, the first and fourth with ankle stimulation, the second and third with upper arm. This will generate two ankle and two upper arm mass reaction times (record these in Part III of the data sheet).

Each reaction time represents the sum of twenty-five reaction times (five participants, five times each). Obtain the average individual reaction time by dividing the total reaction times by twenty-five. Now average the two ankle reaction times and, separately, the two upper arm reaction times. Subtract the average arm time from the average ankle time. This is the amount of time it takes the impulse to go the extra distance from the ankle to the level of the shoulder. To calculate the speed of the nerve impulse, you must estimate the magnitude of this distance (in meters).

Measure the distance for the third tallest person in your group of five participants. Measure the distance from the ankle to the base of the neck and from the upper arm to the base of the neck. Take the difference between the numbers, divide by the time difference, and you will have an estimate of the speed of the nerve impulse. How does it compare with Helmholtz's estimate? (Helmholtz estimated a speed of from 50 to 100 meters per second. Modern measurements range from 6 to 122 meters per second, depending on the type of nerve fiber.) (*If your instructor collects the data, fill out the report sheet in Appendix 3.*)

FURTHER EXPERIMENTS

Now that you have calculated an estimate of the speed of the nerve impulse, you might want to test whether some fairly common variables will affect this speed. Consider fatigue for instance. If a person is tired, does his or her nerve impulse speed slow down? To test this, design your own experiment, using the same measurement technique you used to get your main estimate of nerve impulse speed. To test whether fatigue has an effect, measure the speed both at a time when participants are well rested and at a time when the same participants are tired (e.g., in the morning and at night, or before and after exercise). Does fatigue affect nerve impulse speed? Note, by the way, that given the way the estimate is obtained, it is possible to find that fatigue may well slow down reaction time in general, yet have no effect on the speed of the nerve impulse.

Can you think of other variables that might affect (speed up or slow down) nerve impulse speed? If so, design experiments to test your hypotheses.

Report Sheet

Practice   Time in seconds*

Part I   Trial 1 ankle = _____
           Trial 2 ankle = _____
           Trial 3 ankle = _____
           Trial 4 ankle = _____
           Trial 5 ankle = _____

Part II   Trial 1 upper arm = _____
           Trial 2 upper arm = _____
           Trial 3 upper arm = _____
           Trial 4 upper arm = _____
           Trial 5 upper arm = _____

Test
Part III   Trial 1 ankle time = _____
           $\div 25 =$ _____ (a)
           Trial 2 upper arm time = _____
           $\div 25 =$ _____ (b)
           Trial 3 upper arm time = _____
           $\div 25 =$ _____ (c)
           Trial 4 ankle time = _____
           $\div 25 =$ _____ (d)

$\dfrac{a + d}{2} =$ _____ (average ankle time)

$\dfrac{b + c}{2} =$ _____ (average upper arm time)

Average ankle time – average upper arm time = _____ (difference 1)

(1) Distance of ankle to base of neck
    (for third tallest person) = _____

(2) Distance of upper arm to base of neck
    (for third tallest person) = _____

    Distance 1 – distance 2 = _____ (difference 2)

$\dfrac{\text{difference 2}}{\text{difference 1}} =$ (speed of nerve impulse)

*Record time accurate to .1 second.

CHAPTER 3

Motivation

Learning Objectives

1. Describe the organization of individual motives into those that serve self-regulation, self-preservation, and self-restoration.
2. Indicate the relation between potentiation and motivation.

MOTIVATION AS DIRECTED ACTION
3. Can directed action be reconciled with Descartes' notion of humans and animals as reflex machines?

Control systems
4. Describe the action of negative and positive feedback systems. Give examples of negative and positive feedback systems from modern technology.

Homeostasis
5. What is homeostasis?

TEMPERATURE REGULATION
6. Distinguish endotherms and ectotherms.

Temperature control by internal adjustment
7. Know how reflexes and behavior function to maintain body temperature. Define setpoint.

Temperature control by externally directed behavior
8. Provide examples of how behavior affects body temperature.

The autonomic nervous system and temperature control
9. Describe the way the two branches of the autonomic nervous system function in temperature regulation.

Sensing the internal environment: the hypothalamus
10. Describe how thermoreceptors in the hypothalamus separately motivate behavioral heat loss and gain.
11. What are pyrogens and where do they act?

THIRST

Extracellular water volume
12. Describe how the brain is informed about extracellular water volume, and the role of vasopression and angiotensin in this system.

Intracellular water volume
13. What is intracellular water volume and what and where are osmoreceptors?

HUNGER

Body weight nutrition and energy
14. What is the evidence indicating that animals regulate calorie (energy) intake? What is basal metabolic rate?

The signals for feeding
15. Indicate the internal and external signals that influence hunger and satiety.
16. Contrast signals that indicate short-term (e.g., stomach) and long-term (e.g., adipose tissue) needs for food.
17. What evidence makes it likely that animals and humans stop eating in anticipation of the arrival of sufficient nutrients in the cells?

Hypothalamic control centers
18. Describe the role of the hypothalamus in feeding.
19. What is the dual-center theory? How do the phenomena of aphagia and hyperphagia support this theory?
20. How does the idea of setpoint help account for the regulation of temperature and food intake, and how does it account for the behavior of hyperphagic rats?
21. Review the evidence indicating that the hypothalamic control of eating acts both directly on eating and indirectly through effects on insulin and fat deposition.
22. Review evidence that the hypothalamus is involved in the control of feeding (e.g., orexins) but that other brain areas are also involved (e.g., neuropeptide Y studies).

Food selection
23. Indicate how different species with different ranges of acceptable foods (carnivores, omnivores, etc.) have different solutions to the problem of identifying foods.
24. Describe the roles of innate preferences, learning, culture, and neophobia in omnivore food selection.

Obesity
25. Indicate bodily factors that may contribute to obesity, and review genetic evidence that establishes a role for bodily factors.
26. What behavioral factors may be involved in obesity? Describe the externality hypothesis and the alternative idea that dieting (restraint) causes externality.
27. What aspects of obesity can the setpoint hypothesis explain?
28. Review the success of treatments for obesity. What are some factors that interfere with treatment success?

29. Is being overweight a disorder? What are its health and social consequences?

Anorexia nervosa
30. Describe the symptoms and possible causes of anorexia nervosa.

Bulimia nervosa
31. Describe the symptoms of bulimia nervosa, and contract it with anorexia nervosa.

THREAT

32. Evaluate the relevance of homeostasis and potentiation to fear and rage.

Threat and the autonomic nervous system
33. What are the functions of the parasympathetic and sympathetic systems?
34. Describe the emergency reaction. What role does the sympathetic arousal system play in the flight-or-fight response? Understand the biological survival value of the emergency reaction.
35. Discuss the polygraph approach to lie detection, and the advantages and shortcomings of this technique.

Central controls
36. How are fear, rage, and predatory attack responses organized in the central nervous system? What is the role of the limbic system?

Disruptive effects of autonomic arousal
37. Describe the immediate disruptive effects of sympathetic arousal, and possible long-term effects on health.

Pain and the endorphin system
38. Describe adaptive and maladaptive aspects of pain.
39. Indicate the evidence for nervous system mechanisms to modulate pain. What stimulates them, and what is the role of the endorphins in producing analgesia?
40. What is the placebo effect? How has it been shown that some of the placebo effect for pain is mediated by the endorphin system?

SLEEP AND WAKING

Waking
41. Describe the role of subcortical and cortical areas in wakefulness.

42. Describe the EEG and its relation to sleep.

The stages of sleep
43. Be able to describe the stages of sleep and the two kinds of sleep.

The functions of sleep
44. What are the effects of sleep deprivation? What is known about the functions of sleep and the determinants of the sleep cycle?

Dreams
45. What is the relation between REM sleep and dreaming? Why is our memory for dreams so poor?
46. Discuss whether dreaming has a function, and if so, what it might be. What is the activation-synthesis hypothesis?

WHAT DIFFERENT MOTIVES HAVE IN COMMON

The psychology of reward and the arousal level
47. Describe Hull's theory of drive reduction. Be able to criticize this theory.
48. What is meant by optimal arousal level, and how does it relate to drive reduction? What is the evidence for an optimal arousal level above zero?
49. Explain how drugs can be used to manipulate arousal. Give examples of depressant and stimulant drugs, and contrast the effects of these two types of drugs.
50. Describe drug addiction and the phenomena of tolerance and withdrawal.
51. Describe the opponent process theory of motivation. How do studies of drug addiction support this theory?

The biology of reward
52. What do studies of electrical stimulation of the brain tell us about motivation? Are there both general and motivation-specific pleasure centers in the brain?
53. Explain the dopamine hypothesis of reward, and indicate how it may account for the rewarding effects of stimulant drugs.
54. What might all motives have in common? Include consideration of potentiation, dopamine, and redundancy.

THE NATURE OF MOTIVES

55. Indicate how the biological basis for motives interacts with individual experience (learning).

Programmed Exercises

1. Temperature maintenance, hunger, and thirst involve motives aimed at self-_____. Fear and rage are associated with motives of self-_____, whereas sleep is directed at self-_____.

   regulation

   preservation, restoration

2. Motives increase the tendency to perform specific groups of behaviors. This tendency is sometimes called _____.

   potentiation

MOTIVATION AS DIRECTED ACTION

3. In _____ _____ systems, the feedback strengthens the initial behavior.

   positive feedback

4. In a _____ _____ system, the feedback stops, or even reverses, the original behavior.

   negative feedback

5. The maintenance of a stable equilibrium in the body is called _____.

   homeostasis

TEMPERATURE REGULATION

6. As opposed to _____, _____ can control their temperature internally.

   ectotherms, endotherms

7. Vasoconstriction and piloerection are two forms of _____ responses to _____ in body temperature.

   reflexive, decreases

8. Voluntary and reflexive heat-loss responses are brought into play when the body temperature drops below a temperature standard determined internally, which is called the _____.

   setpoint

9. The autonomic nervous system sends its commands to _____ and _____ _____.

   glands, smooth muscles

10. The _____ and _____ divisions of the autonomic nervous system work in opposite directions to control temperature. The _____ division acts to generate heat, to counteract low temperatures.

    sympathetic, parasympathetic, sympathetic

11. The activation of the divisions of the autonomic nervous system is determined by _____ located in the part of the brain that controls these divisions, the _____.

    (thermo)receptors hypothalamus

12. _____ are chemicals released into the bloodstream that raise the temperature setpoint.

    Pyrogens

THIRST

13. The brain detects the body's need for water from _____ receptors located in the brain and some blood vessels, and _____-receptors, which detect the concentration of minerals in the body fluids. These latter receptors are located in the _____.

    volume
    osmo
    hypothalamus

14. Drops in blood pressure or fluid volume typically cause increased secretion of the hormones _____ and _____.

    vasopressin, angiotension II

HUNGER

15. The fact that animals increase intake of foods that are diluted with nonnutritive substances suggests that they regulate _____.

    calories (energy)

16. Basal _____ _____ refers to the body's expenditure of energy to maintain basic body and cell functions.

    metabolic rate

17. Receptors sensitive to the metabolic state (energy need) of the organism have been postulated to exist in the _____ and _____.

    liver, brain

18. These receptors respond to blood levels of the basic source of short-term energy, which is _____. The liver controls the level of blood_____ (same as above) by reversibly converting it to the stored animal starch, _____.

    glucose, glucose glycogen

19. Satiety signals also originate in the gastrointestinal system, from nutrient receptors in the _____, and as a result of release of _____ when food passes into the duodenum.

    stomach, CCK

20. The brain may also be informed about the state of long-term energy stores (fat) in the body, by detecting the level of _____, secretion of _____ cells, in the blood.

    leptin, adipose

21. _____ stimuli, like the attractiveness of food, can influence the amount ingested, but their effectiveness depends in part on the _____ state of the organism.

    External internal (metabolic)

22. The dual-center theory is supported by the fact that lesions in the lateral hypothalamus produce _____, while lesions in the ventromedial hypothalamus produce _____.

    aphagia, hyperphagia

23. According to dual-center theory, "on" and "off" feeding centers in the hypothalamus are mutually _____.

    inhibitory

24. The fact that hyperphagic rats gain weight and then maintain themselves at the new, higher weight suggests that they are regulating their body weight around an elevated _____.

    setpoint

25. The ventromedial hypothalamus affects eating directly, but also indirectly by affecting fat metabolism through influence on levels of the hormone _____.

    insulin

26. In favor of hypothalamic control of eating, neurochemicals called _____ are secreted by the lateral hypothalamus and initiate eating.

orexins

28. The human infant has a few innate taste preferences, including an avoidance of _____ tastes and an attraction to _____ tastes.

bitter
sweet

29. Because nutritive quality and toxicity vary widely from one type of food to another, animals that eat a wide variety of foods, or _____, have to _____ about what is edible and what is not.

omnivores (generalists)
learn

30. The tendency to be suspicious of new foods is called _____.

neophobia

31. One nonpsychological difference among people that can affect obesity involves _____ "efficiency."

metabolic (digestive)

32. The high resemblance in obesity and body distribution of fat in _____ argues for a _____ determinant of obesity.

twins
genetic

33. According to the _____ _____, obese people are relatively unresponsive to their own internal hunger signals and more susceptible to signals from the outside, like taste.

externality hypothesis

34. Alternatively, externality is a result of being on a _____; that is, being below _____.

diet, setpoint

35. Restrained eaters and obese people may have, on the average, higher _____ than the rest of the population.

setpoints

36. A justification of getting treatment for obesity is that thinner people are more attractive, and hence are more _____ successful. There are also _____ benefits for not being very obese.

socially,
health (medical)

37. _____ _____ is an eating disorder characterized by extreme and self-imposed underweight, caused by an extreme desire to be thin.

Anorexia nervosa

38. _____ _____ is an eating disorder characterized by repeated binge and purge bouts.

Bulimia nervosa

THREAT

39. The parasympathetic system handles the _____ functions of the body.

vegetative

40. The sympathetic system has an _____ function.

activating

41. Sympathetic action is supported or amplified by the secretion of the hormone _____ (or _____).

adrenaline
epinephrine

42. The emergency reaction results from activation of the _____ nervous system.

sympathetic

43. Decreased electrical resistance of the skin, or the _____ _____ _____, is sometimes used as an index of autonomic arousal, as in lie detector tests.

galvanic skin response

44. "Lie detector" tests measure autonomic arousal using a device called the _____.

polygraph

45. The portion of the brain that governs the autonomic system and is responsible for the control of emotional reactions is called the _____ system.

limbic

46. Evidence indicates that there are different brain control centers for _____ attack and _____.

predatory
rage (counterattack)

47. _____ arousal can have disruptive effects, which, if maintained, can compromise health.

Autonomic

48. _____ can trigger fear and rage, and serves as an indicator that something is wrong or damaged.

Pain

49. Reduced feeling of pain, or _____, is produced by secretion of opiatelike substances in the brain called _____.

analgesia
endorphins

50. A chemically inert substance that a person believes will have an effect is called a _____.

placebo

51. Some placebo effects on pain seem to be mediated by endorphins, since their effects are eliminated or reduced by the drug _____, which blocks endorphin action.

naloxone

SLEEP AND WAKING

52. The record of the voltage changes occurring in the brain over time is called the _____ ( ).

electroencephalogram (EEG)

53. An EEG associated with waking relaxation shows _____ waves. The lower voltage, higher frequency EEG associated with alertness is called _____ waves.

alpha

beta

54. Rapid eye movements (REM), a waking EEG, relaxed muscles, and low sensitivity to external stimulation all characterize _____ sleep.

REM

55. In contrast, a more restful type of sleep occurs for most of the night; this _____-_____ sleep goes through a number of _____.

slow-wave

stages

56. The specific need for both REM and non-REM sleep has been shown through experiments in selective _____ _____. These results suggest that sleep of both types is a _____ process.

sleep deprivation, restorative

57. The 90- to 100-minute intervals between REM episodes are described as an _____ rhythm.

ultradian

58. The tendency to sleep varies across any 24-hour period, suggesting that sleep is _____-_____ or _____. This may be mediated by the hormone _____.

clock-driven, circadian, melatonin

59. Dreaming typically occurs during _____ sleep.

REM

60. According to _____, dreams have a function of allowing expression of unacceptable wishes in a disguised form.

Freud

61. According to the _____-_____ hypothesis, the dream is simply a reflection of the brain's aroused state during active sleep.

activation-synthesis

WHAT DIFFERENT MOTIVES HAVE IN COMMON

62. Hull believed that all built-in rewards produce some decrease in tension, or _____ _____.

drive
reduction

63. The fact that animals will learn to press a lever to engage in sexually arousing behavior argues for an _____ _____ of _____ that is greater than zero.

optimal level, arousal

64. Alcohol, barbiturates, and opiates are examples of _____ drugs.

depressant

65. Amphetamines and cocaine are examples of _____ drugs.

stimulant

66. Addiction is associated with decreased sensitivity to a drug. This effect is called _____.

tolerance

67. Addiction is also characterized by effects opposite to a drug's effects when the drug is discontinued. This is called _____.

withdrawal

68. According to _____-_____ theory, withdrawal symptoms can be explained as a result of action by the nervous system to neutralize the effects of the drug.

opponent-process

69. Hot peppers produce unpleasant pain in people who try them for the first time. Yet many come to like the "burn" after many experiences. This could be accounted for by _____-_____ _____, which might hold that the body counteracts this pain by generating pleasure internally.

opponent-process theory

70. Rats will learn to press a lever if it is followed by _____ _____ of certain _____ _____ in the brain.

electrical stimulation pleasure centers

71. There is evidence that brain stimulation reward mimics _____ rewards.

specific

72. According to the _____ hypothesis, _____ release in the nucleus accumbens may account for reward in general, including the effects of _____ drugs.

dopamine, dopamine stimulant

Self Test

1. Potentiation is:
   a. electrical in nature
   b. selective facilitation of certain responses
   c. hunger and thirst
   d. self-restorative
   e. the shift from one motive-state to another

2. Motivated behavior presents a serious problem to some machine models of behavior, because:
   a. motivated behavior involves a whole set of different reactions, any of which may lead toward the same goal
   b. motivated behavior involves direction, and this assumes a type of feedback that cannot be incorporated into machines
   c. motivated behavior assumes the operation of at least one type of feedback
   d. all of the above
   e. none of the above

3. In human sexual behavior, sexual foreplay seems gradually to increase sexual arousal of the partners. This would be an example of:
   a. homeostasis
   b. negative feedback
   c. a reflex
   d. positive feedback
   e. none of the above

4. Which of the following is a reflexive thermoregulatory response to high temperature?
   a. shivering
   b. constriction of the blood vessels in the skin
   c. sweating
   d. piloerection (ruffling of fur)
   e. moving to a colder place

5. The word pair *reflexive-voluntary* represents a relationship paralleled by which of the following pairs?
   a. homeostasis-whole organism
   b. vasoconstriction-vasodilation
   c. sweating-panting
   d. vasoconstriction-building a shelter
   e. none of the above

6. A dog is in a room comfortably heated to 75°F. His hypothalamus is cooled experimentally. The result will be:
   a. he will shiver and his body temperature will go up
   b. he will shiver and his body temperature will go down
   c. he will pant and his body temperature will go up
   d. he will pant and his body temperature will go down
   e. no change in temperature, because his skin temperature remains unchanged

7. A rat's hypothalamus is cooled, and it learns to settle down over a warm air current in one part of its cage. This behavior illustrates:

   a. the operation of hypothalamic thermoreceptors
   b. the mobilization of voluntary behavior by the hypothalamic thermoregulatory system
   c. that directly manipulating hypothalamic temperature can cause an animal to make a response that is inappropriate to its actual body temperature
   d. all of the above
   e. none of the above

8. Maintenance of the body's water supply is affected by all except:
   a. regulation of the volume and concentration of body fluids
   b. changes in reabsorption of water and minerals by the kidneys
   c. drinking in response to signals from internal receptors
   d. a substance secreted by the kidneys and sensed in the hypothalamus
   e. extent of piloerection

9. In both thermoregulation and thirst:
   a. receptors in the hypothalamus sense important aspects of bodily needs
   b. homeostasis occurs
   c. there is both reflexive and voluntary control
   d. all of the above
   e. none of the above

10. When rats are given a great deal of exercise, their intake of food increases; that is, they eat a larger amount of food. Rats also decrease their intake of a food if it is enriched, so that it contains more calories per gram. These findings suggest that:
    a. stomach fullness must be critical in regulating the rat's food intake
    b. the rat is regulating the volume of food consumed
    c. the rat is regulating the caloric or energy value of the food consumed
    d. all of the above
    e. a and c

11. Which of the following statements best summarizes the way that internal and external signals influence food intake?
    a. Signals from various internal structures (brain receptors, liver, etc.) determine the amount eaten; external factors have almost no effect.
    b. Metabolic information from receptors in the brain controls about half of food intake, and external stimulation the other half.
    c. Metabolic information from receptors in the liver, brain, and possibly other locations interacts with external stimulation to determine the amount eaten.
    d. Internal signals determine levels of leptin and glucose; external signals determine levels of glycogen.
    e. Hypothalamic receptors for internal and external events have a dual role in maintaining caloric intake.

12. Leptin, blood glucose, and CCK have in common:
    a. they are all produced by the liver
    b. they can all be converted to glycogen
    c. when levels are high in the blood, they promote satiety
    d. a and b
    e. all of the above

13. Food intake usually ceases before significant amounts of food have been absorbed from the bloodstream. This suggests that:
    a. the stomach may play an important role in satiety
    b. learning may play an important role in satiety
    c. oral factors (e.g., monitoring how much has gone into the mouth) may play a role in satiety
    d. a and c
    e. all of the above

14. Initiation of eating is most likely to be associated with:
    a. high blood glucose
    b. excitation of the lateral hypothalamus
    c. inhibition of the lateral hypothalamus
    d. high liver glycogen
    e. excitation of the ventromedial hypothalamus

15. Dual-center theory makes all but one of the following assumptions or predictions. Which assumption is not a necessary part of the theory?
    a. Information from internal and external receptors is integrated in the hypothalamus.
    b. The relation between the two hypothalamic feeding centers is one of mutual inhibition.
    c. The liver is the primary source of information concerning the metabolic state of the organism.
    d. Damage to the "on" center should produce aphagia.
    e. Damage to the "off" center should produce hyperphagia.

16. Two rats (or people) differ greatly in weight and fatness, but each of them holds its weight rather constant over a period of months. These results suggest that the two differ in:
    a. setpoint
    b. stomach size
    c. ability to regulate body weight
    d. ability to regulate food intake
    e. size of hypothalamus

17. Evidence suggests that hypothalamic control of eating operates:
    a. directly
    b. indirectly via control of metabolism
    c. exclusively through the process of inhibition
    d. primarily to control the type of food eaten
    e. a and b

18. Consider three types of animals: those that eat only one narrow type of food ("univores"), those that eat a variety of animal foods (carnivores), and those that eat a variety of plant foods (general herbivores). Which of the following arranges these types in terms of the increasing importance of learning in their food selection?
    a. univore, general herbivore, carnivore
    b. general herbivore, carnivore, univore
    c. carnivore, univore, general herbivore

    d. univore, carnivore, general herbivore
    e. b or d

19. Which of the following is not a likely example of neophobia?
    a. the rejection of corn, when it came from the Americas, by most cultures in Europe
    b. the avoidance of a new food by a wild rat
    c. the avoidance of a food by a rat after it consumed that food and became ill
    d. the tendency of many young children to accept only a few foods
    e. a and d

20. Which one of the following has not been suggested as a cause of obesity in humans?
    a. damage to the lateral region of the hypothalamus
    b. high digestive efficiency
    c. a high setpoint
    d. overresponsiveness to the palatability of food
    e. high metabolic efficiency

21. Externality and high setpoint are:
    a. both hypotheses about the cause of obesity
    b. both ways of reducing dieting
    c. both consequences of obesity
    d. a and b
    e. all of the above

22. Which of the following findings supports a setpoint as opposed to an externality account of obesity?
    a. Obese people eat relatively more of highly palatable foods.
    b. Obese people tend to maintain a steady weight.
    c. Obese individuals who are not dieting are no more external than are normal-weight individuals.
    d. b and c
    e. all of the above

23. Effective therapy (including better adjustment) for obese individuals might be accomplished by:
    a. drugs that effectively reduce setpoint
    b. a consistent pattern of dieting
    c. curbing the ideal of thinness in western society
    d. b and c
    e. all of the above

24. A major distinction between anorexia nervosa and bulimia is that:
    a. females predominate only in anorexia nervosa
    b. only anorexics are well below normal weight
    c. only bulimia is commonly found in people in the 15–25-year age range
    d. all of the above
    e. none of the above

25. The sympathetic branch of the autonomic nervous system is responsible for which of the following?
    a. decreased heart rate
    b. crying after a sad movie
    c. vegetative functions, such as digestion
    d. emptying of the colon and bladder
    e. none of the above

26. The responses of a cat about to do battle with a dog are mediated by:
    a. the parasympathetic system
    b. the sympathetic system
    c. vegetative functions
    d. the galvanic skin response
    e. b and c

27. Which of the following is *not* associated with activity of the sympathetic system?
    a. the emergency reaction
    b. epinephrine
    c. secretion by the adrenal medulla
    d. increased heart rate
    e. secretion of digestive enzymes

28. Imagine a person who has an unusual amount of voluntary control over her autonomic nervous system. Such a person should be able to:
    a. markedly reduce her weight
    b. successfully "beat" lie detector tests
    c. never experience fear
    d. get along without sleeping
    e. a and d

29. The shaded area of this cross-section of the brain represents a part of the brain that is involved in motivation and emotion. It is called the:
    a. hypothalamus
    b. limbic system
    c. cerebellum
    d. pituitary gland
    e. corpus callosum

30. Which of the following statements about pain is false?
    a. Experience of chronic pain is adaptive.
    b. Experience of acute pain is adaptive.
    c. Endorphins often reduce pain.
    d. Naloxone may block the pain-reducing effects of endorphins.
    e. a and b

31. Imagine a new pain-relieving drug that reduces rated pain by 80%, in comparison to a 50% reduction with a placebo.

Suppose that the placebo effect was completely caused by endorphin secretion, but the residual effect of the new drug was not. Then, for naloxone-treated participants we would predict _____% pain reduction in the placebo condition and _____ % in the drug condition.
    a. 50, 80
    b. 50, 50
    c. 0, 30
    d. 0, 0
    e. 50, 0

32. REM sleep is sometimes called paradoxical sleep because:
    a. behaviorally the person seems to be sleeping, but his or her brain waves show a pattern of activity usually associated with a waking EEG
    b. it occurs at unexpected times (e.g., in a noisy environment or during the day)
    c. the person is easily roused, yet his or her EEG consists of slow, large amplitude, synchronous waves
    d. all of the above
    e. a and b

33. Which of the following pairings represents a contrast between REM sleep and slow-wave sleep?
    a. rapid eye movements—no rapid eye movements
    b. dreaming—lack of dreaming
    c. EEG waking activity—EEG slow waves
    d. all of the above
    e. a and c

34. Restorative functions for slow-wave sleep are suggested by:
    a. increased duration of quiet sleep after quiet sleep deprivation
    b. linkage of quiet sleep to subcortical centers
    c. increased duration of quiet sleep after bodily exhaustion
    d. the existence of active sleep
    e. a and c

35. When research participants are awakened after fifteen minutes of REM they relate longer dreams than when they are awakened after five minutes of REM. This result is evidence that:
    a. dreams are not only better remembered during REM, but actually unfold during REM
    b. dreams are rarely influenced by external sensory stimulation
    c. as dreams progress, they are related to memories of waking life
    d. dreams are mediated by the cerebral cortex and subcortical centers
    e. all of the above

36. The activation-synthesis hypothesis of dreaming differs from the Freudian theory in that:
    a. it holds that dreams are always meaningless
    b. it considers memories important as the raw materials of dreams
    c. it does not focus on dreams as unconsciously motivated ways of solving problems
    d. it links dreaming to REM sleep
    e. c and d

37. According to which formulation is pleasure simply the absence of pain?
    a. opponent-process theory
    b. Hull's theory of drive reduction
    c. the externality hypothesis
    d. the dual-center theory
    e. none of the above

38. The fact that nonnutritive saccharin serves as a reward for rats, and that solving a puzzle seems to be its own reward for monkeys and humans, suggests that:
    a. drive reduction is not the only mechanism of reward
    b. Hull's conception of reward was correct
    c. drive reduction does not depend on electrical stimulation of the brain
    d. organisms seek to diminish their arousal levels
    e. a and d

39. The mechanical puzzle is used to demonstrate that monkeys:
    a. will be motivated by drive reduction
    b. will perform some acts as ends in themselves
    c. will only work for drive reduction
    d. can be stimulated
    e. none of the above

40. Suppose a person is drowsy and inactive much of the time. Which of the following drugs is most likely to reverse these effects?
    a. alcohol
    b. barbiturates
    c. opiates
    d. cocaine
    e. heroin

41. A person addicted to a specific euphoria-producing drug suddenly stops using this drug. He goes into a deep depression. This reaction is an example of:
    a. the effects of tolerance
    b. the effects of addiction
    c. a withdrawal symptom
    d. drive reduction
    e. a and c

42. Withdrawal results from the same forces that produce tolerance to drugs, according to:
    a. opponent-process theory
    b. optimal arousal theory

c. studies on electrical stimulation of the brain
    d. drive-reduction theory
    e. b and d

43. According to the opponent-process theory account of tolerance and withdrawal, the effects of opiate withdrawal should be most like the effect of:
    a. alcohol
    b. barbiturates
    c. amphetamines
    d. cocaine
    e. c and d

44. Studies on electrical stimulation of the brain have indicated:
    a. the existence of motivation-specific "pleasure centers" in the brain
    b. the possible presence of general "pleasure centers"
    c. the importance of the medial forebrain pathway in reward
    d. all of the above
    e. none of the above

45. According to the dopamine hypothesis of reward:
    a. stimulant drugs directly cause reward by initiating dopamine activity in the nucleus accumbens
    b. dopamine is responsible for opponent processes
    c. there is a common neurotransmitter basis for all rewards
    d. a and c
    e. all of the above

46. Food sometimes tastes better after the first few bites, and then gradually becomes less tasty as we consume substantial amounts. This sequence can be accounted for as:
    a. an effect of brain stimulation
    b. increasing levels of dopamine
    c. positive feedback followed by negative feedback
    d. opponent processes, in which endorphins are secreted more and more during a meal
    e. an instance of drive-reduction theory

47. Which of the following can be considered a homeostatic motive?
    a. hunger
    b. sex
    c. curiosity
    d. a and b
    e. none of the above

48. Animals and humans continue to experience hunger after stomach removal, although the stomach clearly contributes to the hunger experience. This type of finding suggests that a basic feature of many motivation systems is:
    a. dopamine activity
    b. potentiation
    c. redundancy
    d. opponent processes
    e. a and b

Answer Key for Self Test

1.	b p. 71	25.	e p. 92
2.	a p. 71	26.	b p. 93
3.	d p. 72	27.	e pp. 92, 93
4.	c p. 74	28.	b p. 94
5.	d pp.74, 75	29.	b p. 95
6.	a p. 76	30.	a pp. 96–98
7.	d p. 76	31.	c p. 98
8.	e pp. 78, 79	32.	a p. 101
9.	d pp. 74–79	33.	d pp. 100, 101
10.	c p. 80	34.	e p. 102
11.	c pp. 80–82	35.	a p. 105
12.	c pp. 80–82	36.	e p. 106
13.	e pp. 81–83	37.	b p. 107
14.	b p. 83	38.	a p. 107, 108
15.	c pp. 83, 84	39.	b p. 108
16.	a p. 84	40.	d p. 109
17.	e pp. 84, 85	41.	c p. 110
18.	d p. 85	42.	a p. 110
19.	c p. 86	43.	e p. 110
20.	a pp. 87, 88	44.	d pp. 111, 112
21.	a p. 88	45.	d pp. 100–101
22.	d p. 88, 89	46.	c p. 112
23.	e p. 89	47.	a p. 112
24.	b p. 91	48.	c p. 112

Investigating Psychological Phenomena

EFFECTS OF MENTAL PROCESSES ON AUTONOMIC ACTIVITY

Equipment: Stopwatch or watch with second indicator
Number of participants: Three
Time per participant: Ten minutes
Time for experimenter: Forty minutes

As part of its role in the control of bodily functions, the autonomic nervous system (ANS) controls heart rate. In this way it can influence the rate of delivery of oxygen and nutrients to the cells of the body. In times when the body is stressed, increased heart rate (and other changes) increases the delivery of nutrients to cells, as well as increasing the rate of disposal of waste products. The changes in heart rate are produced directly by nerve impulses sent to the heart. They are also produced indirectly by stimulation, through autonomic pathways, of the release of epinephrine (adrenaline) and related substances from the adrenal glands.

Arousal of the sympathetic system, and hence increased heart rate, occurs when the organism is undergoing physical exertion. But it can also be produced by mental events. Such a pathway would allow an organism to mobilize its physiological resources in anticipation of a physical stress. On the other hand, it also allows for high and ultimately damaging levels of sympathetic arousal based on chronic anxiety or mental tension.

In this study we will demonstrate the effectiveness of the sympathetic nervous system link between mental activity and heart rate. Participants will be asked to increase their heart rate by thinking about either a strenuous physical activity or something that is mentally exciting.

Make sure that your participant is seated comfortably, has been relaxing for at least ten minutes, and did not engage in any strenuous activity in the last half hour. Before reading the instructions make sure you can find the participant's pulse on his or her wrist. The unit of recording for heart rate will be a thirty-second interval. You will record the number of beats every thirty seconds on the data sheet on the next page. Allow fifteen seconds to pass between each thirty-second interval or recording so that you will have enough time to record the pulse and give the instruction. If you have an instruction to give the participant (e.g., "Relax," "Increase Mental"), give the instruction as soon as you have recorded the pulse rate, but wait the full fifteen seconds before counting heartbeats.

Instructions to read to the participant:

This is a short, ten-minute experiment to determine whether you can control the rate of beating of your heart. When I say "Begin," you should close your eyes and relax while I take your pulse. After a minute I will say "Increase physical activity," and you should try to increase your heart rate by thinking about some physical activity in which you are personally engaged and which requires a lot of exertion. After I record your pulse I will say, "Relax," and you should stop trying to increase your heart rate and relax again. I will take your pulse for another minute and then I will say "Increase mental activity." This time you should try to increase your heart rate by thinking of something that is exciting but that does not involve a lot of physical activity. This could be a fearful experience that you have had, the excitement from watching a sports event, preexamination anxiety, and so on. Following this one-minute episode I will say, "Relax," and you should stop trying to increase your heart rate and relax. I will take your pulse for one final minute. Before you begin the experiment decide on each image you will think about for the physical activity and the mental activity. After you have decided, stop thinking about the images until I give you the instruction during the actual experiment.

Give the participant a few minutes to decide on images and then to stop thinking about them before you begin the experiment. Wait one minute after the participant has selected the two images, to allow any excitation that this may have produced to go away.

DATA FROM THREE PARTICIPANTS (A, B, AND C)

Instruction and time	A	B	C
"Begin and Relax"			
00:00–0:30			
0:45–1:15			
"Increase physical activity"			
1:30–2:00			
2:15–2:45			
"Relax"			
3:00–3:30			
3:45–4:15			
"Increase mental activity"			
4:30–5:00			
5:15–5:45			
"Relax"			
6:00–6:30			
6:45–7:15			

List for each participant the basic situation that they imagined in the "increase" minutes.

	Physical	Mental
A	_____	_____
B	_____	_____
C	_____	_____

Plot the data for each participant on the graph below. Use a different symbol for each participant, and connect the symbols for each participant by lines. Since heart rate is usually expressed as beats per minute, double each of the numbers you have recorded (since you recorded beats per thirty seconds) before plotting. We have plotted the results from ten undergraduates (mean). In our study nine of the ten undergraduates showed the increased heart rate effect.

Do all of your participants show an ability to increase heart rate by mental activity? Which procedure, thinking of physical activity or something mentally exciting, is more effective? (*If your instructor collects the data, fill out the report sheet in Appendix 3.*)

FURTHER PROJECTS

Lowering heart rate is much more difficult than raising it. You might see if you can get some participants to do that.

Some people have great difficulty in raising their heart rate. If one of your participants is such a person, you could try to get an increase by having the participant *talk* about physical activity or something exciting during a one-minute period.

You could also explore whether certain kinds of "exciting thoughts" (e.g., fear, excitement of a spectator at a sports event) are more effective in raising heart rate.

CHAPTER 4

Learning

Learning Objectives

1. Describe the point of view of learning theorists, their fit with American values, and the reason that most of their work focused on nonhuman animals.

HABITUATION

2. Define habituation and discuss its adaptive significance.

CLASSICAL CONDITIONING

Pavlov and the conditioned reflex
3. Explain the basic procedure (paradigm) of classical conditioning, and define conditioned and unconditioned stimuli and responses.
4. Distinguish between classical conditioning and habituation.

The major phenomena of classical conditioning
5. Describe the three measures of conditioned response strength: response amplitude, probability of response, and response latency.
6. Draw a curve to represent the acquisition and extinction of a conditioned response.
7. Be able to define: reinforcement, second-order conditioning, extinction, and spontaneous recovery.
8. Describe generalization and discrimination, and contrast the two processes.

Extensions of classical conditioning
9. Indicate how classical conditioning can account for acquired fears and phobias, and describe how conditioned fear is measured.
10. Show that the conditioned response often functions to prepare the organism for the unconditioned stimulus, and hence that the CR and UR often differ. Illustrate this with the example of the compensatory-reaction hypothesis and its account of drug tolerance and addiction.

INSTRUMENTAL CONDITIONING

11. Review the major similarities and differences between classical conditioning and instrumental conditioning.

Thorndike and the law of effect
12. Explain the law of effect and indicate the evidence that supports it.
13. What is the relation between the law of effect and the evolutionary principle of survival of the fittest?

Skinner and operant behavior
14. What additions and modifications did Skinner propose to Thorndike's view of instrumental conditioning?

The major phenomena of instrumental conditioning
15. How do the phenomena of instrumental conditioning parallel those of classical conditioning?
16. Describe the processes of generalization, discrimination, and shaping in instrumental conditioning.
17. Give examples of conditioned and primary reinforcers, and describe how a conditioned reinforcer can be produced or eliminated.
18. Evaluate the importance of information, behavioral contrast, and intrinsic motivation as extensions or modifiers of the concept of reinforcement.
19. Define and describe schedules of reinforcement and their properties, and indicate the effect of the schedules on resistance to extinction.
20. Indicate the ways in which aversive stimuli influence learning, by describing punishment, escape, and avoidance learning.
21. Why does avoidance learning present a problem for learning theory?

COGNITIVE LEARNING

22. Compare learning theory with cognitive learning theory, contrasting learning of responses to learning of cognitions (representations).

A cognitive view of classical conditioning
23. Discuss the effects of different times of onset of the conditioned and unconditioned stimulus. What is the most effective CS–US interval, and why is this adaptive?
24. Distinguish contiguity and contingency, and explain the studies that indicate that contingency is a critical factor in the formation of conditioned responses.

25. Explain the role of surprise in learning, and show how blocking demonstrates this.

A cognitive view of instrumental conditioning

26. Review the evidence supporting the position that what is learned in instrumental conditioning is act-outcome associations, as opposed to the strengthening of specific responses. Describe latent learning.
27. Explain the role of contingency in instrumental conditioning, and its relation to learned helplessness.
28. How has learned helplessness been used to explain some types of depression in humans?

VARIETIES OF LEARNING

Biological constraints on associative learning: belongingness

29. What is the equipotentiality principle, and what is the evidence against it? Describe belongingness or preparedness.
30. Describe the phenomenon of taste aversion learning, and indicate why it illustrates biological constraints. Describe acquired taste aversions in humans.
31. Discuss belongingness in response–outcome relations in instrumental conditioning.
32. In what sense is key-pecking by pigeons not an arbitrary operant? In what sense is key-pecking classically conditioned?

Adaptive specializations of learning

33. Summarize the argument that there are specialized types of learning in particular species and ecological niches. Provide an illustration.

Similarities in what different species learn

34. Indicate some similarities across situations and species in properties of learning. How do these relate to environmental "universals"?

THE NEURAL BASIS FOR LEARNING

35. Explain the advantages of studying a simple system, like the nervous system of Aplysia.

Presynaptic facilitation

36. What is presynaptic facilitation, and how might it account for learning?

Long-term potentiation

37. What is long-term potentiation, and how might it account for learning and, in particular, contingency detection?

COMPLEX COGNITION IN ANIMALS

Cognitive maps

38. What are cognitive maps and what is the evidence that animals have them?

Insightful behavior

39. Describe the phenomenon of insight in animals, and indicate why it presents problems for traditional learning theory.
40. How do we determine whether insight or trial and error is a better way of describing a particular learned behavior? What is the role of transfer of training in making this distinction?
41. Distinguish between generalization and transfer.
42. Describe complex perceptual concepts, like the concept of "water" in pigeons.
43. Explain what abstract concepts are and how they differ from complex perceptual concepts. Illustrate this with results from matching to sample and same-different symbol studies.

TAKING STOCK

44. Evaluate the strengths and shortcomings of accounts of all learning based on habituation, classical conditioning, and instrumental conditioning.

Programmed Exercises

1. _____ _____ believe that a few simple laws of learning can account for most of human and animal behavior.	Learning theorists

HABITUATION

2. _____ is a decline in the tendency to respond to stimuli that have become familiar due to repeated exposure.	Habituation

CLASSICAL CONDITIONING

3. Unlike habituation, classical conditioning involves the formation of _____ between events.	associations
4. _____ _____ was first demonstrated in the laboratory by Ivan Pavlov.	Classical conditioning
5. After classical conditioning, the salivation of a dog upon presentation of a previously neutral bell would be called a(n) _____ _____. The previously neutral bell is now called a(n) _____ _____.	conditioned response conditioned stimulus
6. In Pavlov's laboratory, food in the mouth was a(n) _____ _____, and the salivation it produced was a(n) _____ _____.	unconditioned stimulus unconditioned response
7. Salivation to meat powder in the mouth is a(n) _____ _____. Salivation to a tone paired with meat powder in the mouth is a(n) _____ _____.	unconditioned reflex (response), conditioned reflex (response)
8. According to Pavlov, when the CS is followed by the US, the connection between them is _____.	reinforced

9. Response strength in classical conditioning can be measured as the amount of response, that is, the response _____, the time from onset of CS to the onset of the CR, called the _____, or the proportion of trials on which the CR is made when the CS is presented, the _____ of response.

amplitude

latency

probability

10.

Reinforced trials

This graph is an example of an idealized _____ _____.

learning curve

11. A light is paired with shock. Subsequently, a tone paired with the light comes to elicit fear. This is an example of _____-_____ _____.

second-order conditioning

12. If after a CR has been established, the CS is presented but is not followed by the US, the result will be _____ of the CR.

extinction

13. If time is allowed to pass, the CR will reappear when the CS is presented. This is the phenomenon of _____ _____.

spontaneous recovery

14. Horizontal stripes on a card (CS) are paired with a puff of air to the eye (US), resulting in a conditioned eye blink response. Now, the first time vertical stripes are presented, a conditioned eye blink is observed. This is an example of _____ _____.

stimulus generalization

15. The greater the difference between a CS and another test stimulus, the weaker the CR to this test stimulus. This relationship is described as a _____ _____.

generalization gradient

16. Reinforcement (US presentation) after CS^+, and nonreinforcement (no US) after CS^-, leads to _____.

discrimination

17. Animals show _____ _____ when a stimulus paired with shock is presented to them. This is called the _____ _____ _____.

response suppression
conditioned emotional response

18. According to a classical conditioning analysis, the object of a phobia or fetish can be considered a _____ _____.

conditioned stimulus

19. In many instances, the CR does not duplicate the UR, but rather _____ the animal to deal with the UR.

prepares

20. Sometimes the CR has the opposite effect from the UR, as when the CS signals drug arrival (US). This is accounted for by the _____-_____ hypothesis, and explains the phenomenon of drug _____.

compensatory-reaction
tolerance

INSTRUMENTAL CONDITIONING

21. In classical conditioning, a relation between two stimuli is learned. In instrumental conditioning, however, the relation that is learned exists between a _____ and a _____.

response, reward

22. The experimental study of instrumental learning was begun by _____ in the context of a debate over the mental continuity of humans and animals, which was stimulated by the evolutionary theories of _____.

(Edward L.) Thorndike

(Charles) Darwin

23. Thorndike's _____ _____ _____ states that the consequences of a response determine whether it becomes strengthened or weakened.

law of effect

24. The most prominent figure in modern learning theory was _____.

(B. F.) Skinner

25. Skinner emphasized distinctions between classical conditioning and instrumental learning. In the former, responses are _____, while in instrumental learning they are _____.

elicited, emitted

26. Skinner used the term "_____" to describe the "voluntary" or "emitted" responses that are studied in instrumental learning. He preferred to measure _____ _____ as a measure of response strength.

operants
response rate

27. In instrumental conditioning, the delivery of an _____ stimulus (some preferred situation or substance; e.g., food) following a particular response is one form of reinforcement. appetitive

28. In instrumental conditioning, the situation in which an instrumental response eliminates an _____ stimulus is another form of reinforcement. aversive

29. Although operants are not elicited by external stimuli, the stimuli can control behavior as _____ _____. discriminative stimuli

30. Animals can be trained to perform difficult responses by the process of _____, using the method of _____ _____. shaping successive approximation

31. After a neutral stimulus is paired with a reinforcer such as food, the neutral stimulus acquires reinforcement properties. This is called _____ _____. conditioned reinforcement

32. Conditioned reinforcement is established by a procedure that seems to be the same as _____ conditioning. classical

33. Animals and humans can be reinforced not only by events that reduce biological needs, but also by _____ from the environment. information

34. The effectiveness of a reinforcement depends on the context of reinforcement; whether prior reinforcements were larger or smaller than the current one. This is called _____ _____. behavioral contrast

35. Behaviors performed for their own sake, providing their own reward, are described as cases of _____ motivation. intrinsic

36. The rule set up by the experimenter (or society) that determines the occasions on which a response is reinforced is called a _____ _____ _____. schedule of reinforcement

37. An animal that is reinforced for every five responses is on a _____ _____ schedule. fixed ratio

38. Responses acquired with intermittent reinforcement exhibit greater resistance to extinction. This is termed the _____ _____ _____. partial reinforcement effect

39. Loud noises, painful stimuli, bitter tastes, and social rejection are examples of _____ stimuli. aversive

40. In _____ training, an aversive stimulus follows a particular response. punishment

41. _____ learning is a type of instrumental learning in which the organism is required to perform a response which terminates or reduces an aversive stimulus. Escape

42. Avoidance learning presents problems for behavior theory because it is not easy to identify the _____ for the avoidance response. reinforcer

43.

This graph illustrates the transition from _____ to _____ learning. escape, avoidance

COGNITIVE LEARNING

44. Learning theorists emphasize that learning modifies _____. In contrast, cognitive theorists argue that learning involves acquisition of _____.

responses (action)
knowledge (cognitions, representations)

45. Learning of a conditioned response (CR) occurs most efficiently when the _____ precedes the _____ by a small time interval. This is called _____ pairing.

CS, US, forward

46. Pavlov and others claimed that togetherness in time, pairing, or _____ forms the basis for classical conditioning.

(temporal) contiguity

47. Later research suggests that what is critical for conditioning is that the CS predicts the US, so that there is a _____ between CS and US.

contingency

48.

The pattern of shock and signals shown in A above is most likely to give rise, in the presence of the tone, to the state of _____, whereas the _____ shock shown in B is likely to give rise to the state of _____.

fear, unsignaled (uncontingent), anxiety

49. According to several theorists, the greater the _____ at the onset of the US, the more learning will occur.

surprise (unexpectedness)

50. A stimulus (CS-1) is presented contingently with a US. Then, a second stimulus (CS-2) is also presented at the same time as CS-1, and both are followed by the US. Often, only CS-1 will show classical conditioning. This phenomenon is called _____.

blocking

51. Two conditions that seem necessary for classical conditioning to occur are that the CS must show a _____ relation to the US, and the CS must provide _____ that the organism did not have before.

contingent, information

52. Evidence indicates that rather than strengthening specific responses, instrumental reinforcement creates _____-_____ associations.

act-outcome

53. Learning in the absence of reward indicates that responses need not occur for learning to occur. This is called _____ learning.

latent

54. Just as is the case with classical conditioning, what is learned in instrumental learning is a _____.

contingency

55. Dogs given inescapable shocks are then placed in an avoidance situation shuttlebox where they could learn a jumping response to escape and avoid shock. Instead, they lie quietly and take the shocks. Their behavior has been interpreted as learning that the presence or absence of shocks is not contingent on their behavior, a state called _____ _____.

learned helplessness

56. The symptoms shown by helpless dogs resemble those seen in the human disorder of _____.

depression

VARIETIES OF LEARNING

57. Traditional learning theory assumes that the relation between stimuli in classical conditioning, or between response and outcome in instrumental learning, is _____. This assumption is known as the _____ principle.

arbitrary
equipotentiality

58. One criticism of traditional learning theory holds that there are certain built-in limitations called _____ _____ that determine what a given animal can easily learn.

biological constraints

59. _____ _____ aversions are an example of belongingness, and their rapid acquisition makes them an example of _____-_____ learning.

Learned taste
one-trial

60. Belongingness in animal learning, as illustrated by taste aversion learning, seems to fit well with the survival needs of animals. Thus, rats, who rely heavily on _____ in feeding, tend to associate that with the aftereffects of eating, while birds, which rely on _____ in feeding, tend to associate this type of stimulus with the aftereffects of eating.

taste
vision (sight)

61. The fact that it is easier to train a pigeon to flap its wings to escape shock than to receive food is an instance of _____ in _____-_____ relations in instrumental learning.

belongingness (preparedness),
response (act)-outcome

62. It is easier to teach built-in reactions to danger, or _____-_____ _____ reactions, in escape or avoidance experiments.

species-specific defense

63. Acquisition of bird song, navigational abilities, and memories for sites where food has been stored all represent _____ _____ of learning.

adaptive specializations

64. Similarities in properties of learning across species and situations suggest _____ features of the world across environments.

common (universal)

THE NEURAL BASIS FOR LEARNING

65. The capacity for neurons to change the way they function as a consequence of experience is called _____ _____.

neural plasticity

66. The study of the marine mollusk, Aplysia, is advantageous for research on the neural basis of learning because the nervous system of Aplysia is a relatively _____ system.

simple

67. One form of neural plasticity, as demonstrated in Aplysia, involves activation of one pathway increasing the transmitter release at the synapse of another pathway. This is called _____ _____.

presynaptic
facilitation

68. In the process of _____-_____ _____, activation of a synapse makes that synapse more sensitive for periods lasting for days or weeks.

long-term potentiation

69. Inputs to the same neuron that occur roughly simultaneously may mutually increase the sensitivity of the _____ neuron receptors for the other input neuron, perhaps accounting for the process of _____ detection.

postsynaptic
contingency (correlation)

COMPLEX COGNITION IN ANIMALS

70. Tolman's original work, later work on the radial-arm maze with rats, and food retrieval by chimpanzees suggest that animals have _____ _____.

cognitive maps

71. Köhler claimed that animals can acquire _____, as well as responses.

cognitions

72. The photograph below represents a situation studied by Köhler in which he demonstrated the phenomenon of _____.

insight

73. A chimpanzee solves the problem of knocking down a piece of fruit hung above the cage by throwing a ball at it. When the ball is taken away, it throws a piece of fruit. This demonstrates _____ _____ _____.

transfer
of training

TRADITIONAL LEARNING

74. Traditional learning theory interprets transfer effects as instances of _____ _____, but transfer often seems to be based on abstract _____ relationships.

stimulus generalization,
conceptual (meaningful)

75. The concepts of water or tree in pigeons are examples of _____ _____ concepts.

complex perceptual

76. An animal is shown one stimulus and, below it, two other stimuli. One of these two is identical to the upper stimulus. The correct response is to indicate this stimulus. This procedure is called _____ _____ _____.

matching to sample

77. The idea of "sameness" developed by Sarah, the chimpanzee, is an example of an _____ _____.

abstract
concept

78. A major criticism of behavior theory that emerges from recent work is that we must explore not only what animals (and humans) *do*, but also what they _____.

know

Self-Test

1. Learning theorists share with Descartes the conviction that:
   a. one must study the nervous system to understand behavior
   b. learning is the most important aspect of animal behavior
   c. complex behavior can be analyzed into simpler, more elementary processes
   d. almost all behavior can be described as hardwired (innate)
   e. c and d

2. An animal startles when it is exposed to the sound of either a door slamming or a gong ringing. It is then exposed, about ten times, to the gong ringing followed by the door slamming. Now, when the gong rings, the animal does *not* startle. This is an example of
   a. habitation
   b. classical conditioning
   c. extinction
   d. associations
   e. a learning curve

3. Classical conditioning and habituation have in common the fact that both:
   a. involve associations
   b. require a conditioned stimulus
   c. are built-in responses that animals show in laboratory situations
   d. involve a change in response to a stimulus
   e. occur primarily in dogs, though they may occur in some other species

4. In a classical conditioning experiment in which a tone is paired with meat in the mouth, a dog comes to salivate to the sound of the tone. The tone is called the:
   a. conditioned stimulus
   b. unconditioned stimulus
   c. unconditioned response
   d. stimulus generalization
   e. reinforcer

5. Ivan Pilaff developed a fear of German shepherds because, on a few occasions, he was bitten by them. Some weeks later, he became friendly with someone who had a German shepherd as a pet. After a few visits to this friend plus shepherd, he became fearful of the friend, even though this particular German shepherd never bit him. This is an example of:
   a. discrimination
   b. extinction
   c. reinforcement
   d. learning with a long delay
   e. second-order conditioning

6. A dog is first classically conditioned to seven stimuli (A–G) until he responds equally to all. He then gets some further training. At the end he produces the unusual generalization curve shown above, right. What was the further training the dog received?

   a. extinguished stimuli A, B, D, F, and G
   b. extinguish B, D, and F; further condition A and G
   c. extinguish C and E
   d. extinguish C, D, and E
   e. further condition A and G

7. This figure illustrates the phenomenon of:

   a. conditioning
   b. generalization
   c. extinction
   d. reconditioning
   e. spontaneous recovery

8. Classical conditioning has been:
   a. shown to occur only with salivation
   b. used to explain responses to music, in conjunction with Romantic conditioning
   c. demonstrated only in vertebrates
   d. suggested as an explanation for phobias
   e. a and c

9. During World War II, air raid sirens preceded bombing raids. A person who, as a result of fear, stopped her ongoing activity (e.g., eating, working) when sirens sounded showed:
   a. response suppression
   b. a siren phobia
   c. extinction
   d. spontaneous recovery
   e. a generalization gradient

10. An experienced skydiver does not show nearly as much arousal, on entering the plane from which he will jump, as does a novice skydiver. Consider an experienced skydiver who is just about to enter the plane, but is called back at the

last minute. If he shows a conditioned compensatory response, we would expect that:
a. his arousal would be about the same as that of the novice
b. he would show a bigger increase in arousal than the novice
c. he would show the same decrease in arousal as the novice
d. he would show the same increase in arousal as the novice
e. he would become less aroused than he normally is in daily life

11. The relation between a UR and a conditioned compensatory response is like the relation between excitation and:
a. conditioning
b. reconditioning
c. extinction
d. response suppression
e. inhibition

12. Instrumental learning differs from classical conditioning in that:
a. in instrumental learning, a response-reward association is learned, while in classical conditioning, a relation between stimuli is learned
b. associations are formed only in classical conditioning
c. responses are never involved in classical conditioning
d. instrumental learning always occurs gradually, in trial-and-error fashion, whereas classical conditioning occurs very rapidly
e. a and c

13. According to the law of effect, responses followed by reward:
a. increase in latency
b. are not always reinforced
c. become trials or errors
d. are strengthened
e. all of the above

14. The parallel between Darwin's theory of evolution and instrumental conditioning is between:
a. mental continuity and trial-and-error learning
b. learning and extinction
c. survival of the fittest and the law of effect
d. a and b
e. all of the above

15. As described by Thorndike, instrumental learning:
a. is gradual
b. involves no complex, uniquely human processes
c. is accomplished on a trial-and-error basis
d. is a means of strengthening particular responses
e. all of the above

16. Skinner added to Thorndike's conception(s) the idea that the responses conditioned in instrumental learning were:
a. emitted or voluntary, as opposed to elicited as in classical conditioning
b. increased in strength by the process of reinforcement
c. selected from all responses emitted on the basis of the law of effect
d. a and c
e. all of the above

17. Skinner and Thorndike share in common a belief in:
a. the importance of schedules of reinforcement
b. the law of effect
c. the idea that instrumental behavior is emitted
d. the superiority of instrumental training with discrete trials
e. all of the above

18. A rat is placed in a chamber and is given a number of pellets of food, each preceded by a clicking sound. It is later trained to lever press, with the reinforcement only the sounding of the click, but no food. Every other day the rat receives pairings of click and food, and on the alternate days, it presses only for the click. Eventually, it stops pressing the lever on the "click" days. This cessation could be explained as:
a. generalization
b. loss of conditioned reinforcement properties by the click
c. discrimination between clicks in two different situations
d. an illustration of the importance of extinction
e. spontaneous recovery

19. In order to shape an animal to perform a difficult response, all but one of the following procedures should be followed. Which procedure is *not* appropriate?
a. Provide a clear signal for the arrival of reinforcement.
b. Present the reinforcement immediately after the response is performed.
c. Initially reinforce approximations to the desired response.
d. At first, reinforce those parts of the desired response sequence that come at the end of the sequence.
e. Work with the most difficult component in the response sequence first.

20. The desire for good grades illustrates the phenomenon of:
a. stimulus generalization
b. simultaneous discrimination
c. conditioned reinforcement
d. successive approximation
e. a and d

21. The idea that reinforcement can be understood completely by reduction of biological need is challenged by:
a. intrinsic motivation
b. behavioral contrast
c. schedules of reinforcement
d. a and b
e. all of the above

22. Consider each swing by a baseball player as an operant response, and every successful hit (single, double, etc.) as a reinforced swing. What schedule of reinforcement is a baseball batter on?
a. continuous reinforcement (fixed ratio 1)
b. fixed ratio
c. variable ratio
d. extinction
e. variable interval

23. Paradoxically, when an operant is reinforced on a schedule (e.g., every third response is reinforced), the response shows a greater resistance to extinction than when it received an

equal number of reinforced responses on *every trial*. This effect (partial reinforcement effect) is paradoxical because:
a. the nonreinforced trials in partial reinforcement training are extinction trials and should weaken the response
b. CS-US contingencies must be precisely controlled in order for good conditioning to occur
c. the animal on partial reinforcement performs more responses in training
d. the organism is learning a discrimination during training
e. all of the above

24. Avoidance learning typically:
a. involves extinction
b. is preceded by escape learning
c. involves aversive stimuli
d. b and c
e. all of the above

25. In a classic experiment (appropriately) on classical conditioning, it was shown that classical conditioning could occur when animals were temporarily paralyzed with a drug, so that they could not respond. (Of course, when testing for conditioning with a CS, the animals were no longer paralyzed.) Which position does this result support?
a. the cognitive learning view
b. the learning theory view
c. Pavlov's position
d. Skinner's position
e. b and c

26. This figure demonstrates that it is very difficult to produce conditioning with:

Stimulus intervals (seconds)

a. forward pairing
b. second-order conditioning
c. extinction
d. simultaneous pairing
e. all of the above

27. Consider the following table of occurrences of CS and US. What predictions would the contiguity and contingency accounts make of whether conditioning would occur in this case?

	US	No US
CS	9	1
No CS	9	1

a. both predict conditioning
b. both predict no conditioning
c. only contingency predicts conditioning
d. only contiguity predicts conditioning
e. neither predicts conditioning

28. Consider the following table of occurrences of CS and US. What predictions would the contiguity and contingency accounts make of whether conditioning would occur in this case?

	US	No US
CS	7	3
No CS	3	7

a. both predict conditioning
b. both predict no conditioning
c. only contingency predicts conditioning
d. only contiguity predicts conditioning
e. neither predicts conditioning

29. In the case of unsignaled shock (a random relation between a signal and shock), the relation between a signal and the shock is one of:
a. anxiety
b. absence of contingency
c. contingency
d. contiguity
e. blocking

30. Some properties of classical conditioning suggest that it functions to make predictions about events in the world, somewhat like a scientist makes. Which feature(s) of classical conditioning suggests(s) this property?
a. sensitivity to contingency
b. forward pairing
c. blocking
d. all of the above
e. b and c

31. Harriet gets very excited whenever she approaches the house of her boyfriend, Milton. She notices that her heart starts beating when she turns his corner and sees the name of his street on the corner sign. But she is surprised one day to note that the sign is down, and that she does not get excited on turning the corner, nor on passing Milton's street mailbox, just twenty feet from the corner. Why doesn't the mailbox cause her heart to increase beating?
a. blocking
b. backward pairing
c. Harriet is in extinction
d. the mailbox doesn't have a contingent relation with Milton
e. fear suppresses her response

32. A rat learns to run down a runway when reinforced with a sugar solution in the end box. After learning this, it is then fed a bitter (negatively reinforcing) solution in this same end box. When put back in the start box of the runway, it runs to the end less quickly than before. This illustrates:
    a. second-order conditioning
    b. blocking
    c. learned helplessness
    d. the law of effect
    e. cognitive learning

33. Studies on learned helplessness in dogs and infants' responses to mobiles that they could or could not control are evidence for the importance of:
    a. the law of effect
    b. contiguity
    c. contingency
    d. belongingness
    e. none of the above

34. Animals exposed to lights randomly paired with shock (hence, unsignaled shock) sometimes develop pathologies related to stress. The relation of this finding to learned helplessness is the same as the relationship of:
    a. conditioning to extinction
    b. the optimum CS-US interval to contingency
    c. generalization in classical conditioning to generalization in instrumental conditioning
    d. extinction to the partial reinforcement effect
    e. extinction of instrumental conditioning to establishment of classical conditioning

35. A simplified version of John Garcia's belongingness experiment would present bright-noisy tasty water to rats, followed by X-ray produced illness. The rats would show an aversion only to the taste (one of the groups in the experiment described in the text). However, without the use of a second group in which shock is the US, this experiment could be criticized by a learning theorist, because:
    a. bright-noisy type of stimuli don't associate well with USs like those induced by X-rays
    b. the bright-noisy stimuli might have been generally less effective as CSs than the taste stimulus
    c. this result would contradict the bird studies, showing selective association of visual stimuli and gastrointestinal effects
    d. the selective association could have been previously learned by the rats
    e. all of the above

36. Rats have a special ability to associate tastes with illness. Pigeons learn to peck a key for food, but have difficulty learning to peck a key to avoid shock. Both of these phenomena demonstrate belongingness. However, they differ in that the belongingness in the case of learned taste aversions occurs between _____ while in the pigeon example it occurs between _____.
    a. species-specific stimuli, general stimuli
    b. stimuli, responses
    c. responses, stimuli

d. stimuli, responses and outcomes
e. stimulus and response, responses

37. Which of the following instances of human learning most clearly represents arbitrary, as opposed to biologically specialized or prepared, learning?
    a. acquisition of grammar
    b. learning to catch a ball
    c. learning the rules of chess
    d. learning to judge distance
    e. a and b

38. Differences in types of learning in different species or situations are referred to as:
    a. convergent evolution
    b. insight learning
    c. adaptive specializations of learning
    d. a and b
    e. all of the above

39. Some similarities in the properties of learning across species and situations result from:
    a. universal properties of environments
    b. misbehavior of organisms
    c. adaptive specializations of learning
    d. a and b
    e. all of the above

40. Both presynaptic facilitation and long-term potentiation are possible neural bases of learning because:
    a. both are examples of neural plasticity
    b. both involve changes in the presynaptic neuron
    c. both have shown some contingency sensitivity
    d. a and c
    e. all of the above

41. Presynaptic facilitation and long-term potentiation:
    a. have been demonstrated only in the marine mollusk, Aplysia
    b. involve changes in sensitivity of the presynaptic neuron
    c. do not show activity dependence
    d. produce a net increase in sensitivity by acting at different sites
    e. a and b

42. What do classical conditioning, instrumental conditioning, presynaptic facilitation, and long-term potentiation all have in common?
    a. contingency sensitivity
    b. a cognitive explanation
    c. they contribute to explanation of act-outcome relationships
    d. a and b
    e. none of the above

43. Which of the following phenomena presents a serious problem to traditional learning theory?
    a. learning without performing a response or without getting a reward
    b. taste aversion learning
    c. insight learning
    d. cognitive maps
    e. all of the above

44. Which of the following statements describes a fundamental difference between learning and cognitive theorists?
    a. Learning theorists think a response is necessary for learning, while cognitive theorists think responses may be merely an index of learning.
    b. Learning theorists believe in reinforcement, and cognitive theorists believe in belongingness.
    c. Learning theorists believe in belongingness, while cognitive theorists believe in preparedness.
    d. all of the above
    e. none of the above

45. In his attempts to demonstrate higher mental processes in animals, Köhler's experiments differed from those of Thorndike in that:
    a. Köhler used an animal that might have greater reasoning power
    b. Köhler used situations in which it was possible to "reason" a solution
    c. Köhler used problems that could be gradually understood
    d. a and c
    e. a and b

46. Köhler suggested that a way to distinguish insightful from trial-and-error learning is that only insightful learning would:
    a. generalize
    b. show transfer of training
    c. be arbitrary
    d. be accomplished by apes
    e. show belongingness

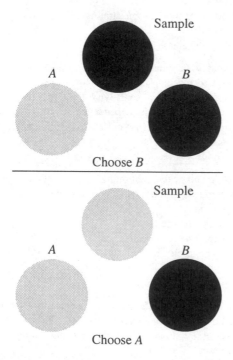

Sample

A   B

Choose B

Sample

A   B

Choose A

47. The figure sets out a problem used frequently in studies with primates. The problem is called:

a. discrimination
b. symbol manipulation
c. learning to learn
d. matching to sample
e. generalization

48. Complex perceptual concepts differ from abstract concepts in that only the former:
    a. do not show transfer of training to very different stimuli
    b. show belongingness
    c. can only be demonstrated in pigeons
    d. depend on insight
    e. none of the above

49. Critical evidence for a concept of "sameness" in chimpanzees comes from the demonstration of:
    a. discrimination
    b. generalization
    c. belongingness
    d. matching to sample
    e. transfer of training

50. Which of the following pairs best expresses a distinction between learning theory and cognitive theory?
    a. discrimination versus generalization
    b. same versus different
    c. biological constraints versus abstract concepts
    d. insight versus out of sight
    e. doing versus knowing

51. Cognitive theorists criticize learning theorists on the grounds that learning theorists:
    a. assume animals are able to learn any arbitrary relationship
    b. underestimate the ability of some animals to show sophisticated learning in some specific situations
    c. rely too much on the response as a necessary part of learning
    d. a and c
    e. all of the above

52–54. For the following three questions, the same set of answer alternatives are relevant.

Each question describes a major principle of traditional learning theory. For each one, choose the answer that describes a finding that casts doubt on this principle. The possible answers are listed below.
    a. learning sets
    b. random pairing of CS and US leads to no conditioning
    c. insight learning
    d. learned helplessness
    e. taste-aversion learning

52. Contiguity in time of two stimuli is sufficient grounds for conditioning.

53. Any CS can be associated equally well with any US.

54. Learning occurs gradually.

Answer Key for Self-Test

1.	c p. 117	28.	a p. 142
2.	a p. 118	29.	b p. 143
3.	d p. 118	30.	d pp. 141–43
4.	a p. 119	31.	a p. 143
5.	e p. 122	32.	e pp. 144–45
6.	c p. 123	33.	c pp. 145–46
7.	c p. 122	34.	c p. 146
8.	d p. 125	35.	b pp. 148–49
9.	a p. 125	36.	d pp. 148–49
10.	e p. 126	37.	c p. 151
11.	e p. 126	38.	c p. 152
12.	a p. 128	39.	a pp. 153, 154
13.	d p. 130	40.	d pp. 156, 157
14.	c p. 130	41.	d pp. 156, 157
15.	e p. 130	42.	a pp. 156, 157
16.	a p. 131	43.	e p. 158
17.	b p. 131	44.	a p. 144
18.	c p. 132	45.	e p. 159
19.	e p. 133	46.	b p. 160
20.	c p. 134	47.	d p. 161
21.	d pp. 134–35	48.	a p. 162
22.	c p. 136	49.	e p. 162
23.	a p. 137	50.	e p. 162
24.	d pp. 138–39	51.	e p. 162
25.	a p. 140	52.	b p. 142
26.	d pp. 140–41	53.	e p. 148
27.	d p. 142	54.	c p. 159

Investigating Psychological Phenomena

MAZE LEARNING

Equipment: Stopwatch or watch with second indicator
Number of participants: One (yourself)
Time per participant: Twenty to thirty-five minutes
Time for experimenter: Twenty to thirty-five minutes

This experiment illustrates a basic feature of learning: the acquisition curve, or the gradual acquisition of a skill or task. It employs a technique that was commonly used with animals in the earlier part of this century. The task is to find a way through a maze, presumably through learning a series of correct choices at the various choice-points. In the experiment you will proceed through the same maze four times: each time, a record will be kept of both your total time to completion and the number of errors (false entries). Learning would be demonstrated by a drop in either time to completion or the number of errors, as the number of trials increases.

Beginning on page 49, a maze is reprinted four times. In each case, using the second indicator on a wrist watch or a stopwatch, time yourself from the time you begin with a pencil at the starting point to the time you leave the maze. You should never pick your pencil off the paper until the maze is completed. If you make an error, simply retrace your steps with the pencil. Upon completion

of the maze, record the total time taken at the bottom of the page. Do not record the number of errors until you have finished all the mazes, since calculation of errors would be like another trial (you would have to work through the maze again).

Finish all four trials and then calculate errors for each trial. An error is defined as the crossing of the imaginary line at the mouth of an "alley" that leads to a dead end. One such entry can only count for one error, no matter how far you go up the blind alley before realizing that it is blind. In other words, once you have entered an alley that will ultimately be blind, you can only score one error, even if there is a further choice-point along this path (both of these choices would of course have to be blind alleys). The only way you can score two errors for the same blind alley is if you enter it twice.

Plot the time/trial and errors/trial on the two graphs provided below. Do you show evidence for gradual mastery of the maze? Compare your results with those from a group of undergraduate students that we have plotted on the same graph. We have plotted the mean (the average) scores. Individuals vary a lot; not all individuals show smooth curves like these averaged curves. In the graph, •——• represents the mean for eight participants. H and L represent the range. H is the highest value of eight participants; L is the lowest score of eight participants.

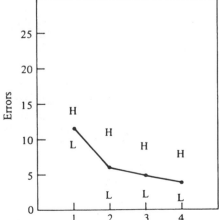

In the earlier part of this century, psychologists speculated about what exactly is learned when a rat or human learns a maze. Some, like John B. Watson, took a "molecular" position and claimed that a sequence of responses is learned. The most critical responses would be those at the choice-points: From this point of view, the learning would be represented as a series of turning instructions (e.g., left, right, right), one for each successive choice-point. Others, such as Edward Chace Tolman, argued that the participant, rat or human, developed a spatial representation of the maze in his or her head, a "cognitive map," rather than a sequence of responses. What do you think you actually learned in this task?

You should realize that this type of maze differs markedly from the mazes used for rats, or the life-size mazes for humans. In these cases, the participant does not get a direct picture of the whole layout; rather, the participant can only see the part of the maze in the immediate vicinity of the choice-point. This, of course, would make it much harder for the participant to build up a map of the maze. To get a feeling for the difference, cut out a hole about 1/2" square from the center of a full-sized piece of paper. Place it at the beginning of the fifth duplication of the maze, and attempt to move through the maze with the pencil again, moving the hole along as you move the pencil. If you had learned a series of turns or choices, this procedure should not seriously affect your performance. On the other hand, insofar as you used a "map," or some sort of larger view of the shape of the maze and your path through it, this procedure would seriously affect your performance.

(If your instructor collects the data, fill out the report sheet in Appendix 3.)

FURTHER ACTIVITIES

We have included one extra copy of the maze. You can use this copy for further experiments: If you need more than one maze, you can make a copy of this unused maze.

You might wish to text the idea of a map of the maze versus a set of turning responses, by trying to run the maze backward (start at finish and end at start). What predictions would you make? A cognitive map view would hold that the backward run would be a lot easier than the first run in the "proper" direction, since the same maze map would work in both directions. But a response-learning view would not predict that having learned the maze in the original order would aid in the learning of the reversed maze. The sequence of turns (e.g., left, left, right, left, etc.) would be entirely different when running the maze backward.

Of course, there is a problem here. How do you know how long it would have taken to run the maze backward if you did that on your first trial? You don't. One possibility would be to run a few people on one trial forward and a few others on one trial backward. One could then see if one direction was harder than the other. Another possibility, not as satisfying, is just to assume that it should be about as easy forward as backward, since it wasn't designed to be more difficult one way than the other.

Another activity would be to look at forgetting. Do the final maze in a few days or a week and compare your time and errors to your performance today. Would you expect you performance to be about the same as Trial 4? Better than Trial 1?

On the following three pages, cover the top (completed) maze while doing the bottom one.

Finish

Start

Finish

Start

Read the rest of the experiment before going on.

Finish

Start

Finish

Start

LEARNED TASTE AVERSIONS

Equipment: None
Number of participants: Five to eight
Time per participant: Five minutes
Time for experimenter: Sixty minutes

One of the basic assumptions of behavior theory is that any conditioned stimulus (CS) could become associated with any unconditioned stimulus (US). That is, it is assumed that the relation of the CS to the US is arbitrary. This assumption has been seriously challenged by the discovery of the phenomenon of learned taste aversions in rats. As first documented by John Garcia and his colleagues, rats can learn in one trial to associate a taste (CS) with illness (US). They will subsequently avoid the taste. This learned taste aversion was of particular importance because Garcia and his colleagues showed that this rapid learning would only occur with tastes as the CS and certain types of illness as the US. This specificity of association between tastes and illness is an illustration of belongingness, the nonarbitrariness of associations.

Because learned taste aversions differ from most of the frequently studied types of learning, they were investigated in some detail. We now know that:

1. The specificity (belongingness) is between tastes and specific types of illness: symptoms from the upper gastrointestinal system, especially nausea, seem by far the most effective.

2. The learning typically occurs in one trial (thus allowing rats to avoid poisons without too many life-threatening trials).

3. The rat can accomplish this learning even if the illness follows the taste by more than one hour. This challenges the view that two stimuli must occur close together in time in order to be associated. CS-US intervals of more than an hour rarely, if ever, support conditioning in traditional classical conditioning, using salivation or startle responses, and tones, bells, and lights.

4. Novel tastes show much more conditioning than familiar ones. This makes sense: If eating of the familiar food has not been followed by illness, it is reasonable to associate the illness with the new food. This is true in other types of classical conditioning as well: There is generally more conditioning to novel stimuli.

It often happens that after a new phenomenon is described, it is found to be common, and one wonders how it could have escaped notice before. So it was with learned taste aversions. A phenomenon similar to that described by Garcia in the rat seems to occur in humans. Most commonly, someone eats a (usually new) food and gets ill within a few hours. Nausea and vomiting are particularly common symptoms. After this one experience, a person finds the food distasteful. Garb and Stunkard (1974) distributed a questionnaire about such experiences to about 700 people. They found that somewhat over one-third of people have had at least one such experience. The analysis of the results of their questionnaire confirmed the presence of the basic properties of learned taste aversions in humans:

1. Belongingness. Aversions were almost always limited to the food and its taste. Rarely were there reports of aversion to the restaurant, tablecloth, accompanying people, or other stimuli that were also associated, in time, with the illness. Furthermore, the illness in question almost always (87 percent of the time) involved the gastrointestinal system.

2. One-trial learning. The aversions usually occurred after one food-illness pairing.

3. Long CS-US intervals. There was often an interval measured in hours between food ingestion and illness.

4. Novelty. Novel foods (tastes) seem more effective. In spite of the fact that almost everything eaten on any given day would be familiar, 45 percent of the aversions involved foods that had been eaten no more than twice before the pairing with illness.

5. "Irrationality." In many cases, a participant knew that the food did not cause the illness (e.g., other people eating the same food did not get ill, and/or other friends not at the meal came down with the same viral illness at about the same time). Yet, this knowledge that the food did not cause the illness did not weaken the aversion.

We will attempt to confirm the phenomenon of learned taste aversion in humans and highlight its unusual properties. Since, according to Garb and Stunkard, about one-third of people show this phenomenon, we will ask you to interview five to eight people, in the hope that you will find one to four participants with aversions. We will use an interview protocol that asks many of the same questions covered in Garb and Stunkard's questionnaire. Read the introduction, below, to each participant. If the participant has an aversion, ask each of the questions indicated and record the answers.

LEARNED TASTE AVERSIONS: INTERVIEW PROTOCOL

If a person becomes sick after eating a particular food, he or she may develop an intense dislike, called an aversion, for that food, whether or not it was responsible for the illness. For example, one person developed a high fever after eating pizza in a restaurant, and found that he did not like pizza any more. Another person became very nauseous after eating a breakfast with hash-brown potatoes, and found the potatoes distasteful after this experience. She also found she did not want to eat from the plate that the potatoes were on. Have you ever come to dislike a food because you became ill after eating it? If so, please answer the following questions:

1. Your current age.
   (Participant A) _____ (B) _____
   (C) _____ (D) _____

2. Age when the aversion experience occurred.
   (A) _____ (B) _____ (C) _____ (D) _____

3. What is the food? (A) _____ (B) _____
   (C) _____ (D) _____

4. Describe the experience in terms of what and where you were eating, and the symptoms of the illness. (*Use extra sheet of paper if necessary.*)
   (A) _____
   _____
   _____
   (B) _____
   _____
   _____
   (C) _____

_____

_____

(D) _____

_____

_____

5. Did this happen only once? If more than once, how many times? (A) _____, _____ (B) _____, _____ (C) _____, _____ (D) _____, _____

6. What was the most important symptom you had?

(A) _____ (B) _____

(C) _____ (D) _____

7. Were you nauseous? Did you vomit (if not mentioned in answer above)? (A) _____, _____

(B) _____, _____ (C) _____, _____

(D) _____, _____

8. About how long after you ate the food did the symptoms appear? (A) _____ (B) _____

(C) _____ (D) _____

9. Do you believe that the food actually caused your illness?

(A) _____ (B) _____

(C) _____ (D) _____

10. List all the foods that you can remember at the meal before you got sick. Indicate for each food whether it was relatively unfamiliar (you ate it no more than three times in your life). Indicate if you developed an aversion to any of these foods:

Food	Unfamiliar	Aversion
(A)		
_____	_____	_____
_____	_____	_____
_____	_____	_____
_____	_____	_____
(B)		
_____	_____	_____
_____	_____	_____
_____	_____	_____
_____	_____	_____
(C)		
_____	_____	_____
_____	_____	_____
_____	_____	_____
_____	_____	_____
(D)		
_____	_____	_____
_____	_____	_____
_____	_____	_____
_____	_____	_____

11. List all the other things or events that you can remember at this same meal and in the time after the meal and before the illness (e.g., the restaurant, table settings, people with you, books read, and so on). Indicate if you acquired an aversion to any of these items.

(A) _____

_____

(B) _____

_____

(C) _____

_____

(D) _____

_____

12. Do you still have this aversion? (A) _____ (B) _____ (C) _____ (D) _____

13. Was (Is) the aversion to the taste, smell, and/or sight of the food?

Taste	Smell	Sight
(A) _____	(A) _____	(A) _____
(B) _____	(B) _____	(B) _____
(C) _____	(C) _____	(C) _____
(D) _____	(D) _____	(D) _____

Summarize the results from all of your participants below. You decide which questions are relevant to each feature of learned taste aversion, and summarize your results with respect to each of the features listed below.

BELONGINGNESS Relevant questions (Nos.)

_____

_____

ONE-TRIAL LEARNING Relevant questions (Nos.)

_____

_____

LONG CS-US INTERVAL Relevant questions (Nos.)

_____

_____

NOVELTY EFFECT Relevant questions (Nos.)

_____

_____

"IRRATIONALITY" Relevant questions (Nos.)

_____

_____

OTHER INTERESTING RESULTS

_____

_____

_____

Do your data confirm the basic properties of learned taste aversion?

Comment: Interview protocols like this are quite common in psychological research. They are essentially questionnaires, but they are administered by a researcher or someone on his or her staff. In a way they are more subjective than questionnaires because the interviewer could influence the answers of the participant, especially if there is embarrassing material in the protocol. On the other hand, the interview allows for an interaction between the researcher and the participant: If a participant misunderstands a question, he or she can be corrected. If the participant says something that is ambiguous, it can be expanded. Similarly, if the participant says something of unusual interest, it can be followed up.

The introductory statement in the interview is critical. We tried to write it so as not to guarantee that participants would only describe specific food aversions based on gastrointestinal illness. Note that we gave one example of another sort of illness and also suggested the possibility of an aversion to items other than tastes. This certainly does not guarantee an "unbiased" sample of aversions, but it allows for exceptions to the phenomena as described by Garcia and, later, by Garb and Stunkard. Garb and Stunkard's introductory paragraph was more suggestive of gastrointestinal illness than is the paragraph we use here. *(If your instructor collects the data, fill out the report sheet in Appendix 3.)*

PROBLEMS AND FURTHER ACTIVITIES

Garb and Stunkard's questionnaire and our interview are not experiments. They can demonstrate that one-trial taste-illness aversions occur in humans. But by themselves they cannot demonstrate belongingness. Remember that Garcia's experiments with rats showed that although lights and tastes were equally paired with both illness and electric shock, the taste was much more strongly associated with illness and the lights with shock. Our introduction for the participants (and more so Garb and Stunkard's) pointed the participant toward taste-illness associations.

We did not ask the participants if they ever got to dislike a restaurant or a person because they were "followed by" illness or whether they ever got to dislike a food because it was followed by pain or a variety of other unpleasant events. On the contrary, we could ask whether, as a consequence of a very unpleasant event such as a death in the family or painful injury, a participant developed an aversion to any object, event, or food. Such questions have not been asked systematically. Do you have any such aversion? Do any of your friends? If there are many aversions linking food with unpleasant events "outside of the body" or outside of the gastrointestinal system, or if there are aversions to visual or other objects paired with illness, then there is little evidence for the belongingness effects in humans. We don't think there *are* many such effects, but we are not sure at this time.

We have suggested that nausea and vomiting are especially important in generating taste aversion. See if you can get evidence for this. If you know anyone (including yourself) with a food allergy, interview that person, using a protocol like the one we have used for aversions. (You will have to make a few modifications.) The critical question is whether people with food allergies develop aversions to these foods. In particular, if the allergy produces no symptoms in the gastrointestinal system, is there an aversion? There is some data (Pelchat and Rozin, 1982) that suggest that people with food allergies outside of the gastrointestinal system do not have aversions to these foods—that is, they don't dislike these allergenic foods.

References

Garb, F., and Stunkard, A., 1974. Taste aversions in man. *American Journal of Psychiatry* 131:1204–07.

Logue, A. W., Ophir, I., and Strauss, K. E., 1981. The acquisition of taste aversion in humans. *Behavior Research and Therapy* 19:319–33.

Pelchat, M. L., and Rozin, P., 1982. The special role of nausea in the acquisition of food dislikes by humans. *Appetite* 3:341–51.

PART TWO

COGNITION

CHAPTER 5

Sensory Processes

Learning Objectives

THE ORIGINS OF KNOWLEDGE

The empiricist view
1. Be familiar with the viewpoint of the British empiricists.
2. What is the distinction between proximal and distal stimuli?
3. What are sensations?
4. Understand the role of association in the empiricists' view of perception.
5. What is the relevance of linear perspective in a discussion of association?

The nativist rejoinder
6. How does nativism differ from empiricism?
7. What is the sequence of events leading from the stimulus to the reported sensation? What is the psychophysical approach to this problem?
8. Why is the just-noticeable difference (jnd) important in measuring sensory intensity?
9. What is Weber's law? How is Weber's fraction used to compare the sensitivities of different sensory modalities?
10. Why is Fechner's law biologically plausible?

Detection and decision
11. What is the relevance of "background noise" to weak stimulus detection? How does setting a criterion play a role in this?
12. What sorts of errors might result from setting a criterion? How do payoff manipulations affect response bias?
13. How can an analysis of the proportions of "yes" and "no" responses measure the separate effects of sensitivity and response bias?
14. How is signal-detection theory applicable to problems other than the detection of weak stimuli?

Sensory coding
15. How is stimulus intensity coded?
16. Explain the doctrine of specific nerve energies as it applies both within and between sensory modalities. Explain how specificity and pattern theories account for sensory coding.

A SURVEY OF THE SENSES

Kinesthesis and the vestibular senses
17. Define kinesthesis.
18. Describe the function of the semicircular canals.

The skin senses
19. Be familiar with the four basic skin sensations. What is known about the receptors that correspond to these sensations?

The sense of taste
20. What are the four basic taste qualities? What coding processes underlie these taste qualities?
21. How is taste coded?
22. Be familiar with the principles of adaptation and contrast as illustrations of sensory interaction.

The sense of smell
23. What are examples of olfactory sensations? Are these coded by particular receptors?
24. How do smell and taste combine?
25. As a distance sense, why is olfaction a minor sense in humans? Of what importance is smell to humans?
26. Be familiar with the various functions of pheromones in animals and discuss whether pheromones might play a role in human behavior.

Hearing
27. What is the stimulus for hearing? How do sound waves vary?
28. Know how the amplitude and wavelength of sound stimuli are measured.
29. What is the difference between simple and complex auditory stimuli? How does the brain treat complex stimuli?
30. Describe the structure of the ear as it collects the auditory stimulus. How does this structure help in the perception of sounds?
31. How is the cochlea designed?
32. Describe the place and firing frequency theories of pitch perception. Why does each seem important to perception, and what triggers each?
33. Give an example of how evolutionary pressure has led to the development of a sensory system.

The senses in overview
34. What are four principles that govern the structure of all sensory systems? Give examples.

VISION

The stimulus: light
35. What are the characteristics of light, and what are their visual consequences?

Gathering the stimulus: the eye
36. How is the eye like a camera?

The visual receptors
37. Describe the retina.
38. Be familiar with the following terms: rods, cones, bipolar cells, ganglion cells, optic nerve, and blind spot.
39. Where is visual acuity greatest, and why?
40. Understand the duplex theory of vision. What is the evidence for two types of receptors, and why are they needed?
41. How does spectral sensitivity help to distinguish rods from cones?
42. How are visual pigments similar to and different from the emulsions on film?

Interaction in time: adaptation
43. What is sensory adaptation? What does the organism gain by sensory adaptation?
44. Explain the technique used to show that stabilization of the retinal image leads to visual adaptation.
45. What is the biological significance of involuntary eye movements?

Interaction in space: contrast
46. Recall that brightness contrast increases with progressive intensity difference between two regions and with decreasing distance between them. How is this phenomenon important to visual perception? How do Mach bands illustrate this?
47. What is the physiological mechanism that underlies Mach bands?
48. Be familiar with the effects of lateral inhibition.

Color
49. What are the dimensions of color?
50. Describe the "unique" colors.

51. Are differences in brightness best observed in chromatic or in achromatic colors?
52. How can colors be varied in saturation?
53. Describe the color solid. How are different dimensions of color represented in it? What is its relationship to the color circle?
54. Differentiate between additive and subtractive mixture of colors. Give examples illustrating each.
55. What are complementary colors? How do their complementary characters account for simultaneous color contrast and negative afterimages?

The physiological basis of color vision
56. Explain the differences among the three cone types in human color vision.
57. It is important to understand the opponent-process theory thoroughly. Be aware of the relevance of primary colors, color antagonists, and inhibition in the perception of hue and brightness.
58. What is the physiological evidence for the opponent-process theory?
59. Describe different types of color blindness.

Perceiving shapes
60. How do electrophysiological studies of the action of single neural cells tell us about the perception of contours?
61. Define a receptive field.
62. What is the significance of studies of "bug detectors"?
63. How can adaptation studies inform us about the perception of complex attributes of forms?
64. Be familiar with the aftereffect of visual movement and how studies of it can uncover the site of neural adaptation.
65. Understand how the perception of complex forms such as faces might be related to the use of feature detectors.

Programmed Exercises

THE ORIGINS OF KNOWLEDGE

1. John Locke postulated that all knowledge comes by way of experience. This school of thought is known as _____.

   empiricism

2. Locke used the metaphor of a _____ _____ in describing the human mind at birth.

   tabula rasa (blank slate)

3. An object in the real world is known as a _____ stimulus.

   distal

4. When the energy from an object impinges on a sensory surface, we say that this pattern of energy has become a _____ stimulus.

   proximal

5. Empiricists assumed that the raw materials of knowledge are _____.

   sensations

6. According to the empiricists, complex ideas are perceived by the linking together, or _____, of two or more sensations.

   association

7. Two identical objects have different retinal sizes. This clue that one object is closer than the other is known as _____ _____.

   linear perspective

8. Kant believed that a number of aspects of perception are innate. This view has since been labeled _____.

   nativism

9. The study of the relationship between properties of the stimulus and sensory experience is known as _____.

   psychophysics

10. When a stimulus is converted to a nerve impulse, it is said to be _____.

    transduced

11. Noticing the mere presence of a stimulus is called _____ .

detection

12. Telling two stimuli apart is called _____.

discrimination

13. Determining the magnitude of a stimulus is answering a question of _____.

scaling

14. Noticing whether a stimulus is one that you have encountered before is_____.

recognition

15. You find that you are unable to tell the difference between a 25-lb. weight and a 28-lb. weight, but you can differentiate the 25-lb. weight from any other weight over 28 lbs. Something slightly over 3 lbs. is your _____ _____. It will produce a _____-_____ _____ in this weight range.

difference threshold, just-noticeable difference (jnd)

16. A difference threshold is 2 lbs. when the standard is 40 lbs. _____ law predicts that the difference threshold with a 20-lb. standard would be _____ lb(s).

Weber's
1

17. The jnd divided by the standard stimulus is known as _____ _____ and, in general, seems to be constant.

Weber's fraction

18. Imagine that for a certain psychophysical task we found that sensation grew as a function of the logarithm of the physical stimulus intensity. This would be support for _____ law.

Fechner's

19. Imagine that we toss a coin 100 times, each time asking a research participant to predict the outcome (heads or tails). We find that 73 times he predicts heads. We also find that he knows that on the average, 100 tosses will result in approximately 50 heads. We can then attribute his deviation from this figure to a _____ _____.

response bias

20. One duty of air traffic controllers is to watch a radar screen and determine what planes are in the area. There are two kinds of errors they might make in this task. First, they may not see a small dot on the screen, thus committing a _____, as it is often called in signal-detection theory. On the other hand, they may report a plane when there is none there. This is called a _____ _____. Considering the costs of these two errors, the _____ _____ error is probably more common than the _____.

miss

false alarm
false alarm
miss

21. Corresponding to the two types of errors, there are also two kinds of correct responses. When an event occurs in the world and we say that the event occurred, that is known as a _____. When an event hasn't occurred in the world and we say that it hasn't, we have given a _____ _____.

hit
correct negative

22. We have looked at response bias that is caused by the costs of making various types of errors and response bias due to unspecified internal preferences. In a detection experiment, response bias can be altered by varying the _____ _____.

payoff matrix

23. According to proponents of signal-detection theory, the reason that research participants have trouble telling whether a low intensity stimulus was presented or not is due to _____ _____.

background noise

24. If you make a selection error during the admission of a student to medical school that results in a student who cannot complete the degree requirements, you have made a _____ _____ error .

false alarm

25. The theory that accounts for performance when participants are trying to determine whether a weak stimulus was presented is called _____-_____ theory.

signal-detection

26. When a weak stimulus is presented, participants must set a _____ to determine whether the level of activity within their sensory system warrants saying that the stimulus was present.

criterion

27. There clearly are qualitative differences in sensations (e.g., smells are different from sounds). These differences are due to differences in sensory _____.

quality

28. According to the doctrine of _____ _____ _____, differences in subjective quality are caused by differences in associated nervous structures rather than by differences inherent in the stimuli.

specific nerve energies

29. There are two theoretical approaches that explain the neural processes that underlie sensations. The _____ theory states that different sensory qualities are signaled by different quality-specific neurons. The other theory, the across-fiber _____ theory, asserts that substances produce a pattern of activation across a set of fibers, and that this pattern is the neural code that gives rise to sensory quality.

specificity
pattern

A SURVEY OF THE SENSES

30. The _____ canals indicate rotation of the head. They are located in the _____ _____ .

semicircular, inner ear

31. The four basic skin sensations are: _____ , _____ , _____ , and _____ .

pressure, warmth, cold pain

32. It is believed that pressure sensations are produced by specialized _____ in the skin that sense movement and vibration of skin and hair.

receptors

33. Sensations of _____ and _____ are probably signaled by free nerve endings in the skin.

temperature, pain

34. The four basic taste qualities are: _____ , _____ , _____ , and _____ .

sour, sweet, salty, bitter

35. The basic taste sensations are caused by stimulating taste _____ that carry messages from the taste receptors to the brain.

fibers

36. Sensory interaction in taste is manifested in _____ to continually presented stimuli as well as in the influence of _____ on taste.

adaptation smell

37. The technical term for smell is _____ .

olfaction

38. The olfactory receptors are located in a part of the nasal cavity called the _____ _____ . Here, olfactory quality is not coded by particular receptors, but rather by a _____ of excitation across different receptor groups.

olfactory epithelium pattern

39. The sense of smell can be valuable in communication for organisms employing _____ .

pheromones

40. One line of evidence suggesting that pheromones are important to humans comes from the study of _____ synchrony.

menstrual

41. Light intensity is to vision as _____ is to hearing.

amplitude

42. Hue is to vision as _____ is to audition.

pitch

43. Many different _____ _____ , differing in both frequency and amplitude, combine to form a _____ _____ .

sine waves complex wave

44. The purpose of the middle ear, oval window, and inner ear is to _____ and _____ sound waves.

conduct, amplify

45. The structure that actually contains the auditory receptors is known as the _____ .

cochlea

46. The actual auditory receptors are the _____ _____ , which are stimulated by deformation of the _____ _____ .

hair cells basilar membrane

47. Pitch perception seems to be based on two mechanisms. High frequencies are coded using _____ of excitation, while lower frequencies are coded by _____ firing rate.

place, neural

48. _____ pressure has caused the development of specialized sensory equipment for different species.

Evolutionary

49. The processing of sensory stimuli begins when they impinge on _____ structures of the body.

accessory

50. For all modalities, stimulus energy must be converted into a form that can be used by the senses. The translation is termed _____ .

transduction

51. Higher neural centers process all sensory input and _____ this input into various quantitative and qualitative dimensions.

code

52. Any part of a sensory system is in _____ with the rest of that system.

interaction

VISION

53. Objects can either _____ or _____ light.

emit, reflect

54. Light energy can vary in _____ , thus giving rise to perceived brightness, and in _____ , which determines perceived hue.

intensity, wavelength

55. The visible spectrum extends from roughly _____ to roughly _____ nanometers.

360, 750

56. The first place at which light energy from the world interacts with the senses is at the _____.　retina

57. The focusing of the eye is affected by _____ of the lens.　accommodation

58. _____ are most densely packed in the fovea, while _____ are most frequent in the periphery.　Cones, rods

59. The first cells to be stimulated by light are the _____, which activate the _____ cells, which in turn stimulate the _____ cells.　receptors, bipolar ganglion

60. The axons of the ganglion cells form a bundle, which is known as the _____ _____; this exits the eyeball at the _____ _____.　optic nerve blind spot

61. One person is able to distinguish a one-inch "F" from a one-inch "E" at a distance of 300 feet. Another person is only able to make the same discrimination at 200 feet. These two people have different visual _____.　acuity

62. The fact that primarily nocturnal animals have no cones and many rods, while animals that operate in daylight have many cones and few rods, is evidence for a _____ theory of vision.　duplex

63. The fact that sensitivity to dim light is greater in the periphery of the visual field (where rods are) than in the fovea (where cones are) supports the _____ theory of vision.　duplex

64. The chemical reaction in which the visual pigment rhodopsin breaks down and then reforms into rhodopsin takes place in the _____ .　rods

65. _____ _____, as examples of visual adaptation, illustrate the role of temporal interaction in vision.　Stabilized images

66. _____ _____, a phenomenon of brightness contrast, are examples of spatial interaction.　Mach bands

67. The physical resolution of the eye is not very good. In terms of physics, we shouldn't be able to see as clearly as we do. However, the exaggeration of contrast through _____ _____ enhances the visual message.　lateral inhibition

68. The three attributes used to describe color are _____, _____, and _____.　hue, brightness, saturation

69. _____ colors cannot be distinguished on the basis of hue.　Achromatic

70. Unique red is the red that appears to have neither any _____ nor any _____ in it.　blue, yellow

71. Only _____ colors can differ in saturation.　chromatic

72. The _____ _____ equates spatial relationships along three dimensions with the three dimensions of color.　color solid

73. Colored filters placed over two different lights that are focused on the same spot produce an _____ color mixture.　additive

74. A _____ hue is one that, when mixed with another hue in the correct proportion, will produce the color gray.　complementary

75. A gray color, when surrounded by green, appears reddish. This is known as _____ _____ _____ and is evidence for antagonistic pairing of colors.　simultaneous color contrast

76. _____ _____ have the complementary hue and the opposite brightness of the original stimulus.　Negative afterimages

77. Human vision is termed _____, since there are three cone types.　trichromatic

78. According to the opponent-process theory of color vision, it should never be possible to see a red hue with a trace of _____ in it.　green

79. Color blindness is most common in _____ and could entail the _____ of one of the opponent-process pairs.　males, absence

80. _____ have contributed significantly to the study of form perception by studying the behavior of single nerve cells in the visual system.　Electrophysiologists

81. In recording from a single nerve cell, you discover that its firing rate varies when a stimulus is presented at a certain place in the visual field. This is the cell's _____ field.   receptive

82. A nerve cell that selectively responds to some characteristics of a stimulus but not to others is often called a _____ _____.   feature detector

83. One of the characteristics that visual nerve cells respond to selectively is _____.   orientation

84. Studies of _____ in humans provide some evidence for the importance of feature detectors in visual perception.   adaptation

85. The aftereffect of visual _____ is a phenomenon that reveals a feature detector for a visual characteristic that is not lodged in the retina.   movement

86. It has been shown that monkeys have feature detectors that are selectively sensitive to very complex stimuli, such as _____.   faces (or hands)

Self Test

1. John Locke, the British empiricist, would most likely agree with which of the following statements?
   a. "All knowledge is determined by innate mechanisms."
   b. "We are born with a fair amount of innate knowledge, with experience playing a small role."
   c. "Knowledge arrives through the senses."
   d. John Locke was not an empiricist and would not have agreed with any of the above statements.

2. The metaphor that best describes the empiricists' view of the human mind at birth is:
   a. a camera
   b. an encyclopedia
   c. a pad and pencil
   d. a blank slate

3. An example of a distal stimulus would be:
   a. the pattern of light energy hitting the retina
   b. a Chevrolet
   c. the sensation produced by a distant mountain
   d. a hallucination

4. An example of a proximal visual stimulus is:
   a. the activity of the retina hit by an array of photons
   b. an object situated very close to the retina
   c. a distant object that appears closer than it really is
   d. all of the above

5. According to the empiricists, linear perspective serves as a depth cue because:
   a. it produces a memory of an associated movement and an experience of depth
   b. it mitigates the effect of convergence
   c. its use by painters has familiarized us with its symbolic representation of depth
   d. we are classically conditioned to accept it as such

6. Immanuel Kant believed:
   a. in innately determined categories of perception
   b. that all knowledge came through the senses
   c. that associations of sensations determined perception
   d. in none of the above

7. Which of the following is an example of transduction?
   a. sound waves in the air being translated into electrical energy by a microphone
   b. electrical waves being translated into sound waves by a loudspeaker
   c. light energy being converted into nerve energy by the retina
   d. all of the above

8. Psychophysics studies the relationship between:
   a. the distal and proximal stimulus
   b. the distal stimulus and sensory experience
   c. nativism and empiricism
   d. the proximal stimulus and sensory experience

9. It can be argued that sensations cannot be measured directly. It should be possible, though, to compare sensations. For instance, we should be able to determine whether one sensation is the same as or different from another. This viewpoint would most likely be expressed by:
   a. Kant
   b. Locke
   c. Fechner
   d. Berkeley

10. You are shopping for a new car. You have test-driven a number of cars to determine which models have the best performance. You discover that you cannot tell the difference between models A and C. The difference (however measured) between cars A and C is below your:
    a. difference threshold
    b. response bias
    c. criterion
    d. sensitivity

11. Which of the following agrees with Weber's law? (In each case, the first number represents the weight difference needed to produce a jnd, and the absolute stimulus energy is specified by the second number. Two pairs are provided for each possible answer.)
    a. 1, 10/2, 100
    b. 20, 50/1, 2.5
    c. 5, 100/5, 50
    d. All of the above are in agreement with Weber's law.

12. As in 11 above, each of the pairs of numbers below represents a hypothetical difference threshold with its associated stimulus energy value. Which of the Weber fractions that results from these values represents the greatest sensitivity?
    a. 1, 100
    b. 1, 10
    c. 100, 1000
    d. 50, 1000

13. Fechner's law states that the strength of the sensation increases _____ with stimulus intensity.
    a. inversely
    b. minimally
    c. logarithmically
    d. linearly

14. A doctor is scanning a lung X-ray. She sees something that may be either the beginnings of a tumor or harmless scar tissue. It is likely that response bias will come into play when the doctor decides whether to operate or not. Which of the following factors might influence this response bias?
    a. probability that it is a tumor
    b. risks associated with surgery
    c. risks associated with an untreated tumor
    d. all of the above
    e. none of the above; response bias is fixed and cannot be easily changed

15. In the above example, what type of error is worse to make?
    a. false alarm
    b. miss
    c. a and b are equally important
    d. cannot be determined without knowing associated costs and benefits

16. Still considering the example in question 14, imagine that there are five different types of tumors such that each is associated with a different death rate when left untreated. Type I has the highest death rate, and Type V has the lowest rate (with the others falling between I and V, in order). Imagine further that these five tumors can be distinguished from each other with X-rays, but none of them can be distinguished from scar tissue (which is harmless). Assuming that everything else is constant from one tumor type to another, under which condition would the doctor be most likely to operate and risk putting the patient under the dangers of surgery?
    a. The patient has either scar tissue of Type III tumor.
    b. The patient has either scar tissue or Type V tumor.
    c. The patient has either scar tissue or Type I tumor.
    d. If the doctor was good, the probability of her operating would be constant, despite the type of tumor.

17. If, under certain circumstances, a participant's hit rate went up while his false alarm rate stayed the same, we could conclude that his:
    a. response bias changed
    b. sensitivity decreased
    c. sensitivity increased
    d. sensitivity and response bias both changed

18. In which of the situations represented by the following graphs would a participant produce the highest ratio of hits to false alarms?

A

B

C

D

19. Differences among the taste of a cold beer, the sound of a Mozart quartet, and the sight of a fireworks display are due to:
    a. our past experiences with these stimuli
    b. differences in the sense organs that respond to the stimuli
    c. physiological differences in the conduction velocities of the neurons attached to the various sense organs
    d. all of the above

20. If, by some freak of nature, the optic and olfactory nerves were crossed and led to the opposite sense organ, the law of specific nerve energies would predict the following result:
    a. smelling red
    b. normal sensations
    c. the law of specific nerve energies makes no predictions in such a case
    d. any of the above

21. Kinesthesis is:
    a. information from the muscles, tendons, and joints
    b. a function of the ossicles in the inner ear
    c. the movement of hair cells in the cochlea
    d. the crystallization of the viscous liquid in the semicircular canals

22. Head rotation is sensed via:
    a. the pressure of crystals on hair cells in the vestibular sacs
    b. the deformation of hair cells in the semicircular canals
    c. dynamic tension of the relevant musculature
    d. the movement of the world relative to ourselves as we walk through it

23. Pressure:
    a. is assessed via the two-point threshold
    b. is one of the four basic skin sensations
    c. depends on the allocation of cortical space
    d. is the sensation elicited by stimulation of capsule receptors
    e. both b and d

24. Jack eats a piece of candy. The receptors in his mouth stimulate a particular "sugar-best" fiber, which carries the message to the brain. Which neural code is being used to give rise to the sensory quality of sweetness?
    a. the receptor code
    b. the across-fiber pattern code
    c. the sensory interaction code
    d. the specificity code

25. A little sucrose and quinine are placed simultaneously on opposite sides of the tongue. What will be the primary result?
    a. The bitter taste produced by the quinine will make the sucrose taste sweeter.
    b. Sensitivity to taste will decline rapidly as the taste buds adapt.
    c. The sweet taste produced by the sucrose will enhance the bitterness of the quinine.
    d. Since the sense of smell was not employed, both the quinine and the sucrose will be tasted equally.

26. The sense of smell, or olfaction, exhibits which of the following characteristics?
    a. It could classify odors as fragrant, spicy, and putrid.
    b. It could classify odors as aromatic, acrid, and rancid.
    c. It detects chemicals suspended in air.
    d. a and c

27. Rats working in a Skinner box are exposed to air taken from the vicinity of a group of rats that suffered electric shock. What will be the probable result?
    a. The rats will exhibit aggressive behaviors.
    b. There is no effect.
    c. The rats' bar-pressing performance will be disrupted.
    d. The pheromone present in the air will render the rats immobile.

28. You are given an acidic solution of lemon and water to drink. After continuously drinking this solution, it appears to be almost tasteless. What phenomenon is being demonstrated?
    a. specificity
    b. adaptation
    c. difference threshold
    d. receptor interaction

29. The sense of taste is enhanced by which of the following senses?
    a. smell
    b. sight
    c. hearing
    d. touch

30. The physical stimulus for hearing is described in terms of amplitude and frequency. The corresponding psychological dimensions are:
    a. loudness and tone
    b. amplitude and pitch
    c. loudness and timbre
    d. loudness and pitch

31. Which pair of the following representative sound waves includes both a simple and a complex wave?

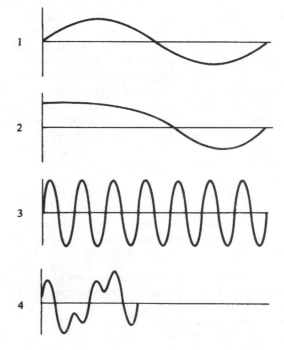

    a. 1 and 3
    b. 2 and 4
    c. 2 and either 3 or 4
    d. either 1 or 2 and 3

32. The correct ordering of anatomical structures in the ear (from outside in) is:
    a. eardrum, middle ear, oval window, cochlea
    b. oval window, middle ear, eardrum, cochlea
    c. eardrum, oval window, middle ear, cochlea
    d. none of the above

33. For low frequency tones (below 400 hz), pitch is detected by:
    a. the eardrum
    b. localization on the basilar membrane
    c. firing frequency of the auditory nerve
    d. none of the above

34. For frequencies above 5000, pitch is detected by:
    a. the eardrum
    b. localization on the basilar membrane
    c. firing frequency of the auditory nerve
    d. none of the above

35. A praying mantis needs only one ear because:
    a. it uses its ear to detect only loud sounds
    b. it needs only to detect an ultrasonic sound, not to localize it
    c. it needs to localize an ultrasonic sound, not to detect it
    d. it needs to detect the sound only of another mantis

36. Which of the following are characteristics common to most of the senses?
    a. the presence of anatomical structures
    b. the transduction of the physical stimulus to a neural impulse
    c. the translation of the neural impulse to a dimension of sensation
    d. the interaction of all parts of the sensory system
    e. all of the above

37. One light source appears bluish and another appears greenish. This difference in appearance is due to differences in:
    a. intensity
    b. wavelength
    c. opponent processes
    d. none of the above

38. Intensity is to brightness as wavelength is to:
    a. sensitivity
    b. darkness
    c. wattage
    d. hue

39. Which of the following wavelengths is not considered to be part of the visible spectrum?
    a. 650
    b. 400
    c. 300
    d. 575

40. The structure that bends light rays so that they are projected onto a light-sensitive surface is the:
    a. retina
    b. iris
    c. lens
    d. all of the above

41. During the process of accommodation, a close object will result in _____ of the lens.
    a. thickening
    b. flattening
    c. no change
    d. increased transparency

42. You arrive late to a movie theater and are forced to sit in the far right-hand seat of the first row. You must then look to your left to see the rectangular screen. What is the image of the screen that is projected onto your retina?

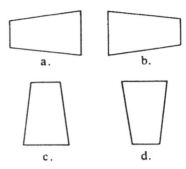

43. The two types of receptors in the human eye are known as _____ and _____.
    a. bipolars, horizontals
    b. ganglions, bipolars
    c. rods, cones
    d. bipolars, cones

44. An area near the center of the retina has virtually no rods, consisting entirely of cones. It is approximately two degrees in diameter and is known as the:
    a. periphery
    b. optic nerve
    c. optic chiasm
    d. fovea

45. In order to maximize visual acuity you should:
    a. stare slightly away from the thing that you are trying to see
    b. use only one eye at a time (to reduce interocular rivalry)
    c. reduce the luminance of the area, in order to engage the more sensitive rod system
    d. look directly at the object

46. Which of the following is not in agreement with the duplex theory of vision?
    a. The rods are the receptors for night vision, while cones serve day vision.
    b. Rods respond to low light levels, cones to high levels.
    c. Rod vision provides good acuity, cones provide poor acuity.
    d. Rods result in achromatic vision, cones provide color vision.

47. In a psychophysical task, we ask a participant to tell us when she can see a dim light. We vary the intensity until she reports that she sees it. We then record the luminance level. Now we change the wavelength and plot sensitivity again.

This figure is known as the:
a. dark adaptation curve
b. spectral sensitivity curve
c. receiver operating characteristic (ROC)
d. sensory adaptation curve

48. What happens when light hits a visual receptor?
a. Silver bromide molecules combine with light to release silver.
b. Light strikes the retina and generates rhodopsin.
c. Energy is converted to nervous impulses via a photochemical process which bleaches rhodopsin.
d. The reflected light from the receptor causes a photochemical alteration leading to neural excitation.

49. Which of the following is an example of sensory adaptation?
a. The cold ocean feels warmer after we've been in it for a while.
b. Being able to see in a dark room after a period of adjustment.
c. Increasing sensitivity to salt with continued exposure.
d. all of the above
e. a and b

50. The first time you see a friend's new car, it is parked against a black wall. Later you see that same car parked against a white backdrop (at the same time of day) and comment that you remember the car as being much brighter. This is an example of:
a. brightness contrast
b. adaptation
c. temporal interaction
d. none of the above

51. Lateral inhibition is responsible for which phenomenon?
a. color vision
b. Mach bands
c. stabilized image
d. all of the above

52. Which of the following is not used to classify colors?
a. brightness
b. hue
c. amplitude
d. saturation

53. White and black can be distinguished only on the basis of which dimensions?
a. brightness
b. hue
c. wavelength
d. saturation

54. Red and green must differ on which dimension (at least)?
a. brightness
b. hue
c. amplitude
d. saturation

55. White and black cannot possibly differ on which dimension?
a. hue
b. saturation
c. both of the above
d. none of the above

56. The extent to which a color of some fixed hue is mixed with an achromatic color is represented by a value on the _____ dimension.
a. brightness
b. hue
c. intensity
d. saturation

57. An example of a subtractive color mixture is:
a. two spotlights, each with a different filter, trained on the same location
b. the use of two filters on one spotlight
c. the light as it enters the human eye
d. all of the above

58. All of the following are examples of additive color mixtures except:
a. color printing
b. color TV
c. human color vision
d. mixing of paints

59. In an additive color mixture, equal amounts of complementary hues mixed together will produce:
a. a unique hue
b. a color with a hue intermediate to the two original hues
c. a color without hue
d. could be any of the above, depending on the choice of hues

60. All of the following are used as evidence for color antagonism except:
a. complementary colors
b. retinal bleaching
c. simultaneous color contrast
d. negative afterimages

61. Any wavelength will stimulate:
a. all three receptor types, but unequally
b. all three receptor types, and equally
c. only one or two receptor types
d. from one to three receptors, depending on the intensity and wavelength

62. In the opponent-process theory, the three pairs of receptors are:
a. red-blue, green-yellow, black-white
b. red-yellow, blue-green, black-white
c. red-green, blue-yellow, black-white
d. never specified

63. An achromatic color results when which system(s) is(are) in balance?
   a. red-green
   b. blue-yellow
   c. red-green and blue-yellow
   d. black-white

64. Which of the following would be predicted by the opponent-process theory?
   a. the dark gray appearance of black pepper placed against a gray background
   b. chromatic contrast
   c. negative afterimages
   d. all of the above

65. A person who is color-blind will probably:
   a. use color names appropriately
   b. be female
   c. be unable to distinguish any hues at all
   d. be unable to imagine how ultraviolet looks to a bee

66. The presence of "bug detectors" in frogs indicates that feature detectors:
   a. can be responsive to quite complex objects
   b. cannot be wired to detect anything but simple attributes of shapes
   c. cannot be shaped by evolutionary pressure
   d. are a minor part of the visual response to objects

67. Adaptation effects in humans can be demonstrated for the perception of:
   a. color
   b. movement
   c. both of the above
   d. none of the above

68. Suppose you had a participant close his left eye, and view a visual field filled with vertical lines with his right eye for several minutes. Then suppose you had him close his right eye, and you flashed him briefly presented, single vertical lines for detection. If his sensitivity for detecting the vertical lines was lower than it had been before he had viewed the lines with his right eye, you could conclude:
   a. that adaptation to vertical lines was restricted to a retinal site
   b. that adaptation to vertical lines was at a site more central in his brain than the retina
   c. that there are no feature detectors for vertical lines in the visual system
   d. none of the above

69. Cases of prosopagnosia and the preference of infants to view faces as opposed to other stimuli suggest that:

   a. there are feature detectors in the human visual system for faces
   b. there is no similarity in how humans and monkeys perceive faces
   c. the perception of faces may be handled by a different part of the visual system than the perception of other objects
   d. none of the above

Answer Key for Self Test

1.	c p. 170	36.	e p. 192
2.	d p. 170	37.	b p. 194
3.	b p. 170	38.	d p. 194
4.	a p. 170	39.	c p. 194
5.	a p. 172	40.	c p. 194
6.	a p. 173	41.	a p. 194
7.	d p. 173	42.	a p. 194
8.	b p. 173	43.	c p. 195
9.	c p. 174	44.	d p. 195
10.	a p. 174	45.	d p. 196
11.	b p. 174	46.	c p. 196
12.	a p. 174	47.	b p. 196
13.	c p. 175	48.	c pp. 196, 197
14.	d p. 178	49.	e p. 197
15.	d p. 178	50.	a p. 198
16.	c p. 178	51.	b p. 200
17.	c p. 179	52.	c p. 201
18.	b p. 179	53.	a p. 201
19.	b p. 180	54.	b p. 201
20.	a p. 180	55.	c p. 201
21.	a p. 181	56.	d p. 201, 202
22.	b p. 181	57.	b p. 203
23.	e p. 182	58.	d p. 204
24.	d p. 183	59.	c p. 206
25.	c p. 183	60.	b pp. 206, 207
26.	d p. 184	61.	a p. 207
27.	c p. 185	62.	c p. 207
28.	b p. 184	63.	c p. 207
29.	a p. 185	64.	d pp. 207, 208
30.	d p. 187	65.	a p. 209
31.	b p. 188	66.	a p. 210
32.	a p. 190	67.	c p. 211
33.	c p. 192	68.	b p. 212
34.	b p. 192	69.	c p. 212
35.	b p. 192		

Investigating Psychological Phenomena

MEASURING BRIGHTNESS CONTRAST

Equipment: Stimuli are included; one sheet of black construction paper needed
Number of participants: One or more
Time per participant: Ten minutes
Time for experimenter: Twenty minutes

In this "Sensory Processes" chapter, the authors describe a phenomenon that clearly illustrates the effect of context on perception. The phenomenon is brightness contrast. Examine Figure 5.20 in the text once again. Note how sharply different in brightness the four central gray squares appear to be; yet they are identical. (You can prove this to yourself by laying a sheet of paper over the figure with holes cut out where the squares are located.) The difference in brightness is apparently a result of interaction between each central square and its surrounding light or dark border. As the text explains, the surrounding border induces a contrast effect such that a patch will appear lighter when surrounded by a dark border, and darker when surrounded by a light border. The greater the difference in lightness between the center and its surroundings, the greater the illusion.

Of course, as you have probably already suspected, brightness contrast has limits. That is, there is just so much illusion that can be produced by a surrounding context, no matter how great the difference between the center and its surroundings. The present experiment provides an opportunity to examine the extent to which the visual system can be fooled by context. More importantly, however, in this exercise you will have a chance to conduct an actual psychophysical experiment to measure quantitatively the relationship between physical stimuli and psychological experience.

The purpose of the experiment is to measure the magnitude of brightness contrast for a particular test patch of a given, fixed lightness. This test patch will be surrounded by several borders that differ in their lightness, one from another. With this arrangement, we should be able to produce different degrees of brightness contrast. But how do we measure the extent of the effect? One way would be to ask a participant to assign numbers to the test patch corresponding to how bright she thought it was. But we shall use a more accurate technique: Each time we present a border around the test patch, we shall ask the participant to match the apparent brightness of the test patch by choosing another patch that seems to match it. The matching patch that is chosen, having been carefully measured for its lightness, will then serve as an index of how light the participant perceived the test patch to be.

First, cut out the matching patches and the borders on the insert for Chapter 5. The matching patches are the ten squares on the left. Note that there is a number on the back of each that corresponds to its lightness. (The units for these numbers have to do with how various lightnesses are actually created by printers,

and it is not necessary to know them for this exercise. It is sufficient that the patches are ordered correctly.) Now cut out the six borders on the right side of the insert, and cut out the central square area of each. Note that the borders are also marked with a lightness code on the back. Be very careful with both matching patches and borders to trim away any gray from the adjoining figures so that each cutout is an even gray. On the bottom of the insert is the test patch that has already been placed on a white surrounding region. The test patch has a lightness value of 6. *Do not cut out the test figure!* Leave it on its background and place this in turn on a sheet of black construction paper.

Now you are ready to run the experiment. The procedure is to select one background, place it over the test patch, and ask your participant to select a matching patch from among her ten choices that appears to match the test patch in brightness. (Be sure that she lays down the matching patch on the black area to the right of the background to be certain of her choice.) Be careful to tell the participant not to hesitate to select different matching patches with different backgrounds if she feels this is appropriate. Participants may think that because the test patch remains the same, they should always select the same matching patch. Do not let the participant see the test patch without a border between trials. as this may also cause a bias toward a particular matching patch.

Place the matching patches at the top of the black construction paper haphazardly. Run the participant through eighteen trials of the experiment, three trials with each background. In order to have the backgrounds presented in a random order in each set of six, here are three random orders that you may use to determine the order in which the backgrounds are presented: 5, 10, 3, 1, 4, 7; 4, 3, 10, 7, 1, 5; 10, 4, 1, 5, 7, 3 (the numbers refer to the lightness codes on the back of each background).

After you have presented a background over the test patch and the participant has chosen her matching patch, place the value of the matching patch in the appropriate space in the table that follows. After the experiment is complete, add up the values in each column and divide by three to get an average matching patch value for each background.

Now you can plot these data in the graph provided. Along the x-axis are the six values of background that you used. Above each find the average value of matching patch that you calculated from the table, and place a dot at the value (as determined from the y-axis). Now connect the dots and note the shape of the function.

Recall that the test patch has a lightness value of 6. Given this, what shape should the function have? How much of a brightness contrast were you able to obtain? How could you improve the experiment to get an even larger effect?

Reference

Heinemann, E. G. 1955. Simultaneous brightness induction as a function of inducing- and test-field luminance. *Journal of Experimental Psychology* 50:89–96.

Background values:	1	3	4	5	7	10
Matching value 1:	_____	_____	_____	_____	_____	_____
Matching value 2:	_____	_____	_____	_____	_____	_____
Matching value 3:	_____	_____	_____	_____	_____	_____
Total matching value:	_____	_____	_____	_____	_____	_____
Average matching value:	_____	_____	_____	_____	_____	_____

Test patch lightness value = 6

Background lightness values

CHAPTER 6

Perception

Learning Objectives

THE PROBLEM OF PERCEPTION

1. Know that the central issue of perception is not why a stimulus is recognized as an object, but why it is even seen as an object.
2. Keep in mind the characteristics of the proximal stimulus in comparison with the distal stimulus.
3. Understand that to organize the sensory world, three questions must be asked of any given stimulus: Where is it? Where is it going? What is it?

THE PERCEPTION OF DEPTH: WHERE IS IT?

Binocular cues
4. Be aware of the significance of binocular disparity in depth perception.

Monocular cues
5. What are the monocular cues to depth perception? How is texture important?

The perception of depth through motion
6. How do motion parallax and optic flow contribute to our perception of depth? How do they differ?

The role of redundancy
7. Why do we have multiple mechanisms for perceiving depth?

THE PERCEPTION OF MOVEMENT: WHAT IS IT DOING?

Retinal motion
8. Remind yourself about motion-sensitive cells discussed in Chapter 5.

Apparent movement
9. Be familiar with the phenomena of apparent and induced movement, and the relevance of these phenomena to the study of real movement.

Eye movements
10. How are we able to distinguish between a moving world with a stationary self (e.g., watching a car go by) and a stationary world with a moving self (e.g., looking out the window of a moving train)?
11. Understand the difference between relative displacement and absolute displacement of objects in the world and how this relates to an automatic compensation system in the brain.

Illusions of motion
12. Describe some motion illusions.

FORM PERCEPTION: WHAT IS IT?

13. Why is form perception not simply a matter of accumulating a checklist?
14. What is transposition and how is it important to the study of form perception?
15. Be aware of the central assumption of Gestalt psychology as it applies to perception.
16. Why does one need to understand both the perception of parts and the relationships among the parts to account for form perception?

The information-processing approach
17. What is the central assumption of the information-processing approach and how is this related to the analogy between mind and computer?
18. What is the role of flow charts in developing psychological theory about perception?

The elements of form
19. Review the evidence for mechanisms in the physiology of the brain that underlie the perception of features.
20. Describe some behavioral evidence for the existence of elementary feature detectors in the visual system.
21. Be aware of the later stage of processing at which features are assumed to be conjoined. How does the study of illusory conjunctions pinpoint the stage of processing that is at work in pattern recognition?

Perceptual segregation
22. What is the role of perceptual segregation in scene perception? Why is it important?
23. Give examples of how perceptual segregation occurs in vision and audition.

24. How is the segregation of figure and ground an example of perceptual segregation?
25. Be familiar with reversible figures and how they contribute to our understanding of perceptual segregation. What proposal has been made about the perception of reversible figures?
26. What are the laws of perceptual grouping and how do they relate to each other?
27. How does the principle of maximum likelihood support the laws of perceptual grouping?

Pattern recognition
28. Describe the feature net model as an approach to pattern recognition. Be familiar with its elements of activation and deactivation.
29. What phenomena show that context affects pattern recognition? What is priming?
30. How does bidirectional activation combine to yield pattern recognition?
31. Why is an intermediate step corresponding to the use of geons necessary in some perception? What are geons?
32. How do patients with visual agnosias inform us about the creation of structural descriptions and the interpretation of them in perception?

The processing sequence in form perception
33. Review the major steps in form perception. Be prepared to discuss how these may be arranged in sequence or in parallel in actual perception.

PERCEPTUAL PROBLEM SOLVING

34. What purpose does the perceptual hypothesis serve? How does it involve bidirectional processing?

The logic of perception
35. Describe a study of stroboscopic movement that illustrates the constructive nature of perception.

When logic fails: impossible figures
36. The perceptual system follows rules of logic. Explain how and why impossible figures pose a perceptual problem for us.

FORM PERCEPTION AND THE NERVOUS SYSTEM

Early stages of visual processing
37. Know the difference between magno and parvo cells. How do they function differently in perception?

Visual processing in the brain
38. Review the difference between simple and complex cortical cells.
39. Be able to distinguish between the "what" and "where" pathways in the brain. How are they different anatomically and in function? What evidence supports these differences?

The Humpty-Dumpty problem
40. Be aware of the binding problem and how it is created by a visual system that is based on component analyses of scenes.

PERCEPTUAL SELECTION: ATTENTION

41. What is attention?

Selection through orientation
42. How can the study of orienting movements inform us about attention?

Central selection
43. Be familiar with the concept of central selection and its manifestations in the auditory and visual modes. What is visual search?
44. What are the conditions that permit parallel visual search, and what are those that require serial search?
45. Be familiar with studies showing that even in vision, attention can be moved internally without moving the eyes.
46. How is priming relevant to attention?
47. How does the study of shadowing inform us about attention?
48. What evidence is there about a "filter" theory of attention?

PERCEIVING CONSTANCY

49. What is the relationship between distal objects and the proximal stimuli they cause that gives rise to the problem of constancy?

Size and shape constancy
50. Be able to describe the phenomena of size and shape constancy.
51. What is meant by higher-order patterns, and how can these be used to solve the problem of size constancy?
52. What role is played by distance cues such as motion parallax in the perception of constant size?
53. Helmholtz's principle of unconscious inference is a powerful explanation of size constancy. Describe it and give an example.

Lightness constancy
54. Describe the phenomenon of lightness constancy and explain how the principle of reflectance is related to lightness constancy.
55. How is lightness constancy achieved? Explain the role of the ratio of reflected light from an object and its surroundings.

Empiricism and nativism revisited
56. Defend this statement: On balance, it appears that our perceptual systems are a function of both native endowments and the role of experience.

THE REPRESENTATION OF REALITY IN ART

Seeing and knowing
57. Explain the odd appearance of figures in Egyptian art. What does this signal about the artist's rendition of reality?

The Renaissance: scenes through a window frame
58. What is the parallel between the struggle of Renaissance painters to represent reality and the psychologist's struggle to understand the perception of reality?

The Impressionists: how a scene is perceived
59. What was the aim of the Impressionists? How is this realized in their paintings?

The Moderns: how a scene is conceived
60. How is the aim of introducing conceptual representations in art achieved by the Moderns?

Programmed Exercises

THE PROBLEM OF PERCEPTION

1. The properties of a three-dimensional distal stimulus are perceived as constant despite continuing variation of the _____ stimulus.

    proximal

2. In order to perceive an object, the observer must _____ the sensory world into a coherent, meaningful scene.

    organize

THE PERCEPTION OF DEPTH: WHERE IS IT?

3. The two eyes look out on the world from slightly different positions and thus obtain a somewhat different view of any solid object on which they converge. This is called _____ _____.

    binocular disparity

4. Relative size is an example of a _____ depth cue.

    monocular

5. Abrupt change in a _____ _____ produces the impression of a sharp drop, a "visual cliff."

    texture gradient

6. Far-off objects are blocked from view by other opaque objects that obstruct their optical path to the eye. This is a depth cue called _____.

    interposition

7. As we move our head or body from right to left, the images projected by the objects outside will move across the retina. The direction and speed of this motion is an effective monocular depth cue called _____ _____.

    motion parallax

8. The phenomenon that causes an apparent change in the size of objects as we move toward or away from them is known as _____ _____.

    optic flow

THE PERCEPTION OF MOVEMENT: WHAT IS IT DOING?

9. Suppose we briefly turn on a light in one location in the visual field, then turn it off, and after an appropriate period of time (somewhere between 30 and 200 msec), turn on a second light in a different location. The resulting phenomenon is called _____ movement.

    apparent

10. If the ground is moving and a figure is stationary in the visual field, the figure is seen as moving. This phenomenon of illusory movement is called _____ movement.

    induced

11. The perception of movement in one of two stimuli depends on which is seen as a stationary _____ of reference.

    frame

12. Perceived _____ seems to be a result of the brain's compensation for the retinal displacement caused by voluntary eye movements.

    stability

13. To perceive movement, the perceptual system must solve the _____ problem, matching current elements in the field of view to elements in the immediate past.

    correspondence

FORM PERCEPTION: WHAT IS IT?

14. One theory of form perception is that observers consult a mental _____ to see if an object has certain properties.

    checklist

15. The fact that a triangle appears as such regardless of the elements that make it up is called _____ of form.

    transposition

16. A form is perceived as a _____, a whole that is different from the sum of its parts.

    Gestalt

17. Many investigators believe that form perception is the result of a series of _____-_____ steps that transform an input to a perceptual experience.

    information-processing

18. A _____ chart allows one to represent a series of information-processing transformations.

    flow

19. A task used frequently to study form perception requires a research participant to indicate whether a certain target appears in a briefly presented array. This is called a _____ _____ task.

    visual search

20. Examples of features that are processed automatically are _____, _____, and _____.

    color, curvature orientation

21. An _____ _____ occurs when a participant mistakenly ties together two features in an object that did not occur together.

    illusory conjunction

22. The process known as _____ _____ enables us to separate figure from ground.

    visual segregation (or perceptual parsing)

23. _____ figures are ones in which either of two figure-ground organizations is possible.

Reversible (ambiguous)

24. Proximity, similarity, and good continuation are examples of the laws of _____ _____.

perceptual grouping

25. Contours that continue smoothly along their original course follow the law of _____ _____, a principle that is illustrated by _____ contours (perceiving contours when they don't exist).

good continuation, subjective

26. The underlying principle of all the laws of perceptual grouping is known as the principle of _____ _____.

maximum likelihood

27. The model of feature analysis that uses activation and deactivation to recognize stimulus patterns is known as the _____ _____ model.

feature net

28. A feature net model is an example of _____ -_____ processing, an approach to pattern recognition that begins with component features and builds up to larger units.

bottom-up

29. The _____ -_____ process of pattern recognition begins with higher units, because it is often affected by higher-level knowledge and expectations.

top-down

30. _____ effects demonstrate that there is some top-down processing in the perceptual process.

Context

31. Perceptual processing is necessarily _____: It is affected by the stimulus and also by prior knowledge.

bidirectional

32. One model by Biederman uses approximately 30 geometric primitives called _____ as the basis for recognizing all objects.

geons

33. The total of the primitives plus the relationships among the primitives for an object is called its _____ _____.

structural description

34. If a patient is able to perceive an object but not recognize it, her or she has a visual _____.

agnosia

35. The processing steps that occur during the course of object recognition may occur all at once or sequentially, demonstrating _____ and _____ processing, respectively.

parallel, serial

PERCEPTUAL PROBLEM SOLVING

36. A _____ _____ is constantly compared to new stimuli in order to test its validity.

perceptual hypothesis

37. An _____ figure poses a perceptual contradiction for a research participant. It poses a perceptual problem that cannot be solved.

impossible

FORM PERCEPTION AND THE NERVOUS SYSTEM

38. There are two sorts of ganglion cells that exit the retina. One is responsible for detecting movement in the periphery and is composed of _____ cells, and the other is responsible for carrying pattern and form information from the fovea and is composed of _____ cells.

magno
parvo

39. Remember that _____ cortical cells fire most strongly to edges or lines, while _____ cortical cells are sensitive to line movement.

simple, complex

40. The _____ system, located in temporal cortex, codes for object identity, while the _____ system, located in parietal cortex, is responsible for detecting object location.

what
where

41. The _____ problem is caused by the visual system's analysis of scenes by breaking them up into parts; the consequence is that there must be a mechanism that puts the parts back together again.

binding

PERCEPTUAL SELECTION: ATTENTION

42. The ways by which we perceive selectively are grouped under the label "_____."

attention

43. On the average, our eyes move three or four times per second to fixate objects. These fixations are _____, not random. Our eye movements serve the purpose of _____ us to salient stimuli.

purposeful, orienting

44. If a stimulus is defined by a _____ of features in a visual search task, the search for it must be serial.

conjunction

45. During _____ _____, the mind's eye moves although there is no physical movement of the eyes.

central selection

46. When stimuli are presented over earphones so that each ear receives a different message, this is called a _____ presentation.

dichotic

47. When participants are asked to _____ a message, they are repeating it aloud, word for word, as it comes over one of their earphones.   shadow

48. The attentional _____ attenuates irrelevant messages as a whole, but may pass items from them that are important or familiar.   filter

PERCEIVING CONSTANCY

49. The perceptual system responds to real objects outside regardless of variations in their proximal images. This is best illustrated by the perceptual _____: lightness, size, and shape.   constancies

50. Gibson has stressed the importance of _____ relationships within a stimulus pattern in explaining perceptual organization.   invariant (higher-order)

51. A Boeing 747 at a distance of 1,000 feet will look larger than a single-engine two-seater at a distance of 50 feet despite the fact that the retinal image of the latter will be greater than that of the former. This is called _____ _____. An analogous phenomenon occurs in the perception of _____.   size constancy
shape

52. According to Gibson, an important influence on size constancy is the proportion of _____ elements that are occluded by an object. This remains constant regardless of the distance of the observer from the object.   texture

53. An alternative view of Gibson's is that of Helmholtz, who argued that size constancy is achieved by a process of unconscious _____, making a sort of internal calculation of the relationship of distance and image size.   inference

54. The apparent lightness of an object remains fairly constant despite rather drastic changes in the amount of illumination that falls upon it. This is called lightness _____.   constancy

55. The perception of lightness depends on the lightness _____ between a figure and its background.   ratio

THE REPRESENTATION OF REALITY IN ART

56. Artists came to appreciate the use of pictorial cues to depth during the _____.   Renaissance

57. The _____ tried not to depict reality in their art, but to create certain perceptual experiences in the observer, experiences that would be evoked by a scene on canvas.   Impressionists

58. _____ try to add conceptual representations such as ambiguity or tension in their art.   Modernists

Self Test

1. Which of the following is not true of the proximal stimulus?
   a. It is two-dimensional in vision.
   b. It can vary in size and shape.
   c. It alone enables us to perceive the constant properties of objects.
   d. It is the retinal image of the distal stimulus in vision.

2. Binocular disparity is caused by:
   a. a slight difference in the size of the two eyes
   b. small imperfections in the lens and/or cornea
   c. the slightly different position of each eye
   d. the favoring of one eye over the other

3. Binocular disparity:
   a. is an effective cue to depth for long distances
   b. is due to the fact that our eyes receive virtually the same image
   c. is not by itself a sufficient cue to depth
   d. can be simulated by viewing specially designed two-dimensional drawings
   e. is only effective for familiar objects

4. The figure at the right illustrates all of the following monocular cues to depth except:

a. linear perspective
b. relative size
c. binocular disparity
d. texture gradients
e. interposition

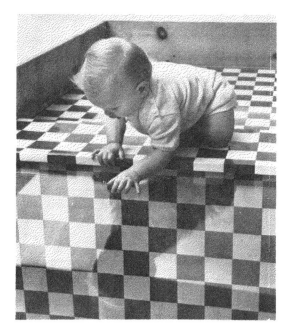

5. The impression of a "visual cliff" is accounted for by which depth cue?
   a. linear perspective
   b. relative size
   c. texture gradients
   d. interposition

6. Which of the following is not true of motion parallax?
   a. Nearby objects move in a direction opposite our own as we move through space.
   b. Objects farther away move in a direction similar to our own as we move through space.
   c. Objects farther away move at a lesser velocity.
   d. Objects closer to us move at a greater velocity.

7. The change in the size of objects as we move closer or farther away from them is known as:
   a. optic flow
   b. motion parallax
   c. linear perspective
   d. apparent movement

8. One of the most effective monocular depth cues is _____, which is absent in pictorial representations but present in real life.
   a. linear perspective
   b. relative size
   c. interposition
   d. motion parallax

9. The results of the visual cliff experiment (illustrated on this page) suggests that:
   a. infants cannot use motion parallax as a cue to depth
   b. infants' eye fixations tend to be directed to edges and vertices
   c. depth perception is largely innate
   d. texture gradients are not useful cues to distance
   e. none of the above

10. Apparent movement refers to:
    a. the perception of movement when two stimuli are presented in alternation at the proper temporal and spatial intervals

    b. the perception of movement of a target when in fact it is stationary but the background is moving
    c. the perception of self-movement when you are stationary but the scene that you are watching is moving
    d. none of the above

11. Induced movement differs from apparent movement in that:
    a. in the former case it is the figure that moves, while in the latter case it is the ground that moves
    b. the former is a physical phenomenon, while the latter is a retinal phenomenon
    c. induced movement is based on relative displacement, while apparent movement is based on absolute displacement
    d. none of the above

12. Which two of the following are examples of induced movement?
    a. the moon moving through the clouds
    b. perceiving movement of a stationary spot of light in darkness
    c. perceiving movement of a stationary spot of light when the rectangular frame around it moves
    d. perceiving that the moon moves when you move with respect to it
    e. perceiving movement in the successive frames in a movie

13. When several investigators temporarily paralyzed their eye muscles and then tried to move their eyes, they saw objects move in their visual field even though their eyes did not actually move (nor did the objects). This suggests that:
    a. paralyzing the eye muscles doesn't affect motion perception
    b. perceived stability is produced by compensating for motor movement
    c. perceived motion is produced by compensating for motor movement
    d. none of the above

14. One of the most interesting features of form recognition is that forms are recognized in spite of:
    a. transpositions of pattern
    b. the fact that their apparent lightnesses change with changes in illumination
    c. the change in perceived shape that occurs when the angle of regard of an object is changed
    d. none of the above

15. According to the Gestalt point of view, the perception of an object depends on:
    a. the perception of the relations among parts of the object
    b. the perception of the elementary features of the object
    c. the perception of the object's geons
    d. the flow of information as an object is transformed with successive process steps

16. The information-processing view of object recognition draws on an analogy between:
    a. the brain and a telephone switchboard
    b. steps in mental processing of an object and the workings of the brain during processing
    c. input and retrieval processes
    d. a flow chart of mental processes and a computer program

17. Object recognition begins with:
    a. recognition of Gestalt properties
    b. visual search

c. selective attention
d. conjunction of features
e. feature detection

18. If a target in a visual search task differs from the background items on a feature such as color or curvature, participants will:
a. struggle to detect the target
b. engage in a conjunctive search for the target
c. perceive the target quickly with little search required
d. none of the above

19. If a participant were presented with a display of letters printed in colored inks that included a blue G, a red M, and a yellow B, and if this display were presented briefly, he or she might see:
a. a blue D
b. a red T
c. a yellow R
d. a blue M

20. Which of the following statements about perceptual parsing is *not* true?
a. It is also called visual segregation.
b. It is contributed by the individual and is not a part of the stimulus.
c. It is the first stage of perceptual organization and separates the stimuli into various subcomponents.
d. It occurs only in the realm of visual perception

21. Segregating figure from ground (as in a reversible figure):
a. is a high-level perceptual process that requires a good deal of preliminary analysis
b. can only be done with reversible figures
c. is accomplished by perceiving the contour separating two regions as belonging to the ground
d. is too elementary a perceptual process to be used effectively by artists
e. none of the above

Reversible figure that can be perceived either as two faces in profile or as a white vase.

22. For reversible figures such as the one above, which of the following is false?
a. the figure is generally seen in front of the ground
b. a reversible figure-ground display is characterized by two adjoining regions alternately acting as figures
c. a contour can be seen as simultaneously belonging to figure and ground
d. none of the above

23. All of the following are "laws of perceptual organization" *except*:
a. proximity
b. similarity
c. good continuation
d. simplicity

24. The law of proximity states that:
a. the closer an object is to an observer, the easier it is to identify it
b. the closer two objects are to each other, the greater the chance that they will be grouped together perceptually
c. given any two objects, one is always nearer (perceptually) to an arbitrary third object than the other
d. none of the above

25. The principle of maximum likelihood:
a. states that we will interpret the proximal stimulus as the external stimulus that most likely produced it
b. opposes the laws of perceptual grouping
c. assumes that we are able to better discriminate between stimuli that are closer together
d. accounts for our ability to form new cognitive constructions when presented with novel and disorganized stimuli

26. Feature net and other similar theories of pattern recognition are based on the principle that:
a. feature detectors can be in competition and the correct one can win out
b. feature detectors are all independent of one another in their analysis of a pattern
c. feature detectors work on an object only after the relationships among the parts have been determined
d. top-down and bottom-up processes cannot work together in object recognition

27. Pattern recognition is a:
a. top-down process
b. horizontal process
c. bottom-up process
d. a and c
e. a and b

28. A professor is giving a lecture on the state of the U.S. economy. His lecture is suddenly broken up by several coughs, which interrupt but do not stop his speech stream. Although there are physical gaps in the utterance, the students hear and understand the presentation. This is an example of:
a. feature analysis
b. context effect
c. bottom-up processing
d. attention

29. All of the following are true about geons, *except*:
a. About 70 geons serve as the geometric primitives of the perceptual system.
b. Geons can be combined with other geons to make up many different objects.
c. The recognition of geons is accomplished by an early stage of pattern recognition.
d. The relationships among geons are an important part of perceptual recognition.

30. A person with an agnosia would:
    a. be able to recognize an object but not perceive its parts
    b. be unable to recognize an object even though he or she could perceive its shape
    c. be unable to recognize the color or shape of an object
    d. be able to write a structural description of an object but be unable to copy the object

31. When people make sense of a previously unknown and meaningless stimulus:
    a. they have trouble perceiving it in its original unorganized form
    b. they must constantly reinforce the new pattern in order to retain it in visual memory
    c. they have formed a perceptual hypothesis
    d. a and c

32. A perceptual hypothesis:
    a. once formed, provides fundamental and unchanging laws of perceptual organization
    b. represents the bottom-up aspect of perceptual processing
    c. is formed for every new stimulus encountered
    d. serves as the top-down aspect of visual processing that is compared to the stimulus

33. The problem in perceiving impossible figures is that:
    a. the individual features of the figures cannot be accurately detected
    b. the parts of the object individually don't make any sense
    c. top-down processing plays too little a role in their perception
    d. the parts cannot be reconciled together into a whole figure

34. Given the properties of magno and parvo cells, and given the two flows of information in the visual system into the "what" and "where" streams, it seems likely that:
    a. magno cells feed into the "where" system
    b. parvo cells feed into the "what" system
    c. magno cells feed into the "what" system
    d. parvo cells feed into the "where" system
    e. magno and parvo cells feed into both systems
    f. a and b
    g. c and d

35. The binding problem is caused by the visual system's breaking up of:
    a. proximity and similarity information
    b. form and location information
    c. size and shape information
    d. location and movement information
    e. information about large and small objects

36. Orienting movements, like turning of the head, are external manifestations of:
    a. differentiation
    b. attention
    c. recalibration
    d. adaptation

37. During a visual search procedure:
    a. a participant is asked to pick out the most relevant component of a stimulus pattern as quickly as possible
    b. participants may employ methods of physical orientation and central selection to locate the target

    c. the orienting movements that a participant makes show little relation to the features of objects that are attended to during scanning
    d. the internal selection process often hinders accurate scanning and location of the correct target

38. In a visual search task, if the target is a blue T that is embedded among green Rs, blue Gs, and red Ts, participants would have to engage in:
    a. a serial search for the target
    b. a parallel search for the target
    c. either a serial or a parallel search for the target, depending on their choice
    d. none of the above

39. Which of the following is not true of the effects of selective attention?
    a. Some information gets in from an unattended message.
    b. It primes certain feature analyzers.
    c. It helps prepare us for an upcoming stimulus.
    d. It is restricted to vision only.
    e. all of the above

40. Two proposals have been made about the perception of constancies. One is based on the idea that:
    a. there are invariant relationships among elements of the distal stimulus
    b. there are invariant relationships among elements of the proximal stimulus
    c. there is an unconscious inference made about the relationships between elements of a proximal stimulus
    d. there is an unconscious inference made about the relationships between invariant features of a distal stimulus

41. The other proposal about the perception of constancy is based on the idea that:
    a. we perceive constancy in shape by making an unconscious inference about orientation of a retinal image and texture elements from the background
    b. we perceive size constancy by making an unconscious inference about the size of a retinal image and the distance we are from an object
    c. we perceive lightness constancy by making an unconscious inference about the size of a retinal image and the reflectance of that image
    d. none of the above

42. It appears that lightness constancy is achieved by:
    a. noting the reflectance of an object of interest
    b. noting the illumination coming from an object of interest
    c. noting the reflectance of an object of interest compared to the reflectance of background objects
    d. noting the reflectance of an object of interest under two conditions of illumination

43. It is likely that infants exhibit some measure of:
    a. angle constancy
    b. depth constancy
    c. lightness constancy
    d. size constancy

44. The fact that a white object in the shade appears lighter than a gray object in the sunlight (even though the gray object has greater luminance) is called:
    a. relative luminance
    b. perceived intensity
    c. lightness constancy
    d. none of the above

45. The representation of reality in art, especially three-dimensional reality, became a feature in which of the following schools?
    a. early Egyptian art
    b. the Renaissance
    c. Modernism
    d. Impressionism

Answer Key for Self Test

1.	c p. 217	24.	b p. 231
2.	c p. 218	25.	a p. 232
3.	d p. 219	26.	a p. 235
4.	c p. 219	27.	d pp. 235, 236
5.	c p. 220	28.	b p. 236
6.	b p. 221	29.	a p. 237
7.	a p. 221	30.	b p. 238
8.	d p. 221	31.	d pp. 238, 239
9.	c p. 219	32.	d p. 239
10.	a p. 223	33.	d p. 240
11.	c p. 225	34.	f pp. 241, 242
12.	a, c p. 225	35.	b pp. 243, 244
13.	b p. 224	36.	b p. 244
14.	a p. 226	37.	b p. 245
15.	a p. 226	38.	a p. 246
16.	d p. 227	39.	d pp. 245–47
17.	e p. 228	40.	a p. 247
18.	c p. 228	41.	b p. 248
19.	d p. 228	42.	c p. 251
20.	d p. 228	43.	d p. 249
21.	e p. 230	44.	c p. 251
22.	c p. 230	45.	b pp. 254, 255
23.	d pp. 231, 232		

Investigating Psychological Phenomena

THE EFFECT OF MENTAL SET

Equipment: Stimuli are included
Number of participants: One
Time per participant: Twenty minutes
Time for experimenter: Twenty minutes

The issue of how past experience influences perception (an example of top-down processing) is an important one in psychology and has generated quite a bit of research. This is a difficult issue to resolve because there are many ways in which past experience might influence perceptual processes. In this problem you are asked to consider a series of hypothetical experiments (modeled after a study by Epstein and Rock, 1960) and to provide alternative interpretations of the hypothetical results. As you

move through the experiments, try to develop one hypothesis which will account for all of the results described. The stimuli for all the experiments are the ambiguous and unambiguous versions of Leeper's old woman-young woman figure shown below.

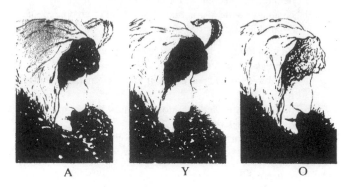

Notice that the first picture (A) can be seen either as a young woman or as an old woman—that is, it is ambiguous. The second picture (Y) is quite similar to the first (A) except that some detail has been changed so that it has become a fairly unambiguous picture of a young woman. Likewise, the third picture (O) is a fairly unambiguous version of an old woman. The purpose of all the experiments is to determine how prior exposure to the unambiguous versions of the figure influences whether participants call the ambiguous version an old woman or a young woman. Imagine that twenty participants are run in each hypothetical experiment.

EXPERIMENT 1

Each participant is shown the following series of slides (at a rate of one slide every eight seconds) and asked to name each picture as "young" or "old" as it is presented: YYOOOOOOOOA (Y refers to a presentation of the unambiguous young woman, O refers to a presentation of the unambiguous old woman, and A refers to the presentation of the ambiguous image.) All participants name the Y and O versions of the figure correctly. On the critical trial, the ambiguous picture A, the results are as follows: Twenty participants call it "old," no participants call it "young." One interpretation of this result is that the more frequently presented unambiguous version determined the perception of the ambiguous picture. This is listed as Hypothesis 1 on the answer sheet. What alternative explanations can you propose to explain the responses of participants in this hypothetical experiment? Write them on the answer sheet. There are at least three other plausible possibilities.

Before you go on to experiments 2 through 4, check to see whether the hypotheses you have developed coincide with those given in the answers to the problem. If not, use the given hypotheses as the basis for your answers to the questions posed in Experiments 2 through 4.

EXPERIMENT 2

A new set of twenty participants receives the following series: YYYYYOOOOOA. Again the responses to all the Y and O stimuli are correct, and the responses to the A stimulus are as follows: Twenty participants respond "old woman," none respond "young woman." Consider each of the four hypotheses raised to account for the results of Experiment 1 and evaluate how each fares with the results of the experiment. Record your responses under Experiment 2 on the answer sheet.

EXPERIMENT 3

Twenty participants each receive the series: OOOOOOOYYYA. All respond correctly to the Y and O stimuli; the responses to A are: Twenty participants call it "young woman," none call it "old woman." Again evaluate the success of each of the four hypotheses at accounting for these results.*

EXPERIMENT 4

Twenty new participants are shown the series: YYOYYOYYOA. All Os and Ys are identified correctly; the data on the A presen-

tations are: Eighteen participants respond "old woman," two participants respond "young woman" (a reliable difference). Which of the four hypotheses can explain these results? Is one of the four hypotheses confirmed by the results of all four experiments?

*We continue to consider hypothesis 1 even though experiment 2 cannot be explained by it; scientists do not typically discard an hypothesis because of a single contradictory finding.

ANSWER SHEET

Experiment 1

Hypothesis 1   Frequency of presentation determines the response to the ambiguous figure

Hypothesis 2   _____

_____

Hypothesis 3   _____

_____

Hypothesis 4   _____

_____

Experiment 2

Hypothesis 1   _____

_____

Hypothesis 2   _____

_____

Hypothesis 3   _____

_____

Hypothesis 4   _____

_____

Experiment 3

Hypothesis 1   _____

_____

Hypothesis 2   _____

_____

Hypothesis 3   _____

_____

Hypothesis 4   _____

_____

Experiment 4

Which of the four hypotheses can account for these results? _____

_____

Which hypotheses can account for the results of all four experiments? _____

_____

Answers to Problem

EXPERIMENT 1:

Hypothesis 2: It is possible that the interpretation of the ambiguous picture was entirely influenced by the perception of the immediately preceding picture of the old woman. If so, this would be called a "recency effect," because the most recently presented picture would have had the strongest influence on perception of the ambiguous picture.

Hypothesis 3: An alternative possibility has to do with what the participant might be expecting to be presented on the last trial. He or she has just seen eight consecutive pictures of the old woman and so might reasonably expect that the next picture will also be that of an old woman. Thus, if this were the case, the participant's cognitive expectations would be guiding his or her perceptions.

Hypothesis 4: A final possibility is that participants in general have a bias to respond with the name "old woman." One might suppose that such a bias exists (for some reason) even independently of what the participant actually sees. That is, participants are biased to call the ambiguous version an "old woman" regardless of what precedes it.

EXPERIMENT 2:

This experiment rules out Hypothesis 1, the frequency hypothesis. Both unambiguous versions were presented equally frequently before the ambiguous version was presented. Thus, a participant's perception of the ambiguous version could not have been influenced by the more frequently presented unambiguous version. None of the alternative hypotheses is ruled out by these results: (a) The response to the ambiguous version was the same as that to the most recently presented unambiguous version. Thus, recency is a viable interpretation of these results. (b) Because the responses to the sixth through tenth stimuli were "old woman," the participants may have built up an expectation that the eleventh stimulus would be an old woman as well. So cognitive expectations may well have guided their response to the ambiguous item. (c) The fact that most participants identified the ambiguous picture as an old woman is consistent with the possibility that they have a bias to call it that regardless of their immediately prior perceptual experience.

EXPERIMENT 3:

Once again this experiment disconfirms the frequency hypothesis. This time participants responded to the test picture with the name of the *least* frequently presented unambiguous picture. Also, the experiment rules out Hypothesis 4, which states that participants have a predisposing bias to call the ambiguous version an old woman. Both the recency and the cognitive expectation hypotheses can account for the results.

EXPERIMENT 4:

The cognitive expectation hypothesis probably is ruled out. In responding to the unambiguous versions, participants were following a regular pattern of two "young woman" responses followed by one "old woman" response. The last unambiguous picture was that of the old woman; thus participants should have been expecting a young woman next. Instead most responded "old woman," a result that can only be explained by noting that the most recently presented unambiguous picture was that of the old woman. Thus, the recency explanation is compatible with these results. Once again the frequency hypothesis is disconfirmed because the most frequently presented unambiguous picture was the young woman. The response bias explanation might be brought up to explain the results of this experiment except that it was ruled out by Experiment 3. Thus, the only explanation which satisfactorily can explain the results of all four experiments is Hypothesis 2, which claims that the picture which a participant sees most recently will affect his current perception.

This exercise demonstrates how it is sometimes possible to start with several potential explanations of a phenomenon and successfully rule out the incorrect ones with further experimentation. Initially there were four plausible interpretations of the results of hypothetical Experiment 1. The results of hypothetical Experiments 2 through 4, however, rule out all but one of the alternatives.

Even though the experiments described above are only hypothetical, they illustrate this process of narrowing down alternative interpretations. You may want to try out any of these experiments to determine the actual results. On page 81 you will find sets of pictures of both the unambiguous versions and the ambiguous version of the figure. Cut them out and return to the previous pages of this section. Perform the experiments as described there and record the results. Do your results correspond to the hypothetical data? Do the same hypotheses apply?

Reference

Epstein, W., and Rock, I. 1960. Perceptual set as an artifact of recency. *American Journal of Psychology* 73:214–28.

Cut these out to perform the experiments. On the back of each figure are the letters Y (young woman), O (old woman), or A (ambiguous).

Y   Y   Y   Y   Y

Y   Y   Y   Y   Y

O   O   O   O   O

O   O   O   O   O

A   A

CHAPTER 7

Memory

Learning Objectives

1. Understand what it means for perception to be concerned with organization in space, and memory to be concerned with organization in time.

STUDYING MEMORY

Some preliminary distinctions
2. Be aware of the distinctions between working and long-term memory, between explicit and implicit memory, and between episodic and generic memory.

Encoding, storage, retrieval
3. What is meant by the terms encoding, storage, and retrieval? How do these processes differ from one another?
4. Be familiar with the fact that both recall and recognition are used to measure retrieval. How do these two methods differ from one another?
5. What are causes of failures to retrieve?

ENCODING

The stage theory of memory
6. What motivates a stage theory of memory, both historically and introspectively?
7. How is the relationship between desktop and bookshelves relevant to working and long-term memory?
8. What is the capacity of working memory? How is it measured?
9. There are two mechanisms that account for forgetting from working memory. What are they, and how do they work?
10. Rehearsal is a process important to working memory. Describe its function in relation to both working and long-term memory.
11. One of the most robust phenomena in the study of memory is the appearance of primacy and recency effects in free recall. Describe these, and indicate what causes them. Be sure you can cite evidence that supports the presumed causes.
12. What is a chunk, and how does this concept apply to the capacity of working memory? How do chunks get created?

A changed emphasis: active memory and organization
13. How do findings about rehearsal challenge the stage theory of memory?

14. What is maintenance rehearsal? Does the amount of maintenance rehearsal affect the probability of information's entering long-term memory? Cite the relevant evidence.
15. What is the concept of "working memory," and how does it differ from the concept of "short-term memory"?
16. Understand the concept of depth of processing and how it affects memory. Give examples of processing at different depths.
17. How do chunking and reorganization affect the capacity of memory? Give examples.
18. Mnemonics are tools to increase the capacity of memory. Describe some mnemonics, and understand how they work to affect memory capacity. What are the practical limitations of mnemonics?

RETRIEVAL

19. Understand the role of retrieval cues in increasing the accessibility of memory traces.

The relation between original encoding and retrieval
20. What is the concept of encoding specificity, and how does it influence successful retrieval? Understand the range of contexts in which this principle operates.

Elaborative rehearsal
21. Contrast maintenance and elaborative rehearsal. Give examples of elaborative rehearsal.

Memory search
22. How is memory searched? What does the tip-of-the-tongue phenomenon tell us about memory search?

Implicit memory
23. Be aware of the difference between implicit and explicit memory retrieval. What is the essence of an implicit measure, and what are some examples?
24. Describe how repetition priming and fragment completion show implicit retrieval effects.
25. Be aware of how variations in depth of processing and in peripheral aspects of the stimulus produce differential effects on explicit and implicit tests of memory.
26. Be sure you understand the importance of the "overnight fame" experiment and its relation to implicit memory.

27. What are some theoretical accounts of the difference between implicit and explicit memory?

WHEN MEMORY FAILS

Forgetting

28. What is the shape of the forgetting curve?
29. Recount the evidence both for and against a decay theory of forgetting.
30. What is an interference theory of forgetting, and how does it differ from a decay theory?
31. Know the experimental techniques that are used to study proactive and retroactive inhibition.
32. What is the role of similarity in producing interference?
33. Give some accounts of the forgetting of childhood memories.
34. Some memories seem to last quite a long time. Give examples. What factors affect this?
35. How are flashbulb memories claimed to be different from other memories? Are these memories really treated differently by the memory system? Discuss the evidence.

Conceptual frameworks and remembering

36. How does past knowledge help us remember current material? How is this like the use of top-down processing in perception?
37. What effects did Bartlett document in his studies of recollection?
38. Describe some effects that schemas have on memory. What is a "script" and how might it affect memory for some event?
39. Memory is an important issue in the courtroom. What does research tell us about the fallibility of eyewitness testimony? Describe how eyewitness memory may be a reconstruction of earlier events.
40. What is source confusion and when does it occur?
41. Can memories be altered after an event?
42. Is hypnosis a reliable way of helping a witness remember an event? What is the evidence on whether hypnosis improves retrieval?

43. What is the verdict on the tape-recorder theory of memory?
44. Why is there reason to be cautious about the concept of "repressed memories"? What issues should one be concerned about in examining cases of this alleged phenomenon?
45. Discuss the limits to which our memories are distorted. How do top-down and bottom-up processes play a role in enhancing and limiting distortion?

Disordered memories

46. What are the symptoms of anterograde amnesia, and what are some of its causes?
47. How does retrograde amnesia differ from anterograde amnesia? What mechanism has been proposed to account for retrograde amnesia?

What amnesia teaches us

48. What sorts of learning are spared in anterograde amnesia? How is the distinction between declarative and procedural knowledge relevant to this issue?
49. The distinction between implicit and explicit memory has also played a prominent role in accounting for anterograde amnesia. Explain why. Why is it difficult to distinguish between the declarative/procedural versus explicit/implicit accounts of amnesia?
50. Be prepared to give examples of amnesias that selectively disrupt either episodic or genetic memory.
51. Distinguish between associate and strategic retrieval. Give evidence that these two types of retrieval are mediated by different brain circuits. Be sure you understand how evidence from patients who confabulate is relevant to this distinction.
52. How does evidence from brain imaging help us distinguish among different types of memories?

TAKING STOCK

53. Discuss the similarity among perception, memory, and thinking.

Programmed Exercises

STUDYING MEMORY

1. _____ memory holds information for a brief interval. _____-_____ memory stores information for longer periods of time.

   Working, Long-term

2. Instances in which we tap our memory quite consciously to retrieve something are called _____ memory. By contrast, when our memory is used in an indirect way in the service of some other task, this is termed _____ memory.

   explicit

   implicit

3. The first stage of memory is _____, in which information is acquired and brought into the system.

   encoding

4. The records of experience made on the nervous system are called memory _____.

   traces

ENCODING

5. The second stage of memory is _____, during which information is filed away. The final stage is _____, the point at which one tries to remember.

   storage

   retrieval

6. A _____ test is a test of retrieval in which a participant is asked to produce an item from memory.

   recall

7. A _____ test is a test of retrieval in which several items are presented and the participant must decide which ones were presented earlier as part of a studied list.

   recognition

8. The theory of memory that argues for separate memory systems working together is called the _____ theory.

   stage

9. The _____ capacity of working memory has been estimated as about 7 items.   storage

10. The _____ _____ is the number of items an individual can recall after just one presentation.   memory span

11. If it was found that items faded from working memory even though no new information entered, this would support a _____ theory of forgetting.   decay

12. If one found that forgetting in working memory occurred only when new material came into the system, one would have evidence for a _____ theory of forgetting.   displacement

13. _____ is one way of either keeping an item in working memory or allowing it to pass into long-term memory.   Rehearsal

14. The method of _____ _____ allows a participant who is presented with a list of unrelated items to report them in any order desired.   free recall

15. Of a long list of presented items, a participant is most apt to remember the first few (known as the _____ effect) and the last few (known as the _____ effect).   primacy, recency

16. The process that allows the contents of working memory to expand is called _____. Using this process results in the creation of _____ of information.   organization chunks

17. _____ rehearsal consists of repeating items over and over to keep them in memory for a short time, as in repeating a telephone number.   Maintenance

18. _____ memory refers to a working memory that is involved in processing the information that is held.   Working

19. One theory of memory asserts that the extent to which information is subject to semantic analysis, as opposed to analysis of its surface features, will determine how firmly the information will be held in memory. This theory attributes permanence in memory to _____ of _____.   depth, processing

20. The various devices designed to improve memory are collectively called _____.   mnemonics

21. The method of _____ requires learners to visualize each of the items they want to remember in a different spatial location.   loci

22. The most effective kind of image for remembering is one in which the elements of the image are _____.   interacting

RETRIEVAL

23. When you know a piece of information (i.e., you have stored it), but you cannot retrieve it at the moment, the trace is said to be _____.   inaccessible

24. A stimulus that provides a trigger to get an item out of memory is called a(n) _____ _____.   retrieval cue

25. The principle of _____ _____ states that retrieval success is most likely if the context at the time of retrieval approximates that during original encoding.   encoding specificity

26. _____ rehearsal consists of the organization of information in working memory so that it can be transferred to long-term memory.   Elaborative

27. Many investigators believe that retrieval is generally preceded by an internal process called _____ _____.   memory search

28. The _____-_____-_____-_____ phenomenon is an example of unsuccessful retrieval in which the participant comes close to the searched-for item in his or her memory but cannot quite find the right memory location.   tip-of-the-tongue

29. Recall and recognition are both _____ measures of memory, while word fragment completion is an _____ measure.   explicit implicit

30. _____ priming is a technique used to study implicit memory; words that appear on a study list are identified more readily than words that do not.   Repetition

31. Subjective _____ can be influenced merely by presenting some material during a study phase so that it is retrieved at the time of judgment, but so that the source of familiarity is forgotten.   fame

WHEN MEMORY FAILS

32. The _____ curve was first plotted by Ebbinghaus who tested himself on the relearning of lists of nonsense syllables.

forgetting

33. The fact that animals forget when their internal temperatures are higher is evidence for a _____ theory of forgetting.

decay

34. One cause of forgetting is _____, in which some items in memory cause the forgetting of others.

interference

35. One example of an interference effect is _____ inhibition, in which new learning hampers recall of old material. Another example is _____ inhibition, in which interference is from old material on the recall of newly learned items.

retroactive
proactive

36. One possible reason that we can't recall childhood memories is the drastic change in _____ cues between childhood and adulthood. This phenomenon is called childhood _____.

retrieval
amnesia

37. When one learns a language in school, at least some of this material seems to enter a _____, lasting many years after the learning has ceased.

permastore

38. Certain salient and emotional events produce what are called _____ memories, which are quite vivid.

flashbulb

39. As Bartlett demonstrated with participants' recall of stories, retrieval is often a _____ event, since partial knowledge of an event is pieced together in recall.

reconstructive

40. The conceptual framework that a person builds on the basis of his or her knowledge of the world is called a _____. A special case of this is a _____, which describes a scenario for a familiar event.

schema, script

41. Eyewitnesses to crimes seem to _____ the past from their partial knowledge of it in the process of trying to remember it.

reconstruct

42. Sometimes an observer can recall an event but not the origin of that event. This is called _____ confusion.

source

43. The effect of _____ seems to be to make people overly willing to cooperate with their questioner, not to substantially improve retrieval of information from memory.

hypnosis

44. The _____-_____ theory of memory asserts that all we have heard or seen is stored in memory.

tape-recorder

45. _____ memories are alleged to occur when an emotionally traumatic event occurs in early childhood and can't be easily retrieved.

Repressed

46. Lesions in the temporal cortex result in _____ amnesia, in which the patient has difficulty learning new material.

anterograde

47. _____ syndrome occurs after extended bouts of alcohol abuse.

Korsakoff's

48. A patient has suffered an accident involving trauma to the head. Following this, his ability to learn things is unimpaired, but he seems to have forgotten some things that happened prior to the accident. This is an example of _____ _____.

retrograde amnesia

49. One theory to account for the loss of prior memories after a trauma to the brain is based on the notion of _____ _____, according to which newly acquired memories undergo gradual change until they become more firmly established.

trace consolidation

50. An amnesic's memory is relatively unaffected when the memory task involves _____ knowledge, but her memory is drastically impaired when it involves _____ knowledge.

procedural
declarative

51. _____ tests of memory show great performance declines in amnesics, while _____ tests show little difference from the performance of normals.

Explicit, implicit

52. There are amnesic patients who lose _____ memory while preserving episodic memory.

generic

53. Sometimes retrieval is effortless and automatic while other times it is quite effortful. The former is called _____ retrieval and the latter is called _____ retrieval.

associative, strategic

54. The _____ plays a role in memory of emotional events.

amygdala

Self Test

1. In order for us to remember something, we must first engage in the process of:
   a. storage
   b. rehearsal
   c. encoding
   d. recall

2. An enduring physical record of a memory is called:
   a. a memory trace
   b. a chunk
   c. short-term memory
   d. none of the above

3. Suppose you are given a choice between a multiple-choice test and a short-answer test for the final exam in this course. You want to maximize the chance of doing well. Based on what you know about recall and recognition, all other things being equal, which test should you choose?
   a. short answer
   b. multiple choice
   c. either, there is no difference
   d. it depends on the difficulty of the material

4. Complete the following analogy: Multiple-choice questions are to fill-in-the-blank questions as:
   a. recognition is to recall
   b. recall is to retention
   c. recognition is to retention
   d. learning is to memory

5. In principle, the stages of memory processes must be arranged in which of the following orders?
   a. memory trace—encoding—storage—retrieval
   b. encoding—memory trace—storage—retrieval
   c. encoding—storage—memory trace—retrieval
   d. encoding—memory trace—retrieval—storage

6. The following are all characteristics of working memory except:
   a. limited capacity
   b. contents lost without rehearsal
   c. displacement causes forgetting
   d. none of the above

7. It has been found that people can hold about seven items in working memory. When more items are presented, complete recall is generally not possible. This demonstrates the _____ of working memory.
   a. retention interval
   b. memory trace
   c. displacement
   d. memory span

8. What is true about forgetting from working memory?
   a. It can be caused by erosion of the memory trace with time.
   b. The memory trace can be knocked out of short-term memory by another trace.
   c. It can be inhibited by rehearsal of the material stored there.
   d. all of the above

9. Suppose you are given driving directions by a gas station attendant and you repeat them over and over to yourself, "First left, second right, left at the first light, third right." Now suppose that your repetition of the directions is interrupted by an emergency driving maneuver. This would likely cause you to forget the directions, thereby demonstrating the importance of _____ in preserving working memory.
   a. storage capacity
   b. retrieval
   c. accessibility
   d. rehearsal

10. Suppose cryogenics (freezing patients and awakening them at some future time) were possible. If you were to discover that after being awakened, the patients had retained very accurate memories of what they had experienced immediately before freezing, this would be evidence for which hypothesis of forgetting in working memory?
    a. interference
    b. decay
    c. neither displacement nor decay
    d. either displacement or decay

11. At a party you are taken around the room by the host and are introduced to the other guests. Some time after the introductions are finished, one of these people comes up to talk to you. All other things being equal, you have the best chance of remembering her name if she was one of the _____ people you met. This phenomenon is called _____.
    a. first, primacy
    b. middle, inhibition
    c. last, recency
    d. first or last, the opposition effect

12. Now imagine the same situation (as in No. 11) except that the person comes up to you immediately after you have been very quickly introduced to everyone. Again, other things being equal, you would have the worst chance of remembering her name if she was one of the _____ people you met and the best chance if she was one of the _____.
    a. first, last
    b. middle, last
    c. first, middle
    d. last, first

13. Suppose a participant is asked to memorize the following list of words: *apple, horse, desk, carpet, mug, milk, parrot, disk, street, tree.* Which of the following will occur?
    a. The word *street* will be rehearsed more than the word *horse*, causing *tree* to be stored in long-term memory.
    b. The word *parrot* will be rehearsed more than the word *mug*, causing *parrot* to be stored in working memory.
    c. The word *apple* will be rehearsed more than the word *carpet*, causing *apple* to be stored in long-term memory.
    d. The word *desk* will be rehearsed more than the word *parrot*, causing desk to be stored in working memory.

Percent recalled (y-axis)

I

II

Item's position on list

1   16

14. The figure above depicts recall curves for a list of 16 items. Two conditions were employed, I and II. What was the difference between the conditions?
    a. The interval between each item was longer for II than I.
    b. The interval between each item was longer for II than I.
    c. The interval between the last item and the recall test was longer for I than II.
    d. The interval between the last item and the recall test was longer for II than I.

15. Increasing the capacity of working memory is a misnomer because:
    a. all one does is to rehearse the material already there, keeping it fresh while new material is added
    b. the number of items stored is the same, about 7, just the content of each item has changed
    c. it is the number of chunks that has changed, not the capacity of working memory
    d. it is not possible to increase the capacity of working memory

16. Suppose you run an experiment in which you present one word, say *rabbit*, and the participant has to repeat it. Then you present another word, say *pear*, and the participant has to repeat *rabbit, pear*. Then you present a third word, and the participant has to repeat all three, and so on. At the end of your list, you test the participant's memory for all words on the list. Based on what you know about the effect of maintenance rehearsal on long-term memory, you predict that:
    a. *rabbit* should be entered into long-term memory with higher probability than the last word on the list
    b. *rabbit* should be entered into long-term memory with lower probability than the last word on the list
    c. *rabbit* should be entered into long-term memory with the same probability as the last word on the list
    d. none of the above

17. Working memory is to short-term memory as:
    a. storage is to processing
    b. processing is to storage
    c. recall is to recognition
    d. recognition is to recall

18. The concept of depth of processing is intended to account for the fact that:
    a. deeper structures in the brain are involved in memory in contrast to the more surface cortical structures that are involved in other aspects of cognition
    b. deeper levels of analysis of material yield better memory for it
    c. deeper organization of material into hierarchically organized chunks produces a better long-term memory for that material
    d. none of the above

19. Which of the following processes will not result in the effective storage of memory traces in long-term memory?
    a. maintenance rehearsal
    b. clustering
    c. elaborative rehearsal
    d. organization by phrases

20. A follow-up to the experiment in which participants recalled the passage about washing clothes found that telling them the title of the paragraph after they had read it did not improve recall compared to not telling them the title at all. This result, taken together with the effect of telling participants the title of the paragraph before it is presented, suggests that:
    a. chunking is not an effective strategy to memorize material
    b. chunking is effective if it can be accomplished at the time of encoding
    c. chunking is effective if it can be accomplished at the time of retrieval
    d. chunking is effective if it can be accomplished during storage

21. Mnemonic devices (memorizing aids) use the principle of:
    a. consolidation of retrieval
    b. recoding
    c. retrieval of consolidation
    d. all of the above

22. Which of the following images would produce the greatest increase in recall performance for the pair of items *horse-rock*?
    a. a horse standing next to a rock
    b. a horse dragging a rock
    c. a horse and rock pictured separately
    d. all of the above would be equivalent

23. You have been trying to remember the name of a street that a friend lives on. Despite all of your efforts you are unable to recall it. While in the kitchen looking for a snack (to console yourself) you reach for a can of nuts, and suddenly the street name comes to you—Walnut. This is an example of the role of _____.
    a. anterograde amnesia
    b. retrograde amnesia
    c. mnemonics
    d. retrieval cues

24. Retrieval cues are most effective if they:
    a. coincide with the way in which a trace was originally encoded
    b. are presented at the time of recall not at encoding
    c. are quite concrete
    d. elicit visual images

25. The kind of rehearsal that establishes long-term memories is _____. The type of rehearsal that holds material in working memory temporarily is _____.
    a. mnemonics, chunking
    b. maintenance rehearsal, elaborative rehearsal
    c. elaborative rehearsal, maintenance rehearsal
    d. method of loci, mnemonics

26. The major role that elaborative rehearsal plays in improving memory, as opposed to maintenance rehearsal, is:
    a. to increase the number of retrieval cues
    b. to increase the number of times an item is rehearsed
    c. to speed up the encoding time
    d. all of the above

27. Repeating word pairs aloud and forming images of words in a pair are respectively examples of:
    a. maintenance rehearsal, and maintenance rehearsal
    b. maintenance rehearsal, and elaborative rehearsal
    c. elaborative rehearsal, and elaborative rehearsal
    d. elaborative rehearsal, and maintenance rehearsal

28. The tip-of-the-tongue phenomenon provides us with evidence concerning:
    a. the hierarchical organization of long-term memory
    b. accessibility in working memory
    c. the search process in long-term memory
    d. the use of retrieval cues in working memory

29. Having something "on the tip of the tongue" indicates a problem:
    a. in the way the item was chunked
    b. with reconstruction
    c. with proactive inhibition
    d. with retrieval

30. What is the relationship between implicit and explicit memory tests?
    a. They must be correlated because they both measure memory.
    b. They can be uncorrelated as shown by demonstrations of implicit memory without explicit memory.
    c. They must be correlated because the tests measure different aspects of memory.
    d. Available evidence does not permit an answer.

31. Evidence that implicit and explicit memory tests may tap at least some different aspects of the memory trace comes from:
    a. studies showing that implicit tests lead to better retrieval
    b. studies showing that forgetting as indicated by implicit tests is slower than forgetting indexed by explicit tests
    c. studies showing that learning instructions affect tests of explicit but not implicit memory
    d. all of the above

32. Each of the following is a test of explicit retrieval except:
    a. fragment completion
    b. repetition priming
    c. free recall
    d. memory span
    e. more than one of the above

33. According to one view, explicit retrieval is to implicit retrieval as:
    a. conscious is to unconscious
    b. bottom-up processing is to top-down processing
    c. repetition priming is to recognition
    d. none of the above

34. It is believed that retrieval is generally preceded by:
    a. chunking
    b. memory activation
    c. memory search
    d. recognition

35. If you read the Memory chapter in the text, which of the following people should you now think of as more famous than you would have if you had not read the text, assuming that you didn't remember having encountered these names in the text itself?
    a. Esther Williams
    b. Ted Williams
    c. Johnny Carson
    d. Sebastian Weisdorf

36. When Ebbinghaus tested himself on memory for nonsense syllables, he found that:
    a. forgetting was fastest immediately after learning
    b. his episodic and generic memory were equivalent
    c. his implicit memory was better than his explicit memory
    d. none of the above

37. According to a decay theory of forgetting, if a participant learning a list of words was then subjected to one of the following procedures, he would forget the greatest number of words if:
    a. he slept for four versus two hours
    b. he learned other lists for four versus two hours
    c. he performed arithmetic problems for four versus two hours
    d. all of the above would be comparable

38. Consider the following experimental design:

    control group:
    learn A → rest → test A
    experimental group:
    learn A → learn B → test A

    This design would be used to test forgetting due to which factor?
    a. proactive inhibition
    b. retroactive inhibition
    c. decay
    d. generalization

39. A college sophomore participates in a nonsense syllable learning experiment. The first list takes him only four trials to learn, the second list takes five trials, and the third list takes eight trials. These results can be taken as a demonstration of:
    a. memory activation
    b. retroactive inhibition
    c. proactive inhibition
    d. retrograde forgetting

40. One hypothesis about forgetting is that it is due to a change in retrieval cues. Which of the following would be counterevidence for this hypothesis?
    a. demonstration of proactive inhibition
    b. demonstration of retroactive inhibition
    c. demonstration that decay caused forgetting
    d. none of the above

41. One of the potential causes of childhood amnesia is that the retrieval cues change massively between childhood and adulthood. Another plausible cause might be:
    a. the poor quality of the initial encoding of memory traces
    b. retroactive inhibition
    c. decay
    d. all of the above

42. The concept of a permastore arises from the fact that:
    a. some memories are not subject to any forgetting
    b. some memories, while they decline initially after learning, remain relatively intact thereafter
    c. some memories have a flashbulb character to them
    d. all of the above

43. The compelling nature of flashbulb memories has caused some to argue that they are caused by a special memory mechanism. Contrary to this hypothesis, though:
    a. the accuracy of these memories may not be all that impressive
    b. some of the good memory may come from conversations about the event after it has occurred
    c. both of the above
    d. none of the above

44. Distortions of memory seem to be accentuated as a function of time between original acquisition of the information and testing. Such distortions could be due to effects of:
    a. encoding
    b. storage
    c. retrieval
    d. b and c, but not a

45. Bartlett's experiments and evidence about the fallibility of eyewitness testimony highlight the importance of which of the following factors about recall?
    a. reconstruction
    b. proactive inhibition
    c. retrieval cues
    d. retroactive inhibition

46. One could have a script for:
    a. mowing the lawn
    b. visiting the eye doctor
    c. going to a fast food restaurant
    d. all of the above

47. Suppose two groups of participants watched a videotape of a minor theft, in which someone in a room full of people reached into a drawer and took a $20 bill. After the video-tape, Group 1 was asked "Did you see the custodian reach into the drawer?" while Group 2 was asked "Did you see a custodian reach into the drawer?" (Actually, there was no custodian in the room.) Which group is more likely to accuse the custodian of the theft?
    a. Group 1
    b. Group 2
    c. Group 1 and Group 2 will be equally likely to accuse the custodian
    d. can't tell from the available detail

48. Suppose an eyewitness to a crime was hypnotized and asked to recall as much as she could of the events of the crime. She would most likely:
    a. recall more of what she had seen
    b. recall less of what she had seen
    c. recall about the same as if she had not been hypnotized, but report more
    d. resist recalling more about the crime because of its emotional impact

49. These are reasons to believe that some of the recent reports of repressed memories of childhood sexual abuse are not correct. Among the factors that may be exaggerating the number of such reports are:
    a. the fact that some of the therapists involved in eliciting them are using hypnosis, which is known to cause the patient to report more things that may be confabulations in the hopes of pleasing the therapist
    b. the fact that some of the therapists who work on this problem have a bias to find childhood causes of adult problems even when there may be no such causes
    c. the fact that highly charged memories such as those of childhood abuse are not likely to be repressed for such a long time without having come out before
    d. all of the above

50. Retrograde amnesia may be caused by:
    a. a disruption in the mechanism that causes new material to be placed into long-term memory, thus preventing any new learning
    b. a disruption of trace consolidation at the time of the trauma
    c. a difficulty in retrieving events that occurred just prior to the trauma
    d. more than one of the above

51. One experiment has shown that while amnesics get better at reading mirror-reversed text, they cannot recognize the words they have read later on, while normals can. This indicates that:
    a. amnesics lose the ability to learn new information
    b. amnesics lose the ability to learn declarative information, but not procedural information
    c. amnesics can learn procedural skills, but only if the very same stimuli are repeated over and over
    d. anterograde amnesics are different from retrograde amnesics

52. Three major symptoms characterize anterograde amnesia. They are:
    a. accurate memory for pretrauma events, normal working memory, inaccurate memory for most posttrauma events

b. inaccurate memory for pretrauma events, normal working memory, inaccurate memory for most posttrauma events

c. accurate memory for pretrauma events, abnormal working memory, accurate memory for most posttrauma events

d. inaccurate memory for pretrauma events, normal working memory, accurate memory for most posttrauma events

53. Milner's patient H. M. (an anterograde amnesic) was tested for his memory span for unrelated nouns. What is your best guess about his span?
a. 0
b. 4
c. 7
d. 10

54. A theory of memory that says that memory needs time to be fixed into a permanent form is called:
a. rehearsal
b. spreading activation
c. trace consolidation
d. memory priming

55. You witness an automobile accident in which one of the drivers hits his head on the windshield. He appears uninjured, but when a police officer asks him what happened just prior to the accident, the man seems confused and is unable to answer. The police officer is about to haul the man off to jail (assuming that he must be drunk) when you step forward and (having studied your psychology text) say, "This man is suffering from _____ _____!"
a. trace consolidation
b. anterograde amnesia
c. retrograde amnesia
d. Korsakoff's syndrome

56. Patients with anterograde amnesia may experience:
a. impaired explicit memory but normal implicit memory
b. impaired declarative learning but normal procedural learning
c. impaired long-term memory processes but normal working memory processes
d. all of the above
e. none of the above

57. Associate retrieval is to strategic retrieval as:
a. explicit memory is to implicit memory
b. anterograde amnesia is to retrograde amnesia
c. working memory is to long-term memory
d. top-down processing is to bottom-up processing
e. none of the above

58. Studies of patients with brain lesions and studies of normals using brain-imaging techniques has revealed a number of regions of the brain that seem to be critical for memory. These include:
a. the prefrontal cortex for working memory
b. the amygdala for emotional memory
c. the occipital lobes for visual memory
d. the temporal lobes for episodic memory
e. all of the above

Answer Key for Self Test

1.	c p. 262		30.	b p. 278
2.	a p. 262		31.	c p. 278
3.	b p. 263		32.	e pp. 278, 279
4.	a p. 263		33.	a p. 279
5.	b pp. 262, 263		34.	c p. 276
6.	c pp. 265, 266		35.	d p. 278
7.	d p. 264		36.	a p. 280
8.	d pp. 265, 266		37.	d p. 280
9.	d p. 266		38.	b p. 281
10.	d p. 265		39.	c p. 281
11.	a p. 266		40.	d p. 282
12.	b p. 266		41.	d p. 282
13.	c p. 266		42.	b p. 283
14.	d p. 266		43.	c p. 284
15.	b pp. 266, 267		44.	d pp. 284–85
16.	c p. 269		45.	a pp. 285–86
17.	b p. 270		46.	d p. 286
18.	b p. 270		47.	a p. 287
19.	a pp. 268, 269		48.	c pp. 288–89
20.	b pp. 271, 272		49.	d pp. 290–91
21.	b p. 272		50.	d p. 294
22.	b p. 273		51.	b p. 295
23.	d p. 274		52.	a pp. 292, 293
24.	a p. 274		53.	c pp. 292, 293
25.	c pp. 275, 268		54.	c p. 294
26.	a p. 275		55.	c p. 294
27.	b pp. 268, 275		56.	d pp. 292, 293
28.	c pp. 276, 277		57.	e p. 296
29.	d p. 276		58.	e p. 297

Investigating Psychological Phenomena

THE EFFECT OF IMAGERY INSTRUCTIONS ON MEMORY

Equipment: None
Number of participants: One
Time per participant: Fifteen minutes
Time for experimenter: Twenty minutes

As the text discusses, there are several mnemonic techniques that will improve memory performance. One of these is the use of images. By now there is a good deal of research that demonstrates the memorial effectiveness of asking participants to create images of the objects or events that they are trying to commit to memory. In the present experiment you will have an opportunity to demonstrate the effectiveness of imagery instructions for yourself in an experiment that involves learning paired-associate lists.

The procedure is quite simple. Below you will find two lists of twenty noun pairs each that you can use as stimuli for the experiment. You will need just one person to participate in the experiment. The procedure is as follows.

First, read the following instructions to the participant:

This is a memory experiment in which you will be required to memorize and recall two lists of words, each of which is composed of twenty pairs of fairly common nouns. First I will read aloud the twenty noun pairs from List 1 at the rate of one pair every seven seconds or so. While I am reading the pairs, just sit quietly and listen to them, trying as best you can to memorize the words in each pair. After I have presented all the pairs, I shall go through the list again, this time reading only the first noun in each pair. As I read each of these nouns, I would like you to recall the appropriate second noun that was paired with it when I originally presented the list. You will have seven seconds or so to recall the second noun for each pair and to write it in the space provided on your answer sheet. Do you have any questions?

After you have read these instructions to the participant, give him or her the report sheet for this chapter in Appendix 3. Then follow the testing procedure outlined in the instructions. After you have completed the procedure for List 1, read the following instructions to the participant:

Now I shall present you with another list of twenty noun pairs that I would like you to memorize. The procedure for this list will be identical to that for the first list except for one change: This time, when you are presented with each pair, try to form a mental image of the words in which there is some sort of interaction. For example, if you were presented with the pair "horse-rock," you might form an image of a horse that is harnessed to a large boulder, dragging the boulder along the ground. Such images should help you memorize the words. Do you have any questions?

Now give the participant another answer sheet for List 2 and present List 2 exactly as List 1 was presented.

To score the participant's performance, simply count up the number of items that were answered correctly on each list. If all went well, the participant should have scored better on List 2 (unless the participant was already forming mental images for the nouns in List 1).

Now at this point you may raise a question. Was the participant's performance on List 2 better because of the influence of the imagery instructions, or could it have been better for some other reason? For example, it may have already occurred to you that performance on List 2 may have been better than List 1 because List 2 was presented *after* List 1, and therefore the participant may simply have been better practiced at memorizing words. Before reading on, try to think of a way that you might have run this experiment that would have avoided this problem.

One way to have avoided a practice effect would have been to use two different participants. This first participant would have received only List 1 with its instructions while the second would have received only List 2 with its imagery instructions. If performance on List 2 was still better than on List 1, you might feel more confident in attributing this difference to the effect of the instructions (assuming that your two participants were fairly comparable in their overall memory ability). At least practice could not account for the difference.

But, you might object, there might *still* be an explanation for the difference between lists that has nothing to do with the effect of imagery instructions. Suppose, for instance, List 2 was composed

of words that were more common or concrete than the words on List 1 (e.g., horse versus liberty). This alone might make List 2 more memorable. There are two ways that one might control for this possibility. The first is to choose words for the two lists that are equated for frequency of usage and concreteness (and, for that matter, whatever else you might think of that would affect the memorability of words). The second method is to balance experimentally which word lists are paired with which instructions. The following table shows one arrangement that should work in which you would have to run at least four participants:

	Neutral instructions	Imagery instructions
Word list 1	Participant 1	Participant 2
Word list 2	Participant 3	Participant 4

If you were to run this experiment, then you could tell whether the word lists differ from one another in memorability and/or whether there is an effect of instructions. If Word list 2 is more memorable than Word list 1, then Participants 3 and 4 should perform better than 1 and 2. If imagery instructions produce better performance than neutral instructions, then Participants 2 and 4 should perform better than 1 and 3. If List 2 is more memorable than List 1 *and* imagery instructions produce better performance than neutral instructions, then Participant 4 should perform best of all.

If you want to check on the possible influence of practice in the experiment that you ran, and if you want to be sure that the word lists are comparable (they have actually been balanced for meaningfulness and commonness of the words), then you should try this last experiment. Whether you do try it or not, however, you should realize that one of the points of this exercise was to show that even a fairly simple experiment such as the one that you ran with the word lists is sometimes open to several interpretations. To find the right one requires careful experimentation.

Noun pairs for List 1	Noun pairs for List 2
1. building-letter	1. sail-bowl
2. grass-meat	2. coffee-lake
3. animal-village	3. girl-flood
4. house-lip	4. corn-river
5. sky-seat	5. stone-bottle
6. dress-apple	6. paper-shore
7. fur-mountain	7. dust-army
8. flag-coast	8. ocean-fire
9. sugar-ship	9. clothing-board
10. mother-city	10. door-king
11. market-church	11. butler-tree
12. plant-baby	12. gold-chair
13. sea-iron	13. flower-car
14. woods-engine	14. bird-skin
15. arm-boulder	15. hall-child
16. woman-forest	16. garden-book
17. table-wood	17. money-shoes
18. queen-college	18. cat-camp
19. bar-diamond	19. wife-storm
20. cotton-street	20. dollar-machine

CHAPTER 8

Thought and Knowledge

Learning Objectives

1. What is directed thinking, and how does it differ from other senses of the word "thinking"?

ANALOGICAL REPRESENTATIONS

2. Be able to define a mental representation and to distinguish it from an external representation.
3. Understand the difference between analogical and symbolic representations. Be able to give examples of each.

Mental images
4. While there are individual differences in imagery, understand that these differences are not clearly related to performance on tasks requiring imagery. Why might this be?
5. Be familiar with the term *eidetic imagery* and what the characteristics of this imagery are.
6. Understand how our visual imagery has some of the qualities of a pictorial representation. Be familiar with the phenomena of mental rotation and mental scanning, but also understand the evidence showing that images are not truly internal pictures.

Spatial thinking
7. Be familiar with the evidence showing that some spatial knowledge is imagelike in quality; but also be familiar with the evidence showing that some spatial knowledge is more symbolic and conceptual.

SYMBOLIC REPRESENTATIONS

Symbolic elements

8. Be able to describe the definition of a concept and to give examples.
9. Be familiar with the term *proposition* and with its elements (the subject and the predicate).

Knowledge and memory
10. Describe the differences between episodic and generic memory. What is semantic memory, and how is it related to episodic and generic memory?
11. What is meant by the claim that semantic memory is organized hierarchically? Explain how judgments of typicality contradict this claim.

12. How is the spreading activation model of semantic memory different from a hierarchical model? Describe how evidence about priming bears on a spreading activation model.
13. What is a parallel distributed processing model, and how does it compare with a spreading activation model? Understand the metaphor of the master spy and how it helps to explicate the principle underlying PDP models.

THE PROCESS OF THINKING: SOLVING PROBLEMS

Organization in problem solving
14. How is problem solving best conceived as a search? How is means-end analysis relevant to this search?
15. How is thinking goal directed?
16. How is thinking hierarchical? How are the concepts of subgoal and subroutine related to the hierarchical nature of thought?
17. What is the shape of the learning curve in the development of a skill, and what does this shape tell us about the course of learning?
18. Be able to describe how chunking ability differentiates novices from experts. What is the role of automaticity in skill development?
19. Describe the Stroop effect and discuss its relevance to automaticity.
20. What are the major differences between masters and beginners in problem solving? What skills do masters have that novices don't?

Obstacles to problem solving
21. Be aware of the effects of set on problem solving. How does set influence solution strategies?

Overcoming obstacles to solution
22. How can the strategy of working backwards help in problem solving?
23. What is the role of analogy in problem solving? What factors govern whether people will retrieve analogies from memory and use them?

Restructuring
24. What is restructuring? How is it related to creative thinking?
25. How is incubation related to the effects of set? Understand how it is related to creative thinking.

26. How is restructuring in problem solving similar to the process required to appreciate certain kinds of humor?

Artificial intelligence: problem solving by computer

27. Why are computers valuable analogs to humans as problem solvers? How is the analogy weak?
28. Understand the goal of the field of artificial intelligence.
29. Define the terms *algorithm* and *heuristic*. Describe some useful heuristics in problem solving. Why are algorithms often inefficient but exact?
30. Why are different strategies required for well-defined versus ill-defined problems? What is the difference between these two kinds of problems, and how is this difference relevant to the comparison of humans and computers?
31. How is the concept of "common sense" important in understanding the limitations in the ability of computers to solve problems?
32. What are expert system (such as MYCIN) and how are they limited in value?

THE PROCESS OF THINKING: REASONING AND DECISION MAKING

33. Are the laws of logic the laws of thought?

Deductive reasoning

34. What is a syllogism? What reasons cause many participants to do poorly in solving syllogisms?
35. What sort of strategies do people use to solve syllogisms?

Inductive reasoning

36. Be able to explain the difference between deductive and inductive reasoning and give examples of each.
37. What is the availability heuristic and how do people use it to make judgments?
38. How is the representative heuristic used to make judgments about instances?
39. What is the confirmation bias? Why are disconfirmations more helpful in testing hypotheses than confirmations? Can you give an example of the confirmation bias?

40. How does formal training in statistics help people to reason inductively?

Decision making

41. Give examples of errors in reasoning that are due to the way a problem is framed. How do people feel about gains and losses in their willingness to take on risk?

THE THINKING BRAIN

42. Be aware of the approach used by the field of cognitive science.

Localization of thought

43. Give some examples of regions of cortex used in different thinking tasks.
44. Be able to describe some of the deficits of patients with damage to prefrontal cortex.
45. What is the role of prefrontal cortex in working memory? What are some theories about the organization of prefrontal cortex?

Cognition and consciousness

46. Why is the study of consciousness so difficult?
47. Be able to distinguish between unconscious and nonconscious.
48. Be familiar with the phenomenon of blindsight and what its implications are for consciousness in perception.
49. What does it mean to use memory unconsciously? Give examples of the use of memory in comprehension that show its influence even when we're not conscious of it.
50. Describe how actions may be taken without conscious awareness.
51. Understand what it means to be aware of the products of processing without being aware of the processing itself.
52. How might consciousness be useful in situations requiring flexibility?

TAKING STOCK

53. How do the broad domains of cognition (perception, memory, and thinking) overlap? Give examples.

Programmed Exercises

1. The word _____ may be used as a synonym for remembering, attention, or belief. thinking

2. If one is talking about _____ thinking, one is referring to reasoning or reflecting on some problem, with some goal in mind. directed

ANALOGICAL REPRESENTATIONS

3. Mental _____ refer to internal codes that stand for external _____. representations
representations

4. An _____ representation is one that captures some of the characteristics of what it represents; a _____ representation stands for what it represents, but does not resemble it in any simple way. analogical
symbolic

5. _____ imagery is sometimes called *photographic memory*, referring to a literal representation of some external visual event. Eidetic

6. Mental _____ seems to be analog in that the time it takes to effect a transformation is related to the number of degrees of transformation. rotation

7. You can show that people can _____ images by showing that the time it takes them to traverse from one part of an image to another is linearly related to the distance that must be traversed, as if they were looking over an actual map of the space.

   scan

8. _____ thinking is sometimes picturelike and sometimes requires conceptual representations. This is illustrated by examining several phenomena of mental maps.

   Spatial

SYMBOLIC REPRESENTATIONS

9. A _____ is an internal representation of a class or category for which some instances can be enumerated.

   concept

10. A _____ asserts a relationship between concepts such that it relates a _____ and a _____, the former of which is what the _____ is about and the latter of which is what is asserted.

    proposition, subject predicate, proposition

11. It is generally believed that there are two kinds of memory representations, ones that tag an event with its time or place of occurrence (called _____ memory), and ones that constitute memory for items of knowledge (called _____ memory).

    episodic
    generic

12. One type of generic memory is _____ memory, which concerns the meanings of concepts.

    semantic

13. One popular type of model for semantic memory involves a representation called a _____, in which various _____ are linked together by lines and arrows in a complex system of relationships to show how they are interrelated.

    network
    nodes

14. A network in which one concept was stored under others that subsumed it throughout would be called _____.

    hierarchical

15. Experiments on semantic _____ reveal that the retrieval of a concept is faster if you have just retrieved a related concept.

    priming

16. Parallel _____ processing models have as one central assumption that the representation of a concept is spread out throughout a network, rather than being concentrated in a single node.

    distributed

THE PROCESS OF THINKING: SOLVING PROBLEMS

17. In an analogy to computer programming, psychologists often call mental operations that are run off under the control of higher-level mental operations _____.

    subroutines

18. The use of master plans to organize subsidiary actions suggests that thought is organized into _____.

    hierarchies

19. The ability to organize many details into larger _____ is one of the crucial features of directed activity, including thinking.

    chunks

20. Much of the difference between a master and an apprentice is in the degree to which subcomponents of an activity have been chunked hierarchically; to the master, the substeps have become _____.

    automatic

21. The _____ and subsequent rise found in many learning curves for motor skills suggest that the learner gradually transforms this task.

    plateau

22. The _____ effect is an example of how reading letter strings has become an automatized activity for adults. Reading incompatible color names interferes with naming colors in which the color words are printed.

    Stroop

23. As Adrian de Groot demonstrated with chess, master problem solvers use _____ that contain more information than do those of beginners.

    chunks

24. When a person becomes _____ on one approach to a task, it is hard for him or her to approach it any other way.

    fixated

25. A person who attempts to solve a problem by thinking along a line of thought created by previous thinking is operating under a _____ _____.

    mental set

26. In general, the greater the motivation toward reaching a solution, the greater the _____ _____ with which the problem is approached.

    mental set

27. _____ _____ is a problem-solving strategy that frequently helps because one can work from the solution.

Working backward

28. When two problems have a similar structure, using one as a(n) _____ to the other can be an effective problem-solving strategy.

analogy

29. Solutions of difficult problems often involve a perceptual _____ of the problem in order to break a false perceptual set.

restructuring

30. The phenomenon whereby one arrives at an insightful solution to a problem after intense preparation followed by rest is called _____.

incubation

31. It has been suggested that both _____ and _____ involve a dramatic shift from one cognitive organization to another.

humor, insight

32. One way in which humans and computers are similar is that both are _____ -_____ systems.

information-processing

33. The field of _____ _____ is concerned with programming computers to solve various intellectual problems.

artificial intelligence

34. A procedure in which all of the operations required to achieve the solution are specified step by step is called an _____.

algorithm

35. A _____ differs from an algorithm in that it is a rule of thumb rather than a fixed sequence of steps.

heuristic

36. A newspaper proofreader is asked to check a piece of text for spelling errors. This is an example of a(n) _____ -_____ problem.

well-defined

37. A student is asked to write a "good" paper. This is an example of a(n) _____ -_____ problem.

ill-defined

38. Some computer scientists feel that the crucial difference between human and artificial intelligence is that computer programs lack _____ _____.

common sense

39. _____ _____ are problem-solving programs that deal with problems in a limited domain of knowledge.

Expert systems

40. _____ is an example of a problem-solving program that helps doctors in the treatment of infectious diseases.

MYCIN

THE PROCESS OF THINKING: REASONING AND DECISION MAKING

41. A _____ contains two premises and a conclusion.

syllogism

42. The statement "All A are B and therefore all B are A" is a(n) _____ inference.

invalid

43. In _____ reasoning we apply a general rule to a particular case.

deductive

44. In _____ reasoning we consider different cases and try to find the rule that covers them all.

inductive

45. When people use the _____ heuristic to make frequency judgments, they rely on ease of retrieval from memory.

availability

46. The _____ heuristic may lead to error if you are making a judgment about an atypical case.

representativeness

47. The fact that people primarily seek evidence that will confirm their hypotheses suggests that there is a strong _____ _____.

confirmation bias

48. One _____ shows that a hypothesis is false, but countless _____ cannot prove that it is true.

disconfirmation, confirmations

49. The way a problem is _____ can influence the way people will solve it.

framed

50. People are more prone to take risks to limit _____ than to achieve _____.

losses, gains

51. There is a good deal of evidence that throws a poor light on human _____; we make all sorts of reasoning errors. But many important intellectual judgments are rational because they come about by _____ effort.

rationality

collective

THE THINKING BRAIN

52. Patients with frontal lobe damage have a difficult time in _____ situations that require some new plan, and they also show distinct patterns of _____, in which they continue the same action repeatedly.

    novel
    preservation

53. One important role of the frontal lobes has to do with _____ memory, the memory that is used in problem-solving and planning situations.

    working

54. The study of _____ has proven very difficult in psychology because mental events are private and not subject to external observation.

    consciousness

55. Major advances in the study of consciousness have come about through the study of when it is _____.

    absent

56. Freud's conception of the _____ included the notion that memories were actively kept out of our awareness.

    unconscious

57. There are patients with damage to the occipital lobe of the brain who experience _____, the ability to make judgments about visual objects with no conscious experience of those objects.

    blindsight

58. By and large, we seem to be unaware of mental _____; but, by contrast, we are sometimes aware of the _____ of mental operations.

    processes
    products

59. In relying on automatic routines, we give up _____.

    flexibility

TAKING STOCK

60. There are no clear boundaries among the domains of _____, _____, and _____.

    perception, memory
    thinking

Self Test

1. All of the following are examples of directed thinking *except*:
   a. discovery of a geometric proof
   b. deciding on the next move in a chess game
   c. daydreaming about last night's meal
   d. trying to figure out why a car will not start

2. A hand drawing of a tractor is what kind of representation, as compared to an actual tractor?
   a. analogical
   b. symbolic
   c. both of the above
   d. neither of the above

3. The relationship between the quality of mental images and the ability to perform tasks that require imagery is:
   a. positive
   b. negative
   c. sometimes positive, sometimes negative
   d. unstudied

4. Eidetic imagery is more prominent in:
   a. young children
   b. older adults
   c. middle-aged adults
   d. no one; it is not a reliable phenomenon

5. You have probably seen standardized tests in which you are given a picture of a flat piece of paper in which folds are drawn in. You have to mentally fold the paper and compare it to several objects shown to determine which of the objects will be formed after the folding is completed. Studies of this skill show that the more folds that have to be executed, the longer it takes to perform the task. The task thus produces performance analogous to:
   a. mental search of a hierarchical network
   b. mental solution of a water jug problem
   c. mental solution of a syllogism
   d. mental rotation

6. It appears that the relationship between scanning mental images and scanning actual pictures is:
   a. symbolic
   b. representational
   c. haphazard
   d. analog

7. Studies of mental images for ambiguous figures show that:
   a. participants can "see" either form of the figure
   b. participants cannot reverse the figure in their mind's eye
   c. participants can see both versions of the figure simultaneously, in contrast to what they see when they are viewing such a figure
   d. none of the above

8. Studies of the time it takes to estimate distance in a familiar environment result in data very much like studies of:
   a. mental rotation
   b. deductive reasoning
   c. mental scanning
   d. functional fixedness

9. A concept:
   a. may designate a quality
   b. must have a finite number of instances
   c. must not refer to a relationship
   d. all of the above

10. A proposition:
    a. can be simply a mental image
    b. can be simply a sentence
    c. has a truth value
    d. none of the above

11. A proposition must have:
    a. a subject and a predicate
    b. a product and a process
    c. a node and a relation
    d. none of the above

12. Remembering what you did on your last birthday is an example of:
    a. semantic memory
    b. generic memory
    c. hierarchical memory
    d. episodic memory

13. A hierarchical network theory of semantic memory won't work because:
    a. *apple* and *olive* are not coequal members of the category *fruit*
    b. *red* is a more typical color than *mauve*
    c. people rate *chairs* as being more representative of the category *furniture* than *ottomans*
    d. all of the above

14. Evidence favoring the spreading activation model of semantic memory comes from studies of:
    a. the time it takes to generate a member of a category, given that you have just generated another member of that category
    b. the time it takes to verify that a string of letters is a word, given that you have just verified that another string of letters is a word
    c. the time it takes to recognize the word *bread* having just seen the word *butter*
    d. all of the above

15. One difference between a parallel distributed processing model of memory and a spreading activation model is that:
    a. the knowledge of a concept in PDP is in single nodes
    b. the knowledge of a concept in PDP is spread throughout the network
    c. the knowledge of a concept in PDP is hierarchical
    d. none of the above

16. Organization in problem solving is often:
    a. lacking
    b. ill-defined
    c. determined working backward
    d. goal-determined

17. Learning curves involving such tasks as receiving Morse code have a characteristic plateau preceded and followed by rises. This is because:

a. people tend to get bored with tasks like this, and so their performance falls off
b. people begin to use mental imagery after a little practice
c. with practice people can make more efficient use of chunks of information
d. none of the above

18. Which of the following is not a characteristic of learning for a new motor skill?
    a. periods in which there is no apparent change in the learning curve
    b. periods of relatively sharp increases in skill
    c. a steady increase in skill from the beginning of learning to the end
    d. a scalloped shape to the learning curve

19. The Stroop effect clearly shows that:
    a. certain mental activities become automatized
    b. colors are named faster than words
    c. words are named faster than colors
    d. none of the above

20. Research has shown that master chess players are better than novices in:
    a. solving algorithms
    b. chunking chess moves
    c. memorizing in general
    d. memorizing random patterns of chess pieces

21. A person is asked to solve a series of math problems. The first five problems can be solved only one way, each the same. The sixth problem can also be solved using this method, but there is also a much simpler solution. The participant solves this problem in the way he solved the first five. This person's problem-solving ability has been hampered by:
    a. working backward
    b. a lack of motivation
    c. mental set
    d. an improper heuristic

22. The use of analogy in problem solving:
    a. seems to be a habitual characteristic of the human problem solver
    b. seems to work only when the analogy is somehow pointed out to the problem solver by someone else
    c. requires that there be several potential analogs in memory for a single problem
    d. depends on the problem solver noticing a structural similarity between two problems

23. All of the following problems discussed in the text require perceptual restructuring for a solution *except*:
    a. the nine-dot problem
    b. the match puzzle
    c. the horse-and-rider problem
    d. unscrambling words (anagrams)

24. All of the following often contribute to insights *except*:
    a. a period of intense preparation
    b. a period of retreat
    c. a different environment
    d. working backward

25. One likely reason that incubation helps in reaching a problem solution is that:
    a. it allows for perceptual restructuring
    b. it helps break mental set
    c. it gives time to set up subgoals
    d. none of the above

26. The concept of an incubation period (in the explanation of insight) is unsatisfactory because:
    a. it tells us nothing of the underlying processes
    b. the term *unconscious thought* is too vague
    c. it has been demonstrated to be false
    d. a and b but not c

27. Insight and humor are similar in that:
    a. both involve heuristics
    b. both can be based on cognitive restructuring
    c. neither will work if the participant is mentally set
    d. none of the above

28. Restructuring seems to be an important component in humor and in problem solving. In both cases:
    a. the person is caught off guard by the unexpected
    b. there is some cognitive reorganization required
    c. there is usually some incongruity between the way things seem to be initially and the way they resolve themselves
    d. all of the above

29. The use of the computer as an analog to the human problem solver depends on:
    a. the sequential nature of computer programs
    b. the fact that computers use algorithms to solve their problems
    c. the fact that computers are limited to solving well-defined problems
    d. the irrelevance of the underlying hardware in humans and computers

30. Humans and computers are similar in that:
    a. both are information-processing systems
    b. both can use heuristics
    c. both can use algorithms
    d. all of the above

31. A food recipe specifies what ingredients are to be added together, in what amounts, and in what order. Such a recipe would be:
    a. a heuristic
    b. an algorithm
    c. a subgoal
    d. a scheme

32. Which of the following would make most efficient use of heuristics?
    i. an initial diagnosis made by a physician
    ii. an architect designing a hotel
    iii. a search for a particular word in the dictionary
    iv. deciding where to hang a new picture

    a. i, ii, iii
    b. ii, iii, iv
    c. iii, iv
    d. i, ii, iv

33. Examples of the appropriate use of subgoals and heuristics might be:
    a. trying for a position in the center of a board in a game of chess
    b. going for a checkmate
    c. finding the general area of an automotive problem (i.e., electrical vs. mechanical)
    d. all of the above

34. Ill-defined problems differ from well-defined problems in that:
    a. ill-defined problems have more difficult and complex solutions
    b. well-defined problems always have solutions, while ill-defined problems are unsolvable
    c. it is hard to define what changes are needed to reach the goal stated in ill-defined problems
    d. all of the above

35. The analogy between computers and the human mind is weak because:
    a. computers are made of transistors
    b. the mind uses nerve signals, not electrical impulses
    c. humans can solve well-defined problems
    d. none of the above

36. One of the limitations of artificial intelligence is its lack of common sense. This could be addressed by:
    a. giving the computer a better set of algorithms to map out all possibilities that might occur in any given situation
    b. providing the computer with better background knowledge so that it can anticipate what might occur
    c. making ill-defined problems well-defined
    d. having the computer stick strictly to relevant information, ignoring any information about a problem that is not directly relevant to its algorithm for the solution

37. Expert systems are limited in their similarity to human problem solving in that:
    a. they are too rigid in their approaches to problems
    b. they are restricted to a narrow area of competence
    c. they are confined to working on well-defined problems
    d. all of the above

38. All A are B
    Some B are C
    Therefore, some A are C. This is a(n):
    a. invalid syllogism
    b. valid syllogism
    c. invalid algorithm
    d. valid algorithm

39. Which of the following statements is true?
    a. People often set out to see whether their hypotheses are false.
    b. People rarely set out to see whether their hypotheses are false.
    c. People do not seek evidence that will confirm their hypotheses.
    d. none of the above

40. In making predictions about the outcome of situations, people seem to make too little use of:
    a. salient information that is presented in the form of a memorable scenario
    b. base-rate information that tells one the past history of a situation
    c. deductive reasoning
    d. none of the above; people appropriately balance these sources of information

41. Consider the following experiment (which is similar to one actually performed): Participants were shown a series of slides on each of which there was a male or female name. The females were relatively famous people, while the males were not. Unbeknown to participants, there were 20 males and 20 females included in the list. At the end of the presentation, participants were asked to judge whether there had been more male names on the list or more female names. According to the availability heuristic, the results should have been:
    a. that female names were judged more frequent because they were more retrievable
    b. that the male names were judged more frequent because they were more retrievable
    c. that the female names were judged more frequent because they were more representative of famous people
    d. that the female and male names were judged equally frequent because they were equally retrievable
    e. none of the above

42. According to the representativeness heuristic, if you were told that Sam L. is hard working, conservative, meticulous, and exact in his behavior, you would be most likely to judge him to be:
    a. a poet
    b. an engineer
    c. a high school teacher
    d. a creative writer for an advertising firm
    e. any of the above

43. Participants are involved in an experiment in which they have to test out whether the following rule is true: If a box contains red, black, or green balls, then it also contains yellow balls. To test out the rule, the participants are given a choice of a number of boxes from which to select. The fact that people are subject to the confirmation bias suggests that they will not select:
    a. a box that they are told contains red balls
    b. a box that they are told contains green balls
    c. a box that they are told contains yellow balls
    d. a box that they are told contains black balls

44. Statistical training does seem to improve people's inductive reasoning. This is probably due to:
    a. its providing them with formal training on such issues as sample size effects
    b. its allowing them to apply their own intuitions more appropriately about such things as chance to situations
    c. its showing them links between their intuitions and formal statistical effects
    d. all of the above

45. When a decision is affected by events that come readily to mind, this is a manifestation of:
    a. inductive reasoning
    b. framing
    c. the representativeness heuristic
    d. the availability heuristic

46. Problem framing has an effect on decision making because:
    a. people are very risk-averse when they face losses
    b. people are not very risk-averse when they face losses
    c. people are risk-seeking when they face gains
    d. none of the above

47. One common marketing technique by consumer electronics stores is to advertise frequent sales (some as frequent as every week!). With sales this frequent, one could think of pricing as not involving discounts on the weeks of the sale, but as price markups on the weeks when no sale is advertised. But marketing would not be as successful this way because:
    a. people are more willing to accept losses than to forego gains
    b. people are more willing to forego gains than to accept losses
    c. people are generally irrational and will not see the symmetry to these two modes of marketing
    d. people will use the marked-up price as the reference point in the alternative scenario

48. All of the following are shortcomings of human rationality except:
    a. people cannot perform the operations of addition, subtraction, multiplication, and division adequately
    b. people make errors in deductive reasoning
    c. people make errors in inductive reasoning
    d. people are not concerned with demonstrating that their hypotheses are wrong

49. Studies of patients with frontal lobe damage have implicated these structures in:
    a. planning novel actions
    b. working memory
    c. being able to switch from one action to another rather than perseverating on just one action
    d. forming strategies
    e. all of the above
    f. a, b, and d only

50. The study of consciousness has been aided by the study of:
    a. blindsight
    b. incubation
    c. functional fixedness
    d. mental set

51. Which of the following phenomena has been instrumental in the study of consciousness?
    a. perception without awareness
    b. memory without awareness
    c. action without awareness
    d. all of the above

52. It has been suggested that consciousness is needed for:
    a. flexibility in processing
    b. automaticity in processing
    c. avoiding the deleterious effects of mental set
    d. promoting the use of analogy in reasoning

Answer Key for Self Test

1.	c p. 301	27.	b p. 321
2.	a p. 302	28.	d pp. 321, 322
3.	c p. 303	29.	d p. 323
4.	a p. 304	30.	d pp. 323–24
5.	d p. 304	31.	b p. 324
6.	d pp. 304, 305	32.	d p. 324
7.	b p. 306	33.	d p. 325
8.	c p. 306	34.	c p. 325
9.	a p. 308	35.	d pp. 323–26
10.	c p. 308	36.	b pp. 325–36
11.	a p. 308	37.	d p. 326
12.	d p. 308	38.	a p. 327
13.	d p. 309	39.	b pp. 329–30
14.	d p. 310	40.	b p. 330
15.	b p. 311	41.	a p. 329
16.	d pp. 312–13	42.	b p. 330
17.	c p. 314	43.	c p. 331–32
18.	c p. 314	44.	d pp. 332–33
19.	a p. 316	45.	d p. 329
20.	b p. 315	46.	b p. 334
21.	c pp. 316, 317	47.	b p. 334
22.	d p. 319	48.	a pp. 334–35
23.	d p. 320	49.	e p. 336
24.	d pp. 320, 321	50.	a pp. 338–39
25.	b p. 321	51.	d pp. 338–40
26.	d pp. 321, 322	52.	a p. 340

Investigating Psychological Phenomena

THE STROOP EFFECT

Equipment: Included (see insert)
Number of participants: One
Time per participant: Thirty minutes
Time for experimenter: Forty minutes

It is frequently observed that as people are given more experience at the task of reading, the skill becomes more and more automatic in character. One symptom of this increasing automatization is that it is difficult to prevent a skilled reader from reading material that he is exposed to. This appears to be a general characteristic of skills that become automated. Given the proper conditions for the occurrence of such a skill, it is difficult to inhibit it.

Since automatization is a prominent characteristic of skilled activities ranging from reading to motor behavior to problem-solving routines, it is useful to investigate it to determine its characteristics. One task that has been studied extensively in this regard is the Stroop task (turn to p. 316 in the text for a full description of the task; Stroop, 1935). The following three experiments are designed to demonstrate the basic Stroop effect and to extend it somewhat so that you can develop some intuitions about why it occurs.

EXPERIMENT 1

First, before performing Stroop's actual demonstration you should conduct a simple version of it that will provide some baseline data on the effectiveness of our ability to ignore irrelevant information

(see Chapter 6, "Perception," for a full discussion of this ability). In this experiment participants are required to name colors. In the control condition of the experiment the colors are simply displayed in patches. In the experimental condition the colors are presented by having randomly ordered letter strings, each string of a different color. The question is whether having the letters present interferes with a participant's ability to name the colors. In principle, if the participant is capable of selectively attending to color, having the letters present should not interfere with his or her color-naming performance. Thus, naming the colors of the letter strings should be as easy as naming the colors of the color patches. On the other hand, the extent to which the participant cannot ignore the letter information is the extent to which his or her performance in color naming will decline.

Your measure of ease of color naming will be the amount of time it takes a participant to name a string of fifteen colors. To obtain reliable data you should have the participant name the colors in five lists of color patches and in five lists of letter strings, alternating between the two kinds of lists (see the number below each list).* The procedure is as follows: Cut out the ten lists of stimuli for Experiment 1. On each trial have the appropriate list in front of the participant turned over so that he or she cannot see the stimuli (see book insert for these lists). Then read the following instructions:

When I say "go," turn over the list in front of you and name the colors in the list from top to bottom. There will be fifteen colors total. Name these colors as fast but as accurately as possible. After you have named the last color, say "Stop!" We will do this with ten different lists. Five have the colors printed in patches of ink the other five have the colors printed in strings of randomly arranged letters. You should *ignore* how the colors are presented and simply name them. Any questions?

You should keep time from when you say "Go" until when the participant says "Stop." Make sure to present the ten lists in the order indicated by the number under the list. Record the time elapsed for each list and the number of errors for each list in the spaces provided on the report sheet.

Average the times for each type of list and total the errors. Does it appear that there is a difference between the average naming time or the total number of errors comparing the two types of lists? How would you interpret the data?

EXPERIMENT 2

In this experiment you are going to duplicate Stroop's demonstration. In the previous experiment you probably found either no effect or a very small effect of list type. The question we now ask is: Are there any conditions under which the participant cannot selectively attend well? In this experiment we have constructed such a condition by having the letters in the experimental condition spell color words themselves. Participants are still required to name the color of the word, not what it spells, but now the name of what it spells is itself going to be a color name. If selective

---

* Notice that the two types of lists are matched for the length of the stimulus,. That is, the color patches of Lists 1, 3, 5, 7, and 9 are matched in length to the Letter Strings of Length 2, 4, 6, 8, and 10. Why is this an important control? How have the lists of Experiments 2 and 3 been matched? Why?

attention is not very effective, these names should interfere with the participant's response and slow him or her down relative to a control condition that has neutral (noncolor) words printed in color.

Following the same procedure as before, but read the following set of instructions:

In this experiment you are going to perform the same task as in the previous experiment. This time, however, the ink colors will be printed in the form of words. For half the lists, the words will be randomly chosen. For the other half, they will be color words. In both lists, however, you are to ignore the meaning of the words themselves and simply name the colors in which they are printed from the top to the bottom of each list. Remember that you should be as fast and as accurate as possible. Don't turn over each list until I say "Go," and when you have finished be sure to say "Stop!"

When you record the data, keep track of both the time to read the list and the number of errors made. Average the time and errors for each type of list. Is the difference in average time and total errors between list types greater than the difference found in Experiment 1? How would you interpret this?

EXPERIMENT 3

Now we will try a somewhat more subtle version of the Stroop experiment to get a better idea of the extent to which the participant can selectively attend. In the experimental condition, the words printed in color represent nouns whose referents themselves have a characteristic color (this color is never the same as the color in which the word is written). If the word suggests the characteristic color of its referent to the participant, this color might interfere with naming the color in which the word is printed (Majeres, 1974).

Follow the same procedure as in Experiments 1 and 2, but read the following instructions to the participant:

In this experiment you are going to perform the same task as in the previous experiment; that is, you will be naming colors. This time the ink colors will be printed in the form of words that themselves are not colors. For example, one of the lists might contain the word "stove" printed in green ink. Disregard the word that is present and simply name the ink color of each word in the list. Remember that you should not turn over the list until I say "Go," you should name the colors as quickly as possible, and you should say "Stop" when you are done.

Conduct this experiment as you did the others. Is there a difference in performance between the lists? It it larger or smaller than in Experiment 2? What does this suggest about selective attention? What does it suggest about the automaticity of the reading process? *(If your instructor collects the data, fill out the report sheet in Appendix 3.)*

References

Stroop, J. R. 1935. Studies of interference in serial verbal reactions. *Journal of Experimental Psychology* 18:643–62.

Majeres, R. L. 1974. The combined effects of stimulus and response conditions on the delay in identifying the print color of words. *Journal of Experimental Psychology* 102:868–74.

Report Sheet

Experiment 1

Color patch list

List 1 _____ sec. _____ errors

List 3 _____ sec. _____ errors

List 5 _____ sec. _____ errors

List 7 _____ sec. _____ errors

List 9 _____ sec. _____ errors

Average = _____ sec.

Total errors = _____

Letter string list

List 2 _____ sec. _____ errors

List 4 _____ sec. _____ errors

List 6 _____ sec. _____ errors

List 8 _____ sec. _____ errors

List 10 _____ sec. _____ errors

Average = _____ sec.

Total errors = _____

Experiment 2

Neutral words

List 1 _____ sec. _____ errors

List 3 _____ sec. _____ errors

List 5 _____ sec. _____ errors

List 7 _____ sec. _____ errors

List 9 _____ sec. _____ errors

Average = _____ sec.

Total errors = _____

Color words

List 2 _____ sec. _____ errors

List 4 _____ sec. _____ errors

List 6 _____ sec. _____ errors

List 8 _____ sec. _____ errors

List 10 _____ sec. _____ errors

Average = _____ sec.

Total errors = _____

Experiment 3

Neutral words

List 1 _____ sec. _____ errors

List 3 _____ sec. _____ errors

List 5 _____ sec. _____ errors

List 7 _____ sec. _____ errors

List 9 _____ sec. _____ errors

Average = _____ sec.

Total errors = _____

Color referent words

List 2 _____ sec. _____ errors

List 4 _____ sec. _____ errors

List 6 _____ sec. _____ errors

List 8 _____ sec. _____ errors

List 10 _____ sec. _____ errors

Average = _____ sec.

Total errors = _____

CHAPTER 9

Language

Learning Objectives

MAJOR PROPERTIES OF HUMAN LANGUAGE

1. Understand the sense in which languages are similar to one another.

Language is creative
2. Describe some phenomena that undermine the view that language is a habit.

Language is structured
3. What are the descriptive rules of language? Explain the difference between descriptive rules and prescriptive rules.

Language is meaningful
4. How do the words and grammar of a language contribute to meaning?

Language is referential
5. What does it mean for language to be referential?

Language is interpersonal
6. Give examples of how an unspoken principle of conversation makes communication successful in different social situations.

THE BASIC UNITS OF LANGUAGE

7. What are the major hierarchical levels of linguistic structure?

Phonemes
8. What is a phoneme? Give examples.
9. Given what you now know about phonemes, and about human perception (Chapter 6), state two reasons why it is difficult for humans to understand unfamiliar speech.
10. Are phonemes combined haphazardly? Give examples to support your answer.

Morphemes and words
11. What is a morpheme? Give examples.
12. How are morphemes combined?

Phrases and sentences
13. How is the organization of words into phrases related to meaning?

The meaning of words
14. What is semantics?
15. Be prepared to argue why meaning is not the same as reference.
16. According to the definitional theory, how are word meanings stored in memory?
17. What convincing evidence exists for the prototype theory? How does this theory differ from the definitional theory?
18. What is a family resemblance structure?
19. How can one reconcile definitional and prototype theories?
20. Discuss how the meanings of some words depend on the meanings of others.

Organizing words into meaningful sentences
21. Describe the subject-predicate structure of sentences and how this conveys meaning.
22. What is syntax, and how is it related to the acceptability of sentences?
23. How is phrase structure related to meaning?
24. What is the difference between surface and underlying phrase structures? How is underlying structure related to meaning?
25. Describe how attitude and proposition combine to form underlying structure.
26. What evidence suggests that people tend to remember underlying structure rather than surface structure?
27. Describe paraphrases in terms of underlying structure.
28. Understand how ambiguities can be explained with reference to underlying structure. What structural properties might give rise to ambiguity?

COMPREHENSION

29. What problem does the listener face in computing the underlying structure of a sentence?

The sentence analyzing machinery
30. Describe how SAM analyzes a sentence, and indicate the first strategy that it uses.
31. What accounts for the reaction time difference in the comprehension of active and passive sentences?
32. Consider the following sentence: "The princess kissed the frog, and the king knighted the frog." Be able to list the steps

that SAM takes in order to understand the two propositions contained in this sentence.

33. Consider the following sentence: "The horse running past the barn fell." Why does SAM have a difficult time analyzing this sentence?

The interaction between syntax and other cues

34. In what type of case is the meaning of a passive sentence recovered as quickly as the meaning of an active sentence?

The extralinguistic context

35. How does the environmental context aid in the interpretation of language? Give examples.

Conversational cooperation

36. What are the unspoken assumptions about cooperation between speaker and listener?
37. Be prepared to describe what Grice meant by *conversational maxims*, and give examples of these having to do with conversational relevance and with quantity.

Interaction among various factors

38. Be able to list the various factors that feed into language understanding and discuss when, in principle, these factors could play a role during conversation.

THE GROWTH OF LANGUAGE IN THE CHILD

Is language learning the acquisition of a skill?

39. Why is imitation insufficient to account for language acquisition?
40. Characterize the kinds of speech corrections that children often receive and what these imply about language learning.

The social origins of speech production

41. Characterize the verbal behavior of the prelinguistic child.

Discovering the forms of language

42. Initially, infants are capable of responding to all sound distinctions made in any language. What change occurs in the later stages of language learning?
43. What is Motherese, and what are its characteristics? What specific uses does Motherese have in language learning?

The one-word speaker

44. What kinds of words do children learn first? What kinds of words do children rarely learn first? Why?
45. Why is it difficult to study the acquisition of word meaning by children?
46. Describe the explanations for early word meaning that a psychologist would give from a functional, a featural, and a prototype perspective.
47. Describe the selective looking experiment and its use in answering this question: Can propositions be conveyed by the child's single words?

The two-word (telegraphic) speaker

48. What changes in language take place around two years of age?
49. How are words ordered in two-word speech? What is the underlying propositional structure of this speech?

50. Cite two factors to explain why children's early sentences are so short.

Later stages of language learning: syntax

51. What are typical language errors made by a two-and-a-half year old? What do these errors indicate about the structure of language?
52. What is a causative verb? What does the study of these verbs tell us about language learning?

Further stages of language learning: word meaning

53. Given what you've learned about syntax and Motherese, suggest some explanations for children's remarkably rapid learning of language.
54. Explain the categorization bias held by most language learners. What evidence helps psychologists to observe this bias?
55. What initial bias about synonyms do young children exhibit?
56. Describe how children use their growing knowledge of word classes, semantics, and syntax to interpret a word meaning.

The capacities needed for language learning

57. Describe an experiment showing that infants are sensitive to the order in which syllables are presented, parsing these syllables into wordlike units. How does this indicate that infants are sensitive to the appearance of patterns?
58. Understand the position that there are genetically programmed predispositions to follow certain language universals and to learn the parameters of one's own language.
59. Be familiar with the evidence that humans are biologically predisposed to be adapted for language production.

LANGUAGE LEARNING IN CHANGED ENVIRONMENTS

60. What characteristics about the course of language acquisition suggest that it is a biological process?

Wild children

61. What does the study of wild children tell us about the nature-nurture controversy?

Isolated children

62. What does the study of isolated children tell us about language acquisition?

Language without sound

63. Describe the characteristics of American Sign Language (ASL). Why is this an important example of language from a theoretical point of view?

Language without a model

64. Describe the language-learner studies with deaf children of hearing parents. What do the results imply?

Children deprived of access to some of the meanings

65. Theoretically, blind children should learn sentence meanings more slowly than sighted children because blind children are cut off from opportunities to observe word referents. Nevertheless, evidence shows that the rate of language acquisition is not significantly different. Explain this finding.

The case of Helen Keller

66. If isolated from language forms, a human infant begins to invent her own language. Describe how Helen Keller and Anne Sullivan invented language. Which characteristics of communication were carefully developed by Sullivan?

LANGUAGE LEARNING WITH CHANGED ENDOWMENTS

67. What do cases of children with specific language impairment and Williams syndrome reveal about the relationship between language and other cognitive functions?

The critical period hypothesis

68. Summarize the evidence that points out the importance of critical periods in language learning.
69. Describe the initial difference between young learners of a second language and old learners. How does this difference change over time?
70. How does age relate to achieving native-level fluency?

Language in nonhumans

71. Compare vocabulary learning in chimpanzees and humans. Which method works best to teach chimpanzees vocabulary?

72. What evidence has suggested early syntax acquisition in chimpanzees? Be able to evaluate the quality of this evidence.
73. If we say that trained chimpanzees use language, what does our definition of language exclude?

LANGUAGE AND THOUGHT

74. Understand the basis of the idea that language may shape thought.

Whorf's claims

75. What did Whorf claim about the relation of words in the language to the way we think about things? How did this claim extend to syntactic structure? Is there evidence to support the claim?

Experimental studies of language's influence on thought

76. Describe the data on perception of such dimensions as color, shape, or facial expression, and the bearing they have on Whorf's claims.
77. Be able to describe phenomena having to do with memory for spatial position that are relevant to the relation of language to thought.
78. In contrast to the color and space domains, there are many cases where language does influence thought. Describe some.

Programmed Exercises

MAJOR PROPERTIES OF HUMAN LANGUAGE

1. There are about _____ human languages now in use on earth.

   4,000

2. Although animal and human languages are similar in that both have sounds and words (or something like words), animal languages do not have _____.

   sentences

3. We are able to make up novel sentences at will. This tells us that language is _____.

   creative

4. An estimate of the number of English sentences that are twenty words or fewer is _____.

   10^{30}

5. A rule such as "it is not correct to say ain't" is a _____ rule.

   prescriptive

6. Each _____ in a language expresses a meaningful idea or concept.

   word

7. We are able to understand which words refer to which things, scenes, and events in the world. This tells us that language is _____.

   referential

8. A communicating pair takes the utterance and its context as the basis for making a series of complicated inferences about the meaning of a conversation. This tells us that language is _____.

   interpersonal

THE BASIC UNITS OF LANGUAGE

9. We can think of language as existing at a number of levels, from sounds to ideas. The structure of language, then, is _____.

   hierarchical

10. The spoken words *bed* and *dead* differ only in the "b" and "d" sounds at the beginning. This is a difference in one _____.

    phoneme

11. English uses about _____ speech sounds.

    forty

12. Some of the facts about how phonemes combine in words are accidental choices. Others are _____ choices.

    systematic

13. Morphemes are the smallest language units that carry _____.

    meaning

14. "Strange," "er," and "s" are all _____.

    morphemes

15. An organized grouping of words is known as a _____, the unit from which sentences are composed.

phrase

16. An old (and insufficient) view of word and phrase meaning is that meaning is whatever a word or phrase points to in the real world. This view equates meaning and _____.

reference

17. Another theory says that the meaning of a word is synonymous with a list of characteristics, or _____. This theory of meaning is called the _____ theory.

features, definitional

18. The _____ theory of meaning is similar to the feature theory, except that no one feature is necessary or sufficient. Instead, a whole group of features may be present. This theory accounts nicely for the fact that certain words are better examples of their respective categories than other words.

prototype

19. Words are related through groups of features shared unequally among word meanings. This concept is termed the _____ _____ structure.

family resemblance

20. When we say, "The girl climbed the tree," "climbed the tree" is the _____ of the sentence, and "the girl" is the _____.

predicate
subject

21. A tree structure of phrases and words is referred to as a _____ _____ _____ of a sentence.

phrase structure
description

22. Two sentences that are different, but are nearly identical in meaning, share a common _____ phrase structure.

underlying

23. Two sentences that are different in their ordering of phrases differ in _____ phrase structure.

surface

24. In the sentence, "The boy saw the ice cream truck," the phrase "the boy " is called the _____ phrase.

noun

25. A _____ _____ is a useful way of partitioning a sentence to show its hierarchical structure.

tree diagram

26. The subtle difference in meaning of sentences like "The boy played with the ball" and "The ball was played with by the boy" is due to differences in _____.

attitude

27. People often forget the _____ structure of sentences in a story, but they usually remember the _____ structure.

surface
underlying

28. Two sentences whose meanings are essentially equivalent are called _____ of each other.

paraphrases

29. An ambiguous sentence is ambiguous because it is decomposable into more than one _____ representation.

underlying

COMPREHENSION

sentence analyzing
machinery

30. SAM is the name given to the _____ _____ _____.

31. SAM's first assumption is that it will encounter a simple complete sentence. This consists of a _____ phrase, a _____ phrase, and another _____ phrase.

noun, verb, noun

32. The phrases in Question 31 represent the _____, the _____, and the _____ _____.

doer, act, done to

33. Studies show that it will take longer to understand a _____ sentence than an active sentence.

passive

34. The sentence "The princess kissed the frog, and the king knighted the frog" contains two _____.

propositions

35. The sentence "The princess kissed the frog the king knighted" is leaving out a _____ word.

function

36. _____ cues can help the listener process the meaning of a passive sentence as rapidly as an active sentence.

Semantic

37. Various _____ factors, such as the context in which a conversation occurs, have pronounced effects on comprehension.

extralinguistic

38. Grice has proposed that a number of conversational _____ govern normal speech, such that speaker and listener have unwritten rules governing their interaction.

maxims

39. One conversational rule is that speakers and listeners will include things in conversation that are _____, and they will leave out unnecessary information.

relevant

40. Another rule that speakers and listeners adhere to has to do with _____, such that a speaker will say neither more nor less than is necessary.   quantity

41. Somehow syntax, semantics, extralinguistic context, and inferential activity all _____ to produce successful comprehension.   interact

THE GROWTH OF LANGUAGE IN THE CHILD

42. Language learning by _____ is not a sufficient explanation, since children often speak novel sentences.   imitation

43. _____ cannot account for language learning, because children are not corrected for grammatical accuracy.   Reinforcement

44. Childish sounds that make no real sense, but often sound like real words, are called _____.   babbles

45. Even deaf children of signing parents babble. They do so with their _____.   hands

46. Speech production is preceded by _____ interactions such as looks, gestures, and caresses.   social (interpersonal)

47. Although infants can respond to all sound distinctions made in any language, they learn to _____ the distinctions that don't matter in their language.   ignore

48. A specific speech style that is adopted by adults when talking to infants is called _____.   Motherese

49. Two-word speech is known as _____ speech.   telegraphic

50. Even though children utter only two-word sequences at one stage in their acquisition of language, there is reason to believe that they have _____ parts to their propositional ideas.   three

51. After a child learns that the past tense of the verbs *play* and *walk* are *played* and *walked*, *runned* may be given as the past tense of *run* although *ran* was previously used. This phenomenon is known as _____.   overgeneralization

52. By two years of age, the child is seeking _____ rules that operate over the whole vocabulary or set of sentence structures.   general

53. When a child says "Mommy eated me" to mean "Mommy fed me," her or she is inventing a _____ verb.   causative

54. Young children have a bias that new words stand for new objects. They don't believe that some new words are simply _____.   synonyms

55. Evidence that children use _____ to guide word learning comes from a study in which they interpreted "sebbing" to be an action.   syntax

56. Evidence indicates that infants are sensitive to _____ that appear in utterances that they hear; thus, they detect the repeated appearance of a sequence of syllables.   patterns

57. Some have claimed that language learning is governed by sensitivity to the _____ structure that governs all languages, with individual languages defined by different _____.   universal parameters

58. The physical structure of human _____ and the human _____ are such that they are maladapted for survival generally, but are well adapted for speaking and language.   teeth, larynx

LANGUAGE LEARNING IN CHANGED ENVIRONMENTS

59. Cases of wild children raised by animals show that a proper environment is _____ for normal language development.   important

60. Evidence that language can develop without sound comes from studies of _____ children.   deaf

61. A widely used manual communication system among deaf people is _____ _____ _____.   American Sign Language (ASL)

62. A biological _____ enables children to learn language, whether they invent the basics themselves (if there is no language model) or follow the model that they are exposed to.   predisposition

LANGUAGE LEARNING WITH CHANGED ENDOWMENTS

63. When language capacities are lost or diminished because of damage to a cerebral hemisphere (usually the left), this state is termed _____.

aphasia

64. Patients who have a deficit in language only may have a _____ language impairment; by contrast, patients with _____ syndrome have other cognitive deficits, but their language is normal.

specific
Williams

65. One hypothesis of language learning postulates an ideal time to learn languages, after which the learning process is significantly more difficult. This time is known as the _____ _____.

critical period

66. In comparing adults with children, it is clear that _____ pick up a second language more effectively than _____ do in the long term.

children
adults

67. After having been taught ASL for four years, Washoe had learned _____ signs. Some of these were acquired by _____, others by having her hands physically molded into a desired position.

130
imitation

68. Even if chimpanzees were shown to have some sense of _____, this would not be sufficient to claim that they have knowledge of syntax.

sequence

LANGUAGE AND THOUGHT

69. Studies of the perception of _____, facial _____, or _____ position suggest that perception is universal, and all that differs among cultures is the words that are assigned to perceptions.

color, expression,
spatial

70. There are some cases, such as the phenomenon of framing discussed in Chapter 8, in which _____ guides thought. In this case, describing an outcome in positive or negative terms influences choice.

language

Self Test

1. A new group of people is discovered possessing a language that has never been studied before. After a good deal of work, linguists are able to translate anything said in this language into English. This is further evidence that all language:
   a. is unrelated
   b. is similar in the ideas that can be expressed
   c. uses the same sounds
   d. uses the same words

2. All of the following describe language use *except*:
   a. it is creative
   b. it has a rule-governed structure
   c. it is imitative
   d. it is interpersonal

3. The fact that there is an infinite number of sentences that can be uttered upon seeing a rabbit is an argument against the behaviorist position and demonstrates the _____ of language.
   a. uncertainty
   b. variability
   c. creativity
   d. rigidity

4. The fact that the words *boys*, *kiss*, and *girls* can be arranged in different orders to give different meanings (i.e., "Boys kiss girls," "Girls kiss boys") demonstrates another universal characteristic of language. Language is:
   a. rule-governed
   b. unpredictable
   c. implicit
   d. prototypical

5. The rules of grammar that structure a language are called:
   a. features
   b. morphemes
   c. semantics
   d. descriptive rules

6. The belief that knowledge of word meanings sets humans above animals is:
   a. a new belief
   b. a belief dating back to antiquity
   c. widely held by psychologists today
   d. both b and c

7. The problem of reference is complex because:
   a. speech is not an automatic response of the nervous system
   b. language is referential
   c. language is meaningful as well as referential
   d. all of the above

8. The actual speech acts that pass between people are merely hints about the thoughts being conveyed. Hidden from the observer are the unspoken, yet guiding:
   a. descriptions of conversation
   b. principles of conversation
   c. dialects
   d. utterances

9. When we say that language is hierarchical, we mean that:
   a. different language uses demonstrate social class differences
   b. language structure exists at many levels
   c. language has developed from other cognitive functions
   d. modern languages are descended from other languages

10. Which of the following represents the actual hierarchy of language structures?
    a. phrase, word, phoneme, morpheme
    b. word, morpheme, phrase, phoneme
    c. phoneme, morpheme, word, phrase
    d. morpheme, phoneme, word, phrase

11. The perceptual units of speech are:
    a. phonemes
    b. morphemes
    c. syllables
    d. words

12. One reason that foreign languages sound strange is that:
    a. the same phonemes are pronounced differently
    b. other languages are spoken more rapidly
    c. there are fewer "gaps" in foreign languages than in English
    d. some of the phonemes are different from those of English

13. New words are being coined every day. Some sound combinations are not used, though. This is due to _____ rules.
    a. syntactic
    b. semantic
    c. pragmatic
    d. none of the above

14. A morpheme is a:
    a. word
    b. single sound
    c. perceptual unit
    d. unit of meaning

15. A phrase is:
    a. several sentences put together
    b. unrelated to the meaning of the sentence
    c. an organized group of words
    d. always delineated by grammatical markings

16. The area of knowledge dealing solely with meaning is called:
    a. linguistics
    b. semantics
    c. phonetics
    d. none of the above

17. The study of semantics proceeds by:
    a. inventing new meanings for words
    b. updating standard dictionaries
    c. eliminating what is false about word meaning
    d. voting on the meaning of words

18. A view of meaning as simply referring to objects in the world is not sufficient, since:
    a. the same object can be referred to in more than one way
    b. it's difficult to describe the reference of words like *truth*
    c. both of the above
    d. none of the above

19. The definitional theory attempts to define the _____ attributes that define a given concept.
    a. necessary
    b. sufficient
    c. both of the above
    d. none of the above

20. One problem with the definitional theory is that:
    a. some attributes are used to describe more than one concept
    b. some concepts involve more than one attribute
    c. some concepts have no attributes
    d. some members of a category seem to be better examples of that category than other members

21. The major characteristics of a prototype theory of meaning is that:
    a. no feature is individually necessary
    b. no feature is individually sufficient
    c. a whole set of features describes word meaning
    d. all of the above

22. A robin will be judged to be an exemplary member of the bird family because:
    a. it has wings
    b. it has feathers
    c. the robin is close to the presumed prototype of a bird
    d. a robin is more like a bird than an ostrich

23. A family resemblance structure is an analogy to support which theory?
    a. prototype
    b. definitional
    c. interpersonal
    d. language attribution

24. Sentence meanings are often called:
    a. propositions
    b. predicates
    c. paraphrases
    d. phonemes

25. A two-branch tree diagram of a sentence structure would include these parts:
    a. principle rules and prescriptive rules
    b. verb phrase and noun phrase
    c. morphemes and phonemes
    d. paraphrases and verb phrases

26. Partitioning of sentences suggests that phrase structure rules:
    a. do not exist psychologically
    b. are psychologically natural
    c. exist but are usually ignored
    d. require more attention than other grammars

27. The two types of phrase structures are:
    a. syntactic, semantic
    b. underlying, syntactic

c. surface, syntactic

d. surface, underlying

28. In which of the following pairs of sentences are the two underlying structures similar?

    a. "The girl kissed the boy." "The boy kissed the girl."

    b. "The girl kissed the boy." "The girl was kissed by the boy."

    c. "The girl kissed the boy." "The boy was kissed by the girl."

    d. all of the above

29. The two sentences "The boy hit the ball" and "The ball hit the boy" differ in:

    a. underlying structure

    b. surface structure

    c. both a and b

    d. neither a nor b

30. Which sentence below has a different proposition from the others?

    a. "The girl kissed the boy."

    b. "The boy was kissed by the girl."

    c. "The girl did not kiss the boy."

    d. all of the above include the same proposition

31. The two sentences "All students like psychology" and "Psychology is liked by all students" represent:

    a. paraphrases

    b. different propositions

    c. the same attitude

    d. different underlying structures

32. The sentences in Question 31 differ in:

    a. attitude

    b. proposition

    c. proposition and attitude

    d. neither proposition nor attitude

33. The sentence "Flying airplanes can be dangerous" is ambiguous because:

    a. there are two possible surface structures

    b. there are two possible underlying structures

    c. there are two possible surface and two possible underlying structures

    d. there is no explanation for the ambiguity of this particular sentence

34. Participants were read a story that contains the sentence "Skinner disagreed with the psycholinguists' view of language." In a subsequent session the sentences below were presented to the participants, who had to determine whether that exact sentence was actually presented. Which sentence is most likely to be mistakenly recognized?

    a. "The psycholinguists disagreed with Skinner about the nature of language."

    b. "Skinner did not disagree with the psycholinguists' view of language."

    c. "The psycholinguists did not agree with Skinner's view of language."

    d. "It was the psycholinguists' view of language that Skinner disagreed with."

35. SAM starts out with a bias to hear sentences in which the order of propositions is:

    a. doer, act, done-to

    b. done-to, doer, act

    c. object, subject, verb

    d. subject, object, verb

36. Some support for the hypothesis that listeners use the "first noun phrase did it" strategy is that participants comprehend _____ sentences faster than they do _____ ones.

    a. active, passive

    b. passive, active

    c. ambiguous, simple

    d. simple, paraphrased

37. Which of the following sentences will take the longest time to understand?

    a. "The boy hit the ball."

    b. "The boy did not hit the ball."

    c. "The ball was hit by the boy."

    d. all of the above will take the same to understand

38. Language comprehension is influenced by more than syntax and semantics. In addition, listeners make heavy use of:

    a. the order of words in the sentence

    b. the meanings of individual words in the sentence

    c. the context in which the conversation occurs

    d. none of the above

39. Speakers and listeners appear to honor a set of unwritten rules when they converse. For example:

    a. a speaker would normally specify which of several possible objects in a room is the topic of an utterance

    b. a listener would normally honor a request that was given indirectly rather than answering "Yes" or "No" to a question such as "Can you pass the butter?"

    c. a speaker would normally not utter a comment that is not relevant to an interchange that is currently occurring

    d. all of the above

40. Which of the following can be used to explain first-language learning?

    a. imitation

    b. reinforcement

    c. correction

    d. none of the above

41. All of the following are forms of preverbal communication *except*:

    a. crawling

    b. babbling

    c. gesturing

    d. touching

42. Which of the following statements is true about sound discrimination in early language learning?

    a. Initially infants respond only to the sounds of their own language.

    b. Initially infants respond to all sounds in all languages.

    c. Initially infants cannot respond to sound distinctions at all.

    d. Initially infants respond only to the most common sound distinctions of their own language.

43. Which of the following is *not* a characteristic of Motherese?
    a. exaggerated intonations
    b. high pitch
    c. infrequent pauses
    d. slow rate of talking

44. Which of the following words is most likely to be among a child's first words?
    a. push
    b. wall
    c. the
    d. pain

45. Which of the following approaches has been used to describe early word meanings in children?
    a. function
    b. features
    c. prototypes
    d. all of the above

46. Two-word speech is known as _____ speech.
    a. functor
    b. telegraphic
    c. syntactic
    d. propositional

47. By two years of age knowledge of _____ begins to develop.
    a. Motherese
    b. propositions
    c. syntax
    d. synapses

48. The use of a word form like "sitted" by a child is known as:
    a. telegraphic
    b. undergeneralization
    c. overgeneralization
    d. syntactics

49. What is an example of a telegraphic utterance that a child might produce?
    a. Mommy on
    b. push baby
    c. Daddy play
    d. under doggie
    e. a and d only
    f. b and c only

50. The invention of _____ _____ explains the appearance of sentences like "Daddy giggled me."
    a. telegraphic speech
    b. causative verbs
    c. word classes
    d. count nouns

51. Which of the following is a "basic level" word?
    a. beagle
    b. animal
    c. poodle
    d. dog

52. Children are disposed to organize the world into broad _____.
    a. categories
    b. syntax

    c. phrases
    d. ideas

53. Which statement(s) describe(s) how children learn language?
    a. They use the forms of new words as clues to their meanings.
    b. They use their knowledge of words to predict their forms.
    c. They use their knowledge of sentence structure to plug in new words.
    d. all of the above

54. One of the theories about the role of genetics in the acquisition of language argues that:
    a. different language communities have somewhat different genetic constitutions, allowing the children in these communities to have specializations that are suited to the particular language in that community
    b. it is very unlikely that language has any genetic basis because there hasn't been sufficient time in the evolution of the human species for this to develop
    c. genetic mechanisms have made humans uniquely suited to learn associations between one concept and another, which is the critical skill necessary to learn word meanings
    d. there are universal features that govern all languages, and humans have some predisposition to be sensitive to these features

55. Which of the following features of human structure seem to be specialized for speech production, even at the expense of survival value?
    a. teeth spacing
    b. larynx functioning
    c. the fact that we can't eat and breathe at the same time
    d. all of the above

56. Evidence from wild children who have been found reveals that:
    a. some can be rehabilitated to use language without problems
    b. some can learn to speak a few words
    c. all can learn to speak a few words
    d. none of the above

57. Language development does not depend on hearing language, as evidenced by:
    a. wild children
    b. ASL
    c. isolated children
    d. retarded children

58. Deaf children whose parents did not teach them sign language demonstrated language development similar to that of hearing children in that:
    a. the children went through one-word speech, two-word speech, and so on.
    b. they invented a communication system
    c. they eventually put signs together in predictable serial order
    d. all of the above

59. The following individuals were deprived of exposure to language since birth. Which one has the best chance of learning to speak?

a. an eight-year-old girl
b. a fourteen-year-old boy
c. a twenty-year-old man
d. a thirty-year-old woman

60. Helen Keller's experience is an example of how, when human infants are isolated from language forms, they will:
a. become incommunicative until adolescence
b. need to be taught how to think
c. begin to invent their own language
d. become permanently incommunicative

61. The loss of language function is known as:
a. aphasia
b. anorexia
c. asphyxia
d. aphaeresis

62. The speech disorder characterized by loss of content in words is:
a. Broca's aphasia
b. expressive aphasia
c. Wernicke's aphasia
d. none of the above

63. First-language learning, second-language learning, and recovery from aphasia may depend on:
a. intelligence
b. the particular language involved
c. generalization
d. the critical period

64. When Washoe teaches some of her human signs to an adopted chimpanzee baby, it is an example of:
a. cultural transmission
b. language acquisition among chimpanzees
c. syntax
d. both a and b

65. The nature of human language can be described by which of the following statement(s)?
a. Fundamentally, languages are the same all over the world.
b. All languages consist of a hierarchy of sentences.
c. Language can flourish in virtually any exposure condition.
d. all of the above

66. Some have argued that the many words that Eskimos have for snow has shaped their perception of snow. However, this argument is flawed because:
a. Eskimos don't perceive snow any differently than do residents of the southern United States
b. Eskimos don't have more than one word for snow
c. Eskimos don't have as many words for snow as English has
d. all of the above

67. Various experimental studies have been conducted that cast doubt on Whorf's claims about the relation of language to thought. For example, studies have shown?
a. that people of different cultures perceive colors the same regardless of the words they use to name colors

b. that people of different languages have similar perceptions of spatial position even if their languages are inconsistent in assigning names to particular spatial relationships
c. that people of different cultures perceive facial expressions similarly regardless of how they name expressions
d. all of the above
e. a and b, but not c
f. a and c, but not b

68. On balance, one would have to say that there is an important influence of language on thought. This is illustrated by:
a. studies showing that using male pronouns that refer to a generic person (e.g., *he*) in text has an influence on how that text is interpreted
b. studies showing that how a problem is framed can influence the choices that people make
c. studies showing that verbalizing thoughts has an influence on later thinking
d. all of the above

Answer Key for Self Test

1.	b p. 345	35.	a p. 364
2.	c p. 345	36.	a p. 364
3.	c p. 346	37.	c p. 364
4.	a p. 347	38.	c p. 363
5.	d p. 347	39.	d pp. 369, 370
6.	d p. 348	40.	d p. 371
7.	d p. 348	41.	a p. 372
8.	b p. 349	42.	b p. 373
9.	b p. 349, 350	43.	c p. 373
10.	c pp. 350–52	44.	a p. 374
11.	a p. 350	45.	d p. 375
12.	d p. 350	46.	b p. 377
13.	d p. 351	47.	c p. 378
14.	d p. 351	48.	c p. 378
15.	c p. 352	49.	g p. 378
16.	b p. 352	50.	b p. 379
17.	c p. 353	51.	d p. 379
18.	c p. 353	52.	a p. 379
19.	c pp. 353, 354	53.	d p. 380
20.	d p. 354	54.	d p. 382
21.	d p. 354	55.	d p. 383
22.	c p. 355	56.	b p. 384
23.	a p. 355	57.	b p. 385
24.	a p. 357	58.	d p. 387
25.	b p. 359	59.	a p. 385
26.	b pp. 359–60	60.	c p. 390
27.	d p. 360	61.	a p. 390
28.	c pp. 360, 361	62.	c p. 390
29.	c p. 361	63.	d pp. 391, 392
30.	d p. 362	64.	a p. 394
31.	a p. 362	65.	d p. 395
32.	a pp. 361, 362	66.	c p. 395
33.	b p. 362	67.	d pp. 397, 398
34.	d p. 362	68.	d pp. 398, 399

Investigating Psychological Phenomena

IMPLICIT LEARNING

Equipment: A stopwatch or a watch that indicates seconds, index cards
Number of participants: One
Time per participant: Thirty minutes
Time for experimenter: Forty minutes

One of the most impressive aspects of language is its acquisition: Children learn an enormous amount about their language without ever being explicitly taught. Consider syntax, for instance. Not until children have already learned a substantial number of syntactic rules do parents correct syntactic constructions that their children use. Somehow the growing child manages to induce the syntactic rules of language from the variety of utterances that he or she happens to encounter. This ability to induce complex rules from examples is an ability that we use all the time, but its use without intention, or even awareness, and with complex linguistic construction is what makes it impressive as a characteristic of language acquisition. Having just learned about language acquisition, you can now begin to appreciate how complex the language-learning process must be, especially since it is largely mediated by implicit induction.

You can demonstrate this implicit induction process using the following experiment modeled after one by Arthur Reber (1967). There are two phases to the experiment. In the first place, your participant will memorize a series of strings letters after being told only that he or she is a participant in a memory experiment. In the second phase, the participant will be told that the letter strings from the first phase were constructed using a rule. Then the participant will be shown twenty-four new strings that she has never seen before and asked to judge which twelve of these were constructed from the same rule used in phase 1. If the participant correctly categorized more of these twenty-four strings than we would expect by chance alone (twelve by chance, since there are only two responses the participant can make), then we can conclude that the participant has learned something about the rule even though he or she wasn't trying to in Phase 1.

PHASE 1

Instruct your participant as follows:

This experiment concerns memory for unmeaningful material. You will be presented with twenty strings of letters that you must memorize and recall. These strings of letters will be presented in groups of four that you can study for fifteen seconds. Then the groups will be taken away and you will be required to recall all four strings (in any order). Following this you will be presented with the same strings again for another fifteen-second study period. This will be followed by another recall attempt. In all, the five groups of strings will be presented five times each for study and recall.

The stimulus materials for this first phase are at the end of this section. Write each of the five lists of strings on index cards and present them to the participant individually. Provide the participant with twenty slips of paper on each of which he or she can recall one quadruplet of strings. Be sure to remove each recall attempt before showing the next repetition of a set of strings or before going on to a new set of strings.

PHASE 2

Instructions:

The strings of letters were constructed according to a rule. The rule dictated the orders in which letters were allowed to follow one another. In the second phase you will be shown twenty-four new strings of letters, and you must decide for each one whether it was or was not constructed according to the same rule for the letter strings in Phase 1. When you decide, you should place your answer in the appropriate place on the answer sheet.

Score the participant's answers after he or she has completed Phase 2, using the answer key provided. Did the participant do better than chance? Ask whether he or she has any guesses about what the rule is. You will probably be surprised to discover how little the participant appears to be aware of the rule even though he or she can use it (in some sense) to make judgments about individual instances.

A diagrammatic representation of the rule is shown below. It works as follows: If you begin at "start" and trace through the diagram along any path in the direction of the arrows, you can get to "end." By noting the order of the letters that you pass along the way, you can construct a string. Notice that because of loops, some strings may be quite long but still permissible according to the rule.

Think about some of the following issues: In what way does this experiment mimic language learning? In what way is language learning different? As a model of language learning, why was it important not to tell participants about the rule until the end of Phase 1? What do the results suggest about language learning?

Reference

Reber, A. S. 1967. Implicit learning of artificial grammars, *Journal of Verbal Learning and Verbal Behavior* 6:855–63.

PHASE 1: STIMULUS LISTS

(Write these on index cards or pieces of paper for presentation to the participant.)

List 1	List 2	List 3	List 4	List 5
VVTRXRR	VVRXRR	VTRRR	VVTRXR	XMVTRX
XMVTTRX	XXRR	XMVRXRR	VTRR	XMTRRRR
XMVRXR	VVRMVRX	VVTTRMT	VVRMTRR	XMVRX
VVTRX	XMVRMT	VVRMTR	XMVTRMT	XXRRR

PHASE 2: LIST OF ALTERNATIVES FOR RECOGNITION TEST

(Write these on index cards as well.)

1.	RXTTVMXR	13.	VVTTRX
2.	XMTR	14.	VVRX
3.	MXXR	15.	VVRRRTX
4.	XMVRXRRR	16.	MT
5.	VVRXR	17.	VVTRMVRX
6.	VTTX	18.	VM
7.	MVTTXVR	19.	XXR
8.	XX	20.	XMT
9.	VRT	21.	RXTMV
10.	VVTTTRX	22.	XXM
11.	TTV	23.	TTRXXM
12.	VT	24.	VTR

RECOGNITION TEST REPORT SHEET

(You can find this report sheet in Appendix 3; cut it out and give it to the participant.)

ANSWERS

1.	no	13.	yes
2.	yes	14.	yes
3.	no	15.	no
4.	yes	16.	no
5.	yes	17.	yes
6.	no	18.	no
7.	no	19.	yes
8.	yes	20.	yes
9.	no	21.	no
10.	yes	22.	no
11.	no	23.	no
12.	yes	24.	yes

RULE FOR LETTER-STRING CONSTRUCTION

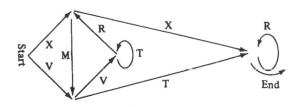

PART THREE

SOCIAL BEHAVIOR

CHAPTER 10

The Biological Basis of Social Behavior

Learning Objectives

THE SOCIAL NATURE OF HUMANS AND ANIMALS

1. Explain Hobbes's conception of human nature.

Natural selection and survival

2. Outline the basic principles of Darwin's theory of evolution.
3. Distinguish personal from genetic survival, and indicate the role of sexual competition in the latter.
4. Does natural selection operate on behavior as well as on physical traits?
5. Are humans an inherently social species? Does Darwin's theory of evolution answer this question?

Built-in social behaviors

6. Describe the basic principles of ethology, including the concepts of display, fixed-action patterns, and releasers.

AGGRESSION

Conflict between species: predation and defense

7. Is aggression a component of predatory attack?
8. Is it fair to describe much of aggressive behavior between different species as defensive? Explain.

Conflict between like and like

9. Discuss the relation between testosterone and aggression, and between serotonin and aggression.
10. Discuss the nature and function of territories.
11. Explain mechanisms for limiting aggression in humans and in animals.
12. What are dominance hierarchies, and what are their functions?
13. Compare functions and characteristics of dominance hierarchies in males versus females.
14. Are humans territorial? Explain. Contrast human and animal territories.

MATING

Why sex?

15. What is the selective advantage of sexual reproduction?

Sexual choice

16. Describe the nature and function of courtship rituals.
17. Discuss the evolutionary origin of displays, and indicate how the comparative method helps to discover this.
19. Explain why the female is more selective in mate selection than the male.

Reproduction and timing

19. Explain the role of sex hormones in sexual behavior in animals and humans. Why is it said that the human female is emancipated from hormonal control?

Evolution and mating systems

20. Define polygyny, polyandry, and monogamy. Explain why most bird species are monogamous, while most mammals species are polygamous.
21. What is the relation between polygyny and sexual dimorphism?
22. What are differences in important characteristics sought in mates by human males versus females? What is the evolutionary account of these differences?
23. What is the evolutionary explanation of the predominance of polygyny in human cultures, and the widespread tendency of men to be more interested in multiple sexual partners than women? What is the culturally oriented rejoinder to the evolutionary explanation?

PARENTING

The infant's attachment to the mother

24. Discuss the function of the infant's attachment to the mother, how it is manifested, and the extent to which the attachment depends on the mother fulfillment of the child's basic biological needs.

The mother's attachment to the infant

25. What is the function of maternal attachment?
26. What characteristics of the infant are important is establishing maternal attachment?

COMMUNICATION

Expressive movements: displays

27. What are displays? How do we determine the messages conveyed in animal displays?
28. Do humans have displays?

Social cognition

29. What are audience effects and why are they relevant to social cognition?
30. Describe evidence indicating that some primates identify individuals in their troop, and are aware of some of the relationships between individuals.
31. What does it mean to say an animal has a "theory of mind"? Cite evidence for a "theory of mind" in nonhuman primates.

Self-sacrifice and altruism

32. Explain how self-sacrifice ("altruism") is consistent with evolutionary theory.
33. Distinguish among enlightened self-interest, kin selection, and reciprocal altruism as accounts for altruistic behavior.
34. What is the relation of mutual grooming to reciprocal altruism and social bonding?
35. Discuss evolutionary accounts of altruism in humans, and the criticism of this approach.
36. What, if any, are the ethical implications of something being a "part of human nature"?

ETHOLOGY AND HUMAN NATURE

37. Indicate the extent to which human social behavior can be explained in biological terms.

Programmed Exercises

THE SOCIAL NATURE OF HUMANS AND ANIMALS

1. The view that humans are an inherently solitary creatures, who invent society as a means of taming their brutish nature, is associated with the British philosopher _____.

    (Thomas) Hobbes

2. According to Darwin, evolution proceeds because variants of a species with superior characteristics are more likely to survive. This process is called _____ _____.

    natural selection

3. Essentially, natural selection is not about literal survival, or _____ survival, but about reproductive success, which amounts to _____ survival. The latter leads to selection of traits that produce an advantage in _____ competition.

    personal
    genetic
    sexual

4. Those characteristics, including behaviors, that confer survival and reproductive advantage are considered to have high _____ _____.

    adaptive value

5. The branch of biology that studies animal behavior, particularly under natural conditions and within an evolutionary framework, is called _____. It focuses on _____-specific behavior.

    ethology, species

6. Genetically programmed, species-specific movements are called _____-_____ _____.

    fixed-action patterns

7. When a female stickleback enters a nest, the male prods her rhythmically at the base of her tail. This action causes the female to deposit her eggs, a species-specific response. We can term such prodding a _____ _____.

    releasing stimulus

8. Since this prodding stimulus is a product of the male's behavior, it can also be called a _____.

    display

AGGRESSION

9. An attack by a lion on a zebra seems qualitatively different from a fight or threat sequence between two members of the same species. We call the former _____ and the latter _____.

    predation, aggression

10. The generally higher level of aggression seen in males of most species has been attributed to higher levels of the male hormone _____.

    testosterone

11. In some species, greater aggression is associated with low levels of brain_____.

    serotonin

12. Animals often defend a particular area against other members of their species. This area probably serves to guarantee them essential _____ and is called a _____.

    resources, territory

13. Animals limit aggression by making ritualized communications, called _____ _____.

    threat displays

14. One mechanism for limiting aggression involves a display that essentially indicates "surrender." Such a display is called an _____ _____.

    appeasement signal

15. In a _____ _____, a group of animals of the same species develops a stable social order based on the establishment of rank as a result of mutual aggressive encounters.

    dominance hierarchy

16. A person walks up to a stranger, approaching her until their bodies are just inches apart. This can be considered a violation of _____ _____.

personal space

MATING

17. Human territoriality expresses itself in many ways, and is not always about _____. In general, human territories are more subject to change by experience, and hence show more _____ than animal territories do.

land (physical space)
plasticity

18. In sexual reproduction, the _____ and _____ unite to produce the fertilized egg, or _____.

sperm, ovum
zygote

19. Sexual reproduction leads to higher _____ across members of a species. This may promote more adaptive responses to _____.

variability
pathogens
(environmental change)

20. The rooster's comb, the stag's antlers, and possibly the enlarged breast of the human female are all instances of structural _____.

displays

21. The relatively complex behavior patterns that constitute sexual displays in many animals are called _____ _____.

courtship rituals

22. Courtship rituals indicate both the animal's _____ and _____.

intentions, species

23. In most species the _____ (male or female) has the major role in "deciding" whether or not to mate.

female

24. Except for primates, mammals mate only when the female is in "heat" or _____.

estrus

25. The most important hormones involved in the mammalian female reproductive cycle are _____ and _____.

estrogen
progesterone

26. Implantations of male hormone, that is, _____, into the part of the brain called the _____, can cause a castrated male animal to show male sexual behavior.

testosterone
hypothalamus

27. While the biological aspects of the human female reproductive cycle are controlled by hormones, in the human female, _____ _____ is relatively independent of hormones.

sexual activity (sexual behavior)

28. In general, in terms of mating systems, bird species are _____, whereas mammal species are _____.

monogamous
polygynous

29. There is usually more _____ _____, that is, structural differences between the sexes, in species that are _____.

sexual dimorphism
polygynous

30. In human mate selection, males are more inclined to emphasize _____ _____, while females are more inclined to emphasize _____ _____ _____.

physical attractiveness (youth), good financial (social) prospects

31. The evolutionary view predicts that, because of the lower investment that male mammals have in any reproductive act, the mating system of _____ will be more common than its opposite, _____, and that males will seek more _____ in sexual partners than will females.

polygyny
polyandry, variety

PARENTING

32. The human infant's cry or the chirp of a newly hatched bird are examples of _____ calls.

distress

33. Human parents have a special sing-song mode of speaking to their infants, called _____.

Motherese

34. The _____ is the human infant's built-in means of communicating with adults and maintaining their attention while indicating a generally positive state.

smile

COMMUNICATION

35. The message of a _____ can be inferred by noting the _____ between the occurrence of the display and the animal's behavior just before and after the occurrence.

display, correlation (relation)

36. Human _____ _____ are displays.

facial expressions

37. Human language differs in many ways from animal displays. One critical difference is that while animals only express specific displays in appropriate contexts, human language constitutes a _____ system necessary for communicating diverse combinations of information.

productive

38. Furthermore, the _____ of messages sent by humans is much more wide-ranging, including conveying information about the world as well as the sender's tendencies to respond. content

39. When the occurrence of a display is related to the presence of appropriate recipients, we say there is a(n) _____ _____. audience effect

40. There is evidence that at least some free-living primates, such as vervet monkeys, are aware of the _____ between other pairs of monkeys in their troop. relationship

41. Demonstrations that chimpanzees can engage in deliberate deception suggest that they have a _____ _____ _____. theory of mind

42. "Self-sacrifice" by a parent animal can be understood within an evolutionary framework, since it may ultimately serve to increase the number of the parent's _____ in the population. genes

43. Certain "altruistic" behaviors, such as _____ calls, may actually promote personal survival, and hence are examples of _____ _____-_____. alarm
enlightened self-interest

44. When this (question 42) is accomplished by sparing the lives of relatives, it is called _____ _____. kin selection

45. "Unselfish" acts may also be adaptive because the recipients of these acts may later return the favor. This is called _____ _____. reciprocal altruism

46. Mutual _____ behavior in animals can be interpreted as reciprocal altruism, and promotes social _____. grooming
bonding

47. The evolutionary view emphasizes genetic relatedness, or _____, in explaining altruism. An extension of this is emphasis by an individual of his or her own group's interests, which is called _____. kinship

tribalism

48. Opponents of sociobiology argue that human altruism derives from _____ as opposed to _____. culture
biology (genes)

ETHOLOGY AND HUMAN NATURE

49. Contrary to the position taken by Hobbes, it now seems clear that the human organism is, in its biological nature, a _____ creature. social

Self Test

1. Hobbes and Darwin agree that:
   a. natural selection is the key to understanding human nature.
   b. humans are basically solitary creatures
   c. humans are basically destructive
   d. humans enter a "social contract" to protect themselves from their brutish nature
   e. none of the above

2. Animal A lives 10 years and has 6 offspring.
   Animal B lives 8 years and has 10 offspring.
   Therefore:
   a. A has greater personal, B has greater genetic survival
   b. B has greater personal, A has greater genetic survival
   c. B is more successful in sexual competition
   d. A is more successful in sexual competition
   e. a and c

3. The Darwinian principle of natural selection implies that:
   a. social behavior cannot be subject to evolution because it is not inherited
   b. in the struggle to survive and reproduce, human beings are self-centered and solitary creatures restrained only by the constraints imposed by society
   c. social or altruistic behavior may evolve only if it serves to increase the frequencies of the genes of the animal showing this behavior
   d. coupled with the principles of ethology and genetics, social and altruistic behavior will evolve as long as there is appropriate display or communication
   e. a and b

4. Ethologists are particularly concerned with the study of:
   a. species-specific behavior
   b. behavior in natural settings
   c. social behavior
   d. all of the above
   e. none of the above

5. Releasing stimulus is to fixed-action pattern as:
   a. species-specific is to general
   b. cause is to effect
   c. learned is to innate
   d. predation is to aggression
   e. house is to door

6. An observer notes that animal A, a male of a particular species, is, at a particular time, more aggressive than animal B. In an effort to increase the aggressiveness of animal B, the observer could:
   a. introduce a dominant animal of the same species into B's environment
   b. inject B with any sex hormone in an appropriate dose
   c. place B in its own territory and arrange for another male to approach the territory border
   d. place B in the territory of another male
   e. raise the level of brain serotonin in B

7. Aggressive encounters between members of the same species are often concerned with the establishment of:
   a. mobbing
   b. predation
   c. appropriate defense mechanisms
   d. territories
   e. displays

8. The adaptive value of territories is that they:
   a. increase the aggressiveness of the territory holder
   b. provide resources for the territory holder
   c. prevent threat displays
   d. decrease personal space and allow for greater reproduction
   e. c and d

9. The damage caused by aggressive encounters within a species is controlled by all but one of the following. Which of the alternatives is not a means of controlling aggression?
   a. appeasement signals
   b. assessing the strength of the enemy
   c. displays
   d. establishment of territories
   e. imprinting

10. Dominance hierarchies:
    a. exist only in males
    b. are the basis of personal space
    c. confer reproductive advantages on those at the top
    d. guarantee equal distribution of resources
    e. increase aggressive encounters

11. Sexual reproduction is particularly advantageous with respect to asexual reproduction when:
    a. fission is nuclear
    b. testosterone levels are high
    c. aggression is common
    d. the environment is not stable over long periods of time
    e. events in the environment are predictable over long periods of time

12. This picture illustrates one stage of:

    a. predation
    b. defense
    c. feeding
    d. courtship
    e. contact comfort

13. Courtship rituals serve all but one of the following purposes. Which of the items below is *not* a function of courtship rituals?
    a. to synchronize the sexual activities of male and female
    b. to attract members of the opposite sex
    c. to increase the size of a territory
    d. to identify the sex and sexual readiness of the partners
    e. all of the above are functions of courtship rituals

14. To the extent that the male of a species spends time and energy in the care of the young, we would expect that:
    a. he would be more selective about mating partners
    b. he would have higher levels of testosterone than expected
    c. he would show more structural sexual displays
    d. he would be less likely to have a territory
    e. he would show more appeasement signals

15. During estrus, the female (nonprimate) mammal is:
    a. secreting estrogen
    b. most receptive to sexual approach of males
    c. fertile
    d. all of the above
    e. none of the above

16. In some species where the female has a clearly defined estrus cycle, the male is always ready for sexual activity. This would make sense if it were the case that in these species:
    a. all females come into estrus at the same time
    b. estrus is dependent on the season
    c. estrus occurs throughout the year and females are not synchronized in their cycles
    d. hormonal factors are especially important in determining the receptivity of the female
    e. a and b

17. Which of the following features of human sexual behavior is shared most completely with other mammals?
    a   the hormone independence of female receptivity
    b. the existence of sexual displays
    c. the importance of learning in the sexual response
    d. the persistence of sexual behavior following castration
    e. b and d

18. Predictions about male-female differences in mammalian mating systems and variety seeking in sexual partners are based on the fact that female mammals have a greater investment in reproduction because they:
    a. carry the offspring during pregnancy
    b. take the greater responsibility for the early care of infants
    c. account for a greater part of the genetic material of their offspring
    d. all of the above
    e. a and b

19. If you knew that in a particular species the males sought more variety in sexual partners than did the females, you would guess that this species had a _____ mating system.
    a. monogamous
    b. polyandrous
    c. polygynous
    d. dimorphic
    e. b or c

20. According to the evolutionary account, a human female is inclined to emphasize financial/social security in selecting a mate because:
    a. this improves the prospects for a successful upbringing of her children
    b. males with higher status are more likely to be fertile
    c. she is likely to give birth to more children
    d. males with higher status are less likely to prefer polygyny
    e. b and c

21. There is a tendency for human males to seek more variety in mates ("male promiscuity") than females. Which of the following is *not* evidence that this difference has a biological basis?
    a. Males have higher economic and social status in almost all cultures.
    b. Male promiscuity appears cross-culturally.
    c. Male promiscuity occurs in most mammalian species.
    d. Male mammals have a lower investment than females in any particular offspring.
    e. Female mammals carry and nurse their young.

22. Features of the human infant, such as the smile, cries, upturned nose, and chubby cheeks, are:
    a. the stimuli through which we learn to recognize specific children
    b. the vehicles for the establishment of basic trust
    c. releasers of parental behavior
    d. instances of distress displays
    e. more common in monogamous cultures

23. Expressive movements (displays) by animal A may inform other members of the species about:
    a. its readiness to behave in a certain way
    b. its presence

c. some of its characteristics
d. a and b
e. all of the above

24. Human language differs from animal displays in that:
    a. it can indicate response tendencies
    b. it has a long evolutionary history
    c. it is a form of communication
    d. it can produce statements about the world as well as about response tendencies
    e. it has more than ten different "displays" that convey different meanings

25. Which of the following is (are) evidence for social cognition in nonhuman primates?
    a. deliberate deception
    b. awareness of kinship relationships between other members of the troop
    c. audience effects
    d. all of the above
    e. a and c

26. The demonstration of deliberate deception in chimpanzees suggests that they:
    a. are aware of kinship relationships
    b. have a theory of mind
    c. recognize that other chimps have thoughts, intentions, or beliefs
    d. b and c
    e. none of the above

27. Consider a case in which an animal risks death from a predator by distracting it from the children of the animal's sister. Which of the possibilities listed below is the most likely account of this "altruistic" behavior?
    a. kin selection
    b. reciprocal altruism
    c. emancipation from hormonal control
    d. all of the above
    e. none of the above

28. Consider a different case, one in which an animal A risks death from a predator by distracting the predator from another adult, B, of its species. And suppose that B is not related to A, and furthermore, that B is not a member of A's group, and is only transiently in A's presence. This apparently altruistic act would be easily accounted for as:
    a. kin selection
    b. reciprocal altruism
    c. emancipation from hormonal control
    d. a and b
    e. none of the above

29. On an evolutionary account, which of the following "altruistic" human acts would be most difficult to explain?
    a. a man sacrificing his life to save four of his sister's children
    b. a woman sacrificing her life to save four of her sister's children
    c. a grandmother sacrificing her life to save one grandchild
    d. a grandchild sacrificing his life to save one grandparent
    e. a and c

30. Which of the following support(s) the cultural critique of the evolutionary view?
    a. Parents leave more money in their wills to their biological as opposed to their adopted children.
    b. Some people list their best friend as the person to be called in an emergency.
    c. Male homosexuals are more promiscuous than female homosexuals.
    d. In some societies, some close relatives (e.g., the maternal side) are ignored.
    e. b and d

31. Hobbes and the evolutionary approach would agree that:
    a. there is something that might be called basic (biological) human nature
    b. humans are inherently social
    c. any apparently selfish act of humans is a result of culture and works against basic human nature
    d. humans are basically aggressive
    e. none of the above

Answer Key for Self Test

1.	e pp. 405–8	17.	b pp. 417–20
2.	e p. 407	18.	e p. 423
3.	c p. 407	19.	c p. 422
4.	d p. 408	20.	a p. 424
5.	b p. 408	21.	a pp. 424–25
6.	c pp. 411–12	22.	c pp. 427–28
7.	d p. 412	23.	e p. 429
8.	b p. 412	24.	d p. 430
9.	e pp. 412–14	25.	d pp. 430–32
10.	c pp. 414–15	26.	d pp. 431–32
11.	d pp. 416–17	27.	a pp. 433–34
12.	d p. 418	28.	e pp. 433–34
13.	c pp. 417–19	29.	d pp. 433–34
14.	a pp. 419–20	30.	e pp. 435–36
15.	d p. 420	31.	a p. 437
16.	c pp. 420–21		

Investigating Psychological Phenomena

PERSONAL SPACE: BEHAVIOR IN ELEVATORS

Equipment: A bank of at least two public elevators
Number of participants: None
Time per participant: None
Time for experimenter: Thirty minutes to one hour

Whatever one's view of the precise way in which the basic phenomena of territoriality in animals are experienced in humans, it is clear that humans prefer to avoid close contact with strangers. Strangers interact at respectable distances, and one typically feels uncomfortable when a stranger approaches to within much less than a meter. Observations of this sort lead to the notion of personal space, a "territory" around the body. The distance spacing of students seated at libraries or riders on public transportation speaks to the same issue.

In this study we will attempt to gather direct evidence for the idea of personal space. To do so, we must find a common situation in which strangers find themselves in close confinement. Elevators seem particularly suited for this study.

Our study will be based on observations of where people stand in elevators. Given that an elevator already requires that all riders stand in close proximity, a personal space approach would certainly predict that *strangers* would maximize the distance between them. In order to test this idea, we will have to make some decisions about where, when, and how to make observations. (Although it would seem easy to just go and observe people in elevators, to do so without some thought, planning, and preliminary casual observation, would almost surely result in unreliable and not very meaningful data.)

What are the predictions? We must realize that elevators are typically asymmetrical: There is a door on one wall, and there is usually a button panel on one or both sides of the door. When people enter, they normally go to the panel to see if their floor has been pressed. Since it is likely that each person who gets on will go to the panel, it would be natural to maximize the distance from the panel in anticipation of the arrival of the next person. A personal space approach would also predict that strangers would not look at each other, but rather would tend to look straight ahead (toward the door) or up or down. On the basis of personal space, we would make the following predictions with respect to the positions in the schematic elevator diagrammed below.

1. In elevators with only one rider, the rider would usually stand along the back wall. In anticipation of a second rider, the first rider would be expected to stand in one back corner, thus leaving the other back corner for the second rider (and keeping both away from the button panels, which an additional rider would approach on entering). In terms of the schematic elevator layouts on the next page, a single person should be located either in Square 7 or Square 9.

2. The second rider would be inclined to maximize distance from both the first rider and a potential third rider, who would be expected to approach the button panel(s) on entering the elevator. Therefore, in the schematic elevator layout below, two people should occupy Squares 7 and 9. (Note: Squares 7 and 6, 4 and 9, and 4 and 6 would also constitute reasonable distributions, but would not be as optimal as 7 and 9.)

Schematic elevator, divided into a 3 × 3 unit array. The door is at 2.

Conditions of Observation: The observer cannot be on the elevator, as he or she would then be influencing the results. Therefore, observations must be made when an elevator arrives or departs and the door is open. Since people are likely to be leaving or entering, quick observations will be necessary at a stable moment: just as the doors open or just as they close. (If you are lucky enough to be near an office or other building with video security monitors for the elevators in the lobby, you can use the monitors to record the positions of people between floors.)

Personal space rules would not necessarily hold among friends, and certainly not between lovers. Therefore, a fair test of personal space should eliminate any data including people who know each other well. To do this as best as possible, we will adopt two policies:

1. We will eliminate any observation (i.e., the data collected from any particular elevator at a particular time) if any two people in the elevator are talking to one another or showing personal involvement in any way (e.g., holding hands).
2. We will try to make observations at places and at times when the number of people knowing each other well would be minimal. Ideal locations would be elevators in department stores or office buildings. Time would also be an important factor. We should avoid taking observations around the noon hour. (Why? Because it is very common to go out to lunch with friends, so the level of friend pairs or groups in elevators might be particularly high. This holds as well for people returning from lunch.)

Finally, precise conditions of measurement must be determined. Only record stable patterns: No one should be moving. Your critical time for observation is the moment before the doors close (it is harder to use the moment they open, because it is likely that a passenger intending to exit has moved toward the door as the elevator comes to his or her floor). If, at the time of departure, the elevator contains one or two people who have settled into position and if they do not appear to be friends (by the criteria above) then record their location on the data sheet. Assign each person to whichever of the nine squares best locates him or her.

To minimize data collection time, try to find a bank of elevators (at least two), and try to go at a time of moderate use, so you won't have to deal with infrequent or empty elevators. But don't use the lunch period, as discussed above. Normally the first floor is the natural place to make observations, but if you have a great deal of trouble with participants moving in the elevator, you could go to another floor and push the call button, so that the elevator will stop on your floor. (The second floor would be best for these purposes. Why?)

Make sufficient observations so that you can get fifteen cases of elevators with one rider and fifteen of elevators with two riders. Indicate on the two data sheets the plan of the elevator, its location, and the time of day. Record one-person elevators on one data sheet and two-person elevators on the other.

When you have fifteen observations of each type, enter your data in the boxes in the table below. Do your data support the personal space theory? In order to help you make this evaluation, we have given you an indication of what would be statistically significant findings.

For the one-person elevator, there are nine possible positions. The theory predicts that one of two positions (7 or 9) will be occupied. If people positioned themselves randomly in the elevator, we would expect them to be at 7 or 9 2/9 of the time, or for fifteen cases, $2/9 \times 15 = 3.3$ times (see table). By statistical calculations, we have determined that if there was actually an equal chance of someone's standing in any square, the chances of finding nine or more participants out of fifteen in Squares 7 or 9 is less than one in 100. This seems highly unlikely, so we would reject the idea that people stand randomly in the elevator and claim that the results supported the personal space hypothesis. These calculations are worked out in the table.

For the case of two people in the elevator, we have made similar calculations. It turns out that there are thirty-six different pairs of spaces that could be occupied in our 9-square elevator. The 7-9 combination is just one of them, and hence, if people were standing in random positions, there would only be one case in thirty-six where the 7-9 position was occupied. Therefore, the expected number of 7-9 locations in fifteen trials would be $15 \times 1/36 = 0.4$. A value of three or more people in this pair of locations would come about by chance less than one time in 100.

We can use one other measure with the two-person elevators. Personal space theory predicts, in general, that these people will stand far apart. We can translate this into the prediction that two people will not stand in boxes that are touching (even on the diagonal). Pairs 7-9, 4-6, 1-9 and others would meet this criterion, although, of the thirty-six pairs of locations, twenty are touching (contiguous). Thus, we would expect that (since there are sixteen nontouching pairs), in $16/36 \times 15$ cases, we would expect people in nontouching pairs, assuming that people distributed themselves randomly. A score of twelve or more pairs in nontouching squares would come about less than one time in 100 by chance and would be evidence for the personal space hypothesis. (See calculations in table below.)

For comparison purposes, we have made measurements like those we asked you to make in this study. We took advantage of a special situation that allows unusually easy data collection. The data we present comes from elevators in an office building in New York City. In this building, there is a video security camera in the ceiling of each elevator. Therefore, we could watch the bank of video monitors, and record the location of people. Furthermore, we could make the measurements between floors, so that there was no movement to or from the door. (*If your instructor collects the data, fill out the report sheet in Appendix 3.*)

Analysis of Results

Elevator type	Location prediction	# in predicted place/Total	Expected random #	# significant[*]
1 person	7 or 9	□/15	3.3	9
2 person	7 and 9	□/15	0.4	3
New York data				
1 person	7 or 9	28/57	12.7	20
2 person	7 and 9	15/32	0.9	5

		# in noncontiguous squares/Total	Expected random #	# significant[*]
2 person	16 noncontiguous pairs out of 36 total pairs	□/15	6.7	12
New York data				
2 person	16 noncontiguous pairs out of 36 total pairs	31/32	14.2	21

* # significant means that one would expect this or a larger number of cases by chance no more than one time in one hundred.

Indicate panel location and other unusual features on diagram below.

Name _____   Location _____

1 Person in Elevator   Time _____

1

2

3

4

5

6

7

8

9

10

11

12

13

14

15

Indicate panel location and other unusual features on diagram below.

Name _____   Location _____

2 Persons in Elevator   Time _____

FURTHER STUDIES

1. You can extend these observations. In elevators with a button panel on one side of the door, you can make the further predictions that: 1. the first person will stand in the back corner opposite to the panel; 2. in three-person elevators, the third person should stand in the front corner that does not have the button panel.

2. You can extend this study to elevators with three persons. In elevators with two-button panels, it is hard to make precise predictions about where people will stand (see item 1 above, for predictions in single-panel elevators). However, personal space theory would predict that people would stand as far apart as possible, so that they should not stand in contiguous squares. There are eighty-four possible arrangements of three people, assigned to three of the nine squares. Only nine of these eighty-four arrangements involve no person in a square contiguous to another (e.g., 1, 3, 9; 6, 1, 7; 1, 3, 8). Run another fifteen elevators, this time with three persons. How many have no one in a square contiguous with any other? We would predict, based on random location of people, $9/8 \times 4 \times 15 = 1.6$ cases of people in noncontiguous squares. A significant result (less than one time in 100, by chance) would be six or more cases out of fifteen with no one in contiguous squares.

3. You can make observations like the elevator observations in any place where strangers are in an enclosed area. Library tables or seats on vehicles of public transportation are natural places to see if distance between strangers are maximized.

4. What do you think would happen if the rules of personal space were purposely violated? How would the desire for privacy and isolation from strangers affect the behavior of the person violated? Also, do you think that the gender of the participants, in cases when there are two or more persons per elevator, would be influential in any way?

CHAPTER 11

Social Cognition and Emotion

Learning Objectives

1. Distinguish human from animal social behavior in terms of complexity, culture, and social cognition.

SOCIAL COGNITION AND SOCIAL REALITY

The interpersonal nature of belief
2. What is social cognition?
3. Describe Asch's experiment on the social basis of physical "reality," and indicate why research participants become upset in this study.

Social comparison
4. What is social comparison, and how does it function in ambiguous situations?

Cognitive processes and belief
5. What is meant by cognitive consistency?
6. Explain cognitive dissonance and give an example.

ATTITUDES

7. Define attitudes and distinguish between attitudes and beliefs.

Attitudes and behavior
8. How good is the relation between attitudes and behavior? Indicate some factors that could explain discrepancies between attitudes and behavior.

Attitude change
9. What accounts for the effectiveness of persuasive communications? Review the role of the message source.
10. Describe the central and peripheral routes to persuasion, and indicate the role of heuristics.
11. Explain how aspects of cognitive dissonance, particularly bringing one's own behavior into line with one's attitudes, causes attitude change. Include justification of effort and forced compliance in the discussion.
12. Describe how protecting the self-picture can account for many instances of attitude change, and distinguish this motivation from cognitive consistency.

Attitude stability
13. What are the factors that account for the stability of most attitudes?

PERCEIVING OTHERS

Forming impressions
14. How is visual perception analogous to social perception?

Impressions of others as patterns
15. Describe Asch's experiments on impression formation.
16. What is a "central trait" and in what sense are people perceived as more than the sum of their attributes?
17. What are primacy effects in impression formation?

Impressions of others as cognitive constructions
18. What are the parallels between cognitive constructions of the physical and social worlds?
19. Indicate the roles of schemas and implicit theories of personality in social cognition and impression formation.
20. What are stereotypes, and what is the role of illusory correlation in maintaining inaccurate stereotypes?
21. Explain how in-group favoritism can account for why stereotypes are often derogatory.
22. Describe the outgroup homogeneity effect.

Impression management
23. Describe impression management, including self-handicapping, and indicate how it adds to the complexity of social perception.
24. What is embarrassment, and how might it relate to impression management?

ATTRIBUTION

Attribution as a rational process
25. Indicate the parallels between scientific thinking and the attribution process.
26. What are situational dispositional factors in the attribution process?

Errors in the attribution process
27. Evaluate the roles of situational and dispositional factors in judgments about other people. What is the fundamental attribution error?
28. What is the actor-observer difference?
29. Why are people more inclined to make situational attributions about their own behavior, as opposed to the behavior of others (the actor-observer difference)? Indicate the role of different information and different perspectives.
30. What is the self-serving attributional bias?

31. What is the above-average effect and how does it relate to the self-serving attributional bias?
32. How can the self-serving attributional bias and the above-average effect be explained?

PERCEIVING ONESELF

The self-concept
33. Describe the factors that contribute to the developing perception of the self.

Self-perception and attribution
34. What is self-perception theory? What is the evidence for the influence of one's own behavior on one's attitudes?

CULTURE AND SOCIAL COGNITION

35. Describe the difference between individualist and collectivist cultures, and how cross-cultural studies might provide a different perspective on social cognition.

Conformity
36. What are the general results of Asch conformity studies when carried out on people from collectivist cultures?

Attribution about causes of behavior
37. How do people from collectivist cultures differ from those from individualist cultures on the balance between dispositional and situational attributions? What might cause this difference?

In-groups and out-groups
38. Under what circumstances are collectivists more influenced by in-groups? Discuss differences in in-group membership and involvement in in-groups.

Above-average effect
39. What might one predict about the above-average effect in collectivist cultures, and what are the results?
40. How does the recent work in cross-cultural psychology relate to the distribution of individual differences within a culture?
41. Discuss the issue of whether or not there are cultural universals in social cognition.

EMOTION

Emotional experience: interpretations of internal states
42. Describe the James-Lange theory of emotion and the major objections to it.

43. Describe the attribution-of-arousal theory of emotion. Contrast this theory with the James-Lange theory. What is the role of physiological state in each theory?
44. Discuss the misattribution of arousal in light of the attribution-of-arousal theory. How do results from excitation transfer effects support this theory?
45. Describe the evidence, from both animals and humans, indicating a special role for the amygdala in the integration of appraisal and arousal, particularly with respect to fear.

Emotional behavior: facial expressions
46. What is Darwin's universality thesis? What is the cross-cultural evidence for it, and what are some problems with the evidence?
47. Describe cultural display rules, and indicate how they relate to the universality thesis.
48. What is the facial feedback hypothesis and why is it difficult to test?
49. Describe the view that facial expressions are communicative displays, in addition to or instead of expressions of an inner state. What is the evidence for this position, including audience effects, and what are some problems with this view?

Are there basic, universal emotions?
50. Explain the idea of basic emotions, and the criteria that have been suggested for distinguishing them. Indicate the problems with the idea of basic emotions.

Complex emotions
51. Indicate the role of attributions of controllability and moral issues in the experience of anger, guilt, and pity.
52. What is regret, and how does the ease of reconstructing a scenario that would have avoided a negative event help to explain the circumstances that elicit regret?

Culture and emotion
53. Discuss cultural differences in emotion lexicons, and the problem of determining whether people in different cultures experience different emotions.

Emotion and the theater
54. Discuss the experience of emotion in the theater, and the idea of "as if" emotions.

TAKING STOCK

55. Evaluate the contribution of motivational (passion) and cognitive (reason) factors in social cognition and emotion.

Programmed Exercises

1. Human social behavior is more _____ than animal social behavior, and includes a major influence from _____.

   complex (flexible)
   culture

SOCIAL COGNITION AND SOCIAL REALITY

2. The way we try to interpret and understand social events, that is, _____ _____, is like the way we comprehend nonsocial events.

   social cognition

3. In Asch's experiment on judging line length, participants become disturbed because the behavior of the confederates challenges their shared sense of _____ _____.

   physical reality

4. When people have to make difficult judgments, they often seek the opinion of others, demonstrating the need for _____ _____.

   social comparison

5. _____ _____ refers to people's tendency to resolve contradictions between their attitudes and beliefs.

Cognitive consistency

6. The perception by a person of inconsistency in beliefs, feelings, or behavior sets up an unpleasant internal state called _____ _____.

cognitive dissonance

ATTITUDES

7. An _____ is a rather stable, evaluative mental position held toward some idea or object or person.

attitude

8. Unlike beliefs, attitudes are _____.

evaluative (or emotionally tinged)

9. Situational pressures are one factor that explain why attitudes measured by _____-_____ often do not predict _____.

self-report (questionnaire), behavior

10. _____ as opposed to _____ attitudes are better predictors of behavior.

Specific, general

11. Messages that openly try to convince us of something, called _____ communications, are more effective if they come from a _____ and _____ source.

persuasive
credible, trustworthy

12. There may be two routes to persuasion. One, the _____ route to persuasion, involves careful consideration of arguments. The other, the _____ route to persuasion, demands less attention and makes use of shortcuts, or _____.

central
peripheral
heuristics

13. According to _____ _____ theory, a goal will be valued all the higher, the harder it was to reach.

cognitive dissonance

14. Attitudes toward a goal often become more positive after a person makes sacrifices to attain the goal. This is called retrospective _____ of _____.

justification, effort

15. If people behave inconsistently with their beliefs under _____ _____, they are unlikely to change their beliefs or attitudes.

forced compliance

16. An alternative to cognitive consistency as an explanation of attitude change involves more emotional or evaluative factors, and is described as protecting the _____ - _____.

self-picture

17. Although attitudes can change, cognitive consistency and the constancy of one's personal environment tend to produce attitude _____.

stability

PERCEIVING OTHERS

18. In both object and person perception, the observer extracts certain _____ from the flow of events.

consistencies (invariances)

19. According to Asch, both form perception and person perception result from combinations of attributes into _____ wholes.

organized

20. Asch's experiments on impressions of others showed that certain attributes had an organizing effect on the integration of other attributes. Such "organizing" attributes were called _____ _____.

central traits

21. The special importance of the first information we receive about a person in forming an impression of him or her is called the _____ _____.

primacy effect

22. Impressions of others can be seen as patterns, based on the relations among elements. One basis for this process is a set of organized expectations about the way in which different behaviors of people hang together, called a _____ or an _____ _____ of personality.

schema, implicit theory

23. Simplified schemas applied to whole groups are called _____. Some inaccurate stereotypes are maintained by a tendency for people to see expected relations, even if these relations do not actually exist. This process is called _____ _____.

stereotypes

illusory correlation

24. As a result of _____-_____ favoritism, stereotypes of others are often derogatory.

in-group

25. The tendency to perceive groups other than one's own as more alike than members of one's own group is called the _____ _____ _____.

outgroup
homogeneity effect

26. Goffman holds that much human behavior is "putting up a front," that is, behaving in accordance with the expectations for some role. This is called _____ _____.

impression management

27. One strategy for impression management is _____-_____, in which, anticipating a poor performance, a person arranges for an excuse in advance.   self-handicapping

28. _____ is an unpleasant feeling that may be related to a loss of public or self-esteem.   Embarrassment

29. Becoming embarrassed for another person, or _____ embarrassment, suggests that embarrassment may involve _____ of a social interaction that no one knows how to repair.   empathic

disruption

ATTRIBUTION

30. _____ is a process through which people infer the causes of other people's behavior.   Attribution

31. Studies of attribution show that in judging others people tend to rely too much on internal causation, or _____ factors, as opposed to _____ factors in explaining behavior. This is called the _____ _____ _____.   dispositional, situational
fundamental attribution error

32. People are more likely to attribute their own (as opposed to others') behavior to situational factors. This is called the _____-_____ _____.   actor-observer difference

33. The tendency to make dispositional attributions for one's own success, and situational attributions for one's own failures, is called the _____-_____ _____ bias.   self-serving attributional

34. The tendency to overrate the self in terms of ability compared to others is called the _____-_____ effect.   above-average

35. One account of this bias is that it is a form of face-saving , or _____ _____.   impression management

PERCEIVING ONESELF

36. Bem and some other cognitive social psychologists believe that conceptions of the self are built up from attribution processes of the same type used in forming conceptions of other people. This position is called _____-_____ _____.   self-perception theory

37. According to this theory, _____ determines attitudes, rather than the other way around.   behavior

38. The "_____-_____-_____-_____" technique is an example of how behavior can lead to attitude change.   foot-in-the-door

CULTURE AND SOCIAL COGNITION

39. In _____ cultures or ethnic groups, the emphasis is on interdependence, and there is a focus on the group.   collectivist

40. In _____ cultures or ethnic groups, the emphasis is on independence, and the self is seen as the central focus.   individualist

41. In general, it is the cultures of _____ or_____ that are more collectivist.   Asia, Africa

42. When Asch conformity studies are carried out with people from collectivist cultures, they show less_____ than do people from individualist cultures.   distress

43. People from collectivist cultures are more likely to explain an individual's actions with _____ attributions than are people from individualist cultures.   situational (external)

44. Individualists tend to have (be members in) more_____-_____, but to be less committed to them than are collectivists.   in-groups

45. Generally, collectivists seem to conform more than individualists to their _____-_____, and are less influenced by _____-_____.   in-groups
out-groups

46. While individuals in individualistic cultures seem to enhance their self-esteem, as shown in the _____-_____ effect, this does not occur for individuals in collectivist cultures.   above-average

EMOTION

47. According to the _____-_____ theory, the subjective experience of emotion results from our awareness of bodily changes in the presence of certain stimuli.

    James-Lange

48. According to Schachter and Singer's _____-_____-_____ theory of emotion, emotion depends on the interpretation of autonomic _____ by an individual, in light of the total situation.

    attribution-of-arousal
    arousal

49. According to attribution-of-arousal theory, when a person believes that arousal actually caused by one factor (e.g., exercise, an arousing drug) is caused by another (e.g., sexual excitation), this is an example of _____ of arousal

    misattribution

50. A part of the brain that is involved in important ways with the integration of appraisal and arousal is the_____. It seems to play a particularly important role in the emotion of _____.

    amygdala, fear

51. In _____ _____ _____ disorder, sometimes called *temporal lobe epilepsy*, overactivity in the amygdala leads to the attachment of inappropriate emotional significance to objects or events.

    complex partial seizure

52. According to Darwin's _____ _____, at least some aspects of emotional facial expressions are present in all humans.

    universality thesis

53. Learned and deeply ingrained conventions that govern what facial expressions should be displayed or suppressed in different situations are called _____ _____ _____.

    cultural display rules

54. According to the _____ _____ hypothesis, one's own facial expressions contribute to the experience and/or appraisal of emotions.

    facial feedback

55. According to the _____ _____ view of facial expressions, they are primarily social signals indicating actions that the displayer is about to take, or actions that the displayer is calling for in others.

    communicative display

56. Evidence for the communicative display view comes form the fact that facial expressions are more common in social situations, called the _____ _____.

    audience effect

57. According to some investigators, such as Ekman, there are certain fundamental emotions, called _____ _____. These can be identified because of universal _____ expressions, specific_____ circuitry devoted to them, or the fact that they cannot be decomposed into other _____.

    basis emotions, facial
    neural
    emotions

58. Whether one experiences pity, guilt, or anger depends in part on whether one thinks the behavior in question was _____.

    controllable

59. The experience of anger and guilt may be related to _____ factors.

    moral

60. _____ is the emotion of the might-have-been.

    Regret

61. The tendency to feel regret is _____ in near-miss situations, as a result of a tendency to replay such situations.

    greater

62. Cultures differ in the words they use to describe emotions. These are called _____ _____.

    emotion
    lexicons

63. We cannot be certain whether differences in the words used to describe emotions mean that different emotions are _____.

    experienced

64. The esthetic flavor and emotional responses produced in a theater audience depend on the creation of an "_____ _____" emotion. This, in turn, depends on a delicate balance between _____ and _____.

    as if
    belief, disbelief

Self Test

1. Primate and human social behavior have in common:
   a. displays
   b. a role for social cognition
   c. some type of territorial defense
   d. all of the above
   e. a and c

2. In Asch's experiment on the effect of social pressure on judgments of noticeably different line lengths, he found that:
   a. many participants yielded to social pressure, but their perception of line length did not necessarily change
   b. the actual perceptions of line length were changed in the participant
   c. the perceptions of line length were changed in the confederates
   d. the shared sense of physical reality can affect perception
   e. a and b

3. Indicate which of the following statements about social comparison is *false*:
   a. Social comparison is more likely to occur when someone is faced with a difficult decision.
   b. Social comparison is more likely to occur in a situation in which there is some ambiguity.
   c. Social comparison is more likely to occur when people feel they need more information.
   d. Social comparison is more likely to occur when the decision involves social issues.
   e. none of the above are false

4. Fred supports the cause of the As, in their war against the Bs. He then sees on television that the As are killing innocent children. He decides that the As must be being forced to do this by the Bs and that the As have no choice. This type of thinking in Fred is an example of:
   a. social comparison
   b. stimulus-response association
   c. resolution of cognitive dissonance
   d. reference to comparison groups to change attitudes
   e. all of the above

5. Sandy maintains that French food is good and Canadian food is bad. These views represent:
   a. attitudes
   b. beliefs
   c. cognitive consistency
   d. cognitive dissonance
   e. actions

6. Attitudes are usually measured by:
   a. questionnaire
   b. observation of behavior
   c. experimental studies
   d. physiological measures
   e. a and c

7. Attitudes do not always predict behavior. This could be because:
   a. attitudes, as measured, are often very general, and behavior deals with specific situations
   b. attitudes are evaluative and behavior is not

   c. specific aspects of situations may prevent attitudes from being expressed
   d. behavior is not affected by cognitive consistency or cognitive dissonance
   e. a and c

8. Someone using the peripheral route to persuasion is likely to:
   a. have cognitive dissonance
   b. use heuristics
   c. show more cognitive consistency
   d. have fewer attitudes
   e. pay special attention to events in the periphery

9. According to cognitive dissonance theory, which of the following would be the best way to cause people to change attitudes?
   a. pay them a lot to make them believe they hold the new attitude
   b. force them to behave as if they support the new attitude for at least a few weeks
   c. tell them that they will be prejudiced of they continue with their current attitude
   d. show them that their current attitude is inconsistent with their actual behavior
   e. urge them to consult with an appropriate social comparison group

10. The accompanying graph illustrates the relation between:
    a. attitudes and beliefs
    b. cognitive dissonance and forced compliance
    c. cognitive dissonance and cognitive consistency
    d. social comparison and ambiguity
    e. cognitive dissonance and beliefs

11. After working as a volunteer for a political candidate for a month, Jonathan finds that his support for the candidate has increased, even though he has never met her. This is an instance of:
    a. forced compliance
    b. justification of effort
    c. persuasive communications
    d. a and b
    e. all of the above

12. Which of the following techniques is *not* considered an effective way to produce a positive change in attitude toward a message?
    a. use of a credible and trustworthy source
    b. use of a message that is regarded favorably by a social comparison group

    c. openly forcing a person to behave in a way that supports the message

    d. linking the message to past behavior by the person that supports the message

    e. c and d

13. An alternative to the view that attitude change results from attempts to create logical consistency invokes emotional factors that motivate creation of:

    a. cognitive consistency

    b. a favorable self-picture

    c. retrospective reevaluation

    d. justification of effort

    e. postdecision dissonance

14. Which of the following is involved both in maintaining stable attitudes and in attitude change?

    a. attitude questionnaires

    b. forced compliance

    c. cognitive consistency

    d. striking and unexpected events

    e. changing reference groups

15. Perception of objects and people have in common the fact that:

    a. both rely almost exclusively on vision

    b. both involve the construction of stable or invariant characteristics

    c. both are fixed in their nature by first impressions

    d. both involve the resolution of cognitive dissonance between the object (or person) and its perception

    e. none of the above

16. After a few encounters, Susan decided that Gary was stupid. She maintained this impression even after she discovered that he got the highest grade on a physical chemistry examination, and assumed that he cheated. Susan's behavior is an example of:

    a. resolution of cognitive dissonance

    b. forced compliance

    c. the primacy effect

    d. a and c

    e. all of the above

17. Stereotypes:

    a. are always inaccurate

    b. may be distorted because of illusory correlation

    c. are not like heuristics, because they lead to incorrect conclusions

    d. may be accurate

    e. b and d

18. Which of the following could explain the outgroup homogeneity effect?

    a. people have more information about their in-group

    b. out-groups actually are more homogeneous

    c. people usually value consistency

    d. a and c

    e. b and c

19. There are parallels between nonsocial and social cognitions. Which of the following processes does *not* appear in both types of situations?

    a. impression management

    b. illusory correlation

    c. use of heuristics

    d. use of schemas

    e. attempts to simplify complex situations

20. A senior lawyer tells a novice lawyer: "It is important to convey to your client on the first meeting that you are extremely experienced and well informed as to the law in the area of the client's problem." This advice illustrates:

    a. stereotypes

    b. the primacy effect

    c. impression management

    d. illusory correlation

    e. b and c

21. Having become bored with the guests at a dinner party, Kermit excuses himself by saying that he has to get up very early the next morning (which is not true) to take a trip out of town. According to Goffman's analysis, this performance can be explained as:

    a. an example of Kermit's theatrical sense

    b. an example of attitude formation

    c. an attempt to leave without seeming rude and without insulting the guests

    d. an attempt to alter the social perception of the audience by providing them with an ambiguous social stimulus

    e. a stereotype

22. In a high school classroom, a teacher selects a student at random and asks her a difficult question. She confidently gives the correct answer but feels embarrassed. This episode is *most* consistent with:

    a. the loss of public esteem theory of embarrassment

    b. the disrupted and irreparable social interaction view of embarrassment

    c. the idea that embarrassment results when attention is called to the self

    d. a and b

    e. b and c

23. The decision by a person that another person's behavior was internally caused (e.g., as a result of his or her aggressive nature) is an example of:

    a. impression management

    b. illusory correlation

    c. stereotypes

    d. attribution

    e. situational factors

24. People have a tendency to believe that actors in the theater are really like the roles that they play. This is an example of:

    a. the resolution of cognitive dissonance

    b. the dominance of dispositional over situational factors in attribution

    c. the primacy effect in impressions

    d. the distinction between the bodily self and the social self

    e. the interaction of social and biological factors in the determination of behavior

25. The actor-observer difference describes the fact that people are *less* likely to make _____ attributions about themselves than others.

a. dispositional
b. correct
c. cognitively consistent
d. situational
e. c and d

26. Explanations of the actor-observer difference include the fact that:
    a. people know themselves better than they know others
    b. people cannot literally see themselves in social situations
    c. attribution theory only applies to judging other people
    d. a and b
    e. all of the above

27. The self-serving attributional bias is designed to explain:
    a. the fundamental attribution error
    b. the actor-observer difference
    c. the greater inclination to make dispositional attributions about the self in cases of success
    d. a and b
    e. all of the above

28. The above-average effect is to self-serving attributional bias as:
    a. behavior is to attitudes
    b. cognitive dissonance is to cognitive consistency
    c. horse is to rider
    d. fundamental attribution error is to actor-observer difference
    e. reality is to social comparison

29. According to self-perception theory:
    a. one's own behavior can influence one's attitudes
    b. cognitive dissonance is a self-fulfilling prophecy
    c. social roles determine behavior
    d. social factors are not involved in the concept of the self
    e. attitudes are formed more or less independent of behavior

30. Which of the following illustrates how one's feelings or beliefs may be the result of one's actions?
    a. the "foot-in-the-door" technique
    b. impression management
    c. the primacy effect
    d. the need for comparison groups
    e. none of the above

31. From what we know about collectivist versus individualistic cultures, we might expect individuals from collectivist cultures to be lower in:
    a. in-group aggression
    b. out-group aggression
    c. parenting
    d. impression management
    e. situational attributions

32. Individualism is to collectivism as:
    a. in-group is to out-group
    b. society is to culture
    c. independence is to interdependence
    d. autonomy is to community
    e. c and d

33. Americans, unlike Japanese, are reported to be more likely to enhance their self-picture. This tendency might be accounted for, at least in part, by:
    a. the smaller number of in-groups among the Japanese
    b. Japanese kinship patterns
    c. a greater tendency to conform among the Japanese
    d. a and c
    e. none of the above

34. Differences between individuals in individualist and collectivist cultures, in the area of social cognition, have been reported for all but which one of the following?
    a. the above-average effect
    b. primacy in impression formation
    c. the fundamental attribution error
    d. degree of conformity
    e. b and c

35. Suppose it was reported that 80 percent of Dutch people show the fundamental attribution error, and 55 percent of Hindu Indians do. This finding would:
    a. be evidence that there is no cultural difference on this characteristic, since both groups score above 50 percent
    b. suggest that increasing college education among Indians makes them more inclined to dispositional attributions
    c. support the argument for cultural difference in an aspect of attributions
    d. cast doubt about the existence of the fundamental attribution error
    e. by itself, be no evidence for anything

36. Bert, after a great deal of effort, convinces Sarah to go to a movie with him. Although Sarah finds Bert's company to be exactly what she expected, she ends up liking him more than she had anticipated. This could be explained in terms of:
    a. the James-Lange theory of emotion
    b. the principle of displacement
    c. either self-perception theory or cognitive dissonance
    d. the notion of emotion as an attribution process
    e. Bert's captivating, but subtle, personality

37. After running for a quarter mile, a person shows increased heart rate and various other signs of arousal but may not feel any strong emotion. This fact is particularly damaging to which of the following theories?
    a. the attribution-of-arousal theory
    b. the James-Lange theory
    c. Cannon's idea that subjective emotion leads to physiological responses
    d. a and b
    e. all of the above

38. An experiment has shown that participants alter their ratings of the attractiveness of nude photos in response to feedback about the increase or decrease of their heart rate. This result can be taken to support:
    a. the attribution-of-arousal theory of emotion
    b. the James-Lange theory

c. Cannon's theory (subjective emotion leads to the physiological responses, but the latter do not cause the former)
d. a and b
e. all of the above

39. Evidence implicating the amygdala in the experience and integration of emotion comes from:
a. animal studies of fear acquisition in animals with amygdala damage
b. effects of seizures in the amygdala in humans
c. misattribution of emotion in humans with amygdala damage
d. a and c
e. all of the above

40. The existence of cultural display rules presents serious problems for:
a. the facial feedback position
b. the communicative display view
c. the attribution-of-arousal theory
d. the idea of impression management
e. none of the above

41. Which of the following is a problem for the universality thesis?
a. There have been few studies of recognition of emotion in different cultures.
b. Facial feedback may influence the experience of emotion.
c. There are no current cultures that have absolutely no exposure to western culture.
d. There have been no cross-cultural studies of spontaneous expressions of emotion.
e. c and d

42. Facial expressions can be considered as primarily communicative displays. Audience effects are used as evidence for this position. Consider the following statements, and then indicate which of the combination of alternatives represents both a criticism of the audience effect evidence, and a counter to that criticism.
   i. Facial expressions are made when people are unobserved.
   ii. An audience of only one observer is sufficient to induce more facial expressions.
   iii. Facial expressions increase when a person is alone but imagines the presence of another.
   iv. Facial expressions are distinctive only for basic emotions.

a. ii, iv
b. i, iii
c. i, ii
d. iii, ii
e. none of the above

43. People in obviously emotional situations are often not expressive. This observation causes problems for the _____ view of emotions, but can be accounted for in terms of _____.
a. communicative display, cultural display rules
b. communicative display, basic emotions
c. facial feedback, cultural display rules

d. James-Lange theory, facial feedback
e. basic emotions, communicative displays

44. Suppose an investigator claims that disgust is a "basic emotion." Which of the following would be evidence for this claim?
a. Disgust has a characteristic, universal facial expression.
b. Disgust is specifically interfered with by certain types of brian lesions.
c. Disgust cannot be decomposed into a combination of other emotions.
d. a and c
e. all of the above

45. Anger and guilt share:
a. the same facial expression
b. a basis in transgression
c. a moral component
d. a sense of near-miss
e. the fact that both evoke pity

46. Regret is enhanced by:
a. near-miss situations
b. a tendency to replay experiences
c. feelings of pity
d. its own unique facial expression
e. a and b

47. Regret and guilt differ from anger and disgust in that regret and guilt:
a. are uniquely human
b. are complex emotions
c. do not have a unique facial expression
d. a and b
e. all of the above

48. Rather unique emotion words, such as *amae* in Japanese or *Schadenfreude* in German, show that:
a. there are actually different emotions in different cultures
b. cultures have different emotion lexicons
c. only basic emotions are constant across cultures
d. there cannot be basic emotions
e. b and d

49. Consider the reasonable finding (probably true, but not yet demonstrated) that the most satisfactory emotional experience in a theater audience is mostly likely to occur in people sitting a moderate distance from the stage. According to the "as if" interpretation in the text, this would be because at this distance there is an ideal balance between:
a. autonomic and somatic arousal
b. distance and closeness
c. belief and disbelief
d. as and if
e. attribution and physiological response

50. Forced compliance, interpretation of emotions, and the self-serving bias all share:
a. cognitive interpretations
b. motivational interpretations
c. an involvement with attitude change
d. a and b
e. a and c

Answer Key for Self Test

1.	d p. 441	26.	d pp. 462–63
2.	a pp. 442–43	27.	c pp. 463–64
3.	e pp. 444–45	28.	b pp. 450–51, 463–64
4.	c pp. 444–45	29.	a p. 466
5.	a pp. 446–47	30.	a pp. 466–67
6.	a p. 447	31.	a pp. 467–69
7.	e pp. 447–48	32.	e pp. 467–68
8.	b p. 449	33.	c pp. 468–70
9.	d pp. 450–51	34.	b pp. 467–70
10.	b pp. 450–51	35.	c pp. 467–70
11.	b p. 450	36.	c pp. 466, 471–73
12.	c pp. 448–51	37.	b pp. 471–73
13.	b p. 451	38.	d pp. 471–74
14.	c pp. 451–52	39.	e pp. 475–76
15.	b p. 453	40.	e pp. 476–80
16.	d pp. 450, 454	41.	e pp. 477–79
17.	e pp. 455–56	42.	b pp. 478–79
18.	a p. 457	43.	a pp. 479–80
19.	a pp. 457–58	44.	e pp. 480–81
20.	e pp. 454, 458	45.	c p. 482
21.	c p. 458	46.	e pp. 482–83
22.	c pp. 458–59	47.	e pp. 481–84
23.	d pp. 459–60	48.	b pp. 484–85
24.	b p. 460	49.	c pp. 485–87
25.	a p. 462	50.	d p. 487

Investigating Psychological Phenomena

PERSON PERCEPTION: THE EFFECT OF CONTEXT OR SET ON FIRST IMPRESSIONS

Equipment: Paper and pencil, a stopwatch or a watch that indicates seconds
Number of participants: At least eight
Time per participant: Five minutes
Time for experimenter: Forty minutes

Social perception bears many analogies to more traditional areas of perception (see pp. 453–54 in the text). In both cases, information is taken in selectively and put together into some organized percept. This aspect of person perception was illustrated in the text with special reference to the classic studies of Solomon Asch. Asch's work argued for an organizational basis for impression formation. This approach is in keeping with the position of Gestalt psychology. In Asch's view, impressions were not formed by "summing" different items of information about a

particular person. One particular aspect of the active process of impression formation is the effect of set. One is constantly forming impressions of people. New information on any person is integrated with an already existing impression: the new information will be interpreted to be as consistent as possible with the existing impression. Under the circumstances, one would expect that the first information one gets about a person would be especially important, since it might color what comes in later. Therefore, an organizational view would predict that the *order* of items of information about a person would affect the resulting impression, whereas a simple *summation* hypothesis would not matter.

Asch tested his hypothesis in a very simple manner: He gave college students a list of six adjectives that ostensibly described someone and recorded the impressions that they subsequently formed of this imaginary person. By manipulating the types of adjectives used and the order of their presentation, Asch attempted to produce systematic changes in the elicited impression formations. We will repeat his experiment on word order in precisely the same way that it was performed by Asch.

Try to get at least eight (student) participants. It might be useful for you to team up with a few friends from the course and run up to twenty participants, so that your results might be more meaningful. Participants must be divided into two groups. You can run as many participants as you want at the same time, so long as they are all from the same group. Since this experiment will compare the results of participants from one group with the results from another group, it is important that the two groups be similar in general characteristics. For example, keep the percentage of females the same in both groups, and try not to run a group of friends together, since they may share many similar characteristics. If you run one participant at a time, simply assign the first participant to Group A, the second to Group B, and so on. This should give you a random and "unbiased" sample.

The list for Group A	The list for Group B
intelligent	envious
industrious	stubborn
impulsive	critical
critical	impulsive
stubborn	industrious
envious	intelligent

Note that the adjectives in Group B are in the reverse order of Group A. This arrangement is designed to enhance any effect of order, by putting adjectives that would lead to quite different impressions on opposite ends of the adjective list.

Participants should be seated comfortably, and should have in front of them a blank piece of paper and a pencil. Make sure to put the group letter (A or B) on the paper and on the checklist. The experimenter reads the following instructions:

> I shall read you a number of characteristics that belong to a particular person. Please listen to them carefully and try to form an impression of the kind of person described. You will later be asked to give a brief characterization of the person in just a few sentences. I will read the list slowly and will repeat it once.

Read the list of six adjectives out loud in a steady voice, with an interval of five seconds between terms. Then say:

> I will now read the list again.

(Repeat the reading of the list)

> Now please write a brief characterization of this person.

(Participant writes)

Finally, tell the participants while handing them the checklist (see pages 143 and 145);

> Here is a list of pairs of adjectives. For each pair, please circle the adjectives that better characterizes the person we have been describing.

After the participant has completed this task, he or she is finished.

NOTES ON PROCEDURE

In setting up any experiment, many decisions must be made. Here, these include selecting the adjectives for the list, and for the checklist, deciding on the number of adjectives in the list, and so on. In most cases there are specific reasons for making these decisions. In this experiment, for example, ask yourself:
1. Why does the experimenter read the list instead of allowing the participant to read the list?
2. Why is the participant asked to write an impression before seeing the checklist rather than after filling out the checklist?

RESULTS

You should end up with eight or more written sketches and eight or more marked checklists. About half should be in each group. There is no simple way to score the written impressions. Read them over and try to summarize the impressions written by the two groups (the procedure used by Asch). You could also give the written impressions to another person and ask that person to sort them into piles, about equal in size. One pile would be for the more desirable impressions (persons) and the other for the less desirable ones. See if the impressions based on the adjective list with more desirable traits first are usually classified as more desirable. (It would be a good idea to fold back the part of the impressions paper with the group letter on it before reading and analyzing the character summaries.)

It is easier to analyze the data from the checklists. Simply record the percent of participants who selected the more favorable adjective of each pair for each group. This is the procedure used by Asch. His results, based on twenty-four student participants in Group A and thirty-four in Group B, are presented in the accompanying table. Record your data in the columns next to his data. Compare your results with his. If we take a difference of 20 percentage points as worthy of note, he reported big differences, in favor of Group A, on happy, humorous, sociable, popular, good-looking, and restrained.

(You can increase the significance of your data by combining it with data from a few friends in the class, so that you would have 20 or more participants in each group.)

Based on your results, what is the conclusion about the validity of the organization (set, Gestalt) versus simple summation explanations of impression formation?

Try to explain why some particular adjectives show clear effects and others do not. Obviously, in real life people form impressions from interactions with other people or by hearing about them from other people. To what extent do you think that Asch's procedure gives an indication of how people actually form impressions? The hallmark of a good experiment is that it simplifies a situation but still preserves its essential features. Is that true of this experiment?

FURTHER STUDY

You can use Asch's technique to address other questions. You can change specific adjectives on the list. You can use brief statements about a person's *behavior* (e.g., John consistently drives over the speed limit; John is always on time, etc.), rather than general characteristics. You can see which types of adjectives cause a participant to guess that a person is male or female. There are many possibilities, should this problem interest you. Some of the possibilities that you will come up with may never have been investigated.

Reference

Asch, S. E. 1946. Forming impressions of personality. *Journal of Abnormal and Social Psychology* 41:258–90.

Percent of participants checking favorable adjective at left

| | Asch's data | | Your data | |
| | Group A | Group B | Group A | Group B |
Adjective pair	(24 students)	(34 students)	(__ students)	(__ students)
generous	24	10		
wise	18	17		
happy	32	5		
good-natured	18	0		
humorous	52	21		
sociable	56	27		
popular	35	14		
reliable	84	91		
good-looking	74	35		
serious	97	100		
restrained	64	9		
honest	80	79		

CHECKLISTS

There are eight checklists on the next two pages. Cut one out for each participant. (Asch used eighteen adjective pairs. We use twelve of these pairs.)

Circle the most relevant adjective:

generous–ungenerous

shrewd–wise

unhappy–happy

irritable–good-natured

humorous–humorless

sociable–unsociable

popular–unpopular

unreliable–reliable

good-looking–unattractive

frivolous–serious

restrained–talkative

dishonest–honest

Group _____

Circle the most relevant adjective:

generous–ungenerous

shrewd–wise

unhappy–happy

irritable–good-natured

humorous–humorless

sociable–unsociable

popular–unpopular

unreliable–reliable

good-looking–unattractive

frivolous–serious

restrained–talkative

dishonest–honest

Group _____

-------------------------------------- *Cut here* --------------------------------------

Circle the most relevant adjective:

generous–ungenerous

shrewd–wise

unhappy–happy

irritable–good-natured

humorous–humorless

sociable–unsociable

popular–unpopular

unreliable–reliable

good-looking–unattractive

frivolous–serious

restrained–talkative

dishonest–honest

Group _____

Circle the most relevant adjective:

generous–ungenerous

shrewd–wise

unhappy–happy

irritable–good-natured

humorous–humorless

sociable–unsociable

popular–unpopular

unreliable–reliable

good-looking–unattractive

frivolous–serious

restrained–talkative

dishonest–honest

Group _____

Circle the most relevant adjective:

generous–ungenerous

shrewd–wise

unhappy–happy

irritable–good-natured

humorous–humorless

sociable–unsociable

popular–unpopular

unreliable–reliable

good-looking–unattractive

frivolous–serious

restrained–talkative

dishonest–honest

Group _____

Circle the most relevant adjective:

generous–ungenerous

shrewd–wise

unhappy–happy

irritable–good-natured

humorous–humorless

sociable–unsociable

popular–unpopular

unreliable–reliable

good-looking–unattractive

frivolous–serious

restrained–talkative

dishonest–honest

Group _____

--------------------------------------- *Cut here* ---

Circle the most relevant adjective:

generous–ungenerous

shrewd–wise

unhappy–happy

irritable–good-natured

humorous–humorless

sociable–unsociable

popular–unpopular

unreliable–reliable

good-looking–unattractive

frivolous–serious

restrained–talkative

dishonest–honest

Group _____

Circle the most relevant adjective:

generous–ungenerous

shrewd–wise

unhappy–happy

irritable–good-natured

humorous–humorless

sociable–unsociable

popular–unpopular

unreliable–reliable

good-looking–unattractive

frivolous–serious

restrained–talkative

dishonest–honest

Group _____

CHAPTER 12

Social Interaction

Learning Objectives

RELATING TO OTHERS: ONE-ON-ONE INTERACTIONS

Social exchange and reciprocity

1. What is social exchange? Over what range of social interaction might it operate?
2. Explain the reciprocity principle.
3. How is the reciprocity principle used in bargaining and persuasion? What are reciprocal concessions and what is the door-in-the-face technique?
4. Discuss self-disclosure in the context of reciprocity, and gender differences in self-disclosure.
5. Is reciprocity and social exchange in humans rooted biologically in similar phenomena in animals?

Altruism

6. Under what circumstances do people fail to help others in distress? Consider the role of ambiguity, pluralistic ignorance, and diffusion of responsibility.
7. What is the bystander effect?
8. Indicate the possible costs that someone who offers aid might incur.
9. In there any genuine altruism?

Attraction

10. Why is proximity a major determinant of attraction?
11. Review the evidence for similarity and physical attractiveness in attraction.
12. What is the evidence for the importance of physical attractiveness in attraction?
13. Describe the matching hypothesis.
14. Evaluate the roles of biological and cultural factors as determinants of sexual attractiveness.

Love

15. What are the three components that have been proposed to constitute love?
16. Describe the phenomenon of romantic love. What is the role of culture in defining it and establishing its importance?
17. Indicate how the cognitive arousal theory explains romantic love.
18. What factors affect the intensity of romantic love? Include a discussion of the Romeo-and-Juliet effect.

19. Distinguish romantic from companionate love.

SOCIAL INFLUENCE: MANY-ON-ONE INTERACTIONS

20. What is social influence?

Social facilitation: social influence by the presence of others

21. Define social facilitation. Indicate the conditions under which it occurs, and in particular, the role of arousal and facilitation of dominant responses.

Conformity

22. What is conformity? What is the role of cognitive and motivational factors in causing conformity?
23. What is the ally effect?
24. Under what conditions do minorities, whether of one person or of an organized group, successfully oppose the conformity influence of the majority?
25. How might minority influence differ from majority influence?

Blind obedience

26. What characterizes the authoritarian personality? What may cause it? How does the trait relate to prejudice against minorities?
27. Describe Milgram's basic study on obedience.
28. Discuss the importance of seeing oneself as another's agent. Relate this to the Nazi massacre of the Jews or other atrocities.
29. Discuss how dehumanization, psychological distance, and gradual escalation (slippery slope) influence blind obedience. Illustrate these influences with the example of the Milgram experiments.
30. Contrast personality factors with situational factors as causes of blind obedience.

Social impact theory

31. What is social impact theory? What environmental factors increase and decrease social impact?
32. Describe social loafing.

LEADERSHIP: ONE-ON-MANY INTERACTIONS

Great person or social forces

33. Compare situational and dispositional approaches to the determination of leadership.

Leadership in the laboratory

34. Illustrate how leadership has been studied in the laboratory. What personality and situational factors promote leadership?

CROWD BEHAVIOR: MANY-ON-MANY INTERACTIONS

The emphasis on the irrational: deindividuation

35. What is deindividuation? What is the evidence linking it to crowds? What is the role of group size and anonymity?

Cognitive factors and the panicky crowd

36. Describe the circumstances under which panic is likely to spread in a crowd.

37. What is the prisoner's dilemma? Provide examples of payoff matrices as illustrations.

38. Show how the prisoner's dilemma analysis can account for panic in crowds. How does it relate to the rationality-irrationality issue?

39. Discuss the prisoner's dilemma analysis of social dilemmas, such as air pollution, and indicate strategies that might produce more cooperation.

40. Evaluate the statement that "people become 'primitive' or irrational in crowds."

SOME FINAL COMMENTS

Common themes

41. Illustrate how the reason-passion and individual-situation contrasts enter into the accounts of many social phenomena.

The generality of social psychology

42. Evaluate the extent to which principles of social psychology discussed in this and the preceding chapter are general features of human nature, as opposed to principles specific to United States culture in the late twentieth century.

Programmed Exercises

RELATING TO OTHERS: ONE-ON-ONE INTERACTIONS

1. According to the principle of _____ _____, each partner in a relationship gives something to the other, and expects to receive something in return.

    social exchange

2. The notion that favors and gifts must be repaid is embodied in the _____ principle.

    reciprocity

3. An application of this principle is the _____-_____-_____-_____ technique, in which, after a major request is refused, a smaller request from the same source is more likely to be granted. This is based on the principle of _____ _____.

    door-in-the-face

    reciprocal concession

4. In the nonmaterial domain, _____-_____ is an example of reciprocity. At least in the United States, it is more common in _____.

    self-disclosure
    women (females)

5. Some believe reciprocity in humans derives directly from our animal ancestors, and thus is explained by _____ _____. Others account for it in terms of _____ evolution.

    biological evolution,
    cultural

6. Three factors that account for people's failure to help someone in distress are _____, _____ _____, and _____ _____ _____.

    ambiguity
    pluralistic ignorance,
    diffusion of responsibility

7. The larger the size of the group a person is in, the less likely he or she is to come to a victim's assistance. This is called the _____ _____.

    bystander effect

8. The costs of helping include loss of _____ and possible _____ _____.

    time, physical danger

9. Two people who have spent a fair amount of time in physical _____ to one another are more likely than not to become friends.

    proximity

10. In addition to proximity, two major factors that cause one to like another are _____ and _____ _____.

    similarity
    physical attractiveness

11. The strong tendency for people to marry other people very similar to themselves is called _____.

    homogamy

12. The personal characteristic that most influences initial liking for a person in American culture is _____ _____.

    physical attractiveness

13. The view that people select mates who are similar to them on many characteristics (such as physical attractiveness) is called the _____ _____.

    matching hypothesis

14. Although there may be some universal characteristics that lead to sexual attraction, to a large extent the criteria of sexual attractiveness vary in different _____.

    cultures

15. Three factors or components that have been proposed to account for love are _____, _____, and _____.

    intimacy
    passion, commitment

16. According to a cognitive arousal theory, romantic love involves a cultural _____ and a state of physiological, perhaps sexual _____.

context, arousal

17. Parental opposition tends to intensify romantic love. This is called the _____-_____- _____ effect.

Romeo-and-Juliet

18. Two contrasting types of love are a passionate type, or _____ love, and another type that emphasizes mutual trust, care, and sharing, called _____ love.

romantic companionate

SOCIAL INFLUENCE: MANY-ON-ONE INTERACTIONS

19. The study of the way an individual is affected by different social forces acting simultaneously is the study of _____ _____.

social influence

20. The improvement in performance in the presence of other members of one's species is called _____ _____.

social facilitation

21. According to Zajonc, social facilitation operates by producing _____, which strengthens the tendency to perform the _____ response.

arousal dominant

22. Going along with what other people think or do is called _____.

conformity

23. Conformity is more likely if the other persons involved are _____ in the position they take. A single other dissenter may reduce conformity considerably. This is called the _____ _____.

unanimous ally effect

24. A minority group is more likely to be successful in opposing the conformity induced by a majority, if the minority is _____ and _____.

unanimous, consistent (steadfast)

25. People who emphasize the importance of power, dominance, and obedience have been described as having an _____ personality.

authoritarian

26. According to some investigators, people who score high on minority prejudice and authoritarianism often have _____ fathers.

harsh (punitive, stern, all powerful)

27. In Milgram's first experiment on obedience, approximately _____ percent of participants shocked the learner up to the maximum amount.

65 (50–75 percent would be acceptable)

28. Milgram's experiments suggest that it is not necessary to have an _____ personality to exhibit blind obedience.

authoritarian

29. An important factor that causes people to perform acts that they might otherwise consider abhorrent is the feeling that they are another person's _____.

agent

30. Blind obedience is more likely when _____ _____ between the "participant" and the "victim" is increased.

psychological distance

31. The obedient person who causes pain to another person may treat that person as an object. This is called _____.

dehumanization

32. The cognitive reorientation required in producing obedience is best accomplished by a _____ _____ in obedience requirements. This is called the _____ _____.

gradual increase, slippery slope

33. According to _____ _____ theory, social influence can be explained in terms of a combination of the effects of a variety of social forces.

social impact

34. In _____ _____, individuals working as a group on a common task, all doing the same thing, generate less effort than they would if working alone.

social loafing

LEADERSHIP: ONE-ON-MANY INTERACTIONS

35. The most important one-on-many interaction is _____.

leadership

36. Leadership is associated with dispositional characteristics, such as _____ and _____.

(2 of) dominance, intelligence, sociability (extraversion, "outgoingness")

37. Situational factors that encourage leadership include _____ and _____.

(2 of) authority, clear-cut task, good interpersonal relations

38. Evidence suggests that part of leadership depends on dispositional characteristics, so that there is an effect for _____ _____ as well as social factors.

great persons

CROWD BEHAVIOR: MANY-ON-MANY INTERACTIONS

39. _____, a weakened sense of personal identity, disinhibits impulsive actions that are normally under restraint. It occurs more often in _____.

Deindividuation

crowds

40. _____ and _____ _____ _____ promote deindividuation.

Anonymity, large group size

41. The prisoner's dilemma presents an individual with a choice in a situation with mixed risks and benefits, described in a _____ _____.

payoff matrix

42. The prisoner's dilemma analysis is an attempt to explain the apparently _____ behavior of a crowd in terms of the _____ behavior of individuals.

irrational

rational

43. The prisoner's dilemma can be applied to problems of society, such as industrial pollution and other _____ dilemmas.

social

SOME FINAL COMMENTS

44. There are two common themes or "oppositions" that enter into the understanding of many social phenomena. They are _____-_____ and _____-_____.

reason-passion, individual (disposition)-situation

45. Some principles of social psychology described in this and the preceding chapter may be universal aspects of _____ _____, or they may be much more specific to this _____ and this _____.

human nature, culture

time

Self Test

1. The idea of social exchange is:
   a. tit-for-tat (exchange of favors)
   b. the money economy
   c. the slavery system
   d. forced compliance
   e. altruism

2. The relation between the foot-in-the-door and the door-in-the-face techniques is the same as the relation between:
   a. social exchange and the reciprocity principle
   b. altruism and sharing
   c. perception and memory
   d. gradual commitment and downside bargaining
   e. display and communication

3. Both gift-giving and self-disclosure:
   a. are altruistic
   b. encourage reciprocity
   c. encourage ambiguity
   d. are examples of the door-in-the-face technique
   e. a and d

4. The bystander effect is accounted for by:
   a. reciprocity
   b. diffusion of responsibility
   c. altruistic tendencies
   d. a and c
   e. all of the above

5. Diffusion of responsibility is:
   a. an example of social exchange
   b. an example of cost of intervention
   c. less if there are fewer observers
   d. b and c
   e. a and c

6. Which of the following is a possible basis for true altruism?
   a. the bystander effect
   b. hopes for reciprocal altruism
   c. empathy (sharing another's feelings)
   d. social exchange
   e. proximity

7. Proximity is an important factor in attraction. There is evidence that this relation results from the fact that:
   a. one must ordinarily meet someone in order to be attracted to him or her
   b. familiarity promotes attraction, and familiarity is increased by proximity
   c. proximity explains the matching hypothesis
   d. a and b
   e. all of the above

8. Mildred and Herb have been dating for years. Both are physically unattractive, and one acquaintance wonders what they see in each other. Which of the following factors could contribute to their mutual attractiveness?
   a. proximity
   b. similarity
   c. matching
   d. a and c
   e. all of the above

9. In a first impressions study, four groups of participants each hear a different list of adjectives describing a person. The lists are as follows: Group 1: trustworthy, sensitive, subtle, detached, stingy, envious

   Group 2: same as group 1, but in the opposite order

   Group 3: same as group 1, but with physically attractive added as the first adjective (making this a seven-adjective list)

   Group 4: same as group 2, but with physically attractive added at the end of the list

   Participants are then asked to rate how charming the person is. We would expect the participants in which group to give the highest charm rating?
   a. 1
   b. 2
   c. 3
   d. 4
   e. 3 and 4 equally

10. The prediction in Question 9 is based on:
    a. similarity
    b. the primacy effect
    c. the importance of physical attractiveness
    d. the matching hypothesis
    e. b and c

11. In a particular culture, relatively thin males tend to marry relatively plump females. According to the matching hypothesis, this implies that:
    a. relative thinness in males is as desired (attractive) as relative plumpness in females
    b. physical attractiveness is not important in this culture
    c. body shape is not important in this culture.
    d. the plumpness and thinness of relatives is important in this culture
    e. c and d

12. Romantic love:
    a. occurs only in certain cultures and at certain periods in history
    b. is intensified by parental approval
    c. can be completely explained in terms of sexual arousal
    d. differs from companionate love in that romantic love depends heavily on similarity
    e. c and d

13. Romantic love has been described as having three components: intimacy, passion, and commitment. In comparison, companionate love would differ most from romantic love in that it would have less of:
    a. intimacy
    b. passion
    c. commitment
    d. b and c
    e. a and c

14. Baseball Player A is a better hitter in batting practice than in actual games, while Player B shows the opposite pattern. We can say that:
    a. A shows social facilitation and B does not
    b. B shows social facilitation and A does not

    c. hitting optimally is more likely to be a dominant response for Player A
    d. hitting optimally is more likely to be a dominant response for Player B
    e. b and d

15. The situations that lead to conformity are similar to those that lead to failure to help a person in distress. Both conformity and failure to help others in distress are increased by all *except* which of the following?
    a. ambiguity in the situation
    b. a need for additional information
    c. presence of a large number of other people
    d. a desire to be liked by others
    e. a feeling of a lack of competence for the problem at hand

16. A single dissenter in a conformity experiment is likely to have more of an effect on an otherwise lone nonconforming participant if:
    a. the dissenter is in agreement with the nonconforming participant
    b. his or her dissent is clear, but not in agreement with the nonconforming participant
    c. the problem in question is a matter of minimal importance
    d. a and c
    e. all of the above

17. An explanation of blind obedience that emphasizes the authoritarian personality of the person in question relies on:
    a. situational factors
    b. dispositional factors
    c. cognitive dissonance
    d. cognitive consistency
    e. attribution of emotional experience

18. Both Milgram's obedience experiment and Asch's line judgment studies show the importance of _____ in determining behavior.
    a. attribution
    b. cognitive dissonance
    c. compliance
    d. dispositional factors
    e. none of the above

19. Which of the following would tend to *prevent* obedience in a situation of the type that Milgram studied?
    a. making a person feel like the agent of another
    b. dehumanizing the person being punished
    c. describing the experiment as a scientific enterprise
    d. decreasing the psychological distance between the participant and the person being punished
    e. none of the above

20. It is probably easier for a bombardier to drop bombs on an inhabited building than for the same person to kill someone standing in front of him. This presumed fact can be accounted for in terms of:
    a. anonymity
    b. psychological distance
    c. dehumanization
    d. all of the above
    e. none of the above

21. The fact that people underestimate the percent of people who comply in the Milgram obedience study can be accounted for in terms of:
    a. the fundamental attribution error
    b. social exchange theory
    c. social impact theory
    d. conformity
    e. b and c

22. According to social impact theory, which of the following factors contribute to the total social influence in a situation?
    a. number of "influencers"
    b. number of people being influenced
    c. status of "influencers"
    d. a and c
    e. none of the above

23. Social loafing is somewhat contradictory to the principle of:
    a. conformity
    b. attribution
    c. social impact
    d. social facilitation
    e. blind obedience

24. The tendency to account for leadership almost entirely in terms of "great persons" can be explained by:
    a. leadership theory
    b. social impact theory
    c. the fundamental attribution error
    d. the above-average effect
    e. statistics

25. Which of the following makes it *less* likely that Cynthia will emerge as a leader?
    a. She is in a position of authority.
    b. The goal (situation) is ambiguous.
    c. She is sociable.
    d. She is dominant.
    e. There are good relationships among members of the group.

26. Anonymity promotes:
    a. social exchange
    b. the fundamental attribution error
    c. the actor-observer difference
    d. social facilitation
    e. deindividuation

27. Brown suggests that panic is more likely in situations where:
    a. a serious danger is perceived
    b. the escape routes appear to be inadequate
    c. the people involved have well-defined roles
    d. a and b
    e. all of the above

28. The prisoner's dilemma analysis explains:
    a. the use of payoff matrices
    b. how obedience is based on a past history of stern parental treatment

c. how maladaptive crowd behavior can result from rational behavior of individuals
d. the importance of roles in controlling the crowd panic reaction
e. b and c

29. Which of the following does *not* involve the reason-passion theme?
    a. accounts of the nature of leadership
    b. conformity
    c. the self-serving bias
    d. theories of emotion
    e. all of the above involve a reason-passion theme

30. Which of the following does *not* involve the "individual-situation" theme?
    a. the fundamental attribution error
    b. accounts of the nature of leadership
    c. accounts of blind obedience
    d. social facilitation
    e. b and d

31. The cultural critique holds that much of modern social psychology is a description only of twentieth-century people in western-developed countries. Which of the following argues *against* the cultural critique?
    a. absence of a bias to dispositional attributions in Hindu Indians
    b. absence of a word for embarrassment in some cultures
    c. suppression of self for communal concerns in some cultures
    d. our ability to understand narratives from different cultures and times
    e. all of the above argue against the cultural critique

Answer Key for Self Test

1. a p. 491
2. d pp. 492, 493
3. b p. 494
4. b p. 496
5. c p. 494
6. c p. 499
7. d p. 500
8. e pp. 500, 501
9. c p. 501
10. e p. 501
11. a p. 502
12. a p. 504
13. b p. 506
14. e p. 507
15. d pp. 496, 508, 509
16. a p. 509

17. b p. 511
18. c pp. 513, 514
19. d p. 514
20. d pp. 514, 515
21. a p. 516
22. e pp. 516, 517
23. d p. 518
24. c pp. 518, 519
25. b p. 521
26. e p. 522
27. d p. 523
28. c p. 524
29. a p. 526
30. d p. 527
31. d pp. 527, 528

Investigating Psychological Phenomena

MATCHING FOR INTELLIGENCE AND ATTRACTION

Equipment: None
Number of participants: One, yourself
Time per participant: Twenty minutes
Time for experimenter: Twenty minutes

As described in the text, one of the major features of romantic couples is that they are similar along a wide variety of dimensions. Much of this similarity seems to be a reason for the formation of the relationship, rather than a consequence of it. Although certain characteristics may become more similar the longer a couple is together, this cannot be so for the many characteristics unlikely to change in adulthood, such as height. Furthermore, individuals are likely to seek a partner with a high rating on characteristics for which there can be a clear positive or negative evaluation (such as intelligence or attractiveness), with competitive selection and fear of rejection tending to sort people out with others at their own level of achievement, ability, beauty, and so forth. Thus, one would expect similar ratings on almost all traits.

This study will demonstrate the principles of homogamy and matching by examining the similarity of couples on two characteristics: physical attractiveness and intelligence. You will be the one participant in this study. First, select ten heterosexual couples that you know fairly well. The couples should be selected according to the following criteria:

1. All should be romantically involved: married or together for at least one year.

2. The couples should be about the same age in two senses: The members of the couple should be no more than ten years apart in age and the oldest person should be no more than twenty years older than the youngest person of the same gender on the list. (If you cannot generate the ten couples that this study calls for, you can ask a friend to generate the data for you.)

DO NOT INCLUDE YOURSELF IN ANY OF THESE COUPLES.

List the couples (by first name of each partner) in the accompanying tables. Now rank the ten women and the ten men separately for both physical attractiveness and intelligence. Thus, for physical attractiveness, rank the most attractive man number one, the next most attractive number two, and so on until all ten numbers have been assigned. Rank the women in the same fashion.

Now calculate a rank-order correlation, a statistic that represents the correlation between the ranking for men and women in each couple. (See the Statistical Appendix in the text, but use the formula on page 155 to calculate the correlation.) If the members of a couple match perfectly on a characteristic (i.e., if the man ranked number one for attractiveness is involved with the woman ranked number one on this same trait, etc.), the correlation coefficient would equal 1.00—the highest possible value for correlation. If the members of a couple are inversely matched (i.e., if the man ranked number one for attractiveness is involved with the woman ranked number ten on that trait), then the correlation coefficient would equal −1.00 (the lowest possible value). If there is no relation between the ranking of the man and woman in a couple on the trait in question, then the correlation coefficient would be 0. (For a sample calculation and table, see page 155.)

Attractiveness

Couple (man's/woman's name)	Man's Rank	Woman's Rank	Difference	Difference^2
1 _____	_____	_____	_____	_____
2 _____	_____	_____	_____	_____
3 _____	_____	_____	_____	_____
4 _____	_____	_____	_____	_____
5 _____	_____	_____	_____	_____
6 _____	_____	_____	_____	_____
7 _____	_____	_____	_____	_____
8 _____	_____	_____	_____	_____
9 _____	_____	_____	_____	_____
10 _____	_____	_____	_____	_____

Correlation for attractiveness = _____

Intelligence

Couple (man's/woman's name)	Man's Rank	Woman's Rank	Difference	Difference^2
1 _____	_____	_____	_____	_____
2 _____	_____	_____	_____	_____
3 _____	_____	_____	_____	_____
4 _____	_____	_____	_____	_____
5 _____	_____	_____	_____	_____
6 _____	_____	_____	_____	_____
7 _____	_____	_____	_____	_____
8 _____	_____	_____	_____	_____
9 _____	_____	_____	_____	_____
10 _____	_____	_____	_____	_____

Correlation for intelligence = _____

Use the formula below to calculate the correlation, r.

$$r = 1 - \frac{6(\text{sum of the difference in ranking between couple members}^2)}{\text{number of couples (number of couples}^2 - 1)}$$

Sample data on intelligence:

Couple (man's/woman's name)	Man's Rank	Intelligence Woman's Rank	Difference	Difference^2
1 A/B_____	1	2	−1	1
2 C/D_____	5	3	2	1
3 E/F_____	3	1	2	4
4 G/H_____	9	6	3	9
5 I/J_____	2	7	−5	25
6 K/L_____	7	5	2	4
7 M/N_____	4	4	0	0
8 O/P_____	8	9	−1	1
9 Q/R_____	10	8	2	4
10 S/T_____	6	10	−4	16

Sum of difference^2 = 65

Correlation for intelligence = .61

For the sample table, the equation would read:

$$r = 1 - \frac{6(65)}{10(100 - 1)} = -.61$$

Compare your results to those in the list below generated by other students in introductory psychology. These correlation coefficients were calculated by eleven students for intelligence and thirteen students for attractiveness and have been arranged in order of increasing correlation. How do your values compare to theirs?

Correlations

Attractiveness	Intelligence
−.16	−.01
−.01	.18
.02	.26
.07	.35
.36	.39
.45	.42
.46	.56
.50	.63
.55	.68
.60	.75
.60	.76
.76	
.76	

Finally, try to think of the characteristic that would be most likely to show similarity in mates, as well as the characteristic that might, perhaps because of its lack of importance, not show matching in mates. Calculate the correlation coefficient for each of these characteristics, using the same ten couples you have already used. You might also consider doing a similarity/matching score for ten same-gender couples or nonromantic friends. Would you expect them to show similarity/matching effects as well? Would you expect this on the same characteristics as with heterosexual romantic partners?

PART FOUR

DEVELOPMENT

CHAPTER 13

Physical and Cognitive Development

Learning Objectives

WHAT IS DEVELOPMENT?

Development as differentiation

1. What is differentiation, and how does it account for similarities in the embryos of different species? How is it relevant to behavior?

Development as growth

2. Review the major events in physical growth of humans from conception to adulthood.
3. How does humans' physical growth (especially of the nervous system) compare with that of other animals? What is the effect of the difference?
4. Review the basic sensory and response capacities of the human infant.

Development as orderly progression

5. Describe the sequence of early development of locomotion and language in humans, and indicate how the order of many accomplishments is fixed.

THE PHYSICAL BASIS OF DEVELOPMENT

The mechanism of genetic transmission

6. Define chromosomes. Indicate how gender is determined by chromosomes.
7. Define genes. Distinguish between dominant and recessive genes, giving an example.
8. Distinguish between genotype and phenotype.
9. Describe polygenic inheritance.

Environments at different points in development

10. Review gene-environment interactions in the embryo, including the role of both the cellular and hormonal environments in development.
11. Define and describe critical periods and sensitive periods.

Environment and maturation

12. Define maturation. What is the evidence for maturation of some basic abilities, such as walking?
13. Describe evidence showing facilitation and inhibition of development due to environmental manipulations and practice.
14. What is the role of specific and nonspecific experience?

PIAGET'S THEORY OF COGNITIVE DEVELOPMENT

15. What are the major philosophical positions on development? How does Piaget's theory relate to these? What are the four developmental stages, according to Piaget?

Sensory-motor intelligence

16. Describe the hallmarks of this stage. How do children see themselves and objects around them? What distinctions develop during this period?
17. Why is object permanence seen as an end to this stage of development?
18. What do the terms *assimilation* and *accommodation* mean according to Piaget? What is a schema?
19. What does Piaget mean by the term *representation*? What are some examples of representations?

The preoperational period

20. How is the name of this period derived?
21. Be familiar with various tests of conservation. How does the child's conservation ability develop during this period? Why do children fail to conserve at the beginning of this period? What operations are crucial for conservation?
22. Describe a test that demonstrates egocentrism.

Concrete and formal operations

23. What is the difference between these stages? How does Piaget study formal operations? Give examples of thinking patterns that would qualify for this stage.

WHAT IS THE COGNITIVE STARTING POINT?

24. How is Piaget compared to empiricists?

Space and objects in infancy

25. What is occlusion? How does it affect adult object perception?
26. What is the habituation procedure, and how has it been used to study infant perception?
27. What does the visual cliff procedure tell us about infant perceptual abilities?
28. What evidence suggests that infants have some notions of the principles that govern objects in space?
29. Cite the evidence that indicates that infants do have a notion of object permanence. In what way is this notion of object permanence incomplete?

Number in infancy

30. What is Piaget's position on the conception of number? What do studies of "threeness" in infancy say about this position?
31. Describe an experiment showing that primitive ideas of addition are also present in infancy.

Social cognition in infancy: the existence of other minds

32. Describe the evidence that very young infants are capable of discriminating a face from other stimuli, a skill that is fundamental to early social interaction.
33. A next important step in social interaction is sharing attention with another person. Be familiar with the data showing that this skill develops early as well.

COGNITIVE DEVELOPMENT IN PRESCHOOLERS

The meaning of mental stage

34. What are the characteristics of a developmental "stage" as Piaget uses the term? How is this contradicted by modern evidence?

Numerical skills in preschoolers

35. Even though preschoolers may use idiosyncratic counting terms, how does evidence show that they may nonetheless have a rudimentary understanding of counting principles?
36. Studies of numerical quantity show that young children have an appreciation of number. Describe the evidence for this claim.
37. How do modern studies of number cast doubt on the Piagetian concept of a stage?

Social cognition in preschoolers: developing a theory of mind

38. What are some basic assumptions of a theory of mind?
39. How has it been shown that young children have the rudiments of an understanding of some of these assumptions?
40. In what sense can one claim that young children have a theory of mind?

Sequence or stages?

41. Understand the argument that Piaget's fundamental conception of stages still has plausibility even in spite of modern evidence about his tasks.

THE CAUSES OF COGNITIVE GROWTH

The nativist approach: maturation

42. Be aware of the role of cross-cultural data in evaluating the maturational hypothesis.

Cognitive development as learning

43. Be able to discuss the basic issue distinguishing the positions of learning and maturation. What is Piaget's position? What is the relevant evidence?
44. How does a learning position explain the fairly fixed orders of development that characterize various stages? What are the results of studies to train young children on conservation?

Piaget's approach: assimilation and accommodation

45. Describe how Piaget sees assimilation and accommodation as explanations of cognitive growth.

The information-processing approach

46. What are the memory limitations of young children? How should these be taken into account when questioning children?
47. Describe some strategies for remembering that adults and children use. How do young children approach a memory task, and how does their approach change as they mature?
48. What is meant by the term *metacognition*? How is metacognition manifested in memory, perception, language, thinking, and problem solving?

COGNITIVE DEVELOPMENT FROM A CROSS-CULTURAL PERSPECTIVE

Differences in competence

49. How is the poor performance of non-Western people on standard cognitive tests explained? Are they capable of abstract thought without formal schooling? Give examples.

Effects of schooling

50. What effect does schooling have on thought?

TAKING STOCK

51. What is the proper balance between maturational and environmental factors in development? Discuss.

Programmed Exercises

WHAT IS DEVELOPMENT?

1. The process of _____ involves a progressive change from the more general to the more particular, from the simple to the more complex.

    differentiation

2. Differentiation predicts and accounts for the fact that development occurs in an _____ progression.

    orderly

3. Physical growth continues until approximately the end of the _____ decade of life.

    second

4. The part of the human body that grows at a disproportionately high rate before birth is the _____.

    head (brain)

5. Because of extensive growth of the brain after birth, humans have a longer period of _____ than most other species.

    dependency

6. Human growth does not occur smoothly, but in _____.

    spurts

7. The _____ reflex is elicited in an infant by a touch to the cheek, which makes the infant turn his head toward the stimulating object.

    rooting

8. The _____ reflex is elicited by a touch of the palm.

    grasp

9. In general, the infant's sensory capacities are _____ advanced at birth than are his or her _____ capacities.

    more, response (motor)

10. The human baby begins to walk alone at an age of about _____ months.

    fifteen (twelve to eighteen)

11. The first words typically occur at about _____ months.

    ten (eight to twelve)

12. Although some children develop faster than others, the major motor and language accomplishments occur in a _____ sequence.

    fixed (orderly)

THE PHYSICAL BASIS OF DEVELOPMENT

13. The genetic material of humans is arranged in pairs of structures called _____.

    chromosomes

14. In contrast to a female, who has two X chromosomes, a male has a(n) _____ and a(n) _____ chromosome in each body cell.

    X
    Y

15. The unit of hereditary transmission is the _____.

    gene

16. A gene that exerts its effect regardless of the identity of the other member of its pair is called _____. A gene that will express itself only if the other member of its pair is comparable is called _____.

    dominant
    recessive

17. The observed characteristics of an organism are called its _____, while the underlying genetic blueprint is called its _____.

    phenotype
    genotype

18. When an attribute is determined by multiple genes, this is called _____ inheritance.

    polygenic

19. In mammalian embryos, the genitals will develop as _____ unless the body is exposed to a _____ sex hormone, called _____.

    female
    male, androgen

20. Consider a person with a male (XY) genetic makeup, but whose tissues are not sensitive to male hormone. Such a person will develop female genitals. Unlike a typical male, such a person shows a disparity between _____ and _____.

    phenotype, genotype (either order)

21. During _____ periods in development, certain important events will have an impact that they would not have (or would have to a much lesser extent) at earlier or later times.

    critical (sensitive)

22. The inevitable unfolding of behavior patterns that is genetically programmed into the species and is independent of specific environmental conditions is called _____.

    maturation

23. Behaviors that mature are usually not subject to the influence of _____ experience, but are affected by _____ experience.

    specific
    general

24. Animals reared in darkness show later deficits in their visual system. This rearing process is called _____ deprivation.

    sensory

25. There are some reports that sensory _____ can exert positive effects on development.

    enrichment

PIAGET'S THEORY OF COGNITIVE DEVELOPMENT

26. Jean Piaget and other developmental psychologists usually look for _____ differences between children and adults; they do not see children as adults in miniature.

    qualitative

27. Piaget regards cognitive development as a dynamic process in which the child progresses through several _____.

    stages

28. A child has begun to learn that he lives in a stable world that can be distinguished from his sensory impressions. This child is most likely in the _____-_____ stage.

    sensory-motor

29. Children develop the notion of _____ _____ near the end of the sensory-motor stage as they become aware that objects exist independently of their sensory experience and motor manipulations.

    object permanence

30. Perhaps the most significant accomplishment of children in the last phase of the sensory-motor stage is their ability to _____ objects or events in their absence, rather than merely reacting to their presence.

represent

31. Recurrent action patterns (such as sucking, swallowing, and head and eye movement) are the first mental elements, or _____. It is in terms of these that the infant organizes the world.

schemas

32. According to Piaget, development proceeds by infants _____ new objects to existing schemas and by changing those schemas appropriately, a process called _____.

assimilating
accommodation

33. Representations may be internalized actions, images, or words; in all cases they function as _____, which stand for whatever they may signify.

symbols

34. _____ imitation is a case in which a child imitates an action that occurred in the past, such as a playmate's temper tantrum observed a day before.

Deferred

35. According to Piaget, a conceptual system of thought can only be constructed by means of higher-order schemas. These _____ allow the internal manipulation of ideas according to a stable set of rules and emerge at age seven or so; the period from two to seven is therefore termed _____.

operations
preoperational

36. A characteristic of children in the preoperational stage is their inability to _____ quantity, as shown by their lack of knowledge about relative quantities of liquids in two glasses.

conserve

37. One of the crucial concepts that children must grasp if they are to conserve is that manipulations upon objects are _____.

reversible

38. A preoperational child is incapable of attending to all of the relevant _____ of an object simultaneously.

dimensions

39. Piaget believes that children can learn to chunk dimensions together when they learn to focus upon the _____ from one experience to another rather than upon the individual experiences themselves.

transformations

40. A preoperational child believes his or her point of view is the only one. Such a belief is known as _____.

egocentrism

41. A child can determine whether a given number is odd or even and can also add one to any number. The child finds that 3 + 1 is even, and 5 + 1 is even, but doesn't understand that any odd number added to one results in an even number. This child would be categorized as being in the _____ _____ stage.

concrete operations

42. A child in the concrete operations stage has operations that are applicable to _____ events but which do not work too well when applied to _____ concepts.

concrete
abstract

43. The ability to entertain hypothetical possibilities and deal with potential relationships is characteristic only of the stage of _____ _____.

formal operations

WHAT IS THE COGNITIVE STARTING POINT?

44. The fact that an infant can perceive an object that is partially blocked by another object gives evidence that infants are capable of reacting appropriately to the perceptual effect of _____.

occlusion

45. Infants show surprisingly good evidence of depth perception as revealed by the visual _____ procedure.

cliff

46. The procedure in which a perceptual display is kept in view until an infant becomes bored is called _____.

habituation

47. It appears that young infants have some knowledge of the fact that two objects cannot occupy the same _____ at the same time.

space (place)

48. Modern investigators believe that, although infants may believe that objects exist, they do not actively search for them. Much of the proof for this theory comes from studies on the _____ effect.

A-not-B

49. Studies show that infants have a primitive notion of _____: They can distinguish two items from three items.

number

50. Studies of the knowledge of number in infants have relied on the _____ method, which depends on showing a stimulus repeatedly and then testing with it and a novel stimulus.

habituation

51. Studies of numerical reasoning show that infants as young as five months had a primitive understanding of _____ operations: They could distinguish when a stimulus had been added to an array.

arithmetical

52. Investigations of infants minutes after birth have demonstrated that they have a preference for looking at normal rather than scrambled _____.

faces

53. Infants will turn their _____ in the direction in which the mother is looking.

attention

COGNITIVE DEVELOPMENT IN PRESCHOOLERS

54. According to Piaget, cognitive development is characterized by a series of _____, each qualitatively different from the others.

stages

55. Even though children may use idiosyncratic symbols to denote given numbers of objects, they may still have the basic principle of _____.

counting

56. Piaget had demonstrated failure of young children to _____ number, in that if a number of items was stretched out, the children thought there were more items present.

conserve

57. Recent studies of cognitive development suggest that stages are not _____ or _____ in nature. The demarcations between stages are not sharp.

all, none

58. The fact that young children will turn a photograph in the proper orientation when showing it to another person suggests that they have a rudimentary theory of _____.

mind

59. At about two-and-a-half years of age, children can predict what another child will do. They understand something about the mental state of _____.

motive (desire)

60. There are two crucial components to the notion of a _____. One is that they can be true or false; the other is that different people can have different ones.

belief

61. The _____ _____ test asks a child to predict what another being will know in a certain situation. This test compares the child's own knowledge with what the child knows about another's knowledge.

false belief

62. One critical difference between preschoolers and school age children is that the latter can apply their knowledge to a wider range of _____.

problems

63. Most developmental psychologists would say that Piaget's cognitive milestones are not a succession of mental stages, similar to those found in embryological development, but rather a _____ of mental steps.

sequence

THE CAUSES OF COGNITIVE GROWTH

64. Nativists would state that mental development depends on _____, a preprogrammed growth process based on changes in underlying neural structures.

maturation

65. While children of different cultures may reach each Piagetian stage at different _____, they pass through these stages in the same _____.

ages
order

66. The alternative to the maturation-centered approach is one that emphasizes the acquisition of _____ through exposure to the environment.

learning

67. Piaget believes that at the same time that the environment is _____ to the child's schemas, the schemas _____ to the environment.

assimilated
accommodate

68. A more current approach to cognitive development asserts that it results from a change in _____ _____.

information processing

69. According to this approach, mental growth is partly based on the acquisition of various _____ for thinking and remembering.

strategies

70. As children get older, _____ repetition, also called _____, is used as a strategy for remembering.

rote, rehearsal

71. The fact that adults can reflect on the cognitive operations whereby they gain knowledge shows that they are capable of _____.

metacognition

COGNITION DEVELOPMENT FROM A CROSS-CULTURAL PERSPECTIVE

72. One reason for cross-cultural differences in cognitive performance is the lack of formal _____ in some cultures (e.g., Australian aborigines, New Guinea tribesmen, and Kpelle farmers in Liberia). schooling

73. Another reason for cross-cultural differences in performance may be that some _____ cultures simply do not understand the nature of the answer expected by the Western experimenter. non-Western

TAKING STOCK

74. Development is best characterized as a function of both _____ and _____. maturation, environment

Self Test

1. The fact that, at early stages, embryos of many very different species look very much alike, and have a much simpler structure than adults, can be taken as evidence for:
   a. physical development
   b. differentiation
   c. the inheritance of behavior
   d. all of the above
   e. b and c

2. The accompanying figure corresponds to a human being of about what age (beginning with conception as zero)?
   a. one month
   b. four months
   c. eight months
   d. birth (nine months)
   e. one year (postconception)

3. All but one of the following are distinctive features of human development, in comparison with most other mammals. Which is not a distinctly human feature?
   a. long period of dependency on the parent
   b. being born at a very immature stage
   c. presence of reflex at birth
   d. continuation of growth until about twenty years of age
   e. b and c

4. Major features of motor, language, and other types of development often occur in a fixed order in children who develop at different rates. A major reason for this is that:
   a. development must occur in stages
   b. some capacities depend on the existence of other capacities
   c. sense organs mature before response capacities
   d. language depends on locomotion ability
   e. the infant begins with reflexes like grasping before it can learn

5. The ability to taste a certain chemical called PTC is genetically determined, and controlled by a single pair of genes. All children of nontasters are nontasters, but some of the children with two taster parents are also nontasters. This suggests that the gene that codes for tasting is:
   a. polygenic
   b. on at least two chromosomes
   c. dominant
   d. recessive
   e. rare

6. Phenotype and genotype are not always in close correspondence because:
   a. some genes are recessive
   b. some inheritance is polygenic
   c. only females have two X chromosomes
   d. a and c
   e. all of the above

7. A genetic female who is exposed to androgen as a fetus and develops male genitals illustrates:
   a. that behavior is inherited
   b. that recessive traits can occur in both gender and intelligence
   c. that inborn, genetically determined traits can be changed by environmental factors
   d. that environmental factors, under some circumstances, have no influence on behavior
   e. that behavior is related to gender chromosomes

8. Studies of transplanted embryonic tissue indicate:
   a. important roles for genes in development
   b. a dominant role for genes in development
   c. a dominant role for the environment in development
   d. that up to a certain point, a tissue may be able to develop in many ways, but later (after a critical period) it may be less changeable
   e. a and d

9. The fact that at different ages organisms perceive their environment differently and the existence of critical periods together argue for the view that:
   a. it is not possible to describe the meaningful environment for an animal by just listing all the physical and social events that are occurring
   b. initially behavior is controlled by genes, and later by environment
   c. it is not possible to evaluate the role of environment in determining behavior
   d. b and c
   e. all of the above

10. A behavior appears at adolescence. Evidence for the position that this is a case of maturation would be that the behavior:
    a. depends on specific experience
    b. does not depend on general experience
    c. appears very frequently in adopted children
    d. is present at birth
    e. none of the above

11. Phenotype is to genotype as:
    a. building is to building plan
    b. maturation is to motor development
    c. fetus is to embryo
    d. recapitulation is to differentiation

12. Rats reared in an environment that has been enriched have:
    a. brains that are heavier than rats reared in a deprived environment
    b. brains that have more neurons than rats reared in a deprived environment
    c. brains that have more interneural connections than rats reared in a deprived environment
    d. all of the above
    e. a and c only
    f. a and b only

13. A nativist:
    a. thinks of the child's mind as similar to an adult's, only with fewer associations
    b. thinks of a child's mind as qualitatively different from an adult's
    c. conceptualizes the growth of a child's mind as progression through a series of natural stages
    d. views basic cognitive categories as given *a priori* at birth

14. A child has learned that whether a toy box is open or closed, there are toys inside. It could be said that the child has attained the concept of:
    a. object permanence
    b. representations
    c. directed action
    d. solipsism

15. When a child just becomes aware that objects exist independent of her own sensory experience, she would most likely have completed which Piagetian stage?
    a. sensory-motor
    b. preoperational
    c. concrete operations
    d. formal operations

16. Recurring action patterns, such as sucking and swallowing, are:
    a. simple reflexes that have little developmental interest
    b. the first mental elements with which the infant organizes the world
    c. examples of intentional acts
    d. none of the above

17. The two processes that Piaget sees as being responsible for cognitive development are:
    a. deferred imitation and assimilation
    b. schemas and representations
    c. assimilation and accommodation
    d. none of the above

18. A toy is hidden under a box in the presence of a child. The child is prevented from reaching the box for a few seconds. When he is released he immediately lifts the box off the toy. The earliest stage that this child could be in is _____.
    a. sensory-motor
    b. preoperational
    c. concrete operations
    d. formal operations

19. When a child searches for an object in a location where it was previously present, but from which she saw it moved, she demonstrates:
    a. the A-not-B effect
    b. deferred imitation
    c. object permanence
    d. all of the above

20. Demonstrations of the child's understanding that symbols (i.e., internalized actions, images, or words) may stand for objects but are not equivalent to them include all of the following *except*:
    a. object permanence
    b. deferred imitation
    c. make-believe play
    d. metacognitions

21. The concept unknown to a child who doesn't conserve quantity is:
    a. reversibility
    b. accuracy
    c. size
    d. weight

22. Children who don't conserve are:
    a. unable to attend to all of the relevant dimensions of a stimulus
    b. usually in the concrete operations stage
    c. usually in the formal operations stage
    d. none of the above

23. One of the features of the world for which children fail to show conservation is number. They apparently believe:
    a. that, say, the number 4 is the same as the number 5
    b. that the number of items is equivalent to its length when laid out
    c. that number and quantity are the same thing
    d. that the number of items that are present is the same as the number that were present a few minutes ago
    e. all of the above

24. The social counterpart of an inability to attend to more than one dimension in a conservation task is:
    a. aggressive behavior
    b. having only one friend during a particular time interval
    c. egocentrism
    d. none of the above

25. The major difference between a child in the concrete operations stage and one in the formal operations stage is:
    a. the former is incapable of following the rules
    b. the former cannot deal with numbers
    c. the former cannot deal with abstract concepts
    d. all of the above

26. The idea behind using habituation to study knowledge of occlusion is:
    a. to have an infant habituate to an occluded stimulus and then see whether it sees the whole unoccluded stimulus as novel
    b. to have an infant habituate to an unoccluded stimulus and then see whether it sees the whole occluded stimulus as novel
    c. to have an infant see a stimulus and then see whether it habituates to that stimulus faster when it is occluded
    d. none of the above

27. The experiment showing that infants have knowledge about objects and the fact that two objects cannot occupy the same place at the same time made use of a procedure in which a screen moved over an object and either stopped when it reached the object or seemed to pass through it. This procedure indicated that the infants had a sense of objects because:
    a. they habituated to the moving screen
    b. they spent more time looking at the screen when it stopped at the object behind it
    c. they moved their hands and arms more while the screen was moving, indicating that they anticipated its stopping when it hit the object
    d. they spent less time looking at the screen when it stopped at the object behind it

28. One problem in interpreting results from the A-not-B effect is that:
    a. it gives an infant too many places to search for a hidden object
    b. it does not allow habituation sufficient time to develop
    c. the results may simply depend on an infant's preference to avoid a place where it has just searched for an object
    d. none of the above

29. Some developmental psychologists have challenged Piaget's view on what is given to the infant at the start of life. With which of the following would these critics agree?
    a. Four-month-old infants can perceive partially hidden objects similar to the way adults do.
    b. Young infants have a primitive notion of number, at least for small numbers.
    c. Young infants have a primitive notion of arithmetic operations.
    d. all of the above

30. Studies of number and addition knowledge in young children:
    a. confirm Piaget's view of the young child's cognitive competence
    b. raise the possibility that young children are endowed with more cognitive sense than Piaget supposed
    c. indicate the concrete operations can precede the preoperational period
    d. none of the above

31. Piaget's demonstration of the failure of young children to conserve number:
    a. has been called into question by more recent work on children's ability to focus attention on where the mother is focusing attention
    b. has stood the test of time in that more recent investigations have also found the preoperational child to be unable to conserve number or any other quantity
    c. is inconsistent with his demonstrations of other skills in conservation tasks at the same age
    d. needs to be modified based on more recent evidence of number conservation of small numbers of items

32. There is evidence that infants have primitive social abilities that will later develop more fully. This evidence includes:
    a. the fact that infants are more responsive to faces than to other stimuli with the same features scrambled
    b. the fact that infants are capable of taking another person's perspective in Piaget's problem where he asks children to predict what another person's perspective will be
    c. the fact that infants are sensitive to where another person is concentrating attention
    d. all of the above
    e. a and b, but not c
    f. a and c, but not b

33. What are two characteristics of a developmental stage as Piaget uses the term?
    a. consistent, continuous
    b. continuous, discrete
    c. consistent, concrete
    d. consistent, discrete

34. The fact that children younger than five count with unusually ordered numbers (e.g., one, two, eight, five) but assign a unique label to each item counted:
    a. casts doubt on Piaget's discrete-stage view of development in which these children should be in a preoperational stage
    b. suggests that the preoperational and concrete operational stages are one and the same
    c. forces one to abandon the notion of sequentially ordered stages altogether
    d. is inconsistent with the ability of even younger children to have a primitive notion of number and addition

35. Evidence that young children have a primitive theory of mind is that they have an early sense of:
    a. another person's beliefs
    b. another person's perceptual capacities
    c. another person's motives
    d. all of the above

36. A rudimentary theory of mind has been demonstrated in young children by the result that:
   a. they will appropriately orient a picture they are showing to an adult so that it faces the adult
   b. they will be egocentric in trying to take the perspective of another person in how that person views a scene
   c. they can recognize faces only minutes after birth
   d. none of the above

37. One way of reconciling modern evidence with Piaget's view of stages of development is to say that:
   a. young children begin with very few cognitive capacities and need to learn them all
   b. young children have some cognitive skills but cannot apply them to very many situations
   c. Piaget was essentially correct in all of his assertions about stages, but he was wrong in when the stages begin
   d. none of the above

38. According to the theory of maturation:
   a. behavior change is associated with neurological changes
   b. environmental changes have great impact on the development of the child
   c. learning takes place independently of age
   d. all of the above

39. According to simple learning theories:
   a. learning is the acquisition of specific associations
   b. most things could be learned at any time
   c. the speed with which a child learns depends on his or her age
   d. a and b, but not c

40. Which of the following statements about Piaget is true?
   a. He asserts that development involves a constant interchange between the child and the environment.
   b. He asserts that simple learning causes the progression from one stage to another.
   c. He asserts that the age at which each stage begins is consistent across cultures.
   d. He says that the child's schemas assimilate to the environment, as well as the environment being accommodated to the schema.

41. An approach to cognitive development asserts that mental growth is based partly on the acquisition of better strategies for handling information. This approach explains cognitive development as a change in:
   a. maturation
   b. information processing
   c. specific learning
   d. assimilation

42. Which of the following is *not* an example of metacognition?
   a. being realistic about how many numbers you can recall at one time
   b. recognizing the difference between reality and illusion
   c. using strategies for reaching solutions
   d. reading and following directions for a recipe

43. Which of the following is true?
   a. Unschooled people are incapable of abstract thought.

b. Schooled and unschooled people think alike.
c. Schooled people cannot apply their knowledge to a variety of contexts or situations.
d. none of the above

Answer Key for Self Test

1.	b	p. 534
2.	b	p. 535
3.	c	p. 537
4.	b	p. 538
5.	c	p. 540
6.	a	p. 541
7.	c	p. 542
8.	e	p. 541
9.	a	p. 543
10.	e	p. 544
11.	a	p. 541
12.	e	p. 545
13.	d	p. 546
14.	a	p. 547
15.	a	p. 547
16.	b	p. 548
17.	c	p. 548
18.	b	p. 549
19.	a	p. 547
20.	d	pp. 548, 549
21.	a	p. 550
22.	a	p. 550
23.	b	p. 552
24.	c	p. 551
25.	c	p. 552
26.	a	p. 554
27.	d	pp. 554–55
28.	d	p. 556
29.	d	p. 556
30.	b	pp. 556–57
31.	d	p. 557
32.	f	pp. 557–58
33.	d	p. 559
34.	a	p. 559
35.	d	pp. 561, 562
36.	a	p. 562
37.	b	p. 563
38.	a	p. 564
39.	d	p. 565
40.	a	p. 566
41.	b	p. 566
42.	d	p. 569
43.	d	pp. 570–71

Investigating Psychological Phenomena

CONSERVATION OF NUMBER

Equipment: Thirty-three red poker chips and thirty-four blue ones
Number of participants: One, age four or five (preoperational stage, according to Piaget)
Time per participant: Fifteen minutes
Time for experimenter: Thirty minutes

In Chapter 13, the authors discuss the development of conservation ability as children move into what Piaget calls the stage of concrete operations. The characteristic of this ability is that children come to use a set of mental rules, or operations, to govern their thought about objects in the world. For example, they learn that a certain volume of water is unchanged by the characteristics of the container that happens to contain it. Thus, pouring a certain amount of water from a low and wide container into one that is tall and thin does not change its volume even though the water achieves a greater height in the tall container.

There is also research suggesting that Piaget may have underestimated the ability of children to conserve. Apparently, when faced with somewhat less demanding tasks, which nevertheless are formal tests of conservation ability, young children who should be in a preoperational stage show some signs of conservation.

This has been shown most impressively with the conservation of number. The problem that preoperational children face in conserving number is that they confuse numerosity with the physical length of the series that contains the items whose number must be judged. For example, they frequently judge that a row of items contains more items if it is simply longer than another row of items.

The present exercise allows you to take an empirical look at this issue. One of the variables that may influence whether children show evidence of conservation or not is the number of items that are included in a test. Common sense suggests that the more objects in a set whose number must be judged, the more difficult will be the judgment. We shall test this hypothesis in the context of a number conservation test in which the number of objects whose number must be judged will vary. In both conditions of the experiment, your participants will be asked to judge which of two rows contains more objects. In one condition, the number of objects in each row will be less than in the other condition.

In order to conduct this experiment most efficiently, and with the greatest chance of keeping the attention of your participant, prearrange the stimulus arrays before you begin. The accompanying figure shows you the five stimulus arrangements for each of the two numerosity conditions. Each letter in the figure represents a chip of the appropriate color (B = blue, R = red). On the left are the arrangements for the lower numerosity condition. The first arrangement is the control condition in which each row contains the same number of chips, and in which the two rows are of equal length. In the second figure, the two rows contain the same number, but the lengths of the rows differ. In the third figure, the lengths are equal, but one row contains more chips than the other. The fourth arrangement pits the two variables against one another: The row that is longest also contains fewer chips than the shorter row. On the right are comparable arrangements for the condition in which more chips are used. The four arrangements are in the same order as the ones on the left of the figure.

Make each of the eight arrangements on a separate piece of cardboard, and place them out of sight. Then seat your participant comfortably and explain to him or her that you are going to play a game in which the child has to say which row of chips has more chips. Take out Arrangement 1 first and ask the child, "Which row has more, the one with red or the one with blue, or are they the same?" If the child answers that they are not the same, then lengthen or shorten one of the rows so that the child agrees that they are equal. Be sure that the red and blue chips are equal. Be sure that the red and blue chips line up above one another, so there is a one-to-one correspondence.

Now move on to Arrangement 2. Continue with the same line of questioning, asking which row contains more, the red one or the blue one. After getting an answer, which you should record on the protocol form that is given on p. 169, ask your participant to explain his or her response. That is, ask why the participant judged one of the rows as having more (or less, or equal, depending upon the answer) chips, and record the substance of this answer on the protocol form. Continue with Arrangements 3 and 4, after which you should move on to Arrangements 5 through 8. In each case, record the data in the spaces provided on the answer sheet. For each arrangement decide whether your participant was paying attention to the number or the length of the series in making his or her judgment. Which condition shows better number conservation overall?

The critical comparison that is of interest in this experiment is whether your participant shows evidence of competence in number conservation with fewer chips, but falters with a greater number of chips. If this is so, how does it fit in with the discussion in the text about the development of conservation? What does it imply about a stage theory of development?

Some other questions that might be raised by this exercise are the following: Would your results have been any different if the two conditions had been run in the opposite order, from the more to the less difficult? Is there something inherent in the questioning of the participant that may bias him or her to attend to length rather than number? Why might number conservation be better with fewer chips in the stimuli? What kinds of operations did your participant seem to be using as the basis for his or her judgment? What kinds of tests could be constructed to discover whether other conservation skills might also develop earlier than previously thought?

STIMULI FOR NUMBER CONSERVATION EXPERIMENT

Small Numbers

1. B B B
   R R R

2.   B B B
   R   R   R

3. B   B
   R R R

4. B   B
     R   R   R

Large Numbers

5. B B B B B
   R R R R R

6.   B B B B B
   R R R R R R

7. B   B   B   B
   R R R   R R R

8. B   B   B   B   B
     R R R R R

ANSWER SHEET FOR NUMBER CONSERVATION EXPERIMENT

1. More blue _____
   More red _____
   Both equal _____

   Explanation:

2. More blue _____
   More red _____
   Both equal _____

   Explanation:

3. More blue _____
   More red _____
   Both equal _____

   Explanation:

4. More blue _____
   More red _____
   Both equal _____

   Explanation:

5. More blue _____
   More red _____
   Both equal _____

   Explanation:

6. More blue _____
   More red _____
   Both equal _____

   Explanation:

7. More blue _____
   More red _____
   Both equal _____

   Explanation:

8. More blue _____
   More red _____
   Both equal _____

   Explanation:

CHAPTER 14

Social Development

Learning Objectives

ATTACHMENT

The roots of attachment

1. Describe the view (the "cupboard" theory) that attributes the infant's love for the mother to the fact that she fulfills basic biological needs.
2. Explain Bowlby's theory of attachment, including both positive and negative aspects of attachment seeking. Contrast Bowlby's theory with Freud's "cupboard" theory.
3. How do Harlow's experiments on monkeys cast doubt on the "cupboard" view and support Bowlby's view?

Imprinting and attachment

4. Describe the process of imprinting in animals. Is there imprinting in humans?

PATTERNS OF ATTACHMENT

5. What is separation anxiety and when does it first occur?

Assessing attachment

6. Describe Ainsworth's procedure for measuring attachment. What characterizes the securely attached child?
7. What is the evidence that the early parent-child relationship, as assessed in the Strange Situation, is a major determinant of later social and emotional adjustment? What are some counterarguments?

Attachment to the father

8. What is the evidence of attachment to the father? What is the difference between paternal and maternal attachment, and what are possible causes of this difference?

Early maternal separation and day care

9. What are the effects of maternal separation and the effects of career mothers and day care on later social adjustment?

Disrupted attachment: domestic conflict and divorce

10. Summarize the effect of divorce on child adjustment, and indicate the possible role of domestic conflict as a causal agent.

When there is no attachment at all

11. Summarize the effects of maternal deprivation on young monkeys and humans. To what extent are the effects similar in monkeys and humans?

Are the effects of early social deprivation reversible?

12. Describe the circumstances under which it is possible to reverse effects of early maternal deprivation in monkeys and humans.
13. Evaluate the Freudian claims that early experience is a critical factor in social development, and that its effects are irreversible. Describe the general process of social development.

CHILDHOOD SOCIALIZATION

Cultural values and child rearing

14. What are some values that are socialized in all cultures? How do the characteristics of a culture or social class influence the values that are socialized?

Mechanisms of socialization

15. Describe social learning theory and observational learning. Indicate the way in which this process differs from instrumental learning.
16. Outline the cognitive (developmental) approach. Indicate how it views imitation.
17. Summarize the basic differences among the Freudian-reinforcement, social learning, and cognitive (developmental) approaches to socialization.
18. What are the effects of breast versus bottle feeding and harshness of toilet training on later development?

The first agents of socialization: the parents

19. Describe the autocratic, permissive, and authoritative-reciprocal patterns of child rearing. What are the characteristic behaviors of children raised under each of these approaches? Might there be culture differences?

The child's effect on the parents

20. Explain the interaction between the child's temperament and the parent's pattern of child rearing, and indicate how this interaction complicates the task of relating patterns of child rearing to the child's personality.

THE DEVELOPMENT OF MORALITY

Not doing wrong

21. What does it mean to internalize moral values? What is the role of punishment in internalization, and what is the principle of minimal sufficiency?

Doing good

22. What is empathy, and how does it function in supporting altruistic behavior? Is it sufficient?

Moral reasoning

23. Describe Kohlberg's stages of moral reasoning.
24. According to Gilligan, what is the fundamental sex difference in moral attitudes or reasoning? What is the evidence on this potential sex difference?
25. Discuss cultural differences in moral reasoning and moral behavior.
26. What is the relation between moral reasoning and moral behavior? To what extent do Kohlberg's stages represent the ability to describe principles, rather than guidance of behavior by these principles?

THE DEVELOPMENT OF SEX AND GENDER

27. Distinguish among gender roles, sexual orientation, and gender identity.

Gender roles

28. What is gender typing and what are gender role stereotypes?

Sex differences in gender roles

29. Review physical and physiological differences in male and female development, and in adults.
30. Consider common misinterpretations of the meaning of sex differences.
31. Evaluate the role of nature (biological-genetic) factors and experience, in establishing gender differences in aggression. In what ways is aggression expressed differently in males and females?
32. Review the types of evidence suggesting a biological basis for gender differences in patterns of intellectual abilities, especially spatial abilities. What are suggested roles for testosterone, the hippocampus, and cultural factors?
33. Discuss how small biological differences can be amplified by social forces.

Gender identity

34. Review the development of gender identity in the first six years of life.
35. Describe intersexuals and pseudohermaphrodites, and indicate what they tell us about gender identity. Describe the nature and justification for sex reassignment.
36. What are the effect of early exposure to sex hormones, or their absence, on gender identity and gender role?
37. Is there a critical period for gender identity determination? Include a discussion of the guevedoces syndrome.

Sexual orientation

38. Discuss the incidence of homosexuality at different historical times and in different cultures.
39. What is the psychoanalytic account of homosexuality? What is the evidence on age of onset of homosexuality and the effects of early experience?
40. Discuss some possible biological causes of homosexuality, or, more generally, sexual orientation. Include consideration of genetic effects, brain differences, and effects of prenatal and adult hormone levels.

DEVELOPMENT AFTER CHILDHOOD

41. Describe Erik Erikson's conception of human growth. What are his "eight ages of man"? To what extent do they hold across cultures?

Adolescence

42. Discuss the particular problems of adolescence as a transition to adulthood in the United States and in other cultures. Is adolescence always turbulent?
43. In what sense is there an adolescent identity crisis?

Adulthood

44. Describe the mid-life transition.
45. Indicate how changes in American society have markedly altered the experience of old age.
46. Evaluate the extent to which Erikson's stages may be considered to be universal.

Programmed Exercises

ATTACHMENT

1. According to Freud, love for the mother derives from the fact that she is associated with the _____ of hunger, thirst, and pain.

   alleviation (reduction, decrease)

2. According to Bowlby's theory of attachment, fear of the _____ forms one basis of attachment. Another basis is a tendency to engage in _____ _____.

   unknown (unfamiliar)
   social interaction

3. According to Bowlby, proximity to an attachment figure provides _____ and _____, and separation from it leads to _____.

   comfort, security
   distress

4. Harlow's experiments with terry-cloth mothers suggest that, in monkeys, the nutrient provided by the mother is less important for attachment than the _____ _____ that she provides.

   contact comfort

5. The formation of strong attachments by the young of a species to objects (typically the parent) encountered early in life is called _____.

   imprinting

6. This type of attachment (imprinting) tends to occur during a special time, early in life, called the _____ _____.

   sensitive (critical) period

7. Specific recognition of the mother and distress at her departure, called _____ _____, occur at about the same time across cultures. This time is from _____ to_____ months of age. — separation anxiety, six, eight

8. In Ainsworth's "Strange Situations" measurements, a child who explores freely when the mother is present, shows some distress at her leaving, and greets her return with enthusiasm is called _____ _____. — securely attached

9. In Ainsworth's "Strange Situation" measurements, a child who doesn't explore even in the mother's presence, becomes intensely upset when she leaves, and shows ambivalence during reunion is called _____. — anxious (resistant)

10. In Ainsworth's "Strange Situation" measurements, a child who is distant and aloof toward his or her mother, shows little distress when she leaves, and ignores her when she returns is called _____. — avoidant

11. In the "Strange Situation" disappearance of the father also produces some _____. — distress

12. While mothers are preferred sources of care and comfort for most children, fathers are often the preferred _____. — playmate

13. The consequences of early separation from the mother, such as placement in _____ _____, have not been clearly established. — day care

14. Attachment may be disrupted by_____. This may have a causal effect, or the effect may be explained by _____ conflict. — divorce, domestic

15. Evidence indicates that the effects of maternal separation in humans are _____, and that maternal _____, with consequent day care, may not compromise social adjustment. — reversible, employment (careers)

16. Motherless monkeys and humans reared in some _____ show marked deficits in social performance. — institutions

17. Maternal deprivation has severe long-term effects in both monkeys and humans, but not if it occurs for no more than a few _____. — months

18. Studies using younger monkey therapists with motherless monkeys and studies on children put in nurturant environments after being in institutions indicate that many of the effects of maternal deprivation are _____. — reversible

19. Freud claimed that early experience (in the first six years or so of life) was _____ for appropriate adult social adjustments, and that the effects of normal early experience were _____. — critical, irreversible

CHILDHOOD SOCIALIZATION

20. _____ is the process by which the child acquires the patterns of thought and behavior that are characteristic of the society in which he or she is born. — Socialization

21. In the process of socialization in America, working-class people stress _____ while middle-class people stress _____-_____. — obedience, self-control

22. Both Freudian and reinforcement theories explain socialization in terms of the opposite influences of _____ and _____. — pain (punishment), pleasure (reward)

23. Researchers who believe that the basic Pavlovian and instrumental learning process must be supplemented to explain socialization are called _____ _____ theorists. — social learning

24. Such theorists (see previous question) add to the basic learning processes the mechanism of _____ learning. — observational

25. In order to perform an observed act, there must be something to _____, that is called the model. — imitate

26. The _____ approach to socialization emphasizes the role of understanding or competence in the socialization process. — cognitive

27. The cognitive approach recognizes the importance of _____, but emphasizes its cognitive complexity.

imitation

28. Important early Freudian features of development—such as _____ or_____ feeding, or harsh or relaxed _____ training—seem to have little effect on later development.

breast, bottle
toilet

29. The child-rearing style in which the parent controls the child strictly, and does not explain the justification for the governing rules to the child, is called the _____ pattern. The opposite extreme is called the _____ pattern. An intermediate approach, in which the parents exercise power, but also recognize the child's point of view, is called the _____- _____ pattern.

autocratic
permissive
authoritative-reciprocal

30. Of these patterns (see above), the one that leads to the best-adjusted children is the _____- _____ pattern.

authoritative-reciprocal

31. Some differences in the pattern of child rearing may result from differences in _____ in children, some of which are present at birth.

temperament

THE DEVELOPMENT OF MORALITY

32. We say a moral value is _____ when an individual avoids transgressions because he or she feels that they are wrong, and not because the individual is afraid of being punished.

internalized

33. According to the principle of _____ _____, internalization occurs best under mild social pressure.

minimal sufficiency

34. The _____-_____ child-rearing style is most compatible with the minimal sufficiency principle and successful internalization.

authoritative-reciprocal

35. A direct emotional response to another person's emotions is called _____.

empathy

36. Kohlberg has interviewed both adults and children in an attempt to describe the development of _____ _____.

moral reasoning

37. Kohlberg describes this development in a series of successive _____.

stages

38. According to Kohlberg, moral reasoning develops along a course in which right and wrong are defined by, first: _____ _____ _____; second: _____; and third _____ _____ _____.

1. fear of punishment and/or gain; 2. convention 3. internalized (or abstract) moral principles

39. According to Gilligan, in making moral decisions, men tend to emphasize _____, while women tend to be more influenced by _____.

justice, compassion (caring)

40. A criticism of Kohlberg's cognitive approach to moral behavior is that although it may be able to _____ moral rules, these rules may not actually guide _____. Furthermore, the Kohlberg results may measure one's _____ to describe moral rules, rather than one's tendency to believe them.

describe, behavior
ability

THE DEVELOPMENT OF SEX AND GENDER

41. A definition of maleness or femaleness would have to consider three different "domains" or aspects. One is our inner sense of being male or female, called _____ _____.

gender identity

42. A second aspect (see above) is a group of behavior patterns that our culture deems appropriate for each sex, called _____ _____.

gender roles

43. A third aspect (see above) is our choice of sexual partner, called _____ _____.

sexual orientation

44. The expectation that someone "labeled" as male will be more aggressive and more interested in things than people is an example of _____ _____.

gender typing

45.

This figure illustrates the phenomenon of gender role _____.

stereotypes

46. Characteristics of the female gender role stereotype in American society include (list 3) _____, _____, and _____.

submissiveness, interest in people, emotionality, gentleness

47. There are many physical and physiological differences between males and females, including the fact that their brains are sexually _____.

dimorphic

48. There seems to be a biological basis for some sex differences; for example, in the area of motivation, males tend to be more _____ than females.

aggressive

49. Although males exceed females in _____ aggression, females are at least the equals of males in _____ aggression.

physical
relational

50. There may also be a biological predisposition for male superiority in _____ ability.

spatial (spatial-mathematical)

51. There is evidence that higher _____ levels lead to better spatial abilities, and that this effect may be produced by greater elaboration of the _____, a structure in the brain.

testosterone, hippocampus

52. In many cases, culture or social factors act to _____ existing small constitutional sex differences.

exaggerate (or amplify or increase)

53. By age five or six, children have a basic understanding of fundamental sex differences and their permanence, or _____ _____.

gender constancy

54. A child who has reproductive organs that are difficult to classify as male or female is called a _____.

pseudohermaphrodite

55. People who are genetically male but raised as female from infancy usually show normal female gender _____, but a tendency to a masculine gender _____.

identity, role

56. A female who sees herself as female and is sexually attracted to males but is aggressive and athletic could be said to have some characteristics of the male _____ _____.

gender role

57. Most sex reassignment studies indicate that if the reassignment is made within the first _____ years of life, the child will grow up with a normal gender _____, appropriate to his or her sex rearing. However, studies on the _____ syndrome suggest that successful sex reassignment can occur at _____.

two (three, four)
identity
guevedoces
puberty

58. The majority of men and women are _____ in that they seek sexual partners of the opposite sex. The minority who seek partners of the same sex are called _____.

heterosexual
homosexuals

59. The incidence of exclusive male homosexuality in the United States is about _____ percent of all adult males (as of 1948).

4

60. _____ experience erotic or romantic feelings toward both sexes.

Bisexuals

61. According to Freud, homosexuality follows from the _____ of the young child with the same-sex parent.

identification

62. Research indicates no major differences between homosexuals and heterosexuals in _____ experience. Overall, it seems homosexuals experience an attraction to the same sex _____ (before/after) having sexual experiences.

early
before

63. _____ studies suggest a genetic influence on homosexuality.

Twin

64. There is evidence for a difference in _____ structure between male heterosexuals and homosexuals.

brain (hypothalamus)

65. There is little evidence for differences in _____ hormone levels between homo- and heterosexuals, but it is possible that there is a difference in _____ hormone levels.

adult
prenatal

DEVELOPMENT AFTER CHILDHOOD

66. Erikson's "Eight Ages of Man" span the entire life cycle, each stage accompanied by a critical _____.

conflict (or crisis)

67. The stage of transition from childhood to adulthood is called _____.

adolescence

68. In some cultures, the transition to adulthood is marked clearly, with a ceremony or more extended set of activities called _____ _____.

initiation rites

69. In adolescence, the major conflict is described as a(n) _____ _____.

identity crisis

70. In the _____ _____, people of middle age reappraise what they have done with their lives, and may reevaluate their marriage and career.

midlife transition

71. In Erikson's scheme, although there are some important biological markers in growth past childhood, such as _____, the quality and duration of each stage is substantially influenced by _____.

puberty (or menopause)
culture

Self Test

1. Bowlby's theory of attachment:
   a. focuses on contact comfort
   b. assumes that infants fear unfamiliar objects
   c. assumes that infants enjoy social interaction
   d. all of the above
   e. none of the above

2. Harlow's results, showing a preference by infant monkeys for a "terry-cloth mother" over a wire mother that provides food, argue:
   a. in favor of Freud's view of attachment
   b. in favor of Bowlby's view of attachment
   c. that nutrition has no effect in producing attachment between infant and mother
   d. a and b
   e. all of the above

3. Which of the following statements about imprinting is false?
   a. Imprinting depends on the fact that the parents will be the most salient objects around the offspring in the first part of life.
   b. Imprinting is based on experience.
   c. Animals may lose the capacity to imprint after a certain age.
   d. One would not expect to find imprinting in a "parasitic" species that is typically raised by adults of another species.
   e. none of the above

4. Proximity is to comfort as separation is to
   a. imprinting
   b. critical periods
   c. providing nutrients
   d. distress
   e. satisfaction

5. Attachment theorists suggest that a good parent-child relationship at an early age, as assessed in the Strange Situation, is a major determinant of later social emotional adjustment. However:
   a. later adjustment may result from the current relation between parent and child
   b. the father also plays a major role in adjustment
   c. adjustment involves the parent-child relation, not just the child
   d. imprinting may be the cause of later adjustment
   e. b and c

6. In Ainsworth's Strange Situation, infants show less distress at their father's than their mother's departure. Which of the following would be most likely to increase the infants' distress response to the father's disappearance?
   a. dress the father as a woman
   b. dress the father as a strange man
   c. find a father who had much more contact with his child
   d. find a child who had been severely punished by his or her mother
   e. feed the child bananas

7. The effects of maternal deprivation for more than a few months on subsequent behavior of monkeys and humans are:
   a. severe, and almost the same
   b. severe for humans, mild for monkeys
   c. severe for monkeys, mild for humans
   d. minimal
   e. irreversible

8. A conclusion that can be drawn from monkey and human maternal deprivation studies is that:
   a. adequate nutrition is not sufficient to produce normal social behavior
   b. behavior to peers is unaffected by maternal deprivation
   c. imprinting does not have anything to do with later sexual or maternal behavior
   d. the effects of maternal deprivation are very different in humans and monkeys
   e. maternal deprivation effects are especially severe if the deprivation occurs in the first few months of life

9. Monkeys deprived of mothers in about the first six months of life:
   a. show a temporary depression in social behavior
   b. are abnormal in social behavior, but will usually be successful parents
   c. are permanently deficient in all domains of social behavior
   d. show severe deficits in social behavior that are completely irreversible
   e. show severe deficits in social behavior that can be at least partly cured by carefully designed "therapy"

10. Institutionalized human children and motherless monkeys show social abnormalities characterized by:
    a. a "critical period" beginning at the time of birth and ending at about three months
    b. social withdrawal
    c. long-term effects that are irreversible
    d. a and b
    e. all of the above

11. Freud claimed that early experience had (1) a critical and (2) an irreversible effect on social development. Results from research up to this time suggest that:
    a. these two principles are basically correct
    b. early experiences have important effects, but many are reversible
    c. these two principles are totally incorrect
    d. early experiences have some significant effects, and these effects are irreversible
    e. none of the above

12. Both the Freudian approach and social learning or reinforcement theory agree that _____ is a major factor in socialization.
    a. imitation
    b. toilet training
    c. the child's understanding of the importance of older people
    d. gender identity
    e. none of the above

13. According to social learning theory, a critical aspect of socialization is:
    a. observational learning from models
    b. making models
    c. Pavlovian conditioning
    d. imprinting
    e. none of the above

14. Wendy sees her big sister smoking a cigarette. A few hours later she sneaks over to a pack of cigarettes, takes one out, holds it with two fingers, and puts it into her mouth, looking as debonair as possible. Then she lights it up, and inhales her first breath, coughing and gagging. But she continues to smoke the whole cigarette. This performance presents problems for a simple reinforcement view of socialization because:
    a. there is observational learning without immediate performance
    b. there seems to be negative reinforcement (gagging) for smoking
    c. there seems to be no basic biological reinforcement for her smoking
    d. it is not clear why she would want to imitate her sister
    e. all of the above

15. The cognitive approach emphasizes the difficulty of imitation. Complexities in the process of imitation include:
    a. what the child sees is a reflection (180-degree rotation) of what he or she has to do
    b. the child must determine what of many actions performed by the model is relevant
    c. one has to explain why the child wants to imitate in the first place
    d. a and b
    e. b and c

16. Ironically, children raised in the opposite autocratic and permissive styles share some common behavioral characteristics. Both types of children tend to:
    a. be socially responsible
    b. be more attached to their father
    c. lack independence
    d. be high in originality
    e. a and c

17. Imagine that a study reports that most cranky five-year-olds had parents who closed the door to their infants' bedrooms at night, so the baby wouldn't wake them. What might be possible explanations of this result?
    a. Isolating infants causes them to be cranky later in life.
    b. Cranky infants are more likely to be isolated by their parents.
    c. Parents who isolate their children in this way also do other things in child rearing that cause crankiness.
    d. Crankiness is inherited; cranky parents are more likely to be irritated by a crying child, and so are more likely to isolate it.
    e. all of the above

18. Authoritative-reciprocal rearing style is to optimal adjustment as mild social pressure is to _____.

a. doing good
b. not doing wrong
c. maximum internalization
d. permissive rearing style
e. autocratic rearing style

19. Forced compliance is an ineffective way of producing attitude change. This finding is in accord with:
a. the permissive rearing style
b. the principle of minimal sufficiency
c. the principle of imitation
d. attachment theory
e. none of the above

20. The occurrence of unselfish helping behavior by A suggests that A:
a. experiences empathic distress
b. is at a high stage of moral reasoning
c. knows how to be helpful in the particular situation
d. a and b
e. a and c

21. Consider the following three objections to making three reservations on different airlines at the same time for one person: A. It is against the unwritten rules of the airlines. B. It interferes with the access of others with no tangible gain to the party in question. C. It can be detected, and penalties can be assessed. According to Kohlberg, how would these three reasons be arranged in terms of the development of moral reasoning; indicate the earliest stage first.
a. A, B, C
b. B, C, A
c. C, B, A
d. B, A, C
e. C, A, B

22. A person says that one shouldn't double park because it is against the law. This explanation is an example of:
a. fear of punishment
b. conventional morality
c. abstract principle
d. empathy
e. none of the above

23. According to Gilligan, moral reasoning in men is relatively more influenced by justice, while in women it is relatively more influenced by compassion. But men and women don't differ on scores on Kohlberg's tests of moral reasoning. Why?
a. Kohlberg's tests value compassion as much as abstract principles.
b. Compassion is more abstract than justice.
c. The male-female difference has more to do with emphases than abilities.
d. a and b
e. a and c

24. Seymour speaks eloquently on the issue of equal rights for all races and religions but is actually quite racially prejudiced when he hires workers at his business. This illustrates:
a. the effects of reinforcement
b. the influence of the Freudian unconscious

c. the distinction between moral reasoning and moral conduct
d. the conflict between the social learning view and more traditional reinforcement explanations of moral behavior
e. egocentrism

25. Which of the following is illustrative of gender role?
a. thinking of oneself as a female
b. attraction to the opposite sex
c. submissiveness and emotionality in a female
d. homosexual tendencies
e. none of the above

26. From the clear demonstration of a biological (genetic) component to a gender difference, we can conclude:
a. that all of one gender is superior on this characteristic to all of the other gender
b. that the gender difference cannot be eliminated
c. that the gender difference is irreversible
d. b and c
e. none of the above

27. The finding that, in American culture, females express emotion more readily than do males, should be interpreted to mean:
a. that females are biologically more inclined to express emotions
b. that our society teaches females to be more expressive
c. that the average female is more emotionally expressive than the average male, but that there is a great deal of overlap
d. gender typing is not a sufficient explanation of sex difference, and one must also consider gender identity
e. a and d

28. The idea that there is a biological factor contributing to sex differences in aggression is (or would be) supported by all but which of the following?
a. In early humans, the stronger male was responsible for almost all hunting and fighting.
b. These differences are seen in many cultures.
c. Some of these differences are also seen in animals.
d. Male hormone increases aggression.
e. all of the above

29. Studies of early sex reassignment indicate that:
a. gender identity and role are completely shifted to the new sex
b. sexual orientation is usually not changed
c. gender identity fails to shift, but there are some effects of the original gender role
d. all three aspects of sex (role, gender, and orientation) show significant resistance to change
e. none of the above

30. The presence of hormones of the opposite "sex" in young children is most likely to influence their:
a. gender identity
b. gender role
c. sexual orientation
d. all of the above
e. none of the above

1. Male homosexuality:
   a. is not stigmatized in all cultures
   b. was quite acceptable in ancient Greece
   c. seems to be more common than female homosexuality
   d. is almost always associated with male gender identity
   e. all of the above

32. The psychoanalytic view suggests that male homosexuality may result when the child resolves fears aroused during the Oedipal conflict by identifying with the mother instead of the father. This theory would have difficulty explaining:
   a. the absence of evidence for differences in the early experience of homosexuals and heterosexuals
   b. the occurrence of a normal homosexual phase in adolescents in some cultures
   c. the fact that, typically, male homosexuals have traditional male gender identity and roles
   d. all of the above
   e. a and b

33. The data from sex reassignment and the fact that, in most cases, homosexuals report homosexual tendencies early in life both argue for:
   a. the psychoanalytic approach
   b. attachment to the mother at the time of the Oedipal crisis
   c. a genetic basis for important aspects of sexual orientation and gender identity
   d. all of the above
   e. none of the above

34. Evidence for a biological predisposition to homosexuality comes from all but one of the following. Which of the following is *not* evidence?
   a. twin studies
   b. male hormone level differences between male homosexual and heterosexual adults
   c. male hormone level differences between male homosexuals and heterosexuals prenatally
   d. differences in brain structure between male homosexuals and heterosexuals
   e. a and b

35. The transition from childhood to adolescence:
   a. occurs at the same age in all cultures
   b. is always a turbulent period
   c. usually occurs at the onset of sexual maturity
   d. all of the above
   e. none of the above

36. Initiation rites, retirement parties, and marriages have in common that they:
   a. explicitly mark important life transitions
   b. occur in virtually all cultures
   c. are explicitly predicted by Erikson's scheme
   d. match Freud's views of major life events
   e. make for gradual transitions from one stage to another

37. In some societies, children gradually assume adult responsibilities, and in some societies, old family members live in the home, taking care of grandchildren (or great-grandchildren) and giving advice. These traditions:
   a. emphasize transitions from one stage of life to another
   b. ease transition from one stage of life to another

   c. emphasize the importance of biological factors in life history
   d. prove the correctness of Erikson's stages
   e. none of the above

Answer Key for Self Test

1.	d p. 576	20.	e pp. 597, 598
2.	b pp. 576, 577	21.	e p. 598
3.	e pp. 578, 579	22.	b p. 598
4.	d pp. 579, 580	23.	c p. 599
5.	a p. 580, 581	24.	c p. 600
6.	c p. 582	25.	c p. 601
7.	a p. 586	26.	e pp. 602, 603
8.	a pp. 585, 586	27.	c p. 602
9.	e p. 587	28.	e p. 603
10.	b pp. 586, 587	29.	e p. 607
11.	b p. 588	30.	b p. 607
12.	e p. 590	31.	e pp. 609, 610
13.	a p. 590	32.	d p. 611
14.	e p. 590	33.	e p. 611
15.	d p. 591	34.	b pp. 612, 613
16.	c p. 593	35.	c p. 615
17.	e p. 594	36.	a pp. 615, 616
18.	c p. 595	37.	b pp. 619, 620
19.	b p. 596		

Investigating Psychological Phenomena

SEX DIFFERENCES

Equipment: None
Number of participants: Twelve
Time per participant: Five minutes
Time for experimenter: Sixty minutes

Sex differences can be analyzed into three different categories:
1. Gender identity—thinking of oneself as male or female.
2. Sexual orientation—sex of desired sexual partners, leading to the heterosexual-homosexual distinction.
3. Gender role—behavior patterns or attitudes associated with one or the other sex.

The relative role of experience (nurture) and genes (nature) has been debated for each of these aspects of sex. But before such studies can be done definitively, we must be clear on the nature of the differences to be explained. This is more or less clear for gender identity and sexual orientation. But the major behavioral and attitudinal differences between the sexes are not obvious and surely differ across cultures.

This study is an attempt to define some reliable sex differences among American college students. We have developed seventeen questions that promise to reveal sex differences (we will use as a criterion of a question that discriminates between the sexes a response pattern in which there is at least a 25 percentage point difference between males and females).

First: Answer the questionnaire. *Do not read on until you finish it.*

Questionnaire on Sex Differences

> Sex: Male Female
> (Circle one)

1. Would you be willing to kill a cockroach by slapping it with your hands?
   a) yes   b) no
2. What is Queen Anne's lace?
   a) flower   d) doily
   b) embroidery   e) spice
   c) perfume
3. How many times in the last twenty-four hours have you used the word "shit"?
   a) fewer than 5 times   b) 5 or more times
4. Can you sew well enough to make clothes?
   a) yes   b) no
5. Do you believe in sexual intercourse only after a spiritual love exists between you and your partner?
   a) yes   b) no
6. Do you walk around freely in the nude in a locker room?
   a) yes   b) no
7. How often do you cry?
   a) very often   d) very infrequently
   b) often   e) never
   c) only with good reason
8. At times I feel like smashing things.
   a) true   b) false
9. Do you know your chest measurement?
   a) yes   b) no
10. Can you change a tire easily?
    a) yes   b) no
11. I spend no more than one hour during an average school day playing the radio or listening to records.
    a) true   b) false
12. Would you prefer to be the dominant one in a relationship?
    a) yes   b) no
13. Do you think that you are overweight?
    a) yes   b) no
14. When you get depressed, does washing your hair make you feel better?
    a) yes   b) no
15. Do you sleep in the nude?
    a) yes   b) no
16. Which parent are you closest to?
    a) mother   b) father
17. I try to keep my room as neat as possible.
    a) true   b) false

These questions have been made up by faculty and students in introductory psychology courses. Each question has been "tested" with at least 100 undergraduate students in psychology courses. Therefore, we know how well these questions discriminate between college-age males and females (at least in 1971–1973, when the questions were tested). Of the seventeen questions, we know from past testing that five do not discriminate males from females. Try and guess, in advance, which questions would not discriminate. Then, check your guesses against the data presented on the final page of this study. *Guess before you read on.*

List questions that would not discriminate.

Note the type of successful questions in this questionnaire. Some relate to traditional male-female differences. Thus, males are more aggressive (Item 12 on dominance, but note no difference on Item 8—smashing things). Similarly males are less squeamish (Item 1, cockroach) and more restrained emotionally (Item 7, crying).

Other questions refer to knowledge or abilities that tend to go with gender in our society. This would include information about flowers (Item 2, Queen Anne's lace), sewing ability (Item 4), ability to change a tire (Item 10), and knowledge of body measurements (Item 9).

There are in addition some "miscellaneous" questions that tap into reliable differences (Item 5, attitudes to intercourse; Item 6, attitude to walking around nude in a locker room; Item 13, perception of fatness in self; Item 14, washing of hair as a response to depression; and Item 17, neatness).

Second, collaborate with at least one or two other students in the class, so that you can collect enough data. Give the twelve copies of this questionnaire, located on pp. 183–93, to twelve undergraduates, six males and six females. (Try to get them to fill out the questionnaire when you give it to them; otherwise, you will find that you don't get a very high return rate.) Aim for a minimum of five completed questionnaires for each sex. Combine your results with the results of as many classmates as you can: It would be desirable to end up with at least fifteen students of each sex.

Third, tabulate your results (see p. 180) in the following way. For the "yes" or "no" questions (e.g., Item 1), add up the number of participants who answered "yes." Then calculate what percentage answered "yes." For the "true" or "false" questions (e.g., Item 8), record those who answer "true." For other items (e.g., Item 2), add up the number of participants whose answers are the same as those indicated in parentheses under "Item" (e.g., Item 1— flower).

Fourth, we have devised a "femaleness" score, by indicating the more common female response to each of the questions that discriminates sex. Compute such a score for each of your participants by counting one point for each of the following answers:

1.	no	9.	yes
2.	flower	10.	no
4.	yes	12.	no
5.	yes	13.	yes
6.	no	14.	yes
7.	very often, often, or with good reason	17.	yes

Indicate here the total number of participants of each sex from whom you have collected data:

Male _____   Female _____

Item	Your data (combined with classmates' data)				U. of Pa. Students**	
	Male		Female		Male	Female
	#	%	#	%	%	%
1. Killing cockroach	____	____	____	____	37	*7
2. Queen Anne's lace (correct answer: flower)	____	____	____	____	50	*82
3. Using word "shit" (less than 5 times)	____	____	____	____	49	50
4. Sew clothes	____	____	____	____	4	*59
5. Intercourse only after spiritual love	____	____	____	____	30	*75
6. Nude in locker room	____	____	____	____	72	*31
7. Crying frequently (very often, often, or only with good reason)	____	____	____	____	22	*78
8. Feel like smashing things	____	____	____	____	75	70
9. Chest measurement	____	____	____	____	28	*78
10. Change tire	____	____	____	____	76	*13
11. Playing radio	____	____	____	____	41	42
12. Prefer dominance in relationship	____	____	____	____	72	*10
13. Overweight	____	____	____	____	17	*60
14. Washing hair when depressed	____	____	____	____	19	*53
15. Sleep in nude	____	____	____	____	39	44
16. Closest parent (mother)	____	____	____	____	61	72
17. Keep room neat	____	____	____	____	51	*77

* A male-female difference of a least 25 percentage points.

** Responses to items in the sex difference questionnaire by undergraduate introductory psychology students at the University of Pennsylvania (1971–1973). Responses are based on from 70 to 270 males and from 88 to 292 females, depending on the item.

SCORES OF MALES AND FEMALES ON "FEMALENESS" SCORE

Plot the number of males and females with each score. Use solid lines for the males and broken lines for the females. The graph at the left contains data gathered from fifteen undergraduate males and seventeen undergraduate females in 1980. Plot your data on the blank graph on the right. How well does this score separate biological females from biological males? What percentage of females score less than the highest male? How would you go about making a better behavioral discriminator of the sexes? (Note: We have avoided asking questions that might trivially distinguish males from females, such as: Do you wash the hair on your chest? or Do you ever wear dresses?)

Your (combined) data

You may note some major differences between your data and the data we reported in 1971–1973. In fact, we tried the questionnaire on fifteen male and seventeen female undergraduate students in 1980 (the participants used in the femaleness ratings), and found some differences from our 1971–1973 study. The biggest effects were that male-female differences disappeared for Queen Anne's lace (Question 2), overweight (Question 13: Over half of the men as well as women thought they were overweight), and washing hair when depressed (Question 14: Practically no one in our recent sample answered "Yes" to that).

There are basically three ways to explain discrepancies (our recent data or your data) from the original large sample of 1971–1973.

1. A general change in society over the last decades. It would seem fair to say that female gender roles have become more like male gender roles in this period. Does your data show this trend for any items? (Note that this would mean that female scores could move closer to male scores, and *not* that male scores would move closer to female scores. Of course, it is also possible to argue that the roles are becoming less distinct, but not necessarily moving toward the traditional male role.)

2. A difference in the populations sampled. Students from different parts of the country or from institutions with different styles or emphases might differ markedly in gender roles. Do you think your student sample would be likely to be very different from University of Pennsylvania students? In what ways? Is this reflected in differences on any scores? (Note that the differences might not just appear as male-female differences, but as generally higher or lower levels of response. For example, one might expect a generally higher positive response on sewing or changing a tire in people from rural backgrounds.)

3. Sampling error. Some observed differences may simply result from the fact that all samples from the same population don't have precisely the same scores (see Statistical Appendix to the textbook). With a small sample such as you have collected (as opposed to the large sample that we originally used), a wider variation from sample to sample would be expected. We would ordinarily use statistical methods to indicate how confident we would be that a difference between samples was not due to chance.

FURTHER ACTIVITIES

You might wish to try out some other questions that would relate gender identity to gender role. You could get a suggestion as to whether your questions were good discriminators with samples as low as twenty.

You can also try to use behavior rather than verbal responses to questionnaires. Can you think of obvious differences in such activities as: manner of walking or eating, facial expressions, behavior in front of mirrors, motorcycle riding, and so on. Test your hypothesis by direct observation.

(If your instructor collects the data, fill out the report sheet in Appendix 3.)

Questionnaire on Sex Differences

Sex: Male   Female
(Circle one)

1. Would you be willing to kill a cockroach by slapping it with your hands?
    a) yes   b) no
2. What is Queen Anne's lace?
    a) flower   d) doily
    b) embroidery   e) spice
    c) perfume
3. How many times in the last twenty-four hours have you used the word "shit"?
    a) fewer than 5 times   b) 5 or more times
4. Can you sew well enough to make clothes?
    a) yes   b) no
5. Do you believe in sexual intercourse only after a spiritual love exists between you and your partner?
    a) yes   b) no
6. Do you walk around freely in the nude in a locker room?
    a) yes   b) no
7. How often do you cry?
    a) very often   d) very infrequently
    b) often   e) never
    c) only with good reason
8. At times I feel like smashing things.
    a) true   b) false
9. Do you know your chest measurement?
    a) yes   b) no
10. Can you change a tire easily?
    a) yes   b) no
11. I spend no more than one hour during an average school day playing the radio or listening to records.
    a) true   b) false
12. Would you prefer to be the dominant one in a relationship?
    a) yes   b) no
13. Do you think that you are overweight?
    a) yes   b) no
14. When you get depressed, does washing your hair make you feel better?
    a) yes   b) no
15. Do you sleep in the nude?
    a) yes   b) no
16. Which parent are you closest to?
    a) mother   b) father
17. I try to keep my room as neat as possible.
    a) true   b) false

Questionnaire on Sex Differences

Sex: Male   Female
(Circle one)

1. Would you be willing to kill a cockroach by slapping it with your hands?
    a) yes   b) no
2. What is Queen Anne's lace?
    a) flower   d) doily
    b) embroidery   e) spice
    c) perfume
3. How many times in the last twenty-four hours have you used the word "shit"?
    a) fewer than 5 times   b) 5 or more times
4. Can you sew well enough to make clothes?
    a) yes   b) no
5. Do you believe in sexual intercourse only after a spiritual love exists between you and your partner?
    a) yes   b) no
6. Do you walk around freely in the nude in a locker room?
    a) yes   b) no
7. How often do you cry?
    a) very often   d) very infrequently
    b) often   e) never
    c) only with good reason
8. At times I feel like smashing things.
    a) true   b) false
9. Do you know your chest measurement?
    a) yes   b) no
10. Can you change a tire easily?
    a) yes   b) no
11. I spend no more than one hour during an average school day playing the radio or listening to records.
    a) true   b) false
12. Would you prefer to be the dominant one in a relationship?
    a) yes   b) no
13. Do you think that you are overweight?
    a) yes   b) no
14. When you get depressed, does washing your hair make you feel better?
    a) yes   b) no
15. Do you sleep in the nude?
    a) yes   b) no
16. Which parent are you closest to?
    a) mother   b) father
17. I try to keep my room as neat as possible.
    a) true   b) false

Questionnaire on Sex Differences

Sex: Male   Female
(Circle one)

1. Would you be willing to kill a cockroach by slapping it with your hands?
    a) yes   b) no
2. What is Queen Anne's lace?
    a) flower   d) doily
    b) embroidery   e) spice
    c) perfume
3. How many times in the last twenty-four hours have you used the word "shit"?
    a) fewer than 5 times   b) 5 or more times
4. Can you sew well enough to make clothes?
    a) yes   b) no
5. Do you believe in sexual intercourse only after a spiritual love exists between you and your partner?
    a) yes   b) no
6. Do you walk around freely in the nude in a locker room?
    a) yes   b) no
7. How often do you cry?
    a) very often   d) very infrequently
    b) often   e) never
    c) only with good reason
8. At times I feel like smashing things.
    a) true   b) false
9. Do you know your chest measurement?
    a) yes   b) no
10. Can you change a tire easily?
    a) yes   b) no
11. I spend no more than one hour during an average school day playing the radio or listening to records.
    a) true   b) false
12. Would you prefer to be the dominant one in a relationship?
    a) yes   b) no
13. Do you think that you are overweight?
    a) yes   b) no
14. When you get depressed, does washing your hair make you feel better?
    a) yes   b) no
15. Do you sleep in the nude?
    a) yes   b) no
16. Which parent are you closest to?
    a) mother   b) father
17. I try to keep my room as neat as possible.
    a) true   b) false

Questionnaire on Sex Differences

Sex: Male   Female
(Circle one)

1. Would you be willing to kill a cockroach by slapping it with your hands?
    a) yes   b) no
2. What is Queen Anne's lace?
    a) flower   d) doily
    b) embroidery   e) spice
    c) perfume
3. How many times in the last twenty-four hours have you used the word "shit"?
    a) fewer than 5 times   b) 5 or more times
4. Can you sew well enough to make clothes?
    a) yes   b) no
5. Do you believe in sexual intercourse only after a spiritual love exists between you and your partner?
    a) yes   b) no
6. Do you walk around freely in the nude in a locker room?
    a) yes   b) no
7. How often do you cry?
    a) very often   d) very infrequently
    b) often   e) never
    c) only with good reason
8. At times I feel like smashing things.
    a) true   b) false
9. Do you know your chest measurement?
    a) yes   b) no
10. Can you change a tire easily?
    a) yes   b) no
11. I spend no more than one hour during an average school day playing the radio or listening to records.
    a) true   b) false
12. Would you prefer to be the dominant one in a relationship?
    a) yes   b) no
13. Do you think that you are overweight?
    a) yes   b) no
14. When you get depressed, does washing your hair make you feel better?
    a) yes   b) no
15. Do you sleep in the nude?
    a) yes   b) no
16. Which parent are you closest to?
    a) mother   b) father
17. I try to keep my room as neat as possible.
    a) true   b) false

Questionnaire on Sex Differences

Sex: Male   Female
(Circle one)

1. Would you be willing to kill a cockroach by slapping it with your hands?
   a) yes   b) no
2. What is Queen Anne's lace?
   a) flower   d) doily
   b) embroidery   e) spice
   c) perfume
3. How many times in the last twenty-four hours have you used the word "shit"?
   a) fewer than 5 times   b) 5 or more times
4. Can you sew well enough to make clothes?
   a) yes   b) no
5. Do you believe in sexual intercourse only after a spiritual love exists between you and your partner?
   a) yes   b) no
6. Do you walk around freely in the nude in a locker room?
   a) yes   b) no
7. How often do you cry?
   a) very often   d) very infrequently
   b) often   e) never
   c) only with good reason
8. At times I feel like smashing things.
   a) true   b) false
9. Do you know your chest measurement?
   a) yes   b) no
10. Can you change a tire easily?
    a) yes   b) no
11. I spend no more than one hour during an average school day playing the radio or listening to records.
    a) true   b) false
12. Would you prefer to be the dominant one in a relationship?
    a) yes   b) no
13. Do you think that you are overweight?
    a) yes   b) no
14. When you get depressed, does washing your hair make you feel better?
    a) yes   b) no
15. Do you sleep in the nude?
    a) yes   b) no
16. Which parent are you closest to?
    a) mother   b) father
17. I try to keep my room as neat as possible.
    a) true   b) false

Questionnaire on Sex Differences

Sex: Male   Female
(Circle one)

1. Would you be willing to kill a cockroach by slapping it with your hands?
   a) yes   b) no
2. What is Queen Anne's lace?
   a) flower   d) doily
   b) embroidery   e) spice
   c) perfume
3. How many times in the last twenty-four hours have you used the word "shit"?
   a) fewer than 5 times   b) 5 or more times
4. Can you sew well enough to make clothes?
   a) yes   b) no
5. Do you believe in sexual intercourse only after a spiritual love exists between you and your partner?
   a) yes   b) no
6. Do you walk around freely in the nude in a locker room?
   a) yes   b) no
7. How often do you cry?
   a) very often   d) very infrequently
   b) often   e) never
   c) only with good reason
8. At times I feel like smashing things.
   a) true   b) false
9. Do you know your chest measurement?
   a) yes   b) no
10. Can you change a tire easily?
    a) yes   b) no
11. I spend no more than one hour during an average school day playing the radio or listening to records.
    a) true   b) false
12. Would you prefer to be the dominant one in a relationship?
    a) yes   b) no
13. Do you think that you are overweight?
    a) yes   b) no
14. When you get depressed, does washing your hair make you feel better?
    a) yes   b) no
15. Do you sleep in the nude?
    a) yes   b) no
16. Which parent are you closest to?
    a) mother   b) father
17. I try to keep my room as neat as possible.
    a) true   b) false

Questionnaire on Sex Differences

Sex: Male   Female
(Circle one)

1. Would you be willing to kill a cockroach by slapping it with your hands?
   a) yes   b) no
2. What is Queen Anne's lace?
   a) flower   d) doily
   b) embroidery   e) spice
   c) perfume
3. How many times in the last twenty-four hours have you used the word "shit"?
   a) fewer than 5 times   b) 5 or more times
4. Can you sew well enough to make clothes?
   a) yes   b) no
5. Do you believe in sexual intercourse only after a spiritual love exists between you and your partner?
   a) yes   b) no
6. Do you walk around freely in the nude in a locker room?
   a) yes   b) no
7. How often do you cry?
   a) very often   d) very infrequently
   b) often   e) never
   c) only with good reason
8. At times I feel like smashing things.
   a) true   b) false
9. Do you know your chest measurement?
   a) yes   b) no
10. Can you change a tire easily?
    a) yes   b) no
11. I spend no more than one hour during an average school day playing the radio or listening to records.
    a) true   b) false
12. Would you prefer to be the dominant one in a relationship?
    a) yes   b) no
13. Do you think that you are overweight?
    a) yes   b) no
14. When you get depressed, does washing your hair make you feel better?
    a) yes   b) no
15. Do you sleep in the nude?
    a) yes   b) no
16. Which parent are you closest to?
    a) mother   b) father
17. I try to keep my room as neat as possible.
    a) true   b) false

Questionnaire on Sex Differences

Sex: Male   Female
(Circle one)

1. Would you be willing to kill a cockroach by slapping it with your hands?
   a) yes   b) no
2. What is Queen Anne's lace?
   a) flower   d) doily
   b) embroidery   e) spice
   c) perfume
3. How many times in the last twenty-four hours have you used the word "shit"?
   a) fewer than 5 times   b) 5 or more times
4. Can you sew well enough to make clothes?
   a) yes   b) no
5. Do you believe in sexual intercourse only after a spiritual love exists between you and your partner?
   a) yes   b) no
6. Do you walk around freely in the nude in a locker room?
   a) yes   b) no
7. How often do you cry?
   a) very often   d) very infrequently
   b) often   e) never
   c) only with good reason
8. At times I feel like smashing things.
   a) true   b) false
9. Do you know your chest measurement?
   a) yes   b) no
10. Can you change a tire easily?
    a) yes   b) no
11. I spend no more than one hour during an average school day playing the radio or listening to records.
    a) true   b) false
12. Would you prefer to be the dominant one in a relationship?
    a) yes   b) no
13. Do you think that you are overweight?
    a) yes   b) no
14. When you get depressed, does washing your hair make you feel better?
    a) yes   b) no
15. Do you sleep in the nude?
    a) yes   b) no
16. Which parent are you closest to?
    a) mother   b) father
17. I try to keep my room as neat as possible.
    a) true   b) false

Questionnaire on Sex Differences

Sex: Male   Female
(Circle one)

1. Would you be willing to kill a cockroach by slapping it with your hands?
   a) yes   b) no
2. What is Queen Anne's lace?
   a) flower   d) doily
   b) embroidery   e) spice
   c) perfume
3. How many times in the last twenty-four hours have you used the word "shit"?
   a) fewer than 5 times   b) 5 or more times
4. Can you sew well enough to make clothes?
   a) yes   b) no
5. Do you believe in sexual intercourse only after a spiritual love exists between you and your partner?
   a) yes   b) no
6. Do you walk around freely in the nude in a locker room?
   a) yes   b) no
7. How often do you cry?
   a) very often   d) very infrequently
   b) often   e) never
   c) only with good reason
8. At times I feel like smashing things.
   a) true   b) false
9. Do you know your chest measurement?
   a) yes   b) no
10. Can you change a tire easily?
    a) yes   b) no
11. I spend no more than one hour during an average school day playing the radio or listening to records.
    a) true   b) false
12. Would you prefer to be the dominant one in a relationship?
    a) yes   b) no
13. Do you think that you are overweight?
    a) yes   b) no
14. When you get depressed, does washing your hair make you feel better?
    a) yes   b) no
15. Do you sleep in the nude?
    a) yes   b) no
16. Which parent are you closest to?
    a) mother   b) father
17. I try to keep my room as neat as possible.
    a) true   b) false

Questionnaire on Sex Differences

Sex: Male   Female
(Circle one)

1. Would you be willing to kill a cockroach by slapping it with your hands?
   a) yes   b) no
2. What is Queen Anne's lace?
   a) flower   d) doily
   b) embroidery   e) spice
   c) perfume
3. How many times in the last twenty-four hours have you used the word "shit"?
   a) fewer than 5 times   b) 5 or more times
4. Can you sew well enough to make clothes?
   a) yes   b) no
5. Do you believe in sexual intercourse only after a spiritual love exists between you and your partner?
   a) yes   b) no
6. Do you walk around freely in the nude in a locker room?
   a) yes   b) no
7. How often do you cry?
   a) very often   d) very infrequently
   b) often   e) never
   c) only with good reason
8. At times I feel like smashing things.
   a) true   b) false
9. Do you know your chest measurement?
   a) yes   b) no
10. Can you change a tire easily?
    a) yes   b) no
11. I spend no more than one hour during an average school day playing the radio or listening to records.
    a) true   b) false
12. Would you prefer to be the dominant one in a relationship?
    a) yes   b) no
13. Do you think that you are overweight?
    a) yes   b) no
14. When you get depressed, does washing your hair make you feel better?
    a) yes   b) no
15. Do you sleep in the nude?
    a) yes   b) no
16. Which parent are you closest to?
    a) mother   b) father
17. I try to keep my room as neat as possible.
    a) true   b) false

Questionnaire on Sex Differences

Sex: Male   Female
(Circle one)

1. Would you be willing to kill a cockroach by slapping it with your hands?
   a) yes   b) no
2. What is Queen Anne's lace?
   a) flower   d) doily
   b) embroidery   e) spice
   c) perfume
3. How many times in the last twenty-four hours have you used the word "shit"?
   a) fewer than 5 times   b) 5 or more times
4. Can you sew well enough to make clothes?
   a) yes   b) no
5. Do you believe in sexual intercourse only after a spiritual love exists between you and your partner?
   a) yes   b) no
6. Do you walk around freely in the nude in a locker room?
   a) yes   b) no
7. How often do you cry?
   a) very often   d) very infrequently
   b) often   e) never
   c) only with good reason
8. At times I feel like smashing things.
   a) true   b) false
9. Do you know your chest measurement?
   a) yes   b) no
10. Can you change a tire easily?
    a) yes   b) no
11. I spend no more than one hour during an average school day playing the radio or listening to records.
    a) true   b) false
12. Would you prefer to be the dominant one in a relationship?
    a) yes   b) no
13. Do you think that you are overweight?
    a) yes   b) no
14. When you get depressed, does washing your hair make you feel better?
    a) yes   b) no
15. Do you sleep in the nude?
    a) yes   b) no
16. Which parent are you closest to?
    a) mother   b) father
17. I try to keep my room as neat as possible.
    a) true   b) false

Questionnaire on Sex Differences

Sex: Male   Female
(Circle one)

1. Would you be willing to kill a cockroach by slapping it with your hands?
   a) yes   b) no
2. What is Queen Anne's lace?
   a) flower   d) doily
   b) embroidery   e) spice
   c) perfume
3. How many times in the last twenty-four hours have you used the word "shit"?
   a) fewer than 5 times   b) 5 or more times
4. Can you sew well enough to make clothes?
   a) yes   b) no
5. Do you believe in sexual intercourse only after a spiritual love exists between you and your partner?
   a) yes   b) no
6. Do you walk around freely in the nude in a locker room?
   a) yes   b) no
7. How often do you cry?
   a) very often   d) very infrequently
   b) often   e) never
   c) only with good reason
8. At times I feel like smashing things.
   a) true   b) false
9. Do you know your chest measurement?
   a) yes   b) no
10. Can you change a tire easily?
    a) yes   b) no
11. I spend no more than one hour during an average school day playing the radio or listening to records.
    a) true   b) false
12. Would you prefer to be the dominant one in a relationship?
    a) yes   b) no
13. Do you think that you are overweight?
    a) yes   b) no
14. When you get depressed, does washing your hair make you feel better?
    a) yes   b) no
15. Do you sleep in the nude?
    a) yes   b) no
16. Which parent are you closest to?
    a) mother   b) father
17. I try to keep my room as neat as possible.
    a) true   b) false

PART FIVE

INDIVIDUAL DIFFERENCES

CHAPTER 15

Intelligence: Its Nature and Measurement

Learning Objectives

1. Explain the relationship between the rise of mental testing and the structure of society.

MENTAL TESTS

2. Distinguish between achievement and aptitude tests.
3. Describe the purpose of intelligence, neuropsychological, and personality tests.

The study of variation
4. Define frequency distribution, mean, median, variability, and normal curve.
5. Explain the meaning of correlation, and describe the correlation coefficient.

Evaluating mental tests
6. Explain the concept of reliability and different measures of reliability.
7. Explain predictive and construct validity and the procedure of standardization.

INTELLIGENCE TESTING

8. Indicate the difficulties in defining intelligence.

Measuring intelligence
9. Outline the major events in the history of intelligence testing.
10. Define and explain the rationale behind intelligence quotients (as calculated by Binet) and deviation IQs.
11. Describe the different types of intelligence tests. Contrast the Wechsler, the Binet, and the Kaufman Assessment Battery for Children.
12. How are intelligence tests modified to deal with culture differences, native language differences, and the exploration of neurological impairment?

An area of application: mental retardation
13. Describe mental retardation.
14. Discuss the relationship between retardation and productive functioning in society.
15. What are some causes of mental retardation?
16. What are the dangers of relying completely on IQ test scores in classifying people as retarded? How can this problem be avoided?

WHAT IS INTELLIGENCE? THE PSYCHOMETRIC APPROACH

17. What is the psychometric approach?

The structure of mental abilities
18. What is a correlation matrix and what is factor analysis?
19. Describe the evidence for "g," and differentiate general factor and group factor theories.
20. Distinguish fluid and crystallized intelligence.
21. Discuss the distinction between g as a statistical as opposed to a theoretical entity.

WHAT IS INTELLIGENCE? THE INFORMATION-PROCESSING APPROACH

Simple cognitive correlates
22. Indicate the logic and evidence behind the suggestion that simple cognitive processes, such as performance on simple or choice reaction time tasks or on a lexical search identification task, may be components of intelligence.

Complex cognitive components
23. What are the limitations on explanations of intelligence in terms of simple cognitive processes, and how does involvement of complex cognitive processes solve some of these problems?
24. Explain how analogical reasoning has been analyzed into components, and the possible relation of analogical reasoning to intelligence.

The role of working memory and attention
25. Indicate how working memory and attention may be components of intelligence, and describe active span tasks.

Strategies and intellectual functioning
26. Discuss the role of strategies and strategies for using strategies in intelligence. Compare retardates, normal children, and normal adults on this dimension. Can retardates learn strategies?

WHAT IS INTELLIGENCE? BEYOND IQ

Practical intelligence
27. What are the limitations of intelligence tests, in terms of the range of mental abilities measured?
28. Distinguish among practical, analytic, and creative intelligence.

29. What is tacit knowledge, and how does it contribute to practical intelligence?

The notion of multiple intelligences

30. What are Gardner's multiple intelligences, and what is the evidence for them?

31. How might cultural differences produce different performances on questions on intelligence tests?

32. Explain and evaluate the statement: "We may be able to measure intelligence, but we don't really know what it is."

NATURE, NURTURE, AND IQ

Some political issues

33. Review the history of positions on genetic factors in intelligence differences related to racial groups or social class.

Genetic factors

34. Explain why it is not possible for any trait to be determined completely by the genotype.

35. Review basic terms in genetics (phenotype, genotype) and the relation between genotype and phenotype.

36. Describe the cause and genetic basis of phenylketonuria, and know how it illustrates the fact that inborn characteristics may be changeable.

37. Explain polygenic inheritance.

38. Explain why studies of the similarity in intelligence of members of the same family cannot be used to distinguish between genetic and environmental factors.

39. Explain how twin and adoption studies can be used to make this same distinction. Summarize the results of these studies and indicate problems in interpreting them.

Environmental factors

40. Summarize the evidence for and against genetic and environmental explanations of differences in intelligence (IQ) in American whites, from twin and adoption studies, from situations where major environmental differences were studied, and from trends over time in IQ scores.

Heritability

41. Explain the idea of heritability and why it only makes sense to use it to explain differences across individuals.

Group differences in IQ

42. Describe the mean differences and overlap in IQ between African Americans and European Americans.

43. Explain how heritability within groups can differ markedly from heritability of the same trait between groups.

44. Evaluate each of the following explanations of the reported difference between average IQ scores of African Americans and European Americans:

1. the difference doesn't exist
2. unfairness of the tests and test situations for African Americans
3. differences in environments between the groups
4. genetic differences between the groups

Some final thoughts

45. What would be the consequences of a clear finding that some of the African American–European American IQ differences was attributable to genetic factors?

Programmed Exercises

MENTAL TESTS

1. Tests of _____ measure what an individual can do now—his or her present knowledge and competence in a particular area. achievement

2. Tests of _____ predict what an individual will be able to do later. aptitude

3. _____ tests measure general aptitude. Intelligence

4. _____ tests assess effects of brain injury. Neuropsychological

5. _____ tests assess behavioral dispositions. Personality

6. The frequency with which individual cases are distributed over different intervals of some measure is called a(n)_____ _____. frequency distribution

7. The sum of all cases (observations) divided by the number of cases is called the _____. mean

8. The case located in the "middle" of the frequency distribution, such that 50 percent of cases are smaller and 50 percent are larger, is called the _____. median

9. The more that individual cases differ from one another, the higher the_____. variability

10. Many physical and mental attributes show symmetrical bell-shaped frequency distributions, which are described as _____ _____. normal curves

11. In evolution, _____ provides the basis on which natural selection works. variability

12. Each point in the figure here represents the weight and IQ of one person. This display is called a
_____ _____.

scatter diagram

13. The _____ _____ is a statistic that describes the relations between two sets of measures.

correlation coefficient

14. The correlation between X and Y is –.70, that is, _____ = –.70. This means that the bigger X gets, the _____ Y gets, on the average.

r
smaller

15. The consistency with which a test measures is called its _____.

reliability

16. This can be measured by calculating the _____ between scores on the same test at two different times, or _____-_____ reliability.

correlation
test-retest

17. Reliability can also be measured as the _____ between split halves of the same test.

correlation

18. The extent to which a test measures what it is supposed to measure is called its _____.

validity

19. The higher the positive correlation between the score on a driving test and the number of years driving without an accident, the greater the _____ _____ of this test.

predictive validity

20. A test based on a theoretical scheme that accounts for the attribute being measured is said to have _____ _____.

construct validity

21. In order to obtain _____ against which to evaluate a test score, the test is administered to a large number of people, called the _____ _____.

norms
standardization sample

INTELLIGENCE TESTING

22. According to Binet's system, a six-year-old who passed all the items at the nine-year-old level and none at the ten-year-old level would have a _____ _____ of nine years.

mental age

23. A person who gets the mean score for people of his or her age would have a deviation IQ of _____.

100

24. An IQ score that indicates the location of a person's score in the frequency distribution of scores for persons of the same age is called a _____ IQ.

deviation

25. The Wechsler Adult Intelligence Scale was in part a response to the emphasis on language in the Binet-Simon IQ tests. The Wechsler test has two parts, labeled _____ and _____.

performance, verbal

26. The Kaufman Assessment Battery for Children focuses on intelligence as a form of _____ processing. It has nonverbal scales, which make it particularly appropriate for testing of _____ or _____ children.

information
handicapped, minority
(non-English-speaking)

27. In _____ assessment tests, there are items that analyze why a person gives the answer he or she does.

neuropsychological

28. The majority of people classified as mentally retarded can function _____ in relatively simple life situations.

adequately

29. In order to be fair to disadvantaged groups, tests used to classify people as retarded should compare the children to _____ of children from the same background, and should include _____ items.

norms
nonverbal

30. Retardation can be caused by _____ factors or by an _____ environment.

genetic (biological), impoverished

31. The types of retardation that result from a single cause and clearly defined damage to the nervous system occur _____ frequently, and tend to produce deficits that are _____ severe.

less, more

WHAT IS INTELLIGENCE? THE PSYCHOMETRIC APPROACH

32. In the _____ approach, the results of intelligence tests are studied and analyzed in an attempt to discover the structure of intelligence.

psychometric

33. The fact that scores from a variety of different intelligence tests, specific and general, are positively _____, led Spearman to introduce the factor of _____ _____.

correlated, general intelligence (g)

34. The technique used to try to extract the structure of intelligence from correlation matrices is called _____ _____.

factor analysis

35. The fact that some specific parts of intelligence tests correlate very highly with only some other parts, and that there are clusters of tests that highly correlate with one another, is evidence for the _____ _____ theories.

group factor

36. It seems to be the case that as one goes to older age, ability to deal with new problems or to respond rapidly, called _____ intelligence, tends to deteriorate, while the repertoire of basic cognitive skills, knowledge, and strategy, called _____ intelligence, remains intact.

fluid
crystallized

WHAT IS INTELLIGENCE? THE INFORMATION-PROCESSING APPROACH

37. One possible cognitive correlate of intelligence is the speed with which a person responds to a stimulus, or _____ _____ _____.

simple reaction time

38. A better cognitive correlate is the speed of response when there are several responses and stimuli, or _____ _____ _____.

choice reaction time

39. Some have argued that basic abilities, such as the time it takes to access a word in long-term memory, or the _____ _____ task, are correlates of intelligence.

lexical identification

40. A problem such as "car is to garage as person is to _____ (house)" is an example of _____ _____. Some believe that such tasks can be analyzed into _____ _____.

analogical reasoning
cognitive components

41. Working memory and attention ability are measured in _____ _____ tasks.

active span

42. Humans improve their performance by using flexible _____ to solve problems, learn, or remember.

strategies

43. The idea that strategies are fundamental to intelligence is supported by the fact that retardates do poorly in memory tasks that require _____. Although they can be trained to use these strategies, retardates are poor at _____ them to other types of problems.

rehearsal (of organization)
generalizing (transferring)

44. A higher-order cognitive process that may be a fundamental dimension of human intelligence is _____ for using _____.

strategies, strategies

45. IQ tests measure principally _____ intelligence. But two other "types" of intelligence are _____ and_____.

analytic
practical, creative

WHAT IS INTELLIGENCE? BEYOND IQ

46. _____ _____, derived from experience in specific domains, is an important part of practical intelligence.

Tacit knowledge

47. Gardner's theory of _____ _____ holds that there are six different, _____ mental capacities.

multiple intelligences, independent

48. Evidence for these independent capacities is the presence of retarded people who show outstanding performance on a task related to one of these activities. Such people are called _____.

savants

49. People from different _____ may know different things, respond to tests differently, and make different interpretations of the meaning of the same question.

cultures

NATURE, NURTURE, AND IQ

50. The observed characteristics of an organism are called its _____. But the underlying genetic blueprint is called the _____.

phenotype
genotype

51. At some level, any trait is a result of _____ between genotype and environment. — interaction

52. A form of mental retardation that is caused by a single gene is _____. — phenylketonuria (PKU)

53. Traits that are controlled by genes but show many different values are determined by _____ inheritance. — polygenic

54. The fact that members of the same family have positively correlated intelligence and often share special abilities can be used as evidence for both _____ and _____ factors. — hereditary (genetic), environmental

55. Two basic methods for estimating the role of inherited factors in intelligence or other traits are _____ and _____ studies. — twin, adoption

56. The pattern of a higher correlation of IQ scores in _____ twin pairs that in _____ twin pairs, argue for a role for heredity in intelligence. — identical, fraternal

57. The fact that the IQ of early-adopted children correlates more highly with the IQ of the biological as opposed to adoptive mother is evidence for _____ determinants of intelligence. — genetic (biological, hereditary)

58. The negative effects of poor environments on IQ are illustrated by data showing that the longer a child is in a deprived environment, the lower his or her IQ. This appears as a _____ correlation between IQ and age. — negative

59. A number of studies have shown that _____ environments increase IQ. — enriched

60. Evidence for environmental influence on IQ is the _____ effect, the gradual (few points/10 years) increase in worldwide mean IQ. — Flynn

61. _____ is a concept that describes the percentage of the variation in a population that can be attributed to genetic factors. It does not apply to individuals. — Heritability

62. The difference between the mean IQs of European Americans and African Americans is _____ to_____ points. — 10 / 15

63. Some have argued that at least part of the European-American and African-American difference in average IQ scores can be attributed to the fact that the test was designed for the white middle class, that is to say, that the tests are not _____ fair. The evidence suggests that this _____ (is, is not) the case. — culture, is not

64. One cannot infer that, if a trait has high heritability within two populations, then population differences will also be explainable as largely due to _____. — heredity

65. A number of studies indicate that when differences in the environment of African Americans and European Americans during childhood are markedly reduced or equated, the African-American and European-American IQ difference is markedly _____. — reduced (diminished)

Self Test

1. Mental testing is primarily an American product, dating from the beginning of this century. America was a natural place for mental testing because:
   a. Americans embraced Freudian theory
   b. the American idea that all people are created equal required mental tests to show up their subtle differences
   c. of the high social and occupational mobility in America
   d. reinforcement was a popular concept in America
   e. Binet and Simon were Americans

2. One group of five people gets the following scores on a mathematics test: 85, 85, 90, 95, 95. Another group gets these five scores: 80, 80, 90, 100, 100. Which of the following statements about these groups is true?
   a. Both have the same means and different variability.
   b. Both have the same means and the same variability.
   c. Both have different means and the same variability.
   d. Both have different means and variability.
   e. It is impossible to say which group has a bigger mean.

3. The accompanying diagram represents the hypothetical scores of individual participants on an IQ test and on a history achievement test. The correlation displayed would be closest to:
   a. +1.00
   b. + .50
   c. +0.00
   d. −.50
   e. −1.00

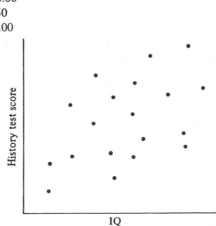

4. For which of the following pairs of variables would one expect to see a negative correlation?
   a. age and vocabulary
   b. height and visual acuity
   c. brain size and intelligence
   d. long-distance running ability and weight (among adults)
   e. social security number and intelligence (among adults)

5. If X is correlated with Y, then:
   a. if we know X, we can guess better than chance at the value of Y
   b. if we know Y, we can guess better than chance at the value of X
   c. there is no variability in X and Y
   d. X causes Y
   e. a and b

6. A hypothetical air force needs a test to help select people for training as pilots. There is no adequate theory of the acquisition of flying skills, but air force investigators discover that the speed with which one can tap with the third finger correlates +.80 with good performance in flying school. On the basis of this observation, one could say that the test had:
   a. high reliability
   b. high predictive validity
   c. high construct validity
   d. good standardization
   e. no mean validity

7. An appropriate standardization sample for a test of artistic talent in elementary school children would be:
   a. elementary school children
   b. elementary school children fifty years ago
   c. older children who have selected art as a career
   d. elementary school children with artistic talent
   e. representative adults from the same country

8. Intelligence testers face special problems because:
   a. intelligence changes with age
   b. intelligence tests are not reliable
   c. all questions require prior knowledge, so that past experience determines the test score
   d. there is no clear basis for determining construct validity
   e. it is difficult to calculate deviation IQs

9. The deviation IQ is a better measure than the older intelligence quotient (mental age/chronological age) because:
   a. it is newer
   b. the deviation IQ is more reliable and is based on better tests
   c. a person's deviation IQ will stay about the same, from age fifteen to fifty, for example
   d. the deviation IQ increases with age, as does intelligence
   e. it is based on the idea of 100 being average

10. Harry is eighteen and has a deviation IQ of 110. Carol is ten and has the same deviation IQ. In comparing them, we can say that:
    a. both have the same position in the frequency distribution of their age group
    b. both have the same mental age

c. both get the same number of questions correct
    d. a and b
    e. none of the above

11. The SATs are a type of intelligence test. The scores are calculated in the same way as deviation IQs, with 500 as the mean score of those who have taken the test over the past few years. The mean deviation IQ of people with SAT scores of 500 is well over 100. This can be explained as a result of:
    a. different types of questions on the two tests
    b. high reliance on verbal ability in most IQ tests
    c. superior intelligence in the standardization population for the SATs
    d. a higher intake of meat and other high protein foods in high school seniors
    e. a and b

12. A student takes the same test of reaction time at 10:00 A.M. on two consecutive days. She gets very different scores on these two days. If this was true of many other test takers, it would suggest that this test is not:
    a. valid
    b. standardized
    c. reliable
    d. none of the above
    e. all of the above

13. A test measuring participants' abilities to do jigsaw puzzles would be a _____ test.
    a. performance
    b. verbal
    c. fluid
    d. unreliable
    e. c and d

14. A neuropsychological assessment differs from other intelligence tests because:
    a. it is designed for minorities
    b. it includes direct measures of brain function
    c. it can be administered to groups or individually
    d. it does not require the use of language
    e. it allows for requestioning to determine why a person fails on a question

15. In classifying people as mentally retarded on the basis of IQ test results, it would be especially important to:
    a. place them in the correct retardation (mild, moderate, etc.) category
    b. use a verbal test
    c. minimize incorrect classifications as retarded
    d. use the mental age/chronological age ratio
    e. avoid using the Kaufman ABC scale

16. Which of the following has *not* been identified as a cause of mental retardation?
    a. chromosome abnormalities
    b. particular genes
    c. severely impoverished environments
    d. trauma in fetal life or at birth
    e. none of the above

17. For someone who is severely (as opposed to mildly) retarded, it is more likely that:
    a. there are complex causes of the retardation
    b. the problem results from a specific biological deficit or environmental trauma
    c. there is more diffuse, as opposed to more specific, damage to the nervous system
    d. b and c
    e. all of the above

18. A psychometrician examines a verbal and a spatial intelligence test, and finds that the scores on these two tests correlate +.38. From this he might conclude that:
    a. performance on both tests is partly determined by "g" but mostly by specific factors
    b. these tests measure very different things, and there is no "g" component here
    c. both of these tests are excellent measures of "g"
    d. these results constitute proof of the group factor theories
    e. none of the above

19. Consider the following matrix of correlations for four subtests of a large intelligence test (the data are made up):

	S	M	C	V
Spatial ability		.88	.38	.46
Mechanical ability			.31	.40
Creativity				.42
Verbal ability				

    A group factor theorist might infer from this pattern that:
    a. there are four basic intelligence factors suggested by these results
    b. there are three basic intelligence factors suggested by these results
    c. there are two basic intelligence factors suggested by these results
    d. the data strongly support general factor, as opposed to group factor theory
    e. a or b

20. Gordon is really pretty ignorant, but he has a way of seeing relationships among ideas and figures and quickly comes up with new ways of doing things. He could be described as:
    a. high in "g"
    b. high in fluid, low in crystallized intelligence
    c. evidence for one-factor theories of intelligence
    d. someone who would do well on vocabulary tests
    e. someone who would do poorly on Raven's progressive matrices

21. Studies indicate that certain types of "intelligence" decline with age in adulthood and others do not. A type that improves or at least holds its own through most of adulthood is:
    a. "g"
    b. fluid intelligence
    c. crystallized intelligence
    d. group factors
    e. none of the above

22. Some believe that one can understand intelligence and predict IQs by analyzing intelligence into simple cognitive components, such as:
    a. strategies of problem solving
    b. reaction times
    c. retrieval time of items from memory
    d. all of the above
    e. b and c

23. Complex intelligence-related tasks, like analogical reasoning, can be broken down into components, such as identifying the common attribute of the first members of each pair in an analogy. This general route to the understanding of intelligence is called:
    a. the simple cognitive component approach
    b. the information-processing approach
    c. the psychometric approach
    d. the analogical approach
    e. none of the above

24. In contrast to retardates, normal children or adults:
    a. are able to learn strategies
    b. use strategies more
    c. generalize learned strategies more
    d. b and c
    e. all of the above

25. Cindy has to memorize the names of all of the American vice-presidents, and the dates that they held office. She considers doing it in alphabetical order, but then decides it would be better to try to remember them in chronological order. She is demonstrating:
    a. analogical reasoning
    b. enhanced working attention
    c. a psychometric effect
    d. simple cognitive components
    e. strategy for using strategies

26. The hypothetical finding that artists and composers are generally poor at solving everyday problems, like organizing a group of people on a task, would argue in favor of:
    a. the distinction between practical and analytic intelligence
    b. the importance of strategies in intelligence
    c. the importance of working memory in only some kinds of intelligence
    d. the separation of practical and creative intelligence
    e. b and d

27. One occasionally finds people who are highly intelligent, but terrible at spatial relations. This fact supports:
    a. Gardner's theory of multiple intelligence
    b. group-factor theory
    c. the concept of "g"
    d. the importance of working memory
    e. a and b

28. One might expect that individuals in non-Western cultures might be superior to Westerners at some types of intelligence, and inferior in others. One major variable might be the degree

of literacy. Which of the following features of "intelligence," broadly conceived, might be relatively unaffected or even improved by an inability to read?
a. spatial relations
b. ability to memorize and repeat long narratives
c. ability to solve analogy problems
d. a and b
e. b and c

29. The observation that people on the political left tend to think of intelligence as more under environmental control, while those on the right tend to think of it as more under genetic control, suggests that:
a. one must distinguish between within- and between-group differences
b. the study of genetic and environmental influences on intelligence is inherently political
c. sociopolitical factors influence judgments about the role of heredity in intelligence
d. there is no way to study scientifically the issue of the role of heredity and environment in intelligence
e. c and d

30. The fact that, in the period between the two World Wars, IQ scores of Eastern European immigrant groups improved the longer the immigrants were in the United States:
a. justified a policy of excluding Eastern Europeans from immigrating to the United States
b. raises questions about U.S. immigration policy in the period between the wars
c. demonstrates that intelligence is primarily under genetic control
d. demonstrates that intelligence is primarily under environmental control
e. none of the above

31. Jane and Phyllis have brown eyes. All of Jane's relatives have brown eyes. Phyllis's father has brown eyes, but her mother has blue eyes (brown eye color is dominant). From this information, we can guess that Jane and Phyllis have:
a. the same genotype and phenotype
b. the same genotype and different phenotypes
c. different genotypes and the same phenotype
d. different genotypes and phenotypes
e. c or d

32. A genetic female who is exposed to androgens as a fetus and develops male genitals, and a person with phenylketonuria who is treated at birth and develops no symptoms, both illustrate that:
a. inborn, genetically determined traits can be changed by environmental factors
b. sex-linked traits can occur in both sex and intelligence
c. behavior is inherited
d. environmental factors, under some circumstances, have no influence on behavior
e. behavior is related to sex chromosomes

33. The clustering of specific talents (e.g., music in the Bach family) or high intelligence in particular families, *across generations*, argues for:

a. a significant role for genetics in these abilities
b. a significant role for environment in these abilities
c. polygenic inheritance
d. a and b
e. a and/or b

34. If, counter to the results actually found, it was reported that fraternal and identical twins had the same high correlation in intelligence and that this was *higher* than the correlation between other siblings (e.g., brothers and sisters of different ages), one would be most justified in concluding that:
a. the higher correlation in twins was due to environmental factors
b. the higher correlation in twins was due to genetic factors
c. fraternal twins are more closely related, genetically, than are other siblings
d. a and c
e. b and c

35. Environmentalists explain the significant correlation between the IQ of adopted children and their biological parents in terms of *selective placement* of these children in adopted homes. (Children with higher-IQ biological parents are placed with higher-IQ adoptive parents.) This argument, however, is strongly weakened by:
a. the studies on identical twins
b. the fact that the IQ of adopted children correlates more highly with biological than adoptive parents
c. the fact that there is a positive correlation between the IQ of adopted children and their adoptive parents
d. b and c
e. none of the above

36. All but one of these findings supports or is consistent with the idea of a hereditary component in intelligence differences. Which finding does *not* support such a view?
a. higher IQ correlation in identical than fraternal twins
b. higher IQ correlation between adoptive children and their biological parents than between these same children and their adoptive parents
c. higher IQ correlation between siblings than between half-siblings (sharing only one parent)
d. higher correlations in IQ between fraternal twins than between other siblings
e. the stability of IQ over decades

37. On the whole, the IQs of biological parents giving children up for adoption are below those of adopting parents (since the latter are screened by agencies). The observation that, whatever the correlation between IQ of adopted child and biological parent, the actual IQ of such adopted children tends to be considerably higher than that of the biological parents, is evidence for:
a. hereditary effects
b. environmental effects
c. a and b
d. a heritability value
e. polygenic inheritance

38. If intelligence (IQ scores) in a particular group showed a heritability of 1.0, this would mean that:

a. existing environments have no effects on intelligence
b. while existing environments have no effects on intelligence, presently nonexistent environments might have significant effects
c. genetic factors account for most of the variation in IQ in this particular group
d. genetic factors account for all of the variation in IQ in this particular group
e. none of the above

39. Which of the following traits would you expect to show the *lowest* heritability?
    a. eye color
    b. height
    c. length of hair
    d. visual acuity
    e. running speed

40. Many have argued that IQ tests and the circumstances under which they are given favor European Americans over African Americans. All but one of the following reported findings argue against this view: That is, all but one indicate that the tests are reasonably culture fair. Select the one reported finding that does *not* argue in favor of the culture fairness of tests or test situations:
    a. the African-American and European-American IQ difference remains about the same when the African-American version of the test is translated into African-American English
    b. the African-American and European-American difference is about the same for verbal tests and for the abstract Raven's progressive matrices
    c. the African-American and European-American difference remains about the same whether the tester is African-American or European-American.
    d. the African-American and European-American difference remains about the same for tests of verbal and tests of spatial intelligence
    e. the African-American and European-American difference decreases in the children in families that have children of both races through adoption

41. Assume two breeds of cattle: In both, size differences within the breed are completely determined by genes (heritability: 1.0). Assume further that one bread is found in New Zealand and the other in central Africa and that the New Zealand breed averages about 10 percent bigger than the African breed. What inferences can be made about the origin of this difference between breeds?
    a. It is certainly due to heredity.
    b. It is certainly due to environment.
    c. The heritability of the population difference would be at least .50.
    d. The heritability of the population difference would be at least .10.
    e. No certain inference can be drawn about breed differences from this information.

42. A fair summary of studies on environmental matching or change, as applied to the African-American and European-American IQ difference, would be:
    a. there is generally a decreased African-American and European-American IQ difference when attempts are made to equalize environments in the comparison groups, and an improvement in African-American IQs when the environment is improved
    b. appropriate manipulation of environments, to provide African Americans with the full advantages of the European-American environment, leads to elimination of the African-American and European-American IQ difference
    c. there is very little effect of environmental change or equalization on African-American IQ or African-American and European-American differences
    d. a and b
    e. none of the above

43. What would be educationally and scientifically *appropriate* sociopolitical responses to a *hypothetical* proof that a fair proportion of the difference in IQ scores between African Americans and European Americans could be assigned to hereditary factors?
    a. curtailment of early enrichment programs
    b. establishment of racial quotas
    c. inclusion of race as an important factor in determining the ability of applicants for jobs involving intelligence
    d. cessation of affirmative action programs
    e. none of the above

Answer Key for Self Test

1.	c p. 625	23.	b p. 646
2.	a p. 627	24.	d p. 648
3.	b pp. 629, 630	25.	e p. 648
4.	d p. 630	26.	d p. 650
5.	e p. 630	27.	e pp. 643, 650
6.	b p. 631	28.	d p. 652, 653
7.	a p. 632	29.	c pp. 653, 654
8.	d p. 631	30.	b p. 654
9.	c p. 633, 634	31.	c p. 655
10.	a p. 634	32.	a p. 655
11.	c pp. 635, 636	33.	e p. 656
12.	c p. 631	34.	a pp. 657, 658
13.	a p. 636	35.	b p. 658
14.	e p. 637	36.	d p. 658
15.	c p. 637	37.	b p. 659
16.	e p. 639	38.	d pp. 660, 661
17.	b p. 639	39.	c pp. 660, 661
18.	a p. 642	40.	e pp. 661, 662
19.	b p. 642	41.	e pp. 662, 663, 664
20.	b p. 643	42.	a p. 664
21.	c p. 643	43.	e pp. 664, 665
22.	e pp. 644, 645		

Investigating Psychological Phenomena

"INTELLIGENCE TESTS"

Equipment: None
Number of participants: One (yourself)
Time per participant: Thirty minutes
Time for experimenter: Thirty minutes

This is an experiment that will help you to understand the construction of intelligence tests. The procedure that you will go through will be like the procedure that might be used in the development of an intelligence test. The main concern is that you understand how a distribution of test scores is generated, and how an individual score is interpreted with respect to that distribution.

For this purpose, rather than making up a so-called intelligence test, we have chosen to try out a measure of a characteristic that is rarely tested: One's knowledge of foods and cooking. In this case, one begins with some idea of the ability or knowledge base that one is trying to assess. Questions or tasks are constructed that seem to measure these. Then, pilot tests, like those we will give you, are distributed to a representative sample of the population for which the tests are intended. In your case, your class might serve as a sample of college undergraduates. Of course, students differ in schools and in different regions, so this would not be anything like the random sample we would actually need were this a real test.

The results of the test are examined. Typically, most of the questions which all participants get right or all get wrong are discarded, because such questions do not help to measure *differences* among people in the abilities under study. Then, some sort of retest studies are done, to make sure the test is reliable, and a validity study is done, to assure that the test measures what it is supposed to measure.

We will only deal with one phase of test construction here. We have made up a test that has never been used by psychologists before. (It is certainly not clear why a food knowledge test would be of interest to anyone in the real world.) We ask each of you to take the test. It is brief. The food knowledge test is in the format of a written test, with unlimited time. It is, of course, "closed book." Fill it out in a quiet place. Then score your answers, using the list of correct answers at the end of this section.

FOOD KNOWLEDGE TEST

Sex _____

Listed below are five countries
    Italy (southern Italy)
    China
    India
    Mexico
    Germany

Each of the following food items (1–14) is particularly characteristic of the cuisines of one of the five countries listed above. Write the name of the appropriate cuisine (country) beside the food item.

1. potatoes _____
2. corn _____
3. sesame oil _____
4. olive oil _____
5. soy sauce _____
6. cumin (two possible answers) _____
7. oregano _____

8. curry _____
9. chili pepper (two possible answers) _____
10. liverwurst _____
11. turmeric _____
12. yogurt _____
13. bean curd _____
14. ghee _____

Write in the name of the country associated with each of the following items:

15. sushi _____
16. lasagna _____
17. taco _____
18. paella _____
19. moussaka _____
20. goulash _____
21. sukiyaki _____

22. mousse _____
23. sate (pron: sā′ • tāy) _____
24. biryani _____
25. mole (pron: mǒ′ • lāy) _____
26. trifle _____
27. kim chee _____
28. champagne _____

29. What is the primary ingredient used in raising (leavening) bread? _____
30. What is yogurt made from? _____
31. What are raisins made from? _____
32. What is meringue made of? _____
33. What animal does bacon come from? _____
34. What are prunes made from? _____
35. What type of fish is lox made from? _____
36. What vegetable are pickles usually made from? _____
37. What fruit is wine usually made from? _____
38. What is sauerkraut made from? _____
39. What are chitterlings made from? _____
40. What does caviar come from? _____
41. What is marzipan made from? _____
42. What is the primary ingredient in guacamole? _____

Indicated below are five common cooking methods:

baking
sautéing or pan frying
braising
boiling
broiling

For each dish or food below, indicate by writing in the correct term from those listed above the primary cooking method used.

43. chicken soup _____

44. bread _____

45. scrambled eggs _____

46. pot roast _____

47. shish-kebab _____

48. spaghetti _____

49. soufflé _____

50. hash-brown potatoes _____

51. collard greens _____

TEST RESULTS AND "IQ" CALCULATIONS

The food knowledge test was taken by 153 University of Pennsylvania undergraduates in the introductory psychology course and twenty-one students in a University of Michigan class in learning and memory. The results were:

Mean score: 35.9 for 174 participants
Standard deviation: 5.03
Range of scores: 22 (lowest) to 47 (highest)

Females do slightly better than males on this test (mean female score: 36.8; mean male score: 35.1).

CALCULATION OF A "CULINARY IQ"

As we will discuss below, much more work would have to be done with this test before it could actually be used in a meaningful way. For the sake of illustrating the scaling of psychological tests, we will use the data generated by undergraduates taking this test to develop a "deviation" scale like that used in IQ tests. You can then calculate your "culinary IQ."

The basic principle behind scaling of tests is the deviation score. Like a percentile score, it expresses where a particular score stands with respect to all of the other scores. The distribution of scores for tests usually falls into what is called a normal distribution. An ideal normal distribution is drawn in the next column. Normal distributions are typically described by their mean value and their standard deviation, a measure of the spread or variability of the curve (see the statistical appendix to the text). In a normal distribution, 68 percent of all observations fall within one standard deviation of the mean, and 96 percent of all observations fall within two standard deviations of the mean (see the accompanying figure). Test scores are measured in units of deviation from the mean. For all IQ type tests, 100 is set as the mean

value and 15 point as the standard deviation. Thus, an IQ of 115 corresponds to the score one standard deviation above the mean (85 to one standard deviation below); 130 corresponds to a score of two standard deviations above the mean (70 to two below), and so on. (An IQ of 105 would then be one-third of a standard deviation above the mean.) In percentile terms, an IQ of 130 would be at the 98th percentile, and an IQ of 85 would be at the 16th percentile (see figure).

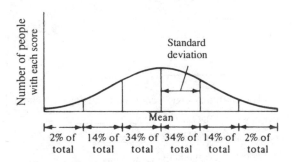

Normal distribution

Applying these ideas to our test, the mean score (35.9) on the food test would be assigned a scaled score of 100. Subtracting one standard deviation (5.03) from this score, we get approximately 31, a score that would be assigned a scaled score of 85 (one standard deviation below the mean corresponds to 15 scaled points). We have performed the appropriate arithmetic for the food test, and provided the raw score (your actual score) and scaled score (converted to deviation units) equivalents in the table on the next page. Because the standard deviation for the food knowledge scores is almost exactly 5, each additional point on the test is worth one-fifth of a standard deviation, or 3 "IQ" points.

FOOD TEST

Raw score (your actual score)	Scaled score ("IQ")
18	46
19	49
20	52
21	55
22	58
23	61
24	64
25	67
26	70
27	73
28	76
29	79
30	82
31	85
32	88
33	91
34	94
35	97
36	100
37	103
38	106
39	109
40	112
41	115
42	118
43	121
44	124
45	127
46	130
47	133
48	136
49	139
50	142
51	145

The nest step in developing a test would be to improve the first version. For example, in the food knowledge test, there are a number of useless items: These are items that do not contribute to the measurement of differences in people. For three items (number 16—lasagna, 37—wine, and 44—bread), all 174 participants got the right answer. Because of this, these items would normally be discarded. Three additional items were missed by less than 2% of the participants and might also be discarded. There were no questions that were missed by all participants. The "hardest" question was about the country of origin of sate (Number 23—Indonesia), and 8.6% of participants were correct on this item.

We would also eliminate any questions that turned out to be ambiguous. In this test, for example, some of the "What is X made from?" questions need clarification. Thus, for Number 39—chitterlings (chitlings), some people answered "pig," and others said "intestine." We scored both as correct, but should have been more specific in the question. Similarly, for Number 30—what is yogurt made from?—we intended that milk be the correct answer. But bacteria cultures are also components of yogurt. We should have asked, "What is the primary ingredient in yogurt?" See if you can find some other ambiguous questions. Finally, we would examine the correlation of correctness on each question with the total score on the test. Are there any items which don't seem to be measuring the same sort of thing as the rest of the test? (See the experiment on personality testing in the next chapter.) Such items might or might not be included but would at least be reexamined. Along these same lines, one might look at any questions which the top performers on the test all missed. Often such items are badly worded, or perhaps even in error. For the food test, there was no single item missed by all of the six top scorers.

Having streamlined the test, we would then use some type of test-retest procedure to determine reliability. (Will the same person score about the same on two different occasions?) The reliability measures would be complicated, since one would expect improvement on the second time through.

We would then perform some sort of validity test. Is the test measuring what it is supposed to measure? If the food knowledge test is supposed to predict likely candidates for success in a cooking school, does it actually do so?

Finally, having satisfied ourselves that we had a reliable and valid test, we would then administer the test to a large sample of people (hundreds to thousands of people) randomly selected from the population of people for whom the test was designed (e.g., high school seniors, all adults, etc.).

Ask yourself whether you believe the food test is meaningful. How would you validate it? What might it be used for? What would it correlate with?

FURTHER ACTIVITIES

Sketch out what you think would be an appropriate test for use in predicting success in a particular profession: for example, fighter pilot, baseball player, or architect. Then ask yourself how you would validate the test.

Answer Sheet

Score one point for each correct answer
(Listed next to each answer are the percentages correct out of 174 students.)

1. potatoes–Germany (83.9%)
2. corn–Mexico (78.7%)
3. sesame oil–China (28.2%)
4. olive oil–Italy (93.7%)
5. soy sauce–China (97.7%)
6. cumin–India or Mexico (78.2%)
7. oregano–Italy (90.2%)
8. curry–India (73.0%)
9. chili–India or Mexico (90.2%)
10. liverwurst–Germany (97.7%)
11. turmeric–India (48.3%)
12. yogurt–India (44.8%)
13. bean curd–China (44.8%)
14. ghee–India (60.3%)
15. sushi–Japan (55.7%)
16. lasagna–Italy (100%)
17. taco–Mexico (98.8%)
18. paella–Spain (40.2%)
19. moussaka–Greece (43.7%)
20. goulash–Hungary (73.6%)
21. sukiyaki–Japan (76.4%)
22. mousse–France (74.7%)
23. sate–Indonesia (8.6%)
24. biryani–India (37.4%)
25. mole–Mexico (14.9%)
26. trifle–England (47.7%)

27. kim chee–Korea (13.2%)
28. champagne–France (80.4%)
29. bread–yeast (97.1%)
30. yogurt–milk (88.5%)
31. raisins–grapes (96.0%)
32. meringue–egg white (74.1%)
33. bacon–pig (99.9%)
34. prunes–plums (77.0%)
35. lox–salmon (66.7%)
36. pickle–cucumber (97.7%)
37. wine–gapes (100%)
38. sauerkraut–cabbage (89.1%)
39. chitterlings–pig or intestine (29.3%)
40. caviar–fish eggs (91.4%)
41. marzipan–almond or sugar (31.0%)
42. guacamole–avocado (48.3%)
43. chicken soup–boiling (96%)
44. bread–baking (100%)
45. scrambled eggs–pan frying (98.3%)
46. pot roast–braising (46.6%)
47. shish kebab–broiling (57.5%)
48. spaghetti–boiling (97.7%)
49. soufflé–baking (83.3%)
50. hash-brown potatoes–pan fry or sautéing (96.6%)
51. collard greens–boiling (55.7%)

CHAPTER 16

Personality I: Assessment, Trait Theory, and the Behavioral-Cognitive Approach

Learning Objectives

1. What are the five orientations from which the subject of personality is approached, and what are their historical origins?

METHODS OF ASSESSMENT

Structured personality tests

2. Understand the construction and the use of the Minnesota Multiphasic Personality Inventory (MMPI). What is the importance of score profiles and validity scales? How is the MMPI-2 updated?
3. Why isn't the MMPI a commonly used test for normal people? What is one of the tests that is used instead?
4. Be familiar with the different types of test validity (predictive and construct) and how personality tests measure up.
5. Why don't the uniformly small correlations between the psychopathic deviance scale of the MMPI and various behavioral patterns invalidate the Pd scale?
6. Be aware of the Barnum effect and why it should be taken into account when assessing the validity of a personality test?

Projective personality tests

7. What is the rationale for projective techniques? Describe some of these procedures.
8. What scoring categories are used in the interpretation of Rorschach inkblots, and what general rules are employed?
9. Be familiar with the difference in interpretation between the Rorschach and the Thematic Apperception Test (TAT) in regard to perceived content.
10. Why is TAT interpretation impressionistic and global?
11. Summarize the issues and arguments in assessing the validity of the TAT and the Rorschach.
12. Of what value are projective tests in a clinical setting? Do they have incremental validity?

THE TRAIT APPROACH

13. What is the trait approach to personality?

The search for the right taxonomy

14. What was Cattell's approach to developing a taxonomy of personality traits? What modifications of Cattell's analysis have been suggested and why?
15. Discuss Eysenck's taxonomy of neuroticism and extroversion-introversion. What personality differences are encompassed by this scheme? Do the two dimensions of Eysenck's classification apply to other cultures?
16. Discuss the five-factor versus two-factor versus three-factor approaches. How are they related to each other?
17. What are the arguments about the validity of a factor-analytic approach to personality?

Traits versus situations: the consistency controversy

18. What is the importance of cross-situational consistency, or inconsistency, in the argument against trait theory? How does this affect the validity of personality tests?
19. What is situationism, and how is it related to personality?
20. How do situationists explain how we see our friends' personalities as consistent?
21. Review the evidence on consistency of behavior across time and situations. Describe how superficially different expressions of a personality trait contribute to apparent behavioral inconsistency. What are the implications for trait theory?
22. What is an interaction effect? Understand the importance of the interaction between a personality and situation in personality assessment. What is the drawback to this approach?
23. Explain the effect(s) of reciprocal interaction, and give an example of this type of interaction.
24. Realize that consistency may be a personality trait. How does Snyder's self-monitoring scale measure behavioral consistency in different situations?
25. How is the study of cross-situational consistency similar to the study of attribution in social psychology?
26. In the light of available evidence, evaluate the concept of person constancy.

Traits and biology

27. What is the definition of the word *temperament*, and what effect does it have on a person's personality?

28. How stable is an individual's temperament, as demonstrated by Buss and Plomin's temperament scale?
29. Discuss the evidence that personality traits may have a genetic component. What traits are most heritable? What evidence does Loehlin present on the heritability of only certain basic personality dimensions?
30. What studies have been done to show that between-family differences in environment are not important in determining personality traits?
31. How can differences within a family environment affect its children? Be aware of the effect of reciprocal interaction on personality development.
32. In what situations do between-family environment differences matter?
33. Describe how Eysenck compares introverts and extroverts in terms of their arousal systems. What research on sensation-seeking has Zuckerman done that correlates with Eysenck's findings?
34. What is known about the involvement of neurotransmitter systems in sensation seeking?

THE BEHAVIORAL-COGNITIVE APPROACH

35. What is the central assumption of the behavioral- cognitive approach to personality?

Radical behaviorism
36. How have the principles of behavior theory applied to the explanation of personality differences? What is the role of learning and reinforcement?
37. Describe the importance of partial reinforcement in accounting for the consistency of behavior according to a behaviorist.

Social learning theory
38. How is social learning theory related to radical behaviorism, and how is it different?
39. Describe some of the cognitive dimensions on which some social learning theorists think that people differ.
40. What is the evidence that control over a situation is a cognitive dimension that people seek?
41. How does explanatory style have an effect on such conditions as depression?
42. Describe how self-control is seen as an important personality characteristic. Discuss evidence that children can be influenced in their self-control depending on physical and cognitive factors.
43. How is the early ability to delay gratification related to late coping ability?
44. How are social learning theorists still similar to behaviorists in orientation?

TAKING STOCK

45. Summarize the differences between the trait approach and the behavioral-cognitive approach to personality.

Programmed Exercises

1. The way that people differ in their desires, feelings, and in the expression of these feelings reflects their _____ differences.

   personality

2. In the comic dramas that they performed, the Greeks and Romans thought of the different characters and their respective personalities as _____. The same characterizations were used in literature.

   types

3. Some felt that these stock characters were two-dimensional, and that more _____ characterizations were needed.

   rounded (multidimensional)

4. Others were concerned over the _____ versus _____ forces that caused a character to act as he did.

   internal, external

5. These arguments between the different schools of drama and literature are analogous to debates between different psychological theories of personality. The _____ theory holds that personality is best understood by the description and analysis of underlying personality dispositions.

   trait

6. Achieving selfhood and actualizing one's own potential would be consistent with the _____ approach to personality.

   humanistic

7. The behavioral-cognitive approach insists that an individual's actions and thoughts are produced by the _____ that he or she is in at any given time.

   situation

8. According to _____ theory, the important aspects of personality originate from buried unconscious conflicts and desires.

   psychodynamic

9. The _____ approach to personality examines universals and particulars in personalities of different cultures.

   sociocultural

10. Implicit in the use of personality tests is the assumption that personality patterns are essentially _____ over time.

    consistent

11. _____ tests were developed to enable us to predict people's future behavior.

Personality

METHODS OF ASSESSMENT

12. The first personality test was administered to army recruits and was meant to identify _____ _____ soldiers.

emotionally disturbed

13. The MMPI is termed _____ because it assesses a number of personality _____ simultaneously.

multiphasic, traits

14. The MMPI is scored by comparing the scores on each of the ten major scales to those of the relevant _____ group.

criterion

15. The authors of the MMPI emphasize the _____ power of a question in distinguishing between the criterion group and normal individuals.

discriminatory

16. In interpreting scores on the MMPI, it is necessary to examine score _____, which present the scores on all the scales in graphic form.

profiles

17. In order to detect whether or not participants are lying on test items or are trying to fake mental illness, the MMPI uses two _____ scales made up of items no one can honestly deny and of items so bizarre that few would endorse them.

validity

18. It is difficult to interpret MMPI scores for _____ participants since the criterion groups used to define the scales were composed of _____ patients.

normal psychiatric

19. One test that was developed using normal participants as the criterion group is the _____ _____ _____.

California Psychological Inventory

20. The degree to which a test can predict real-world events is called its _____ _____.

predictive validity

21. Devising and testing hypotheses about the relation between an underlying trait and various behavioral effects comprises _____ validation.

construct

22. High scores on the psychopathic deviance scale of the MMPI reflect _____, while low scorers are generally considered _____-_____.

aggressiveness good-natured

23. The _____ effect shows that one criterion that is of little use in assessing test validity is the person's own acceptance of the test interpretation.

Barnum

24. The use of _____ techniques was, in part, a protest against the highly _____ nature of paper-and-pencil techniques.

projective, structured

25. One of the concerns of the originators of projective techniques was that a participant could _____ to _____ when taking a test like the MMPI.

lie himself (or herself)

26. The idea behind projective techniques is that in _____ unstructured materials, a participant will reveal deeper facets of his or her _____.

structuring personality

27. The three categories used in scoring Rorschach inkblots are _____, which concerns the portion of the blot used; _____, which note the attributes of the stimulus that the participant responds to; and _____, which refers to what the participant sees.

location determinants content

28. In interpretations of Rorschach inkblots, use of the entire blot is said to reflect _____ thinking, while attention to details suggests _____.

integrative (or conceptual) compulsiveness (or rigidity)

29. Rorschach responses indicating human movement are interpreted as indicating _____, and those dominated by color suggest _____.

imagination, emotionality (or impulsivity)

30. Traditionally, _____ has been less important than the other categories in the interpretation of Rorschach inkblots.

content

31. The _____ _____ _____, in which people tell stories about pictures, places a major emphasis on content.

Thematic Apperception Test (TAT)

32. _____ scoring of a Rorschach test yields better prediction of pathology than atomistic scoring.

Global

33. In addition to predictive validity, it is desirable for a test to have _____ validity, so that the test provides knowledge not found by other means.

incremental

THE TRAIT APPROACH

34. The major task in determining the proper traits with which to classify personality is the development of a(n) _____ of personality difference.

    taxonomy

35. Cattell's taxonomy of personality is based on _____, using factor analysis to discover how _____ words are interrelated.

    language
    trait

36. A(n) _____ _____ of personality views several lower-level traits (e.g., tidiness) as manifestations of a higher-order factor (e.g., conscientiousness).

    hierarchical model

37. According to Eysenck, both _____ and _____ are unsociable and withdrawn, but the former's unsociability is not tainted by fear of social activities.

    introverts, neurotics

38. Eysenck's two-dimensional theory of personality can be related to the four-fold classification of temperaments by Hippocrates. These temperaments, which corresponded to four different personalities, were: _____ (cheerful and active), _____ (calm and passive), _____ (gloomy), and _____ (angry and violent).

    sanguine, phlegmatic,
    melancholic, choleric

39. A later version of Eysenck's system added the dimension of _____.

    psychoticism

40. Some psychologists have argued that the reason that many tests are not good predictors of future behavior is that most people exhibit a lack of _____-_____ consistency.

    cross-situational

41. _____ maintains that human behavior is largely determined by the situation a person is in, rather than by the actual, internal traits of the person.

    Situationism

42. Contrary to situationistic claims, some _____ studies have shown a fair amount of _____ of personality.

    longitudinal
    consistency

43. Another argument against situationism is that perceived behavior inconsistency may be more _____ than _____ since the expression of a constant trait may vary over time.

    apparent, real

44. When a person's reactions cannot be predicted adequately solely by situation or by individual differences, the critical factor may be the _____ of these two.

    interaction

45. When a person's traits determine the situation that he or she chooses, but the situation also determines that person's behavior, the relation between person and situation is _____.

    reciprocal

46. Since cross-situational consistency varies from person to person, it may be regarded as a _____ that only some individuals possess.

    trait

47. One can assess how much a person adjusts his or her behavior to fit a situation by having that person complete the _____-_____ scale developed by Mark Snyder.

    self-monitoring

48. The intuitive belief that most people remain unchanged over time is known as _____ _____ and is similar to size and shape constancy in perception.

    person
    constancy

49. Trait theory is similar to _____ theory in social psychology in that both emphasize the importance of a person's disposition.

    attribution

50. It is believed that a person's _____ ultimately originates from his or her biological makeup.

    temperament

51. Identical twins show more similarity of personality than do fraternal twins, indicating some _____ of personality traits. Thus, it seems that some traits might be determined more by heredity than others. However, in a study of 1700 identical and fraternal high-school-age twins, the results indicated that almost all personality traits are _____ heritable.

    heritability

    equally

52. It appears that _____-_____ differences in environment are unimportant in determining personality traits such as emotionality and extroversion. However, _____-_____ differences in environment (i.e., birth order and spacing, friends, etc.) faced by children in the same family will cause variations in personality between those siblings.

    between-family
    within-family

53. According to Eysenck, introversion corresponds to a high level of _____; thus, persons of this type are actually more awake than others.

    arousal

54. Zuckerman's research on _____ _____ indicates that those people with a higher arousal system (introverts) have higher levels of the neurotransmitter _____ in their brains. Those with lower levels of this neurotransmitter are underaroused, and as a result are likely to seek thrills and take risks.

    sensation seeking
    norepinephrine

THE BEHAVIORAL-COGNITIVE APPROACH

55. The behavioral-cognitive approach, in contrast to _____ theory, emphasizes the importance of external forces in the determination of behavior.

trait

56. This view is a direct descendent of _____, an important movement early in this century that emphasized the role of learning, and de-emphasized the role of cognition.

behaviorism

57. _____ behaviorism, espoused most forcefully by Skinner, sought to limit psychology to the study of behavior and nothing else.

Radical

58. Behaviorism relies on learning through either _____ or _____ conditioning.

classical, instrumental

59. According to behaviorism, the reason some behaviors are so persistent is a result of _____ reinforcement.

partial

60. Behaviorism accounts for the persistence of classically conditioned responses based on fear by arguing that _____ learning is difficult to extinguish.

avoidance

61. A modification of behaviorism that recognizes the importance of internal cognitive states, such as expectations and beliefs, is _____ _____ theory.

social learning

62. According to Mischel, some of the cognitive qualities on which people may differ are their _____, their _____ strategies, their subjective _____, and their _____-_____ systems.

competencies encoding, values, self-regulatory

63. Patients who are allowed the opportunity to _____ their environments are more active and feel better than patients who are not.

control

64. A person's _____ style indicates the extent to which he or she designates the causes of events as internal versus external.

explanatory

65. Measures of _____ of gratification in young children show that this characteristic predicts behavior in adolescence.

delay

66. Social learning theorists can still be regarded as behaviorists in that they continue to stress the importance of the _____ in determining behavior, and they insist on the importance of _____ in acquiring various personality characteristics.

situation
learning

Self Test

1. Personality differences include:
   a. intelligence, ability, and insight
   b. desires, feelings, and modes of expressing these needs and feelings
   c. none of the above
   d. both a and b

2. The five orientations to personality are:
   a. trait theory, psychoanalytic theory, attribution theory, behavioral-cognitive theory, psychodynamic theory
   b. trait theory, humanistic theory, psychogenic theory, behavioral-cognitive theory, validity theory
   c. psychodynamic theory, humanistic theory, behavioral-cognitive theory, projective theory, Barnum theory
   d. trait theory, humanistic theory, psychodynamic theory, behavioral-cognitive theory, sociocultural theory

3. Trait theory:
   a. is consonant with the beliefs of Aristophanes
   b. assumes consistency of personality patterns
   c. establishes personality prototypes, such as the garrulous person, the flatterer, and so on.
   d. a and b

4. The first personality and intelligence tests were similar in that both were _____ but differed in that the former was _____ and the latter was _____.
   a. diagnostic, unstructured, structured
   b. unstructured, descriptive, normative
   c. diagnostic, poorly validated, well validated
   d. structured, descriptive, diagnostic

5. An appropriate criterion group for a diagnostic test of paranoid schizophrenics would be:
   a. normal individuals
   b. paranoid schizophrenics
   c. a mixture of a and b
   d. no criterion group is needed when the test is used as a diagnostic tool

6. The California Psychological Inventory (CPI) uses _____ criterion groups.
   a. no
   b. pathological
   c. normal
   d. random

7. When a test can foretell some real-world event, it is said to have:
   a. face validity
   b. incremental validity
   c. predictive validity
   d. unproven validity

8. Which of the following illustrates construct validation?
   a. correlating the Nielsen rankings of television shows with the amount of fan mail the stars receive and with the number of articles written about the show
   b. the correct choice of presidential candidates by the Gallup polls
   c. the confirmation of a proposed genetic theory through population studies
   d. the repeated modification and testing of a new car design to ensure safety and good performance

9. Which of the following personality sketches is likely to produce the Barnum effect?
   a. You are friendly and outgoing in some situations and quiet and reserved in others. On the outside you appear to be composed, although there are times in which you are inwardly not self-confident.
   b. You feel that a strange person is following you everywhere. There are times when you find fault with yourself.
   c. You want others to respect and like you. You often feel that life is not worth living.
   d. You are not well-adjusted sexually. You often feel that people are out to get you.

10. Projective techniques differ from tests such as the MMPI and CPI in that the former are more:
    a. structured
    b. quantitative
    c. variable
    d. all of the above
    e. none of the above

11. In structuring unstructured materials, it is expected that a participant:
    a. will reveal his or her capacity for conceptual organization
    b. will be relieved of objective test anxiety and will thus perform most effectively and honestly
    c. will project his or her deepest feelings and conflicts upon the ambiguous stimulus
    d. will be distracted from the psychologist's analysis of the participant's voice tone, body language, and gestures in responding

12. Two examples of projective tests are:
    a. the MMPI and the Thematic Apperception Test (TAT)
    b. the Rorschach and the TAT
    c. the Rorschach and the CPI
    d. all of the above

13. The three categories used in interpreting the Rorschach are:
    a. location, negativism, color
    b. content, attributes, and location
    c. content, impulsiveness, use of white space
    d. impulsiveness, happiness, truth value

14. Which of the following is *not* an established piece of evidence against the validity of the Rorschach inkblot test?
    a. the failure of highly intelligent people to use the entire inkblot more than others do
    b. the lack of relation between Rorschach indices and psychiatric diagnosis
    c. the failure of artists to demonstrate a preponderance of human movement in their perceptions
    d. the fact that individual Rorschach indices show little relation to external validity criteria

15. While the TAT has not fared well as a diagnostic tool, it has shown some promise as an indicator of:
    a. intelligence
    b. motives
    c. hidden fears
    d. imagination

16. A taxonomy is a:
    a. classification system
    b. rating scale used in psychiatric diagnosis
    c. type of mental disorder
    d. class of stable personality traits

17. Eysenck has formed a hypothesis that all personalities can be classified on the basis of a rating on two independent scales. They are _____ and _____.
    a. paranoid, schizophrenic
    b. shy-outgoing, anxiety
    c. neuroticism, extroversion-introversion
    d. psychopathic deviance, extroversion-introversion

18. Introverts differ from extroverts in all of the following ways *except*:
    a. they are solitary
    b. they are cautious
    c. they are slow to change
    d. they have a lower pain threshold
    e. none of the above

19. Which of the following constitute problems for Eysenck's theory of personality based on neuroticism and introversion-extroversion?
    a. the dependence of factor analysis on the existing data set
    b. the possible nonindependence of these two dimensions
    c. the observation that introverted people tend to be more easily aroused than are extroverts
    d. a and b

20. Walter Mischel found that children are _____ in their behavior in different circumstances. He saw this as evidence _____ the validity of personality traits.
    a. consistent, for
    b. inconsistent, for
    c. consistent, against
    d. inconsistent, against

21. The concept of situationism is most opposite to the assumptions underlying:
    a. the MMPI and CPI
    b. the Rorschach and TAT

c. all of the above
d. none of the above

22. Situationists:
a. deny the existence of individual differences
b. believe that social roles play a large role in the situations people get into
c. claim that situations themselves are the best predictors of people's reactions
d. believe that past situational experiences determine personality traits

23. In _____ with Mischel, some authors have claimed that there is a higher level of consistency in people's behavior than previously believed. They hypothesize that reactions that appear _____ in gross analysis are really different manifestations of _____ underlying sources.
a. agreement, dissimilar, different
b. agreement, dissimilar, the same
c. disagreement, similar, different
d. disagreement, dissimilar, the same

24. In defense of trait theory, one could cite evidence that behavior is:
a. consistent over time
b. consistent across situations
c. both of the above
d. none of the above

25. Studies by Endler and Hunt have looked at person-situation interactions. Their results suggest that the practicality of assigning traits like fear to people:
a. is useless
b. has been experimentally validated
c. should be qualified to be more specific to individual circumstances
d. is minimal since internal fluctuations in trait strength cause behavior to vary from situation to situation

26. Tom is a gregarious and talkative person. He enjoys organizing activities with friends. Which of the following choices would not illustrate a reciprocal relation between Tom and the situation?
a. Tom gives a party for his birthday.
b. Tom's job is social director for a large singles' group in his city.
c. On many evenings Tom likes to sit in his room and videotape sports events.
d. Tom shares a house with five other guys from his college graduating class.

27. High self-monitors are:
a. not adaptable
b. inconsistent
c. consistent
d. rigid

28. Person constancy involves the notion that:
a. all people behave in essentially the same way for a particular situation
b. people are not consistent, and we perceive them as being that way

c. we tend to see him or a person in only one situation, so we think of her only in that situation
d. all of the above
e. none of the above

29. Which of the following traits is most heritable?
a. dominance
b. self-acceptance
c. sociability
d. a and c
e. all of the above

30. Studies have found that behaviors such as television watching or tendencies toward divorce are partially heritable. These findings need to be interpreted cautiously, however, because:
a. television watching is so recent that it couldn't have influenced genetic makeup
b. divorce, although hundreds of years old, is still too recent to have influenced genetic makeup
c. other, more fundamental traits such as extroversion may be the ones that are heritable, and they reveal themselves in such behaviors as television watching
d. all of the above
e. a and b, but not c

31. One line of evidence suggesting a strong heritable component to personality traits is that:
a. identical twins have higher correlations (one to the other twin) in measures of personality traits than do fraternal twins
b. identical twins have lower correlations (one to the other twin) in personality traits than do fraternal twins
c. identical twins and fraternal twins have equal correlations (one to the other twin) in personality traits
d. fraternal twins have higher correlations (one to the other twin) than to siblings who are not twins

32. Which of the following statements is true?
a. Identical twins have less chance of being alike on various personality tests than do fraternal twins.
b. Fraternal twins raised apart show a lower correlation of personality traits than do those raised together.
c. Siblings raised in the same family are likely to have different personalities partly because the reciprocal interaction between each child's genetic makeup and his or her environment will be different.
d. Identical twins raised together show a higher correlation of personality traits than do those raised apart.

33. Which of the following is true of sensation seekers?
a. They have underactive norepinephrine systems in their brain.
b. They are overaroused in certain systems of their brain.
c. They have a low pain tolerance.
d. They react more to external stimuli than those who are not sensation seekers.

34. The behavioral-cognitive approach to personality does not attribute differences in personality to:
a. enduring traits in personality that may be a function of hereditary influences

b. differences in how a person will behave in different situations

c. learning that occurs during the life of an individual that may cause certain behaviors to appear in certain situations

d. classical and operant conditioning

35. According to a radical behaviorist view, personality traits appear enduring and stable because behavior doesn't change from moment to moment; this, in turn, is due largely to the phenomenon of:

a. the Barnum effect

b. partial reinforcement

c. the attribution error

d. delay of gratification

36. Social learning theory is a modification of radical behaviorism in that it admits of the influence of:

a. an individual's competencies

b. an individual's encoding strategies

c. an individual's subjective values

d. all of the above

37. The Attributional Style Questionnaire is an important instrument to measure control because:

a. it assesses the extent to which an individual thinks the causes of events are internal to her or due to external forces

b. it has value in predicting clinical depression

c. it is related to the idea of learned helplessness in animals that may be related to depression

d. all of the above

38. The extent to which a child is willing to delay gratification is related to:

a. later academic performance

b. later social competence

c. later coping skills in adolescence

d. all of the above

39. Social learning theory has strayed away from its radical behaviorist origins, but it still shares similarities with that school because:

a. it stresses the importance of learning

b. it stresses the role of traits in determining behavior

c. it emphasizes the value of situational differences in exerting an influence on behavior

d. a and b

e. a and c

Answer Key for Self Test

1.	b p. 669	21.	c p. 688
2.	d pp. 670, 671	22.	c p. 688
3.	b p. 670	23.	d pp. 688, 689
4.	c p. 672	24.	c p. 689
5.	b p. 672	25.	c p. 692
6.	c p. 674	26.	c p. 692
7.	c p. 674	27.	b p. 694
8.	a p. 675	28.	e p. 695
9.	a p. 676	29.	e pp. 697, 698
10.	e p. 677	30.	d p. 698
11.	c p. 677	31.	a p. 699
12.	b p. 677	32.	c p. 699
13.	b p. 678	33.	a p. 701
14.	a p. 680	34.	a p. 702
15.	b p. 681	35.	b p. 704
16.	a p. 682	36.	d p. 705
17.	c pp. 684, 685	37.	d p. 706
18.	e pp. 684, 685, 700, 701	38.	d pp. 707, 708
19.	a p. 686	39.	e pp. 708, 709
20.	d p. 687		

Investigating Psychological Phenomena

CONSTRUCTING A PERSONALITY INVENTORY

Equipment: None
Number of participants: One (yourself)
Time per participant: Forty-five minutes
Time for experimenter: Forty-five minutes

Constructing a test to assess a personality trait is an involved process. It requires the creation of test items and the validation of these items through administration of the test to large groups of participants. While it would be impossible to illustrate all the steps in this process through a short exercise such as this, it is possible to provide an idea about some of the issues that are involved. That is the purpose of this demonstration.

A first draft of a test for a particular personality trait has been created.[*] Before reading on, you should take this test. Listed below are twenty-one questions for you to answer. Try to put yourself in each of the following situations and on the answer sheet mark the choice that would best describe your reactions. Limit your replies to the choices given and answer every question.

* We thank Lisa Lange, John Prevost, Barb Merriam, Laurie Tunstall, and Julie Nuse for their permission to use the shyness inventory that was prepared as part of a course project supervised by Dr. Charles Morris. We also thank Dr. Morris for kindly supplying the correlational data.

Draft Personality Inventory

		strongly disagree	slightly disagree	slightly agree	strongly agree
1.	I am in a crowded bar sitting with some friends. A good-looking individual comes up to me and asks me to dance. I like to dance but I notice that the dance floor is empty and answer no.	1	2	3	4
2.	I get an important exam back and I disagree with the grading on one of the problems. But I accept my grade, avoiding a confrontation with the professor.	1	2	3	4
3.	I enjoy attending seminars and discussion groups as opposed to large lectures.	1	2	3	4
4.	I'm in a restaurant and receive some bad food. Instead of saying something, I stay quiet but leave a small tip.	1	2	3	4
5.	My family is moving to another state and I will be attending a new school. I look forward to meeting new people and making new friends.	1	2	3	4
6.	I find it easy to liven up a dull occasion.	1	2	3	4
7.	I am required to form groups in a class and interact on a subject. The groups are formed but I tend to listen more than offer information.	1	2	3	4
8.	If I were in the waiting room of a doctor's office and a stranger sat down next to me, introduced him- or herself, and started asking me questions, I would feel nervous and uncomfortable.	1	2	3	4
9.	I can usually enjoy myself at a party even if I know almost no one there.	1	2	3	4
10.	A teacher asks questions to which I know the answers, but I never raise my hand for fear that the answers might not be what the teacher is looking for.	1	2	3	4
11.	I become uncomfortable and at a loss for words, usually blushing, when I am given a compliment.	1	2	3	4
12.	I often find myself taking charge in group situations.	1	2	3	4
13.	I prefer being with people and going to parties rather than spending my spare time alone pursuing personal interests or hobbies.	1	2	3	4
14.	If someone was smoking a cigarette in a nonsmoking section and the smoke was bothering me, I wouldn't hesitate to ask the person to put out the cigarette.	1	2	3	4
15.	I often look back at a situation and think of things I should have done or said.	1	2	3	4
16.	I feel proud to be called on to give a toast at a social gathering.	1	2	3	4
17.	I would go out of my way to make a stranger feel comfortable in a group in which the people are unfamiliar to him.	1	2	3	4
18.	When I've been waiting in line for service for a long time and someone cuts in front of me, I feel angry but don't say anything about it.	1	2	3	4
19.	I prefer not to answer the door when I know it's a salesperson because I have a hard time getting salespeople to leave once they're inside the door.	1	2	3	4
20.	When I've struck up a conversation with the person sitting next to me, a long plane flight seems more enjoyable.	1	2	3	4
21.	I consider myself to be a shy person.	1	2	3	4

Now that you have answered the questionnaire, you are probably aware that it is intended to assess shyness. The questions themselves were constructed as candidates that might have something to do with predicting how shy people are. How can one tell if the questionnaire accomplishes its purpose or which questions are the best predictors of shyness?

One possibility is to examine the face validity of each of the questions. Since you have just completed the questions yourself and since you are now aware that its purpose is to test for shyness, you can do this yourself. Examine each question and decide for yourself whether you think that it would be a good predictor of shyness. That is, does the question ask participants about a reaction that should depend on how shy the participants are? Try to pick out the four questions that you think would best predict shyness and the four that would be least relevant. Note, by the way, that the questions are constructed so that for some (Items 1, 2, 4, 7, 8, 10, 11, 15, 18, 19, and 21) a high score (e.g., 4) would indicate more shyness, while for the rest, a low score (e.g., 1) would indicate more shyness. This is only done to provide variety; your assessment of each question should be independent of this point.

Questions that would best predict shyness	Questions that would least predict shyness
1. _____	1. _____
2. _____	2. _____
3. _____	3. _____
4. _____	4. _____

Your judgment of the quality of a question is a measure of face validity (i.e., the extent to which a question, on the face of it, is a good predictor of shyness), but this is not the only possible measure of validity. Another criterion is to have some independent measure of a participant's shyness and correlate responses to each question with the measure (predictive validity). Presumably, if a question were a good predictor of shyness, it would correlate highly with this measure.

One such measure is a participant's response to Question 21. This question directly asks participants for their own assessment of whether they consider themselves to be shy. In order to determine how well each test question correlates with this self-assessment of shyness, sixty-nine participants were given this questionnaire and correlations of each question with Question 21 were calculated. They are presented in Table 1 below.

TABLE 1

Correlations of each question in the questionnaire with Question 21. A low correlation (a positive or negative value close to 0) indicates that there is little relationship between the answer to that question and the answer to Question 21; a high correlation (a value closer to −1 or +1) indicates a relationship between responses to that question and responses to Question 21. For example, Item 10 has a correlation of .42 with Item 21. This means that participants who tend to agree with the statement in Question 10 tend to agree also with the statement in Question 21.

Likewise, participants who tend to disagree with the statement in Question 10, also tend to disagree with the statement in Question 21. A negative correlation, such as in Question 6, indicates that participants who tend to agree with the statement in 6 tend to disagree with the statement in 21. Likewise, those who tend to disagree with the statement in 6 tend to agree with the one in 21 (note that even though a correlation is negative, it still means that there is a relationship between the two items in question, but a reverse relationship).

Question:	1	2	3	4	5	6	7	8	9	10
Correlation:	.23	.08	−.15	−.08	−.20	−.28	.38	−.24	−.24	.42
Question:	11	12	13	14	15	16	17	18	19	20
Correlation:	.29	−.22	−.20	−.27	.32	−.37	−.16	.17	.09	−.07

Compare your judgments of question quality against these correlations to see whether the ones you judged as good have either high positive or high negative values; also, check whether the questions you judged as poor have correlations near 0.

Another validity criterion that may be reasonable is the total score on the test. The logic of using this criterion is that individual questions may vary in how well they indicate shyness, but the test *as a whole* may be a much better indicator. If this were so, then it would be sensible to correlate scores on individual questions with those on the whole test to see which questions best predict the total test score. This was done for the same sixty-nine participants as above; the correlations are presented in Table 2.

TABLE 2

Correlations of each question with the total test score. As in Table 1, a low value means little relationship of that question with the total test score, while a higher value (either positive or negative) means that there is some relationship. For example, the correlation of .55 for Question 10 indicates that participants who tend to agree with the statement in Item 10 tend to have a high total score on the questionnaire, while participants who tend to disagree with the statement in 10 tend to score low on the whole questionnaire. Another illustration is the correlation of −.49 for Question 5. This means that participants who tend to disagree with the statement in 5 tend to get a high total score, while participants who tend to agree with the statement in 5 tend to have a low score.

Question:	1	2	3	4	5	6	7	8	9	10
Correlation:	.45	.41	−.54	.13	−.49	−.44	.46	.42	−.53	.55
Question:	11	12	13	14	15	16	17	18	19	20
Correlation:	.37	−.42	−.35	−.44	.40	−.46	−.27	.35	.25	−.01

Again, see how well your judgments of question quality are related to these correlations. Note also an interesting pattern in the two sets of correlations presented in Tables 1 and 2. Item 10 has both the highest absolute correlation with Question 21 and the highest correlation with the total test score. Also, Item 7 has very high correlations with both criterion measures. This consistency suggests that these two items may well be good, valid indices of shyness. How did you rate these items? Examine the items themselves to see if you can explain why they might be better than others.

Note also that two items, 4 and 20, have very low correlations with both criterion measures. How did you judge these items? Why to you think they have such low correlations?

If we were to continue to develop a "shyness inventory," we might well try to use other validity criteria as well as the three described above. For example, we might try to use the inventory to predict some behavior that is characteristic of shy people. This would allow us to assess the predictive validity of the test. Whatever the criteria, though, the objective of test construction is to find questions that best predict that which you are trying to assess. This exercise should have given you some insight into the process by which this objective is reached.

CHAPTER 17

Personality II: Psychodynamic, Humanistic, and Sociocultural Approaches

Learning Objectives

THE PSYCHODYNAMIC APPROACH: FREUD AND PSYCHOANALYSIS

The origins of psychoanalytic thought

1. How did Freud view the process of taming the savage, selfish human nature?
2. Compare Freud's and Hobbes's views of human nature and its taming.
3. Describe the symptoms of hysteria. Why is this illness termed a psychogenic disorder?
4. What is catharsis?
5. What are repression and resistance, and how do they relate to catharsis?
6. What did Freud mean by the unconscious?
7. How did Freud propose to study the unconscious?
8. What is psychoanalysis, and how does it relate to the understanding of psychopathology and the normal personality?

Unconscious conflict

9. Understand the nature of unconscious conflict and its effect on behavior.
10. What are the three divisions of personality according to Freud? How do these develop, and how do they interact to give rise to conflict and resolution?
11. Be cognizant of the major role of anxiety as a motivating force in keeping unacceptable urges repressed.
12. How does repression affect the realm of thought in addition to that of behavior?
13. What are defense mechanisms?
14. Describe the specific defense mechanisms (repression, displacement, reaction formation, rationalization, projection, and isolation).

Unconscious conflict and the formation of personality

15. What are Freud's stages of psychosexual development, and what is the relation of these stages to sexuality and pleasure?
16. What are oral and anal characters, and how, according to Freud, do they relate to psychosexual development?

17. In Freud's view, the Oedipus complex is the most important aspect of psychosexual development. Discuss this theory with respect to both sexes.
18. What are the difficulties in Freud's view of the psychosexual development of girls?

Windows into the unconscious

19. What is the psychopathology of everyday life, and how does it reflect underlying motives and conflicts?
20. Explain Freud's theory of dreams. Understand the motive of wish fulfillment and its symbolic expression, and the difference between the latent and the manifest dream.
21. How have Freud's theories been used to interpret myths and works of literature?

A critical look at Freudian theory

22. Recount some of the methodological and conceptual difficulties with Freud's theories.
23. What are different conceptions of the role of biological factors, especially sexuality, versus social factors in personality development? What is the position of the neo-Freudians on this point?
24. Review the evidence on the validity of the existence of anal and oral characters, and their link to childhood toilet training and feeding experiences.
25. How universal is the Oedipus complex? Summarize evidence from the Trobriand Islanders.
26. What evidence militates against Freud's emphasis on wish fulfillment in the interpretation of dreams?
27. Freud believed that the manifest dream was a disguised and censored version of the latent dream that deals with unacceptable urges. What is the evidence for this? What is an alternative view?
28. Summarize the issues and arguments against and in favor of Freud's reliance on repression in dealing with unconscious conflicts. What is the evidence for repression, as opposed to a less "motivation-oriented" view of retrieval blocking?
29. What are the basic ideas of psychoanalysis?

30. What are Freud's major contributions to our understanding of human nature and to the field of psychology? What are the shortcomings of his approach and theory?

THE PSYCHODYNAMIC APPROACH: PERSONALITY DIFFERENCES

31. What are dominant patterns of defense, and what, according to the neo-Freudians, is their role in accounts of personality differences?

Patterns of conflict
32. Describe Karen Horney's views about patterns of neurotic conflict, including mention of basic anxiety and vicious circles.

Coping patterns and mental health
33. Distinguish between the Freudian position, Karen Horney's position, and the view of the ego psychologists.
34. What are coping mechanisms and how do they relate to Freudian defense mechanisms?
35. What do longitudinal studies tell us about the importance and consistency of coping patterns? What child-rearing patterns are associated with the best adjustment?

THE HUMANISTIC APPROACH

The major features of the humanistic movement
36. Describe the basic differences between the humanistic approach and all of the other approaches to personality that have been discussed.
37. Explain the hierarchy of needs, including definitions of deficiency needs and self-actualization.
38. What are the conditions of personal growth, according to Rogers, and how can therapy help to establish these?

Evaluating the humanistic approach
39. What are the empirical and conceptual problems of the humanistic approach?
40. Indicate the sense in which humanistic psychology is a protest movement. Relate it to other movements of a similar character in history, especially the Romantic movement.

THE SOCIOCULTURAL PERSPECTIVE

41. What are the basic sociocultural criticisms of the four personality theories already discussed?

Human diversity and personality
42. Indicate important cultural variations in basic personality features and gender roles.

Human sameness and universal patterns of personality
43. Describe the cross-cultural method. What does it indicate about common themes in personality across cultures?
44. How do child-rearing practices differ by type of culture and socioeconomic class?

Collectivism and individualism
45. Describe collectivism and individualism. What are the different features of each? Indicate countries or areas of the world in which one or the other is dominant.
46. Review evidence indicating a different concept of self in some Asian cultures.
47. What are the consequences for current personality theory if the sociocultural critique is basically correct?

TAKING STOCK

48. Summarize the five basic views of personality presented in this chapter. Evaluate their contribution to a total theory of personality, and describe the analog, in drama, for most of these approaches.

Programmed Exercises

THE PSYCHODYNAMIC APPROACH: FREUD AND PSYCHOANALYSIS

1. According to the psychodynamic approach, understanding of human personality requires understanding of _____ psychological forces.

    hidden (deep, unconscious)

2. The psychodynamic approach derives from _____, founded by _____.

    psychoanalysis, Freud

3. Freud has been compared to Hobbes, since both men believed that humans are basically _____. But Freud differs from Hobbes in that Freud believed that the taming force of society is _____ in each of us.

    savage (or selfish)
    internalized

4. A patient exhibiting partial blindness, glove anesthesia, or memory gaps would likely be diagnosed as suffering from _____.

    hysteria

5. If organic damage is ruled out in the above case (Question 4), then the origin of the symptoms must be _____.

    psychogenic

6. Freud and Breuer came to the conclusion that the symptoms of hysteria could not be just suggested away; the underlying _____ that such symptoms block must be recovered. The resulting _____ will then have therapeutic effects.

    memories
    catharsis

7. Although Freud began by using hypnosis, he later abandoned this approach, since not all of his patients were hypnotizable and since the same crucial memories could be obtained in the waking state through the method of _____ _____.

free association

8. A patient is told to say anything that enters his mind, yet struggles at times to change the subject or forgets what he was going to say. This subject is demonstrating _____ to the recovery of _____ memories.

resistance
repressed

9. According to Freud's view, forbidden impulses are never completely controlled, despite repressive measures by the individual. This division of the individual (one part fighting another) gives rise to _____ conflicts.

unconscious

10. According to Freud, repression is a _____ against the intolerable pain that would be caused by becoming aware of unacceptable thoughts and wishes.

defense

11. Repressed wishes are usually related to _____ _____, the direct expression of which is forbidden by society.

biological urges

12. Freud investigated unconscious conflicts: their origin, effects, and removal. He termed his exploration and interpretation of these phenomena _____.

psychoanalysis

13. The three distinct systems of the human personality, according to Freud, are the _____, the _____, and the _____.

id
ego, superego

14. The most primitive portion of personality is the _____. It operates according to the _____ principle, with the single goal being immediate satisfaction.

id
pleasure

15. As id-dominated infants encounter the frustration of the real world, they develop a(n) _____, which attempts to satisfy the urges of the id according to a _____ principle.

ego
reality

16. The young child refrains from doing wrong only through fear of being caught. Because the rules and admonitions of the parents are _____, however, the _____ develops and suppresses forbidden behavior even in the absence of negative consequences.

internalized, superego

17. _____ is the crucial factor in the mechanism underlying repression. Internal thoughts and feelings that evoke this state must be escaped and are thus suppressed.

Anxiety

18. Repression can be regarded as the primary, initial _____ _____ _____.

mechanism of defense

19. When fear of retaliation blocks the expression of anger, a person may vent his or her feelings on another recipient, resulting in _____ _____.

displaced aggression

20. When a repressed thought or wish manifests itself as a diametrically opposite wish or thought, it is a result of _____ _____.

reaction formation

21. _____ is another defense mechanism in which a repressed thought is reinterpreted in more acceptable terms.

Rationalization

22. Cognitive reorganization also plays a role in _____, in which forbidden urges are attributed to others rather than to the self.

projection

23. _____ is another defense mechanism in which memories are back into consciousness, but the emotions that accompany them are not.

Isolation

24. Freud's theory of _____ development postulates biologically determined stages of emotional and sexual development.

psychosexual

25. Freud maintained that the young child seeks pleasure. This pleasure is often obtained by touching body parts which are particularly sensitive, such as the mouth, anus, and genitals. These parts are known as _____ _____.

erogenous zones

26. Seeking pleasure through the mouth is characteristic of the _____ stage, which yields to the _____ stage as toilet training begins. The _____ stage focuses on the stimulation of the genitals, while interest in the satisfaction of others as well as one's own satisfaction characterizes the _____ stage.

oral
anal, phallic

genital

27. A lingering attachment to pleasure seeking of the type characteristic of a particular psychosexual stage is called a _____. This can sometimes by manifested in terms of opposite characteristics, mediated by the mechanism of _____ _____.

fixation
reaction formation

28. The _____ character recapitulates the pleasure and passive dependency of nursing at his or her mother's breast.

oral

29. The _____ character is typically excessively clean, obstinate, and stingy.

anal

30. The family drama from which grows the child's internalized morality and identification with the same-sex parent is called the _____ _____.

Oedipus complex

31. According to the theory of the Oedipus complex, the _____ urges of the boy at ages three and four are directed toward the _____ as the source of previous gratification during the oral stage.

phallic (sexual)
mother

32. The young boy's _____ of the father leads to _____ and a fear of retaliation by the father, which is termed _____ _____.

jealousy, hostility
castration anxiety

33. As the young boy's anxiety about retaliation increases, the boy _____ with the father in the hope that this will eventually secure him an erotic partnership like the father's.

identifies

34. The renunciation of genital pleasures endures from about five to twelve years of age and is termed the _____ _____.

latency period

35. The weakest aspect of Freud's theory of psychosexual development concerns the young girl's progression of sexual interests. Freud called this the _____ complex. Specifically, why does the little girl desire the father instead of the mother? Freud attributed this transference of attachment to _____ _____, because the girl believes she has been _____.

Electra

penis envy, castrated

36. Through his study of dreams, Freud came to the conclusion that dreams are an attempt at _____ _____. Desires suppressed by considerations of reality and by the superego emerge and are gratified in dreams.

wish fulfillment

37. The _____ dream is the disguised expression of the _____ dream, which represents hidden and forbidden wishes.

manifest, latent

38. The manifest dream employs _____ in representing the hidden wishes and concerns of the dreamer.

symbolism

39. Psychoanalytic theory has been applied to the study of _____ and _____.

myths, literature

40. The fact that psychotherapists cannot be totally objective about a patient's behavior patterns and problems is one of the difficulties of _____ theory.

psychoanalytic

41. Freud believed that the progression of emotional development is rooted in _____, and is thus universal.

biology

42. Some psychoanalytic practitioners acknowledge the importance of social factors in development. These psychologists are termed _____-_____.

neo-Freudians

43. The _____-_____ differ from Freud in that they emphasize inner conflicts based on interpersonal as opposed to biological sources.

neo-Freudians

44. Freud maintained that neurotic conflict centers on the repression of _____ impulses. Others, such as Erich Fromm, emphasize the area of _____ relationships.

erotic
interpersonal

45. Evidence from _____ anthropology supports the importance of social as opposed to biological factors in personality development.

cultural

46. Evidence suggests that while some of the supposed features of the _____ character cluster together and run in families, there is no relation between this "character" and _____ _____ in childhood.

anal
toilet
training

47. Studies of Trobriand Islanders have suggested that the hostility of the young boy toward the father in our culture may be a product, not of sexual _____, but rather of the father's role as a _____.

jealousy, disciplinarian

48. Freud's belief that dreams reflect current emotional preoccupations is supported by the dreams of _____ patients.

preoperative

49. The same urge may sometimes be disguised and sometimes be expressed openly in a dream. Freud's assertion that the manifest dream represents a _____ disguise cannot handle this facet, but C. S. Hall's proposal that the dream functions to _____ an underlying idea can.

defensive
express

50. Some laboratory research suggests that memory findings indicating "repression" may not involve motivated forgetting but rather be a particular case of _____ failure.   retrieval

51. Despite the criticisms of Freud's theoretical proposals, his conception of _____ conflict and the sheer scope of his ideas rank him as one of the giants of psychology.   internal (or unconscious)

THE PSYCHODYNAMIC APPROACH: PERSONALITY DIFFERENCES

52. The neo-Freudians describe personality differences in terms of _____ _____ of defense.   dominant patterns

53. According to Horney, neurotic conflicts are caused by _____ _____, an all-pervading feeling of being alone and helpless in a hostile world. These conflicts may harden into personality characteristics, because the conflicts create a self-perpetuating _____ _____.   basic anxiety

    vicious circle

54. In _____ _____, there is an emphasis on cultural and interpersonal factors, as well as stress, on the healthy modes of _____ with the world.   ego psychology

    coping

55. _____ _____ by Vaillant and Block indicate consistency in coping patterns, with more _____ coping patterns in older and better-adjusted people.   Longitudinal studies

    mature

56. The results of Block's longitudinal studies suggest that poorly adjusted adults had parents who were either _____ or _____.   overinvolved, rejecting (dictatorial, indifferent)

THE HUMANISTIC APPROACH

57. In contrast to the behavioristic and psychoanalytic approaches to personality, humanistic psychologists describe themselves as having a _____ view of human motivation.   positive

58. Maslow describes the behaviorists and psychoanalysts as focusing on physiological needs such as hunger, thirst, and escape from pain, which Maslow calls _____ _____.   deficiency needs

59. Maslow places the needs referred to above at the bottom of the _____ _____ _____. At the top is the desire to realize oneself to the fullest, called _____-_____.   hierarchy of needs, self-actualization

60. According to humanistic psychologists, a basic part of one's subjective experience is one's sense of oneself as both agent and object, called one's _____-_____.   self-concept

61. According to Rogers, a solid sense of self-worth depends on a child's feeling of _____ _____ _____.   unconditional positive regard

62. According to Maslow, satisfaction of lower-level needs and a reasonable sense of self-worth allow for the expression of the desire for _____-_____.   self-actualization

63. Self-actualized persons are more likely to report profound and deeply felt moments in their lives, called _____ _____.   peak experiences

64. According to Rogers, humans will grow into emotionally healthy people if accepted with _____ understanding, and if they are with another person who is _____, that is, open and trustworthy.   empathic, genuine

65. One problem with the humanistic approach is that there is little _____ to support the assertions made about human nature.   evidence

66. Another problem is that, in an important sense, people like Adolf Hitler fit the description of being _____-_____.   self-actualized

67. In parallel with the Romantic movement, humanistic psychology can be seen as a _____ movement.   protest

THE SOCIOCULTURAL PERSPECTIVE

68. Evidence from _____ _____ suggests wide difference across cultures in _____ and gender _____.   cultural anthropology

    personality, roles

69. The _____-_____ method compares different cultures, with the aim of extracting common themes.   cross-cultural

70. Evidence indicates that the same _____ of personality exist cross-culturally.

dimensions

71. There is evidence from studies both within and across cultures that higher socioeconomic status is associated with child rearing that emphasizes more _____-_____.

self-control

72. Cultures in which there is more emphasis on relations with and obligations to the family and community are called _____, as opposed to _____.

collectivist, individualist

73. Evidence for different concepts of the self in different cultures comes from the way Asian Indians _____ other persons, and the nature and use of personal _____ in Bali.

describe, names

TAKING STOCK

74. The five different approaches to personality represent five different theoretical _____, each of which may have some validity.

perspectives

75. Some of the different approaches correspond to different approaches to the presentation of character in _____.

drama

Self Test

1. Behavioral-cognitive approach is to psychodynamic approach as:
   a. psychiatry is to psychology
   b. normality is to pathology
   c. surface is to deep
   d. airplane is to surface transportation
   e. pleasure is to pain

2. Which of the following adjectives would *not* be used by Freud to describe basic human nature?
   a. sexually motivated
   b. selfish
   c. pleasure-seeking
   d. conflict-free
   e. b and d

3. At first the child's behavior is based on a fear of direct social consequences. Later he or she will avoid certain behaviors even when there is no chance of punishment. Freud would say that the control put on the child by society is then _____.
   a. eliminated
   b. internalized
   c. externalized
   d. repressed
   e. conflicted

4. Freud and Hobbes agree:
   a. about the basic savageness of human nature
   b. that there is a taming of basic human nature
   c. about the way that human nature is tamed
   d. about the importance of unconscious conflict
   e. a and b

5. Freud made a major contribution to the understanding of human nature when he suggested that the apparent irrationality of much human behavior was a symptom of _____ _____.
   a. basic insanity
   b. severe hysteria
   c. unconscious conflicts
   d. wish fulfillment
   e. internalized standards

6. Which of the following are symptoms of hysteria?
   i. partial or total blindness
   ii. paralysis
   iii. feelings of helplessness
   iv. anesthesia of a body part
   v. uncontrollable urges
   a. i, iii, v
   b. i, ii, iv, v
   c. ii, iii, iv
   d. i, ii, iv
   e. all are symptoms of hysteria

7. Charcot and Freud believed that hysteria is _____.
   a. inherited
   b. psychogenic
   c. the result of physical trauma (injury to the brain)
   d. incurable
   e. unimportant

8. The explosive release of emotions that accompanies the remembrance of certain long-forgotten memories is called _____.
   a. resistance
   b. memory release
   c. transference
   d. catharsis
   e. unconscious conflict

9. A patient is asked merely to say whatever comes to his mind during a therapy session. The term applied to this psychoanalytic technique is:
   a. transference
   b. free association
   c. resistance formation
   d. wish fulfillment
   e. hypnosis

10. All of the following statements (made by a patient during free association) are examples of resistance *except*:
    a. "I really can't think of anything right now."
    b. "I just forgot what I was about to say."
    c. "I'm thinking of something which has nothing to do with my problem."
    d. "I just remembered a terrible experience from my childhood."
    e. "What I'm thinking about now is too unimportant to tell you."

11. According to Freud, repressed thoughts:
    a. are connected to a wish or thought that a person is unable to face without intense anxiety
    b. are linked to basic biological urges
    c. often date back to early life
    d. all of the above
    e. none of the above

12. Which of Freud's subsystems would be responsible for a desire to eat or drink?
    a. ego
    b. superego
    c. id
    d. a combination of ego and superego
    e. all of the above

13. If a child wants a drink, we often find that he or she asks for something rather than just taking it. This is evidence for the operation of:
    a. the ego
    b. repression
    c. the id
    d. a and c
    e. b and c

14. The reality principle controls:
    a. the ego
    b. the superego
    c. the id
    d. a and b
    e. all of the subsystems to one degree or another

15. When children begin to think of themselves as if they were the parent, the _____ has begun to develop.
    a. ego
    b. superego
    c. id
    d. a and b
    e. impossible to tell from this description

16. Conflicts develop because the _____ and _____ often issue conflicting commands to the _____.
    a. id, ego, superego
    b. id, superego, ego
    c. ego, superego, id
    d. superego, ego, id
    e. all three systems issue commands to every other system

17. On what is the mechanism underlying repression based?
    a. irrationality
    b. biological urge reduction
    c. anxiety reduction
    d. fear reduction
    e. ego expansion

18. Why are thoughts and memories repressed as well as actions?
    a. thinking about an act is similar to performing it
    b. young children cannot properly distinguished between thought and action
    c. young children do not realize thoughts are private
    d. a and b
    e. all of the above

19. A child is punished for something she did. She then hits her brother. This is an example of:
    a. repression
    b. transference
    c. hysteria
    d. displaced aggression
    e. anxiety

20. A child has deeply hidden feelings of hostility toward a younger sibling. However, the child treats his sibling with apparent love. This is an example of the defense mechanism known as:
    a. projection
    b. reaction formation
    c. rationalization
    d. displacement
    e. repression

21. A child who displays a behavior diametrically opposed to her frustrated true desires is demonstrating:
    a. reaction formation
    b. displacement
    c. projection
    d. isolation
    e. none of the above

22. After failing to be offered a good job, an applicant decides that he wouldn't have liked the job anyway. This person is displaying a defense mechanism called:
    a. rationalization
    b. projection
    c. reaction formation
    d. isolation
    e. repression

23. When a person attributes his or her own thoughts and feelings to someone else, we call this:
    a. rationalization
    b. projection
    c. reaction formation
    d. repression
    e. isolation

24. The relation of defense mechanisms to unacceptable unconscious thoughts is about the same as:
    a. rationalization to irrationalization
    b. blocking or rerouting to river
    c. track to trolley
    d. predator to prey
    e. oral to anal

25. Parts of the body that are particularly sensitive to touch are called:
    a. arousal zones
    b. pleasure zones
    c. sensitivity zones
    d. erogenous zones
    e. projection zones

26. Which of the following presents the correct stages of psychosexual development in the right order?
    a. oral, anal, erogenous, phallic, genital
    b. oral, anal, phallic, genital
    c. anal, oral, erogenous, phallic
    d. oral, anal, phallic, erogenous
    e. none are in the correct order

27. An adult who dislikes eating, and avoids kissing and smoking, would, according to Freud, be described as:
    a. fixated at the anal stage
    b. showing a reaction formation from the oral stage
    c. an oral character
    d. an anal character
    e. a remnant

28. If a child experienced severe toilet training, and grew up to be messy, generous, and open minded, a Freudian would account for this by using the mechanisms of:
    a. fixation and reaction formation
    b. repression and fixation
    c. projection and displacement
    d. isolation and rationalization
    e. a Freudian could not account for this

29. The critical component(s) of Freud's theory of personality is (are):
    a. psychosexual stages
    b. unconscious conflict
    c. fixation and reaction formation
    d. b and c
    e. all of the above

30. The anal and oral characters have in common:
    a. reaction formation at a stage of development
    b. fixation at a stage of development
    c. a concern for orderliness
    d. a lack of normal sexual interests
    e. none of the above

31. All of the following are components of Freud's family triangle *except*:
    a. love
    b. inadequacy
    c. fear
    d. jealousy
    e. b and d

32. The drama of the Oedipus complex unfolds according to the following progression of events:
    a. identification, love, fear, hate, renunciation
    b. love, fear, hate, renunciation, identification
    c. hate, fear, renunciation, identification
    d. love, hate, fear, renunciation, identification
    e. none of the above

33. The motivation for the young boy's identification with his father is:
    a. perception of sexual similarities
    b. castration anxiety
    c. the father's acts of retaliation
    d. vicarious enjoyment of the mother through the father
    e. penis envy

34. The stage following resolution of the Oedipus complex comprises:
    a. the latency period
    b. increased masturbation
    c. puberty
    d. genital stage
    e. all of the above

35. Freud believed that the basis of every dream was:
    a. projection
    b. schizophrenia
    c. wish fulfillment
    d. day residues
    e. castration anxiety

36. Freud distinguished between two parts of the dream, which he termed:
    a. conscious and unconscious
    b. latent and manifest
    c. normal and deviant
    d. wish fulfillment and disguise
    e. normal and abnormal

37. Dreams, metaphor, and poetry all involve:
    a. displaced activity
    b. repression
    c. resistance
    d. symbolism
    e. internalization

38. Problems with the psychoanalytic view include:
    a. lack of objectivity of clinical practitioners in reporting patient's statements
    b. so much flexibility that an outcome or its opposite can be predicted
    c. suggestion or influence of patients to report certain kinds of events or feelings
    d. a and c
    e. all of the above

39. Neo-Freudians believe that Freud erred in:
    a. emphasizing unconscious conflict
    b. his views of dreams as wish fulfillments
    c. his perception of oral and anal characteristics
    d. his assertion that the key to emotional development is in biology
    e. being concerned about anxiety

40. For which claims of psychoanalytic theory is there specific positive evidence?
    a. universality of the Oedipus complex
    b. link between hostility to the father and his sexual link to the mother
    c. existence of a cluster of traits predicted by the anal character

d. a link between toilet training and the anal character
e. no evidence for any of the above

41. In a recent study, a test was made of Freud's view of the dream as an attempt at gratification. Most very thirsty participants reported:
    a. dreams in which they drank
    b. dreams in which they did not drink
    c. no dreams whatsoever
    d. dreams in which the act of drinking was represented symbolically
    e. dreams about eating

42. Which of the following statements is *not* in accordance with C. S. Hall's view about dreams?
    a. The dream symbol expresses, rather than disguises, an underlying idea.
    b. The dream is a concrete form of mental shorthand that embodies a feeling or emotion.
    c. The dream is an abstract form of mental longhand that elaborates on a feeling or emotion.
    d. The function of the dream is analogous to that of a cartoonist's picture.
    e. There may be a role for the unconscious in dreaming.

43. There is little evidence for all of the following assertions of psychoanalytic theory *except*:
    a. the existence of unconscious conflict
    b. the general theory of psychosexual development
    c. the central importance of biology in determining stages of emotional development
    d. personality is essentially fixed by the age of five or six
    e. the Oedipus complex

44. According to Horney, the vicious circle:
    a. results from facing incompatible demands
    b. is more likely if there is more basic anxiety
    c. occurs in normal people
    d. all of the above
    e. none of the above

45. Block finds that parents who are warm, self-assuring and active, but provide firm guidelines, have the most adjusted children. Which of the following might account for this relation?
    a. The parents' upbringing style leads to good adjustment in their children.
    b. Parents who practice a positive upbringing style are better adjusted, and pass this characteristic to their children via genes.
    c. Children who are disposed to be adjusted prompt good upbringing styles from their parents.
    d. Parents with good upbringing styles are also better educated, and it is the education of the parents that produces the adjustment in the child.
    e. all of the above

46. Repression is to deciding to ignore unpleasant news as:
    a. unconscious defense is to conscious defense
    b. inattention is to reaction formation

c. coping is to ego psychology
d. ego is to superego
e. house is to bedroom

47. Coping is:
    a. like a conscious mechanism parallel to unconscious defense mechanisms
    b. somewhat consistent in style across decades in a given individual
    c. an unsuccessful way of dealing with problems
    d. all of the above
    e. a and b

48. The humanistic approach differs from both the behavioristic and psychoanalytic approaches in all but one of the following ways. Which of the choices below is *not* a difference between these approaches?
    a. emphasis on the positive side of human nature
    b. assumption of a hierarchy of needs
    c. acknowledgment of the existence of deficiency needs
    d. emphasis on self-actualization
    e. emphasis on free choice

49. In contrast to the behavioristic approach, the trait, psychoanalytic, and humanistic approaches all:
    a. emphasize internal causes of behavior
    b. focus on the conflict between biological and social needs
    c. posit a hierarchy of needs
    d. take a basically statistical approach to personality
    e. emphasize the role of the environment in shaping personality

50. Self-actualization is:
    a. at the top of the need hierarchy
    b. associated with a higher frequency of peak experiences
    c. dependent on satisfaction of lower-level needs
    d. all of the above
    e. a and b

51. Unconditional positive regard in the humanistic scheme, and failure to fixate at the oral or anal phases in the psychodynamic scheme, are both:
    a. features of personality
    b. contributing factors to adult psychopathology
    c. dependent on repression
    d. influenced by genetic predisposition
    e. conditions for a well-adjusted adult personality

52. Like the Romantic movement, the humanistic movement can be seen as a protest against:
    a. classical conditioning
    b. an overemphasis on culture
    c. a narrow and mechanical approach to human nature
    d. reliance on the scientific approach
    e. c and d

53. The sociocultural perspective differs from all other approaches considered in that only the sociocultural perspective:

a. does not assume the individual is necessarily the basic unit
b. considers the meaning of experience
c. acknowledges a major role for environmental factors
d. rejects a major role for biological factors
e. b and c

54. Humans across cultures show indications of diversity and common elements. Which of the following show marked commonalities across cultures?
a. dimensions of personality
b. degree of aggressiveness
c. degree of cooperation
d. frequency of common personality types
e. a and c

55. The sociocultural approach compares parallel conditions in different cultures in order to:
a. discover dimensions of human diversity
b. extract common features of human nature across cultures
c. test hypotheses (e.g., about the effect of early experience on later personality)
d. a and c
e. all of the above

56. Collectivist cultures are more committed to:
a. charities
b. the extended family
c. community
d. self-expression
e. b and c

57. Dimensions along which the self might vary in different cultures include:
a. degree of belief in situational determinants of behavior
b. degree of belief in personality traits
c. permanence of personal names
d. degree of interdependence with others
e. all of the above

58. According to the parallel to drama, a rich portrayal of a unique and distinct character would correspond to the _____ approach.
a. trait
b. humanistic
c. sociocultural
d. b and c
e. none of the above

59. Overall, the five approaches to personality each:
a. represent valid alternative perspectives
b. present views that cannot, ultimately, coexist with all of the others
c. overemphasize the importance of culture
d. emphasize reason over feelings
e. assign a different role to the function of drama

Answer Key for Self Test

1.	c p. 713	31.	b p. 723
2.	d p. 714	32.	d pp. 722, 723
3.	b p. 714	33.	b p. 723
4.	e p. 714	34.	a p. 723
5.	c pp. 715, 716	35.	c p. 725
6.	d p. 715	36.	b p. 726
7.	b p. 715	37.	d p. 726
8.	d p. 715	38.	e pp. 729, 730
9.	b p. 715	39.	d p. 730
10.	d pp. 715, 716	40.	c p. 731
11.	d p. 716	41.	b p. 733
12.	c p. 717	42.	c p. 734
13.	a p. 717	43.	a p. 735
14.	a p. 717	44.	d p. 737
15.	b pp. 717, 718	45.	e p. 739
16.	b p. 718	46.	a p. 739
17.	c pp. 718, 719	47.	e p. 740
18.	e p. 719	48.	c pp. 740, 741
19.	d p. 719	49.	a pp. 713, 741
20.	b p. 719	50.	d p. 743
21.	a p. 719	51.	e pp. 721, 743
22.	a p. 720	52.	e p. 745–47
23.	b p. 720	53.	a p. 747
24.	b pp. 719, 720	54.	a p. 749
25.	d p. 720	55.	e p. 748. 749
26.	b p. 721	56.	e p. 750
27.	b p. 721	57.	e pp. 751, 752
28.	a p. 722	58.	b p. 741
29.	e pp. 720, 721, 722	59.	a p. 753
30.	b p. 722		

Investigating Psychological Phenomena

ANALYSIS OF DREAM CONTENT

Equipment: None
Number of participants: One or more
Time per participant: Thirty minutes
Time for experimenter: Thirty minutes

The study and analysis of dream content has been of considerable concern to psychologists at least since the publication of Freud's classic work on dreams in 1900. A variety of hypotheses have been proposed to account for the content of dreams and for the way in which our past experiences and expectations about the future are frequently incorporated into our dreamwork.

Given the sparse evidence concerning dream content, there is still a good deal of controversy concerning the facts. One phenomenon of particular interest that is still controversial is whether present motivational states or expectations about the future (e.g., wish fulfillment) influence our dream content.

The present experiment further tests the hypothesis that dream content is influenced by present motivational state. The test is similar to the experiment of William Dement and Edward Wolpert cited by the authors of your text, in which these investigators induced thirst in their research participants, then analyzed the participants' dreams to determine whether there was evidence in the dream content for increased thirst.

You will be the volunteer in the present experiment. Starting on the next page, you will find eight pairs of dream reports. These are the reports of actual dreams from eight students enrolled in an introductory psychology course. One of the reports in each pair is the report of a dream from early in the term in which these students were enrolled in introductory psychology. The other report in each pair represents a dream that occurred on the night preceding a major midterm examination in the psychology course. The question we ask in this experiment is whether the specific issues involved in this examination or general anxiety about the examination was reflected in the dreams of these eight participants.

In order to address the question, you should read each dream and try to decide which dream in each pair was the one that occurred prior to the examination. Be careful to consider the possibility, as Freud theorized, that conflicts or concerns may be either manifest or latent in dream content. That is, there may be direct or transformed reference to the event in question. For each dream pair, mark your answer sheet A or B according to which member of the pair you think was the dream that preceded the examination. In each case, think about the reason for your choice and assess your confidence in your decision. After listing your choices, check them with the answers given.

DREAM PAIRS

1A Someone was singing a rousing song about a coat. An audience of women, mostly of the type interviewed in commercials, was sitting on the floor of a large room. They were asked to describe how they had put together their outfits. Most were wearing the sweater-and-skirt sort of thing, but one woman in a peculiar-looking caftan told how she had bought the trim first and had then searched for something to use it on. The trim didn't look very good on the caftan.

1B A record store. The stuff that had been pasted up all over the walls (posters, clippings, etc.) had yellowed, creating an antique atmosphere. Some balloons. The store was giving away something for free—furniture I think. There was some argument. Something about a snake who liked a trollop. A young and quarrelsome married couple from a film I'd seen more or less reenacted their roles. I was in a strange room in a hotel or dormitory. There was, to my surprise, a small wrought-iron balcony. Night. From the balcony I could see the lights and reflections of the city gleaming white and yellow all around me. The lights began to go out, all at once—the restaurants and bars were closing. I was seeing into a little restaurant or ice cream parlor, very white and empty. Three people wearily got up and left as the place closed up for the night.

2A I was knocking at the door of my best friend's house. (Earlier in the dream I had seen her working on campus and spoken to her. [She lives in San Antonio, Texas.]) I covered the peephole to the front door, as is my custom, when she became very excited and yelled for her parents. She seemed to be very frightened. This is when the dream ended and I woke up.

2B Someone I didn't recognize was walking down Locust Walk wearing shoes exactly like some of mine, except for the color. Mine are red and blue. Hers were green and blue.

3A I dream I was sitting at a table with several people eating brownies with whipped cream and soap suds, fighting with one of my friends.

3B I dreamed that my kitten looked like a guinea pig. (I went home for the weekend and she had changed.) She wasn't tiger striped, she was only solid black and rust colored. Her ears were not pointed, they were small and flat. She had no tail and her legs were short.

4A I was going to go swimming. I sat on a bench on the side of the street waiting for a taxi or bus. With me were a girl and a German teacher. The man had a beach umbrella. He grew tired of waiting and left. I went to a different beach to look for the father from a foreign family I spent a year with.

4B I was with a boyfriend while he was making sandwiches for a party. Beaded strings were in the crevice between the wall and the ceiling. Another girl was there making coffee with a weird machine. Outside I played catch with a friend. First we used a ball, then an orange, and lastly a key. We almost lost the key in the snow. I was skiing with another girl and she kept complimenting Yamaha skis. I tried to park the car in front of my house but there were no spaces. Two guys who I didn't particularly like from high school were in one of the cars drinking. They were not my type. When they asked me to go drinking I declined. Finally I went to a party. A minister I know said grace. A guest commented that a girl's jewelry didn't match her clothes, yet it really did. A lot of people were talking and eating.

5A The dream opened with me having just had a baby, but for some reason the kid (a boy) was about the size of a year-old baby—maybe a couple of months younger. I didn't recall getting pregnant or delivering the kid. Somehow I knew that the kid (baby) had my boyfriend's nickname. I got extreme pleasure from hugging the baby and knowing he was mine, although I didn't know who the father was. Suddenly I realized that I was in high school and my mother would never let me keep the baby. So I had to give him up for adoption. I was very sad at handing him over to a stranger and the thought that I would never see him grow up was upsetting. This was a pleasurable dream until the last scene.

5B I went back to visit my prep school and I bumped into my favorite teacher there. She was terribly aged and frail, having had some sort of drastic operation. I kissed her hello on the cheek and she was very cold, as though I had misbehaved recently at school or something. I don't remember the rest of the dream clearly except that the teacher kept turning into my mother and back into the teacher, and evidently I had done something awful but no one would tell me what. It was a very anxious and unpleasant dream.

6A I was riding on a trolley coming home from high school. The driver asked me for my fare and I found out I didn't have any money. I ran to the back to try to get out. Then I woke up.

6B I dreamt I had a sexual affair with my psychology professor. He told me I was one of his best friends.

7A Dreamt about color vision. Repeatedly remembered seeing one page in the reading.

7B Dreamt that I woke up late for chemistry lab and that experiment failed.

8A I rode on a short train ride and on the return trip I met a very good friend who is coming to visit me for the weekend. However, the train departure is delayed so I sit down to lunch with my family and another three friends (I don't know where they came from). My family wants me to tell them about school, but I am more interested in seeing one of my friends—

procuring tea bags and knives for my apartment (which I need). Another incident—I pass a stand with two older ladies selling homemade doughnuts (and cake) but I don't buy any, even though I see a girl sinking her teeth into one. Also, while I am walking toward the train station, the sidewalk is being paved (by males and females).

8B I have been waiting three weeks to see my boyfriend. Finally the weekend arrives and he comes to visit me. But, of course, we can't be alone since my best friend also drops in on me. Then I find out my grandmother has passed away (however, she is still among us when we all sit down to a mourning feast). When we finally get a chance to be alone again, my boyfriend and I are walking down a street. A car honks its horn and it turns out to be his old girlfriend asking for a ride home. During this same dream I remember buying a new bicycle and a pair of army boots.

Answer Sheet

Dream pair	Dream preceding examination (A or B)	Reason for choice
1.	_____	_____
2.	_____	_____
3.	_____	_____
4.	_____	_____
5.	_____	_____
6.	_____	_____
7.	_____	_____
8.	_____	_____

ANSWERS

1. B 2. A 3. A 4. B 5. B 6. B 7. A 8. B

QUESTIONS TO THINK ABOUT

1. Were you accurate? What does this suggest about the content of dreams and about how well they blend with life events?
2. Were there certain pairs where the choice seemed more obvious than for other pairs? Were you more accurate on these?
3. How might you improve on the experiment?

CHAPTER 18

Psychopathology

Learning Objectives

DIFFERENT CONCEPTIONS OF MADNESS

1. Contrast statistical versus "qualitative (true illness)" conceptions of psychopathology.

Psychopathology as demonic possession
2. Give examples from historical sources of the treatment of madness as demonic possession.

Psychopathology as a disease
3. Describe the history of the treatment of psychopathology as a disease.
4. Describe the somatogenic view of mental illness, referring to the example of general paresis.
5. Define psychogenic disorders, and explain the historical role of hysteria in clarifying the nature of these disorders.
6. Discuss the value of the psychogenic-somatogenic distinction.
7. Indicate the major features that define mental disorders, as developed in DSM-IV. What is the role of deviance, *per se*, in the definition?

THE UNDERLYING PATHOLOGY MODEL

8. Explain the underlying pathology model of mental illness.

Variations of the pathology model
9. Briefly describe the biomedical, psychodynamic, and learning models as approaches to psychopathology.
10. Distinguish different types of psychodynamic and learning models.

Classifying mental disorders
11. Distinguish among symptoms, signs, and syndromes.
12. Describe the basic course of the diagnosis of mental disorders, including integration of the clinical interview information about symptoms, signs, course, and onset.
13. Describe how psychiatrists used to distinguish among organic brain syndromes, neuroses, and psychoses. Indicate how mental illnesses are now classified, referring to the changes in the latest taxonomy, DSM-IV.

Explaining disorder: diathesis, stress, and pathology
14. Describe the diathesis-stress explanation of mental illness.

15. What does one have to know in order to explain fully a mental (or bodily) disorder?

SCHIZOPHRENIA

16. What is the incidence of schizophrenia?

Signs and symptoms
17. Describe the major symptoms of schizophrenia in the areas of thought, social relationships, motivation, and behavior.
18. Define restitutional symptoms, delusions, hallucinations, and ideas of reference.
19. What are the most salient symptoms of paranoid, catatonic, and disorganized schizophrenia?

The search for the underlying pathology
20. Evaluate the idea that the major psychological disorder in schizophrenia is an inability to maintain a focus of attention.
21. Describe the dopamine hypothesis and indicate the types of evidence in favor of it. Suggest what types of experiments might prove it.
22. What is the evidence suggesting a modification of the dopamine hypothesis—the dopamine-serotonin interaction hypothesis?
23. What is the structural defect theory of schizophrenia, and what is the evidence for it?
24. Describe the two-syndrome hypothesis and indicate how it distinguishes positive and negative symptoms.
25. What is the evidence for three schizophrenic syndromes?
26. What are some problems with each of the accounts of schizophrenia?

Ultimate causes of schizophrenia
27. Review the evidence for genetic factors in schizophrenia, and suggestions that schizophrenia is a neurodevelopmental disorder.
28. Describe the role of environmental effects in schizophrenia, including low social status and family pathology.
29. Evaluate the alternative possibilities that the environmental correlates of schizophrenia are caused by or are causes of schizophrenia.

The pathology model and schizophrenia
30. Review the symptoms, underlying pathology, and remote causes of schizophrenia. Review the evidence for an organic basis for schizophrenia.

31. Apply the diathesis-stress model to schizophrenia.

MOOD DISORDERS

Bipolar and unipolar syndromes

32. Distinguish bipolar disorder from major depression. Compare and contrast mania, hypomania, and depression in terms of symptoms.
33. Describe the symptoms and degrees of depression, including depressive stupor and vegetative signs.
34. What is the relation between suicide and depression?
35. What is seasonal affective disorder?

Organic factors

36. Review the evidence for a genetic involvement in the causation of bipolar and unipolar disorders.
37. What are the biochemical hypotheses to explain depression, and what is the evidence for them?
38. What problems arise for these hypotheses in terms of the time course of recovery from depression after drug treatment?

Psychogenic factors

39. Review the evidence for psychogenic factors in depression.
40. Discuss whether mood or cognitive disorders come first in the causation of depression.
41. Describe Beck's cognitive theory of depression.
42. Describe the learned helplessness theory of depression, and summarize the evidence in favor of it that comes from both animal and human research.
43. Explain how the idea of despondent explanatory style as a cause of depression grew out of the concept of learned helplessness, and review the evidence for this position.

Sex differences in the prevalence of major depression

44. Indicate the explanations for the higher incidence of depression in American females, as opposed to males.

Mood disorders and the diathesis-stress conception

45. Apply the diathesis-stress conception to mood disorders.

ANXIETY DISORDERS

46. What defines the anxiety disorders?

Phobias

47. Describe phobias, including social phobias, and explain how they can be accounted for in terms of conditioning.
48. Describe the problems with conditioning accounts of phobia, the preparedness theory of phobias, and how it accounts for at least one problem with a conditioning approach.

Obsessive-compulsive disorder

49. Describe the symptoms of obsessive-compulsive disorders, and possible causes.

Generalized anxiety disorder

50. Describe generalized anxiety disorder, and both conditioning and psychoanalytic explanations for it.

Panic disorder

51. What is panic disorder, and how does it differ from generalized anxiety disorder? How does it relate to agoraphobia? What is a cognitive explanation of this disorder?

Reactions to extreme stress: acute and post-traumatic stress disorder

52. What is post-traumatic stress disorder? How does dissociation fit into the development of this syndrome? How may low cortisol levels have a causative role?

DISSOCIATIVE DISORDERS

53. Describe dissociative amnesia, dissociative fugue, and dissociative identity disorder. What do they have in common?

Factors underlying dissociative disorders

54. What is believed to be the psychological function of dissociative disorders?

Dissociative disorders and the diathesis-stress conception

55. What are the proposed diathesis and stress for dissociative disorders?

SOMATOFORM AND PSYCHOPHYSIOLOGICAL DISORDERS

Somatoform disorders

56. What are somatoform disorders, and what is the psychoanalytic explanation of them? How can their decline in recent decades be explained?

Psychophysiological disorders

57. Define psychophysiological disorders. What is the critical difference between psychophysiological and somatoform disorders?
58. Review the role of biological and psychological factors in the causation of coronary heart disease.
59. What is the Type A behavior pattern? What aspects of this behavior pattern seem most associated with coronary heart disease?
60. Apply the diathesis-stress model to psychophysiological disorders and to the issue of which type of disorder (e.g., coronary heart disease, peptic ulcer) occurs in an individual.

A CATEGORIZING REVIEW

61. Explain how mental disorders can be classified according to the organic or mental basis of both the symptoms and the underlying pathology.

SOCIAL DEVIANCE

The sociopath

62. Discuss the distinctions between criminals and sociopaths.
63. Review the causes of sociopathy (antisocial personality disorder).

Sociopathy and the disorder concept

64. Discuss the advantages and disadvantages of making no legal distinction between sociopaths and criminals.

THE SCOPE OF PSYCHOPATHOLOGY

65. Discuss the problem of defining psychopathology and uncovering common principles underlying it. What, if anything, do all disorders described in this chapter have in common?

Programmed Exercises

DIFFERENT CONCEPTIONS OF MADNESS

1. According to the _____ conception of psychopathology, it simply refers to deviance, or a relatively high frequency of intensity of certain behaviors.

    statistical

2. A dominant early social response to insanity, which resulted in practices such as trephining the skull, was based on the conception of insanity as _____ _____.

    demonic possession

3. Prior to the nineteenth century, people with severe mental illness were treated more or less as we currently deal with _____.

    criminals (or prisoners)

4. The disappearance of the psychological symptoms of _____ _____ following administration of penicillin provides strong evidence for a view of mental illness as a disease.

    general paresis (or syphilis)

5. Mental symptoms that can be directly explained by malfunction at the organic level are called _____. Those, like hysteria, that are best explained at the psychological level are called _____.

    somatogenic
    psychogenic

6. A disorder that is characterized by symptoms that appear to be somatic but have no organic basis was once called _____.

    hysteria

7. The commonly accepted definition for mental disorders is presented in _____. It does not require _____ as a condition for the diagnosis of a disorder.

    DSM-IV
    abnormality (deviance)

THE UNDERLYING PATHOLOGY MODEL

8. According to the _____ _____ _____, a particular disease is considered as the underlying cause of specific mental symptoms.

    underlying pathology model

9. According to the _____ model, mental illness has an organic basis, to be treated with somatic therapies. According to the _____ model, mental disorders are, in large part, the result of maladaptive learning. According to the _____ model, mental illness results from psychogenic factors. Freud's particular form of this model is called the _____ model.

    biomedical
    learning
    psychodynamic
    psychoanalytic

10. Practitioners who ascribe to the learning model and emphasize classical and instrumental conditioning as causes of disorder are called _____ _____.

    behavior therapists

11. A variant of the learning model, called the _____-_____ model, emphasizes faulty thinking habits. Practitioners of this model are called _____ _____.

    cognitive-behavioral
    cognitive therapists

12. In psychopathology, as in physical medicine, the diagnostic process begins with a _____ _____. This elicits a set of complaints, or _____.

    clinical interview,
    symptoms

13. The diagnostician also looks for _____, that is, indications that are not complaints, but that are consistent with the symptoms.

    signs

14. A _____ is a pattern of signs and symptoms that go together.

    syndrome

15. In the course of the _____ _____, the diagnostician integrates information about _____, _____, _____, and _____ to arrive at a diagnosis.

    clinical interview
    symptoms, signs,
    course, onset

16. As a result of the diagnosis, one can often predict the _____ and _____ (cause) of the disorder.

    outcome (prognosis),
    etiology

17. In the most recent classification or taxonomy of mental illness, called _____, more emphasis is placed on the description of disorders, rather than on _____ about their cause.

    DSM-IV
    theories

18. In the older classification of mental illnesses, _____ were considered to be anxiety-related disorders in which there is good contact with reality, in contrast to the more severe disorders called _____. A third category was _____ _____ _____.

    neuroses
    psychoses, organic brain syndromes

19. According to the _____-_____ conception, mental illness results from the interaction between a predisposition and some set of environmental events.

    diathesis-stress

20. The analysis of mental disorders in the biomedical model includes description of remote and immediate (also called _____) _____, which cause the _____.

    proximate, causes, syndrome (symptoms, signs)

SCHIZOPHRENIA

21. The incidence of schizophrenia is about one American out of every _____. — hundred

22. Schizophrenic symptoms include disorders in thinking and selective _____. — attention

23. Schizophrenic persons often lose contact with other people as a result of social _____. This may lead to progressively worse problems, because they have few opportunities for social _____ _____. — withdrawal / reality testing

24. Schizophrenic symptoms include elaboration of the private world, or _____ symptoms, such as _____ of persecution and hearing voices or other _____. — restitutional / delusions, hallucinations

25. Schizophrenics typically show either _____ or _____ affect. — indifference (apathy), inappropriate

26. Some schizophrenics begin to believe that external events are specially related to them, personally. These beliefs are called _____ _____ _____, and may be elaborated into a _____ _____. — ideas of reference / delusional system

27. Delusions are typical symptoms in a common form of schizophrenia, _____ schizophrenia. — paranoid

28. A schizophrenic with unusual motor reactions, such as remaining motionless for long periods, is classified as _____. If the predominant symptoms are extreme incoherence in thought and inappropriateness in behavior, a person is classified as a _____ schizophrenic. — catatonic / disorganized

29. A cognitive theory of schizophrenia holds that many symptoms result from an inability to keep things in proper focus. This results in an inability to hold on to one _____ of thought or action. Some believe this is the basic _____ _____ in schizophrenia. — line (train) / psychological malfunction

30. One argument for an organic basis for schizophrenia is the effectiveness of a group of drugs called _____ _____ in treatment. — classical antipsychotics (major tranquilizers)

31. The _____ hypothesis of schizophrenia holds that it results from too much brain activity caused by the catecholamine neurotransmitter _____, which may cause the overstimulation characteristic of schizophrenia. — dopamine / dopamine

32. In accord with the theory that holds that neurons in the schizophrenic's brain are oversensitive to dopamine, the _____, which enhance dopamine activity, make schizophrenics worse and can induce a schizophreniclike _____ in nonschizophrenic individuals. — amphetamines / psychosis (syndrome)

33. The superior schizophrenia treatment effects of the _____ antipsychotics, such as Chlorazil, suggests the _____-_____ _____ hypothesis. — atypical, dopamine-serotonin interaction

34. There are often _____ abnormalities in the brain associated with schizophrenia, and sometimes evidence of less total brain tissue, as indicated by enlarged_____. — structural / ventricles

35. A more modern classification of schizophrenia contrasts abnormal behavior, or _____ symptoms, with the absence of normal behaviors, or _____ symptoms. — positive / negative

36. According to the _____-_____ hypothesis, both anatomical deficits and neurotransmitter excess are causes of schizophrenia. The anatomical deficits are thought to be associated with the _____ symptoms and the neurotransmitter excess with the _____ symptoms. — two-syndrome / negative, positive

37. There is evidence that there are three syndromes of schizophrenia, with the positive symptoms divided into those that represent _____ and those that represent _____ symptoms, like delusions and hallucinations. — disorganization, psychotic

38. Twin studies indicate that there is a significant _____ factor in the causation of schizophrenia. — genetic (hereditary)

39. Identical twins show a _____ of 55 percent for schizophrenia. — concordance

40. According to the view of schizophrenia as a _____ disorder, pathological genes cause brain abnormalities in the fetus, which eventually lead to schizophrenia. — neurodevelopmental

41. Studies indicate that schizophrenia is much more common in _____ classes and that class status may be both a cause and effect of schizophrenia. — lower

42. According to the _____ _____ view, there is a higher incidence of schizophrenia in lower classes because schizophrenia causes lower-class status, rather than lower-class status causing schizophrenia. — downward drift

43. There is evidence that _____ pathology may cause schizophrenia, but there is also evidence that it may be caused by schizophrenia.

family

44. There is no strong evidence for family attitudes and problems as _____ of schizophrenia, but they can affect how well schizophrenics _____.

causes
cope

45. In accord with the diathesis-stress model, the evidence for a genetic predisposition for schizophrenia corresponds to the _____, while the demonstrated role of environment events corresponds to the _____.

diathesis
stress

MOOD DISORDERS

46. While schizophrenia can be regarded as essentially a disorder of thought, in the _____ disorders, the dominant disturbance is one of affect or mood.

mood

47. The two major types of mood disorders are _____ disorder and _____ _____.

bipolar, major depression

48. _____ is the opposite of depression, and is characterized, among other things, by endless talking and overabundance of energy. In a milder form it is called _____.

Mania
hypomania

49. Depression is commonly associated with physical manifestations such as weakness, loss of appetite and interest in sex, and sleep disorders. There are called _____ symptoms.

vegetative

50. In severe depression, a person may become entirely unresponsive and may be in a _____ _____.

depressive stupor

51. Depression is associated with a high rate of _____.

suicide

52. Depression associated with decreasing amounts of light as winter approaches is called _____ _____ _____. This may relate to changes in sleep cycles and the level of the pineal hormone, _____.

seasonal affective
disorder
melatonin

53. Twin studies indicate a higher role for genetic factors in _____ than in _____ disorders.

bipolar, unipolar

54. There is evidence that low levels of either of two neurotransmitters, _____ and _____, may account for depression.

serotonin,
norepinephrine

55. _____ _____ take a few weeks to affect depression, but they have an immediate effect on brain neurotransmitter levels.

Antidepressant
medications

56. According to a number of psychogenic approaches to depression, the primary disorder is _____, which leads to changes in _____.

cognitive
mood

57. Beck asserts that depression results from a set of negative beliefs, called _____ _____ _____, and can be treated successfully with _____ therapy.

negative cognitive
schema, cognitive

58. According to the _____ _____ theory of depression, depression is caused by an expectation that one's actions will have no significant effects.

learned helplessness

59. As a result of the difficulty in explaining symptoms such as self-blame in depression, emphasis on psychological causative factors has changed from learned helplessness to despondent _____ _____.

explanatory
style

60. In Western cultures, there is a much higher incidence of _____ _____ and _____ _____ in females.

major depression
bipolar disorder

ANXIETY DISORDERS

61. An irrational and intense fear of an object or situation is called a _____.

phobia

62. According to a _____ view, phobias are produced by a form of Pavlovian or classical _____.

conditioning
conditioning

63. A fear of embarrassment or humiliation in front of others is called a _____ phobia.

social

64. The _____ theory of phobias accounts for why snakes and spiders are more common phobic objects than flowers or pajamas.

preparedness

65. In _____-_____ disorders, anxiety is produced by persistent internal events (thoughts or wishes).

obsessive-compulsive

66. _____ are persistent thoughts. _____ are acts usually performed in an attempt to deal with these thoughts.

Obsessions, Compulsions

67. In phobias, anxiety is focused on a particular object or situation. In _____ _____ disorders, it is all-pervasive.

generalized anxiety

68. _____ disorder is more acute than generalized anxiety disorder, but like generalized anxiety disorder it doesn't focus on a particular object or situation.

Panic

69. Fear of having panic attacks causes some people not to venture away from their home, a condition called _____.

agoraphobia

70. Some have explained panic disorder as an overreaction to the bodily symptoms of _____.

fear

71. Recurrent nightmares and flashbacks about a traumatic event characterize _____-_____ _____ disorder.

post-traumatic stress

72. Immediately after the trauma, people who will develop post-traumatic stress disorder often feel oddly unaffected by the event, or _____.

dissociated

73. Some have suggested that early adverse experiences may serve as a _____ for PTSD, and that this may be mediated by low _____ levels.

diathesis
cortisol

DISSOCIATIVE DISORDERS

74. In dissociative disorders, a whole set of mental events are removed from ordinary _____. These disorders include _____ and _____ (cite two types).

consciousness, dissociative fugue, dissociative amnesia, or dissociative identity disorder

75. Many believe that dissociative disorders are a psychological _____ against something the individual is unable to face.

defense

76. According to one formulation, the tendency to be able to be _____ forms part of the diathesis for dissociative disorders, and _____ _____ is often the stress.

hypnotized
severe trauma (severe abuse, child abuse)

SOMATOFORM AND PSYCHOPHYSIOLOGICAL DISORDERS

77. In somatoform disorders, the principal symptom is a _____ disorder, such as paralysis.

somatic (bodily)

78. The four different types of somatoform disorders include (list two): _____ and _____.

hypochondriasis, somatization disorder, somatoform pain disorder, conversion disorder

79. Conversion disorders are declining in incidence. This probably results from more _____ child rearing and more general _____ sophistication.

permissive, medical

80. In _____ disorders, organic damage is caused by psychophysiological factors.

psychophysiological

81. The _____ _____ behavior pattern is associated with increased risk of coronary heart disease. The component of the personality most associated with coronary heart disease is _____.

Type A
hostility

82. In the face of continued stress, some people get peptic ulcers, some get coronary heart disease, some get other psychophysiological disorders, and some show no obvious effects. These differences may be accounted for in terms of a preexisting somatic _____.

diathesis (predisposition, susceptibility)

A CATEGORIZING REVIEW

83. Psychophysiological disorders have primarily _____ symptoms and primarily _____ underlying pathology.

organic, mental

84. Schizophrenia has primarily _____ symptoms and primarily _____ underlying pathology.

mental, organic

SOCIAL DEVIANCE

85. Someone who behaves antisocially without signs of remorse is called an antisocial personality, or _____.

sociopath

86. Some explanations of sociopathy suggest that it may result from cortical _____, or cortical _____.

immaturity
underarousal

87. Another account of sociopathy holds that sociopaths have little _____ for the consequences of their actions.

fear (concern)

88. The distinction between sociopathy and _____ is often hard to maintain.

criminality

Self Test

1. Treatment of "mental disorders" in the past by such procedures as trephination or flogging is indicative of a conception of these disorders as caused by:
   a. microorganisms
   b. criminal impulses
   c. degeneration
   d. demonic possession
   e. medical malpractice

2. The discovery of a cure for general paresis gave support to the view of mental illness as:
   a. demonic possession
   b. akin to criminality
   c. a disease of society
   d. somatogenic
   e. resulting from medical malpractice

3. If a specific enzyme lack was pinned down as the cause of a previously poorly understood severe mental illness, it would change its classification from _____ to _____.
   a. psychosis, neurosis
   b. disease, pathology
   c. psychoanalytic, medical
   d. psychogenic, somatogenic
   e. minor, serious

4. According to the modern view, as expressed in DSM-IV, abnormality (deviance) is:
   a. part of the definition of mental disorders
   b. a frequent but not necessary feature of mental disorders
   c. unrelated to mental disorders
   d. directly linked to distress
   e. serious only when it is somatogenic

5. Both the biomedical model and the psychodynamic model:
   a. emphasize somatogenic disorders
   b. fail to explain conversion disorders
   c. are limited versions of the pathology model
   d. emphasize psychogenic disorders
   e. emphasize the role of learning

6. It is probably true that most Swiss today are at least bilingual. Then a monolingual Swiss would be deviant or abnormal. Classification of such a person as suffering from a mental disorder would depend, according to the pathology model, on:
   a. the establishment of the deviance
   b. demonstration that monolingualism seriously impairs functioning in Switzerland
   c. description of some underlying pathology that caused monolingualism
   d. b or c
   e. none of the above

7. Which of the following goes along with symptoms, course, and onset in forming a mental disorder diagnosis?
   a. signs
   b. labeling
   c. deviance determination
   d. neurosis evaluation
   e. psychogenic evaluation

8. The diagnosis often leads to information about the:
   a. signs
   b. deviance
   c. outlook
   d. etiology
   e. c and d

9. The fundamental difference between what was known as a psychosis and a neurosis was:
   a. the psychosis involves more detachment from reality
   b. the neurosis is easier to cure
   c. all psychoses have a known biological cause
   d. b and c
   e. a and c

10. Understanding of a disease includes knowledge of its symptoms, underlying pathology, remote causes, and:
    a. proximate causes
    b. psychogenicity
    c. psychoanalytic roots
    d. deviance
    e. a and c

11. Certain types of color blindness occur, invariably, if a person inherits a particular gene or pair of genes from his or her parents. This "disorder" does not fit the diathesis-stress model, because:
    a. there is no diathesis
    b. there is no stress
    c. both diathesis and stress are present, but either is sufficient for manifestation of the disorder
    d. both diathesis and stress are present, but they do not interact
    e. c or d

12. The general idea that schizophrenics have difficulty distinguishing between personal (internal) and external events can be used to explain some of the symptoms of schizophrenia. Which of the following schizophrenic symptoms can be explained in this manner?
    a. delusions
    b. hallucinations
    c. catatonic immobility
    d. a and b
    e. all of the above

13. Delusions differ from hallucinations in that:
    a. delusions are associated with ideas of persecution
    b. delusions are based on interpretations of real events
    c. delusions are primarily visual while hallucinations are auditory
    d. delusions are associated with apathy (indifference)
    e. delusions cause social withdrawal

14. The idea that the fundamental disorder in schizophrenia is a cognitive deficit having to do with failure to keep things in proper focus can explain all but one of the following. Which feature of schizophrenia *cannot* be easily explained?
    a. disconnected thought
    b. rhyming associations
    c. social withdrawal (as a consequence of overstimulation)
    d. apathy (indifference)
    e. c and d

15. Thorazine is a drug in the classical antipsychotic (major tranquilizer) family and is effective as therapy for schizophrenia. Antipsychotics are known to block the action of dopamine at the synapse. Dopamine is a neurotransmitter. Low levels of dopamine in animals lead to the neglect of stimulation. Taken together, these findings suggest:
    a. that schizophrenia results from an excess of dopamine, leading to overstimulation or overload
    b. that there is a strong, enzyme-based hereditary deficit in dopamine in schizophrenics
    c. that schizophrenics have too little dopamine, leading to cognitive and affective symptoms
    d. that there is probably no direct relation between dopamine levels and schizophrenia
    e. that drugs should be given simpler names

16. Penicillin is to general paresis as _____ is (are) to schizophrenia.
    a. dopamine
    b. amphetamines
    c. antipsychotics (major tranquilizers)
    d. norepinephrine
    e. genetics

17. According to the dopamine hypothesis of schizophrenia, a drug that opposes the effect of amphetamines would:
    a. be likely to reduce positive symptoms of schizophrenia
    b. be likely to reduce negative symptoms of schizophrenia
    c. cause schizophrenic symptoms in normal people
    d. oppose the effect of antipsychotics
    e. a and b

18. Delusions in paranoid schizophrenics or bizarre behaviors in catatonic schizophrenics, are examples of:
    a. syndromes
    b. diatheses
    c. ideas of reference
    d. negative symptoms
    e. positive symptoms

19. The two-syndrome hypothesis asserts that:
    a. the positive and negative symptoms of schizophrenia have different causes
    b. anatomical and neurotransmitter disorders produce different types of schizophrenia
    c. there are two anatomical deficits underlying schizophrenia
    d. amphetamines and dopamine are the two causes of schizophrenia
    e. a and b

20. The concordance rate among identical twins for schizophrenia is 55 percent, while the comparable figure for fraternal twins is 9 percent. These results suggest that :
    a. genetic factors predominate as causes of schizophrenia
    b. there is a very weak genetic component in the causation of schizophrenia
    c. schizophrenia is essentially caused by environmental factors
    d. the primary cause of schizophrenia is probably lack of a neurotransmitter, rather than a genetic effect
    e. both genetic and environmental factors play important roles in the causation of schizophrenia

21. The incidence of schizophrenia is higher in the lower classes. This suggests that:
    a. social class is a causal factor in schizophrenia
    b. schizophrenics are lower in social class because they are schizophrenic
    c. schizophrenia does not have a strong organic component
    d. a and/or b
    e. all of the above

22. There are some reports of poorer mental health in the *adoptive* parents of schizophrenics. This, along with studies of differences in the behaviors of mothers to their schizophrenic and normal children, suggests that:
    a. pathological home environments cause schizophrenia
    b. schizophrenic children can induce pathological behavior in parents
    c. there is an organic basis for schizophrenia
    d. there is a psychogenic basis for schizophrenia
    e. a and d

23. The pathology model of schizophrenia presented in the text includes all but one of the following assumptions. Which assumption is *not* included?
    a. Family pathology leads to deficits in the function of brain neurotransmitters.
    b. Some genetic factors contribute to pathology in the function of certain brain neurotransmitters.
    c. Neurotransmitter deficits can lead to inability to focus in time or space.
    d. Inability to focus in time or space can lead to social withdrawal.
    e. Inability to focus in space and time can lead to inappropriate emotions.

24. Manic disorders share with some forms of schizophrenia which of the following symptoms?
    a. hallucinations
    b. social withdrawal
    c. shifting from one subject to another in conversation
    d. blunted affect in response to stimuli that would normally elicit affective responses
    e. enormous amounts of energy

25. A person shows little interest in the world around him. He shows little emotional response and has disconnected thoughts. On this basis, the most likely guess for a diagnosis would be:
    a. mania
    b. major depression
    c. bipolar disorder
    d. schizophrenia
    e. a or c

26. Which of the following is *not* associated with some type of depression?
    a. shortening light cycles in winter
    b. hypomania
    c. disturbed sleep cycles
    d. suicide
    e. changes in levels of melatonin

27. There is evidence for a gene on the X chromosome that is associated with the occurrence of:
    a. seasonal affective disorder
    b. major depression
    c. bipolar disorder
    d. schizophrenia
    e. none of the above

28. Parents with bipolar disorder tend to have children with bipolar disorder, and parents with unipolar disorder tend to have children with unipolar disorder. This suggests that:
    a. parents are a stress
    b. bipolar and unipolar disorders have a different basis
    c. bipolar and unipolar disorders share a common cause
    d. environmental events are the primary cause of mood disorders
    e. bipolar disorder is more likely to be inherited than unipolar disorder

29. According to the biochemical hypotheses, low levels of norepinephrine or serotonin are causative factors in:
    a. mania
    b. depression
    c. schizophrenia
    d. a and b
    e. a and c

30. All but one of the following provide evidence in favor of the theory that low levels of norepinephrine in the brain lead to depression. Which of these findings does *not* support this theory?
    a. Drugs that deplete norepinephrine cause depression in nonschizophrenic individuals.
    b. Helplessness training in animals depletes norepinephrine.
    c. Drugs which increase the availability of norepinephrine are effective in therapy for depression.
    d. Norepinephrine is involved with the systems in the brain that produce arousal and activation.
    e. Dopamine, a neurotransmitter related to norepinephrine, is implicated in the causation of schizophrenia.

31. In terms of the hypothesis that holds that high levels of norepinephrine (or serotonin) cause mania, which of the following should be an effective therapy for mania?
    a. a drug that mimics norepinephrine
    b. amphetamine
    c. a drug that increases reuptake of norepinephrine by the presynaptic neuron
    d. a drug that decreases the rate of breakdown of norepinephrine in the synaptic gap
    e. a drug that increases the rate of synthesis of norepinephrine in the synaptic terminals

32. According to Seligman's helplessness views, the low affect of depression results from:
    a. low levels of norepinephrine
    b. negative cognitions that produce affective changes
    c. a tendency toward suicidal thoughts
    d. bipolar mood change
    e. self-hatred

33. Which of the following symptoms of depression is particularly difficult to explain for both the biochemical and psychogenic (learned helplessness) theories?
    a. negative affect
    b. inactivity
    c. responsiveness to antidepressant drugs
    d. self-hatred
    e. none of the above

34. According to the learned helplessness theory of depression, which of the following would be the most relevant diathesis for depression?
    a. depletion of norepinephrine or serotonin
    b. past experiences in which a person could not control his or her environment
    c. genetic factors
    d. parents who gave the person too much responsibility as a child
    e. c or d

35. The advantage of the explanatory style explanation of depression over learned helplessness is that the former can explain:
    a. inactivity
    b. suicidal thoughts
    c. self-blame
    d. global depression
    e. low levels of norepinephrine

36. Which of the following hypothetical findings would oppose the organic explanations of a higher incidence of depression in adult females?
    a. equal incidence of schizophrenia in both sexes
    b. equal incidence of depression in both sexes in traditional cultures
    c. lower levels of brain norepinephrine in females
    d. lower levels of activity in adult females
    e. a and b

37. Which of the following lists of disorders is arranged in order of *increasing* importance of psychogenic causative factors?
    a. schizophrenia, depression, bipolar disorder
    b. schizophrenia, general paresis, phobias
    c. phobias, depression, mental retardation
    d. general paresis, depression, phobias
    e. schizophrenia, phobias, general paresis

38. One effective treatment for specific phobias is to expose the phobic person to weak instances of the phobic object while the person relaxes. The strength of the stimulus is gradually increased. Under these conditions, many phobias disappear, and no undesirable symptoms seem to replace them. This therapeutic success is an argument in favor of:
    a. the conditioning view of phobias
    b. preparedness
    c. a diathesis-stress model of phobias
    d. a biological basis for social phobias
    e. none of the above

39. A disorder in which anxiety is handled by repetitive and ritualistic acts is called:

a. phobia
b. psychogenic fugue
c. obsessive-compulsive disorder
d. conversion disorder
e. generalized anxiety disorder

40. If phobias are often about objects, and obsessions are about thoughts, then panic disorder can be said to be about:
a. physiological symptoms
b. lack of ability to escape
c. sexual objects
d. denial of fear
e. sympathy

41. Post-traumatic stress disorder and specific phobias share:
a. a conditioning explanation
b. causation by a traumatic event
c. dissociation
d. low anxiety
e. ritualistic behaviors

42. Amnesia, fugue, and/or multiple identities may be symptoms of:
a. obsessive-compulsive disorders
b. psychoses
c. conversion disorders
d. dissociative disorders
e. none of the above

43. There has been a decline in the incidence of diagnosed conversion disorders in the United States. This might result from:
a. greater sophistication in making neurological diagnoses
b. increased medical sophistication of people
c. greater permissiveness in the upbringing of children
d. a and b
e. all of the above

44. The fundamental distinction between anxiety disorders and somatoform or dissociative disorders is that:
a. anxiety disorders are more generalized
b. anxiety is an explanation only for anxiety disorders
c. organic factors are much more heavily involved in anxiety disorders
d. only in anxiety disorders is anxiety expressed overtly
e. a and b

45. Obesity, smoking, and hostility have in common the fact that they are all:
a. components of the Type A behavior pattern
b. risk factors for coronary heart disease
c. associated with a competitive personality
d. a and b
e. all of the above

46. If a study found that, under the stress of threat of terrorism for a period of years, a group of 100 people developed a wide variety of psychophysiological disorders, including ulcers in some, hypertension in others, and asthma in still others, this would be evidence in favor of:
a. a diathesis factor
b. a stress factor
c. a role for neurotransmitters
d. an organic origin for psychophysiological disorders
e. therapeutic use of the antibiotic terrormycin

47. A fundamental difference between a somatoform disorder and a psychophysiological disorder is that:
a. treatment of the organic "complaint" is much more likely to be effective in psychophysiological disorders
b. psychophysiological disorders are much more likely to be accompanied by low levels of neurotransmitters
c. somatoform disorders are mental in origin
d. dissociation is involved only in psychophysiological disorders
e. psychophysiological disorders always involve the nervous system

48. In terms of the model of categorization of mental disorders in the text, diabetes is to psychophysiological disorders as schizophrenia is to _____.
a. general paresis
b. bipolar disorders
c. asthma
d. sociopathy
e. pneumonia

49. A person is apprehended after committing a series of crimes. The question is whether she should be treated as a criminal or a sociopath. All but one of the following characteristics suggest that she is a sociopath. Indicate the characteristic that suggests a criminal, rather than sociopath, diagnosis:
a. she is a loner
b. she feels no guilt for the committed crimes
c. she is anxious
d. she is charming
e. she is intelligent

50. There is actually evidence that low levels of brain serotonin are associated with high levels of violence. This might lead someone to hypothesize that levels of serotonin were a cause of sociopathy. Which of the following hypothetical findings would be evidence for this hypothesis?
a. Drugs that block the action of serotonin reduce antisocial acts in sociopaths.
b. There is a negative correlation between degree of sociopathy and levels of serotonin by-products in the blood.
c. Many sociopaths are not more violent than normal people.
d. There is a positive correlation between degree of sociopathy and levels of serotonin in the brain.
e. None of the above are evidence.

51. Sociopathy differs from almost all other disorders considered as psychopathology in that:
a. there is no evidence that it runs in families
b. there is serious question as to whether it is a mental disorder
c. there is no accepted treatment for it
d. a and b
e. all of the above

Answer Key for Self Test

1.	d p. 758	27.	c p. 784
2.	d pp. 760–61	28.	b p. 784
3.	d pp. 762–63	29.	b p. 785
4.	b pp. 763–64	30.	e p. 785
5.	c pp. 764–65	31.	c p. 785
6.	d pp. 763–64	32.	b p. 787
7.	a pp. 765–66	33.	d p. 787
8.	e p. 766	34.	b p. 787
9.	a p. 766	35.	c pp. 787–88
10.	a p. 767	36.	b pp. 788–89
11.	b pp. 767–68	37.	d pp. 760–61, 784–88
12.	d p. 771		790–92
13.	b p. 771	38.	a p. 791
14.	d p. 772	39.	c p. 792
15.	a p. 773	40.	a pp. 794–95
16.	c p. 773	41.	b p. 795
17.	a p. 773	42.	d pp. 796–97
18.	e p. 774	43.	e p. 800
19.	e pp. 774–75	44.	d pp. 789–800
20.	e pp. 776–77	45.	b pp. 801–2
21.	d p. 777	46.	a pp. 802–3
22.	b p. 778	47.	a pp. 799–803
23.	a p. 779	48.	d p. 803
24.	c pp. 769–70, 780–81	49.	c pp. 804–5
25.	d pp. 769–71	50.	b pp. 803–6
26.	b p. 780	51.	d pp. 803–7

Investigating Psychological Phenomena

DEPRESSION AND NEGATIVE EXPERIENCES

Equipment: Pencil, paper, and stopwatch or watch with second indicator
Number of participants: One (yourself; you will need the cooperation of a friend to serve as a timer for about five minutes)
Time per participant: Twenty minutes
Time for experimenter: Twenty minutes

Depression is a very common disturbance. It can vary from almost universal "blue" moods to a serious, chronic, and incapacitating disorder. Because at least some of the characteristics of deep (psychotic) depression occur occasionally in most people, it is possible to study depression in a general population. In any population, there seems to be a more or less continuous distribution of people along a dimension running from depression to elation.

Severe depression is characterized by depressed mood; loss of interest in others and normally desirable things (such as food); feelings of hopelessness, helplessness, and worthlessness; and slowed-down thought and motor activity. Many of these symptoms appear in mild forms in the general population. It is reasonable to expect that mildly depressed people will show some of the same bases or causes of their symptoms as severely depressed people.

A number of theories of depression are outlined in the text. These include biochemical explanations (e.g., depletion of norepinephrine), and psychological theories emphasizing hopelessness or learned helplessness. In this study we will explore a particularly simple additional theory: People are depressed because bad things happen to them. Clearly, some people get depressed in the face of success and others remain nondepressed following a series of adverse events. Nonetheless, it seems very reasonable that negative experiences would contribute to the causation of depression. We will test the hypothesis that people who are more depressed have had relatively more adverse experiences in the recent past.

A major purpose of this exercise is to illustrate some of the difficulties that arise in the scientific study of psychopathology. More than in previous studies in this study guide, we want to make you aware of the problem of making definitive measurements that clearly support a particular hypothesis. We want you to appreciate the difficulty of research and at the same time realize that progress can be made.

The first problem that we face is this: How do we measure depression? A basic issue that arises is the matter of "subjective" or "objective" measurement. In the case of a mood disorder, one might be inclined to subjective measurement, and indeed, much of the diagnosis of depression is concerned with what people say about how they feel. More objective measurements would involve observation of people (facial expression, level of activity) or having them report on their own activities (e.., how many hours they sleep each night). In this study we look at a totally subjective measure, the participant's rating of his or her own mood. Remember that we are dealing with the range of depression and elation seen in the general population, and not with people actually diagnosed as depressed. In the case of diagnosis, interview and observation by an experienced clinician is involved, sometimes along with administration of a question inventory. We will use only self-ratings of mood and will collect two such ratings: one for the participant's momentary mood (how depressed he or she feels now) and the other for how depressed he or she has felt, in general, over the past year.

The second problem is this: How do we develop a measure of the incidence of negative and positive events in the recent life of each participant? We will use as our measure the participant's recall of negative and positive events over the past year. There are many problems and alternative interpretations of the results of this procedure. We will discuss them after you have served as a participant in this study.

Fill out the two rating scales that follow and enter your self-ratings on the answer sheet at the end of this section. Then continue to the recall task.

Rate what you judge to be your mood, right now. Circle the most appropriate number.

| Extremely depressed 9 | Very depressed 8 | Moderately depressed 7 | Slightly depressed 6 | Neither depressed nor happy 5 |
| Slightly happy 4 | Moderately happy 3 | Very happy 2 | Extremely happy 1 | |

Rate what you judge to have been your mood, on the average, over the last twelve months.

| Extremely depressed 9 | Very depressed 8 | Moderately depressed 7 | Slightly depressed 6 | Neither depressed nor happy 5 |
| Slightly happy 4 | Moderately happy 3 | Very happy 2 | Extremely happy 1 | |

RECALL OF NEGATIVE AND POSITIVE EVENTS

For this measure you will need the assistance of a friend who will time two separate two-minute intervals for you. No one but you will see what you write down.

You will go through two recall tasks, in order. Get a pen or pencil and sit at a table. When you are comfortable, ask a friend to say "Go" when the second hand of a watch crosses 12. When your friend says "Go," turn to the next page, read the sentence at the top, and follow the instructions. Ask your friend to say "Stop" when two minutes have elapsed. You should then stop the task.

The next time the second hand passes 12 (i.e., a minute after you complete the first part of the task), have your friend time another two minutes. When he or she says "Go," turn to the page after the one you had just written on, read the instructions, and follow them for two minutes.

Do not read on until you have completed the above task.

You are asked to perform the following task for exactly two minutes.

Someone will time the two minutes. When he or she says "Go," read the sentence below and follow the instructions. Continue until you hear "Stop" at two minutes.

List below all of the negative things that have happened to you in the last twelve months.

_____

_____

_____

_____

_____

_____

_____

_____

_____

_____

_____

_____

_____

_____

_____

_____

_____

_____

_____

_____

_____

_____

_____

_____

_____

_____

You are asked to perform the following task for exactly two minutes, following the performance of the "bad events" task.

Someone will time the two minutes. When he or she says "Go," read the sentence below and follow the instructions. Continue until you hear "Stop" at two minutes.

List below all of the positive things that have happened to you in the last twelve months.

_____

_____

_____

_____

_____

_____

_____

_____

_____

_____

_____

_____

_____

_____

_____

_____

_____

_____

_____

_____

_____

_____

_____

_____

_____

_____

_____

Add up the number of negative and the number of positive events that you remembered. Put these numbers on the answer sheet at the end of this section. Also enter the difference between the number of negative events and the number of positive events (# negative events minus # positive events), and the total # of events recalled (# negative events plus # positive events).

ANALYSIS OF DATA

We obtained these same data (depression ratings and event scores) from sixty-four undergraduate students at the University of Michigan. We will present these data here. You will add your own results to theirs, and we will then discuss the results.

MEASURES OF DEPRESSION

We used two measures of depression: rated mood now and rated mood over the last twelve months. You might expect that momentary and long-term mood would be related but that the two could sometimes be different. That, in fact, is just what our data show. Below is a scatter plot that presents the data from all sixty-four participants (see the statistical appendix to the text to learn more about scatter plots). Each point on the plot represents the two mood scores for one participant. Enter your own data point.

There is a positive relation between the two measures of depression. All relations described in these results will be expressed as correlation coefficients (see the statistical appendix). A value of +1.00 indicates a perfect positive correlation; a value of −1.00 a perfect negative correlation, and a value of 0.00 indicates no relation at all.

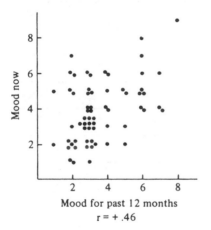

Mood for past 12 months
r = +.46

Our measure of "mood now" correlates +.46 with the measure of "mood over one year."

Looking at the scatter plot, you can see that there is some relation between the two mood measures. The general pattern of dots goes from lower left (happy on both scores) to upper right (depressed on both scores). But there are some exceptions. The correlation is positive, but far from perfect. Mark your point on the graph. Does your point fit in with the general pattern, or is it something of an exception? If an exception, can you explain this (e.g., it has been a very good year for you, but something unpleasant just happened to you)?

EVENT SCORES AND DEPRESSION

Before we test the major hypothesis (relatively more negative events in more depressed people), we can examine another prediction that can be made from the symptoms of seriously depressed people. Such people are characterized by a slowing down of action and thought. If this symptom also appears in milder form, in the low levels of depression in the student population, we would expect slowdown in memory search, along with other mental events. Therefore, we would expect that more depressed students would recall fewer events, positive or negative. (This type of finding would surely be true in a comparison of seriously depressed hospitalized patients versus "normal" participants.) We can test for this possibility by computing the correlation between self-rated depression (mood now) and the total number of events recalled (positive plus negative events). Note that because high scores on the depression rating mean more depression and high scores also represent large numbers of events recalled, we would expect a negative correlation: High depression scores go with low event recall scores.

For our sixty-four participants, the correlation between "mood now" and the total events is −.05: There is no evidence of any relation. Enter your score on these two measures in the scatter plot on the next page. You can see by examining the scatter plot that the two measures do not seem to be related. The relations between "mood over one year" and total events is also small. The correlation is +.14 (this is very small, but also in the direction opposite to the direction we predicted). There are two possible interpretations of our result. One is that our sample is not representative of the population, and that there actually is a negative depression–total event relation. Given the data we have, there is no reason to believe this. Another interpretation is that there is no relation, but that there might well be such a relation if we looked at severely depressed people as well: That is, the slowdown of mental function may only be marked in severe depression.

We now ask whether increased depression goes with a higher relative incidence of negative events. If this was true, we would expect a positive correlation between either depression score and the difference between number of negative and number of positive events recalled. We present below the scatter plot for both depression scores. Enter your own points on each of these plots. Just by inspecting these scatter plots you should be able to see that there is a positive relation: Higher depression scores *tend* to go with higher negative minus positive event scores. In fact, the correlations are:

Mood now vs. negative−positive events r = +.46
Mood over one year vs. negative−positive events r = +.32

Bad events minus good events
r = +.46

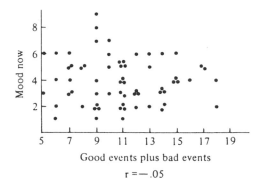

Good events plus bad events

r = −.05

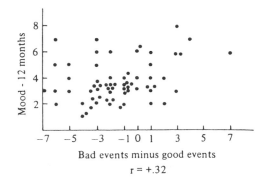

Bad events minus good events

r = +.32

The relations are not overwhelming, but there is a clear relation. For example the .46 correlation is significant at more than the .001 level: This means that a correlation this high could come about less than one chance in 1,000 if there was no relation between mood now and negative–positive events in the population (see the statistical appendix).

DISCUSSION AND COMMENTS

Our hypothesis that in college populations, depression as measured by self-rating is positively related to relative recall of recent negative events, has been confirmed. We will now discuss a few problems in interpreting these results, in order to make you more aware of the type of thinking that must go into research in general, and especially in this area.

First, our measure of events can be interpreted in a number of ways. We did not actually measure the number of positive and negative events that our participants experienced. We measured their *recall* for these events. A predominance of negative events could mean either that the participant experienced more of them or that the participant selectively remembers them . . . presumably because she is depressed. Remember that correlations show relations, but not causes (see the statistical appendix). Our hypothesis was that negative events cause depression. But the results of our study could be taken to indicate that in a relatively depressed mood, a person is more likely to remember negative events. The fact that the correlation was bigger between negative minus positive events and mood now, as opposed to mood over the last year, suggests that current mood may well influence what one thinks about. Of course, it is also possible that both effects exist: Negative events lead to depression and depression leads to selective memory for negative events. There is some evidence in the literature for both of these effects. Under further activities, we will discuss ways of finding out whether both of these effects actually occur.

Second, even if more negative events do occur in more depressed people, the events may not be a cause of depression. By virtue of being depressed, more negative events may occur to a person. For example, a depressed student will be less active, less inclined to study, and will probably not perform as well as he could in school.

Third, the same event that is evaluated as negative by someone who is depressed may not be considered negative by that same person when he is in a good mood (or by another person in a better mood). Many events may be both positive and negative (e.g., receiving a B in a course when one hoped for an A but did very little work and actually worried about getting a C, or the breakup of a relationship that had been unsatisfactory for some years). Read through your own events and decide how many could be seen as positive or negative.

We have just begun to scratch the surface, but we hope that you can appreciate the fact that a study like this would be just a beginning and that many more studies would have to be done to clarify the relation between negative events and depression. It should also be clear that whatever that relation is, there are many factors that influence depression. After all, the correlations we do have between depression and events are significant, but they are not that high. We might improve the correlations by getting better measures of depression and negative and positive events. But we also know from other studies, including those dealing with levels of catecholamines in the brain and specific types of past experiences (e.g., helplessness), that other factors are involved.

FURTHER ACTIVITIES

Try to think of some ways in which you could pull apart the effects of actual negative experiences and selective recall of them. After you decide on a few methods, read our suggestions below.

One approach is to get a more objective measure of the actual negative and positive events that a person has experienced. It is not practical to follow them around for a year. But one could get a fair measure by giving them a checklist of rather objective events, that are clearly negative or positive. Thus you could ask someone whether, over the past year:

A close relative or friend died
A course was failed
A job was lost
A favorite team had a disappointing season
A close relationship was broken

and so on, and, of course, a set of positive events.

One could then compare the negative minus positive recall score to the results of the checklist. What would you administer first to the participants: the free recall or the checklist? Why? You could try to make up an appropriate checklist for college students. It isn't easy.

A second approach is to test whether depressed people selectively remember negative events. For example, you could write a story that included a number of negative and positive events. It could be read to participants and one could measure their recall for the story, say one hour later. One could look at whether people who are more depressed remember relatively more of the negative events.

Answer Sheet

(If your instructor collects the data, fill out the report sheet in Appendix 3.)

Self-rating of mood now (enter number) _____

Self-rating of mood over last twelve months (enter number) _____

Number of negative events recalled _____

Number of positive events recalled _____

Negative minus positive events _____

Negative plus positive events _____

CHAPTER 19

Treatment of Psychopathology

Learning Objectives

BIOLOGICAL THERAPIES

1. Describe some early precursors to therapy for psychological disorders.

Pharmacotherapies

2. Discuss the effects of the classical antipsychotic medications, such as Thorazine, on schizophrenia. What symptoms do they affect and what symptoms do they leave largely untouched? What are the side effects?

3. Discuss the pharmacological effects of the atypical antipsychotics, such as Clozaril. How are they similar to more established antipsychotics, and how are they different?

4. Discuss the effects of the monoamine oxidase inhibitors and the tricyclic antidepressants on the treatment of depression. How do the selective serotonin reuptake inhibitors differ from these? Why are they widely prescribed?

5. What is the effect of lithium salts and other antimanics?

6. What is the action of the anxiolytics and for what maladies are they prescribed?

Evaluating a medication

7. What are the drawbacks to using a before-and-after method to evaluate the effect of a therapy?

8. Describe placebo effects and discuss how they can have an impact in the evaluation of a drug therapy. What might cause placebo effects? How prevalent are they?

9. Discuss the double-blind technique and its usefulness in overcoming expectation effects. What are the limitations of this technique? How are these overcome when the goal of a study is to compare a new treatment with an existing one?

10. How is improvement assessed in the current medical climate?

11. Be aware of the limitations of pharmacotherapy and its impact on mental hospitals.

Psychosurgery

12. What has been the history of psychosurgery? When is it used today?

Electroconvulsive therapy

13. What is electroconvulsive therapy used for, and how effective is it? What are its side effects?

PSYCHOTHERAPY

14. What are the five major types of psychotherapy, and what are the theoretical underpinnings of each?

Classical psychoanalysis

15. What is the theory underlying classical psychoanalysis? What investigative techniques are used in classical psychoanalysis? Of what relevance is transference?

Psychodynamic therapy

16. What are the modern variations on traditional psychoanalysis that have been made by neo-Freudians? How do they differ from Freud's techniques? How are women now viewed?

Behavior therapy

17. What basic assumptions are made by behavior therapists? How are these assumptions translated into treatment techniques? How are women now viewed?

18. Describe the basic assumptions underlying extinction, and explain why this technique is difficult to implement.

19. How does systematic desensitization use response incompatibility to eradicate phobias? How does an anxiety hierarchy figure into this therapy?

20. Describe aversion therapy and give examples of its use.

21. What is the major approach used in the application of operant techniques?

Cognitive therapies

22. How do cognitive therapies differ from traditional psychoanalysis? What are the major assumptions of cognitive therapy?

23. Be prepared to describe the major techniques used in cognitive therapy.

24. There are various techniques that therapists use to improve interpersonal relations. Describe them.

Humanistic therapies

25. How do humanistic therapists approach the topic of mental illness? Characterize Rogerian therapy.

26. Describe the history of existential therapy, and describe the goals of this approach. What is the "encounter"?

Some common themes

27. What common themes underlie the various therapeutic schools? What are their major differences? How have the various schools of therapy become more eclectic?

Extensions of psychotherapy

28. Understand the reasons for the development of group therapy.
29. What are shared-problem groups? Give examples.
30. What are the advantages of therapy groups for the patients who join them?
31. Describe the goals and techniques of couples and family therapy. How are they related to the relationship rather than to the individual? Why might it be difficult to evaluate the effectiveness of family therapy?
32. How has psychotherapy reached beyond the original goals envisioned by Freud?
33. Describe how knowledge of and sensitivity to the cultural background of a patient can enhance the course of therapy.

EVALUATING THERAPEUTIC OUTCOME

34. What extraneous factors might influence the perception of whether a therapy is effective?

Does psychotherapy work?

35. What is the evidence concerning the effectiveness of psychotherapy? Describe the role of meta-analysts in answering this question.
36. Why should there be a deterioration effect?

Comparing different therapies

37. Are there differences in the effectiveness of the various therapies? Describe the "Dodo bird verdict." How do placebo effects bear on this question?
38. What factors do the various psychotherapies have in common? Are there specific effects of individual therapies that go beyond their common effects?
39. How has the implementation of psychotherapy been influenced by practical considerations of accountability?

A CENTURY OF THERAPY

40. What can be said about the effectiveness of psychotherapy? What beneficial effects are likely to be produced by this type of therapy, and what has been the result of advances in biological therapies?

Programmed Exercises

BIOLOGICAL THERAPIES

1. Until the Middle Ages, _____ (the removal of pieces of skull bone) was a popular treatment for mental disorders.

   trephining

2. One of the first major successes of pharmacotherapies was conquering general _____, caused by a syphilitic infection.

   paresis

3. _____ medications have their effects predominantly on mental conditions.

   Psychotropic

4. _____ are drugs that have an effect on mental illness, and the effectiveness of these was among the first lines of evidence of the biochemical basis of schizophrenia.

   Antipsychotics

5. Effective drug treatments for schizophrenia include _____ and _____.

   Thorazine, Haldol

6. The advent of antipsychotic drugs led to the big movement in the 1960s to _____ mental patients.

   deinstitutionalize

7. Atypical antipsychotic drugs, such as _____, have effects on both the positive and negative symptoms of schizophrenia.

   Clozaril (or Risperdal)

8. The effects of the atypical types of antipsychotics seems to be lodged in their impact on the neurotransmitter _____, as well as its impact on the _____ system, which is affected by antipsychotics.

   serotonin, dopamine

9. An individual feels extremely depressed most of the time. We would expect one of two types of drugs to have an effect on her: the _____ _____ _____ and the _____ _____.

   monoamine oxidase inhibitors, tricyclic antidepressants

10. Recently, drugs such as Prozac have been developed for the specific treatment of depression. These drugs are called _____ _____ _____ _____.

    selective serotonin reuptake inhibitors

11. Salts of _____ have an effect on bipolar disorder, both in causing manic episodes to subside, and also in preventing depressive episodes. These are called _____.

    lithium
    antimanics

12. Valium and other _____ have become commonplace in treating anxiety in that they increase the transmission of the inhibitory neurotransmitter GABA.

    anxiolytics

13. The major weakness of using before-and-after assessment techniques to evaluate the effect of a drug treatment is that the patient may _____ spontaneously.

    improve

14. Sometimes merely giving patients what they think is a drug will cause an improvement in their condition; this is called a _____ effect.

placebo

15. It may be that _____ effects are accounted for by the action of _____, which are chemicals in the brain that act like opiates.

placebo, endorphins

16. It is hypothesized that a new drug will alleviate symptoms of air sickness. One hundred volunteers received an injection of this colorless liquid, while another 100 volunteers received an injection of saline solution (a colorless and totally inert liquid). All 200 participants took part in a simulated flight. Both subjective and objective indices of discomfort were recorded. Neither patient nor experimenter knew who received the drug. This study used a(n) _____-_____ technique to guard against any effects of expectations.

double-blind

17. The biggest cost associated with drug therapy is the likelihood of unpleasant _____ _____.

side effects

18. In evaluating the effectiveness of a drug, one must consider multiple _____ measures.

outcome

19. In a prefrontal lobotomy, the connections between the _____ and the _____ lobes are severed.

thalamus, frontal

20. Electroconvulsive shock treatment (ECT) is most effective in the treatment of _____; however, repeated shocks may cause _____ _____ and _____.

depression, brain damage, amnesia

PSYCHOTHERAPY

21. According to the _____ school, neurotic ills stem from unconscious defenses against unacceptable urges.

psychoanalytic

22. A patient is asked to say whatever comes into his mind. This technique is known as _____ _____.

free association

23. During a therapy session involving free association a patient repeatedly changed the subject or forgot what she was about to say. This patient was displaying _____, an indication that she was about to remember something that she had previously tried to forget.

resistance

24. While Freud wanted patients to gain insight into their motives, he didn't want these insights to be merely _____; _____ involvement is necessary for genuine self-discovery.

intellectual, emotional

25. Freud considered _____ as the means for producing emotional involvement.

transference

26. The _____-_____ view emphasizes interpersonal and cultural factors rather than psychosexual development.

neo-Freudian

27. Behavior therapists hold that the condition Freud called neurosis is caused by maladaptive _____, which can be corrected through reeducation.

learning

28. A straightforward way to remove a classically conditioned response is through _____.

extinction

29. The major goal of behavior therapists in treating phobias is to break the link between the _____ stimulus and the _____ response.

conditioned, fear

30. Sequential tensing and relaxing of the major muscles produces muscular relaxation, which is considered incompatible with fear response. Pairing the former with fear-evoking stimuli in order to eradicate phobias is part of the _____ _____ paradigm.

systematic desensitization

31. Since fear-evoking stimuli can seldom be brought into the treatment room, systematic desensitization must depend on the patient's _____ of fear-evoking situations according to a(n) _____ _____.

imagination anxiety hierarchy

32. In order to break compulsive fingernail biters of their habit, we coat their nails with a harmless but extremely bitter liquid so that they experience an unpleasant taste each time they bite their nails. This is an example of _____ therapy.

aversion

33. A _____ _____ uses operant reinforcement techniques to change patient's responses. This technique is usually most effective with in-patients.

token economy

34. One operant technique is _____ management, in which the patient learns of the consequences of his or her actions.

contingency

35. In contrast to behavior therapists, some therapists dispense with all conditioning techniques and, instead, help the patient acquire more appropriate ways of thinking. This is known as _____ therapy.

cognitive

36. Once old, undesirable behavior patterns are eliminated, new patterns must be developed. One technique employs "homework" assignments of increasing difficulty, called _____ _____ _____.

graded task assignments

37. Three techniques that can be used by a therapist to promote healthier interpersonal relations are _____, _____ _____, and _____ training.

modeling, role playing, assertiveness

38. Unlike other forms of therapy, _____ therapists deal with the individual at a global level.

humanistic

39. Rogers believes that people often dislike themselves. In his _____-_____ therapy, an attempt is made to provide a situation in which personal growth can resume.

client-centered

40. Humanistic therapy is characterized by its _____ nature, in which the therapist avoids advising or interpreting.

nondirective

41. _____ therapy is an attempt to cope with the difficulty of some to see meaning in their lives.

Existential

42. One component of existential therapy is the _____, a meeting of two people who see each other as independent entities.

encounter

43. A new trend in psychotherapy is _____ _____, doing whatever works.

technical eclecticism

44. One common feature of various therapies is the creation of a _____ alliance in which the patient feels as if he or she has a friend working with him or her.

therapeutic

45. One common element of all therapists is _____ _____, as the patient is encouraged to rid himself or herself of intense and unrealistic fears.

emotional defusing

46. An important part of therapy helps show patients how they react to others and is called _____ _____.

interpersonal learning

47. One of the important components of psychotherapy is _____-_____, which may mean different things for different schools: For psychoanalysis, for example, it means insight into the patient's past.

self-knowledge

48. All the psychotherapeutic techniques recognize the _____ nature of the therapeutic process. No progress is instantaneous.

incremental

49. There are various _____ gains to be gotten from therapy, such as the development of a close relationship with the therapist, and the hope that one will improve one's condition.

nonspecific

50. In recent years, there has been a large shift in the delivery of therapeutic services from the one therapist-one patient model to _____ therapy.

group

51. One example of _____ therapy is the _____-_____ group, in which a common affliction is present for all the patients.

group, shared-problem

52. A form of group therapy that concentrates on the relationship of the attendees rather than on them as individuals is _____ therapy.

couples

53. An important issue in therapy is the recognition that the _____ background of the patient may have an important effect on what techniques are likely to affect him or her.

cultural

EVALUATING THERAPEUTIC OUTCOME

54. A valuable recent technique for investigating treatment effectiveness is _____, in which a comparison is made of studies that investigate those receiving treatment and those who have not been treated.

meta-analysis

55. In general, a treatment group's scores on a test of emotional well-being will be more _____ following treatment than will a control group's, indicating a _____ effect in addition to improvement.

variable
deterioration

56. The _____ _____ verdict is that all therapies are equivalent in their effects.

Dodo bird

57. By and large, while _____ have an effect on outcome, genuine psychotherapy seems to have more of an effect.

placebos

58. _____ refers to the trend to recommend particular therapies for particular maladies.

Prescriptionism

Self Test

1. Proposed remedies for mental disorders:
   a. are few in number
   b can be divided into biological and psychological intervention
   c. all have a high success rate
   d. all of the above

2. Classical antipsychotic drugs typically have effects on all but which of the following symptoms?
   a. delusions
   b. hallucinations
   c. apathy
   d. none of the above

3. Evidence that Thorazine is an antipsychotic drug and not merely a tranquilizer is:
   a. that it improves the behavior of patients with hallucinations
   b. that it improves the behavior of patients who are apathetic
   c. that true tranquilizers have little effect on the symptoms of schizophrenia
   d. all of the above

4. One of the important drawbacks to the antipsychotic drugs is that they:
   a. have serious side effects such as the production of apathy
   b. must be administered in a hospital setting only
   c. produce side effects that keep patients from taking them
   d. all of the above

5. The new generation of atypical antipsychotic drugs, such as Clozaril, is an advance on standard ones because:
   a. they work on more than one neurotransmitter system
   b. they work on both positive and negative symptoms
   c. they are effective with a larger percentage of patients
   d. all of the above

6. All of the following are effective treatments for depression, either alone or in combination with manic episodes, except for:
   a. monoamine oxidase inhibitors
   b. tricyclic antidepressants
   c. lithium carbonate
   d. selective serotonin reuptake inhibitors
   e. all of the above

7. The action of Thorazine that makes it an effective drug for the treatment of schizophrenia is that it blocks dopamine receptors. This must mean that schizophrenia could be caused by:
   a. too much dopamine being taken up by receptors at synapses
   b. too little dopamine being taken up by receptors at synapses
   c. too little dopamine being produced at synapses
   d. too much dopamine being produced at synapses

8. Antipsychotic drugs (e.g., Thorazine) reduce many symptoms of schizophrenia. Below are characterizations of five patients suffering from some form of mental illness. Which patients would be expected to improve with Thorazine treatment?
   i. this patient suffers from bizarre thoughts and beliefs
   ii. this patient is withdrawn and noncommunicative
   iii this patient has frequent hallucinations
   iv. this patient is easily agitated
   v. this patient is deeply depressed

   a. all of the above
   b. i, ii, v
   c. i, ii, iii, iv
   d. ii, iv, v

9. It has been suggested that lithium carbonate may:
   a. be a general cure for forms of mental illness
   b. be useless, acting only as a placebo
   c. have a general activation and arousal effect rather than a specific treatment effect
   d. effectively treat bipolar disorder

10. Some drugs used to treat mental conditions have their action by increasing the amount of GABA that is released at synapses. This neurotransmitter is largely inhibitory in the nervous system, so one might assume that it reduces the amount of activity to the neurons with which it synapses. In view of this, which of the following drugs do you think have this action?
    a. Valium
    b. Xanax
    c. anxiolytics
    d. all of the above

11. Which of the following sources would be convincing evidence that antidepressants do more than just produce euphoria to counteract the depression that they are meant to treat?
    a. if they did not produce euphoria in normal individuals
    b. if they acted on normal people to increase euphoria
    c. if they had specific action on neurotransmitters
    d. if they had an influence on other illnesses such as panic disorder

12. The main problem in using a before-after design to evaluate the effectiveness of a drug treatment is:
    a. the placebo effect
    b. the effect of expectation
    c. the effect of spontaneous improvements
    d. the Dodo bird effect

13. A researcher finds that after drinking nothing but milk for three months, three patients (out of nine) report that they no longer suffer from migraine headaches. The researcher proclaims the curative powers of milk. What critical questions cannot be answered due to the absence of a control group?
    a. What is the spontaneous recovery rate without treatment?
    b. How did the milk cure the headaches?
    c. Why were only one-third of the patients cured?
    d. Can this finding be repeated?

14. A motorist takes his car to the garage for a tuneup. Unbeknownst to him, the mechanic is dishonest and tells the motorist that he tuned the car when, in fact, he hadn't. The motorist feels that the car runs better. This is an example of:
    a. the placebo effect
    b. schizophrenia
    c. a double blind
    d. desensitization

15. A new drug is believed to alleviate the symptoms of bipolar disorder. The drug is tested in the following manner: One group of patients receives the drug in pill form, and another similar group receives a sugar pill. No patient knows which group he or she is in. A panel of psychiatrists evaluates each patient before and after the treatment period. The panel is not

told whether a patient is getting the drug or the sugar pill. This is an example of:
a. a placebo effect
b. simultaneous control
c. the double-blind technique
d. transference

16. While drug therapy has produced a drastic decline in institutionalized patients, this has occurred at some cost. Patients on Thorazine, for example:
a. experience varying side effects from their drugs
b. make only marginal adjustments to the outside world
c. must continue to take their drugs after release
d. all of the above

17. The original idea behind psychosurgery was to "liberate the patient's thoughts from the pathological influence of his or her emotions." This required:
a. localizing the area of the brain concerned with thought
b. localizing the area of the brain concerned with emotion
c. disconnecting the area of the brain concerned with thought from that concerned with emotion
d. all of the above

18. A treatment that was designed to liberate the patient's thoughts from his or her pathological emotions, but which produced ambiguous results and may impair foresight and attention, is:
a. electroconvulsive shock treatment(ECT)
b. prefrontal lobotomy
c. lithium treatment
d. catharsis

19. ECT was originally used to treat schizophrenia but was later found to be more effective in treating:
a. depression
b. mania
c. compulsive behavior
d. it is still most effective in treating schizophrenia

20. Electroconvulsive shock treatment:
a. is faster than many antidepressant drugs
b. can produce severe memory impairment
c. is generally used only after drug therapy has been tried
d. all of the above

21. In contrast to pharmaceutical approaches to mental illness, psychotherapy:
a. is much more effective
b. involves interpersonal interaction
c. is more relevant to the nature of psychopathology
d. none of the above

22. Orthodox (classical) psychoanalysis:
a. states that illness is a result of unconscious defenses against unconscious urges
b. states that most problems date back to childhood
c. was developed by Freud
d. all of the above

23. The cure for mental illness can be achieved by _____ according to the classical psychoanalysts.
a. the victory of reason over passion
b. a complete suppression of bad memories
c. a reenactment of the cause of the problem
d. none of the above

24. When a patient is asked to say whatever comes into his or her mind, it is believed that sooner or later the memory relevant to the disorder should appear. This technique is known as:
a. resistance
b. repression
c. free association
d. role playing

25. Psychoanalysts believe the emotions are a principal part of therapy. One means for bringing emotions into play involves the relationship between the patient and therapist. The patient begins to behave as if the analyst were an important figure in her life. This is known as:
a. catharsis
b. transference
c. resistance
d. intellectualization

26. Modern day practitioners of psychoanalysis:
a. emphasize interpersonal factors rather than sexual development
b. subscribe to neo-Freudian views
c. focus on the patient's present rather than his or her past
d. all of the above

27. Behavior therapists argue that:
a. the theoretical notions of psychoanalysis are untestable
b. the therapeutic effectiveness of psychoanalysis is unclear
c. neurosis is caused by maladaptive learning
d. all of the above

28. The behavior therapist tends to emphasize:
a. giving the patient insight into the origins of his or her problems
b. righting improper behavior patterns without regard for underlying causes
c. curing the patient by a variety of means, including free association
d. enabling the patient to reach a full realization of his or her human potentialities

29. For behavior therapists, fear:
a. is a classically conditioned response
b. has its roots in early childhood
c. is a manifestation of emotional traumas
d. is an operantly conditioned response

30. Since behavior therapists believe that one of the causes of certain strong fears, such as that of heights, is early classical conditioning, their therapy rests on the principle of:
a. second-order conditioning
b. extinction
c. reinforcement
d. punishment

31. In systematic desensitization, the patient first learns muscular relaxation and then constructs an anxiety hierarchy of fear-evoking situations. The next step is:
a. to imagine the least fearful situation while relaxed
b. to experience the least fearful situation while relaxed
c. to imagine the most fearful situation and then relax as the conditioned link is extinguished
d. to give the patient homework assignments involving exposure to fear-evoking stimuli

32. Systematic desensitization relies on which of the following principles?
    a. extinction
    b. operant conditioning
    c. counterconditioning
    d. none of the above

33. The pairing of an unpleasant stimulus with an undesirable behavior is known as:
    a. paired associate learning
    b. cognitive therapy
    c. response-produced anxiety
    d. none of the above

34. There is some question about the lasting effectiveness of aversion therapy because:
    a. it doesn't even seem to last while the patient is in the therapist's office
    b. the effects wear off even while the aversive stimulus is still applied after some time has passed
    c. without the aversive stimulus, the lasting effects seem to fade
    d. it has been shown to be an ineffective treatment for alcoholism

35. Token economics:
    a. are ineffective with inpatients
    b. are a form of instrumental conditioning
    c. are a form of classical conditioning
    d. are based on the use of extinction

36. All of the following are operant techniques used in therapy except:
    a. token economies
    b. aversion therapy
    c. systematic desensitization
    d. contingency management
    e. b and d
    f. b and c
    g. a and d

37. A therapist confronts a depressed patient with the irrationality of his belief that he cannot get a good job because he thinks he is incompetent despite evidence to the contrary. This therapist is most likely to be a proponent of:
    a. modeling
    b. cognitive therapy
    c. desensitization
    d. could be any of the above

38. Cognitive therapies:
    a. focus on the patient's beliefs and attitudes
    b. are not primarily concerned with the patient's history
    c. do not rely heavily on behavior modification
    d. all of the above

39. One of the features on which cognitive therapies concentrate is:
    a. the behaviors exhibited by patients
    b. the automatic thoughts that patients seem to have
    c. the irrationally of beliefs that patients have
    d. more than one of the above

40. If and when irrational fears and beliefs are eliminated from a patient, new behavior patterns must be developed to substitute. A therapist gives the patient a simple task to perform in her daily life. Once the patient masters this, the therapist gives her a slightly more difficult task, continuing in this way until normal behavior patterns emerge. This is the method of:
    a. modeling
    b. cognitive therapy
    c. graded task assignment
    d. assertiveness training

41. Modeling, assertiveness training, and role playing are all examples of:
    a. desensitization
    b. learning theory tools
    c. classical conditioning techniques
    d. normal interpersonal relations

42. In contrast to traditional psychoanalysis or behavior therapy, humanistic therapists:
    a. are interested in causes rather than effects
    b. deal with only one symptom at at time
    c. treat the individual at a global level
    d. believe that neuroses are a product of society

43. The view that many emotional disorders result from a belief that everything is pointless characterizes the school of:
    a. psychoanalysts
    b. nihilists
    c. existential therapists
    d. all of the above to some degree

44. According to existential therapists, the primary method for initiating a cure involves:
    a. free association
    b. making the patient aware of the importance of free choice
    c. the recall of childhood memories
    d. lengthy philosophical discussions

45. It seems as if the different forms of psychotherapy concentrate on different aspects of the problem. In particular:
    a. cognitive therapy concentrates on the patient's thoughts
    b. psychoanalysis concentrates on the patient's understanding of his or her past
    c. humanistic therapy concentrates on the patient's feelings
    d. all of the above

46. Psychoanalysis can be summarized by the word *unconscious* in the same way that behavior therapy can be represented by *conditioning*. What word best summarizes humanistic therapy?
    a. cause
    b. feeling
    c. directive
    d. rational

47. All of the following are common to the various therapeutic schools except:
    a. interpersonal learning
    b. self-knowledge
    c. emotional defusing
    d. therapy as an all-or-none process

48. A major difference between shared-problem groups and group therapy is:
    a. that shared-problem groups involve more interpersonal interaction
    b. that shared-problem groups work on a single problem that is common to the group members

c. that shared-problem groups incorporate a greater amount of self-knowledge of the problem in question
d. that shared-problem groups involve a more gradual therapeutic process

49. One of the differences between family therapy and classical psychoanalysis is:
   a. family therapists deal with a group of individuals, not just one
   b. family therapists concentrate on relationships, not individual mental health
   c. family therapists don't concentrate on the developmental history of each individual
   d. all of the above

50. Evaluating couples therapy is difficult because:
   a. the patients who decide to see a therapist may not be the most troubled
   b. the patients who decide to see a therapist may need the most individual therapy
   c. the individuals will not get therapy on their own, just in a group
   d. group sessions don't allow one to separate out the effect that the therapist has on any single person

51. Relative to an untreated control group's scores on a test of emotional well being, the scores of a post-treatment group are:
   a. always at least slightly better
   b. seldom significantly different
   c. more variable
   d. less variable

52. Meta-analysis provides a way to compare treatment effectiveness across a wide variety of different treatments and outcomes by:
   a. comparing the percentage of patients who benefit from the treatment of each different kind
   b. comparing the percentage of treated patients who fall above the average of untreated patients
   c. comparing the percentage of success of each of the treatment regimens
   d. comparing the percentage of treated individuals who fall above the treatment average

53. A patient gets worse following therapy. This is known as:
   a. spontaneous remission
   b. the deterioration effect
   c. the placebo effect
   d. desensitization

54. One reason there are deterioration effects is that:
   a. the variability in post-treatment scores is larger than the variability in pretreatment scores
   b. the variability in pretreatment scores is larger than the variability in post-treatment scores
   c. the mean of post-treatment scores is higher than the mean of pretreatment scores
   d. any of the above

55. Evidence that psychotherapies are effective not merely because patients expect them to be effective includes:

a. the fact that patients given placebos score worse than the average score of patients given psychotherapy
b. the fact that patients given one form of psychotherapy improve about as much as patients given another form of psychotherapy
c. the fact that behavioral and cognitive therapies seem to produce more improvement than other techniques
d. the fact that there are no significant placebo effects when it comes to psychotherapies

56. If psychotherapy's only effect is nonspecific:
   a. it may nevertheless have value in providing a shoulder to lean on
   b. it will have proved largely an ineffective treatment course
   c. it will then, by definition, be just a placebo effect
   d. it will be more effective than if its effect had been specific

57. The notion that specific therapies may be most effective for particular mental maladies is called:
   a. the Dodo bird verdict
   b. prescriptionism
   c. existentialism
   d. none of the above

Answer Key for Self Test

1.	b p. 811	30.	b p. 825
2.	c p. 813	31.	a p. 826
3.	d p. 812	32.	c p. 826
4.	c p. 813	33.	d p. 827
5.	d p. 814	34.	c p. 827
6.	e pp. 814, 815	35.	b p. 828
7.	a p. 812	36.	f p. 828
8.	c p. 813	37.	b p. 829
9.	d p. 815	38.	d p. 829
10.	d p. 816	39.	d p. 829
11.	a p. 815	40.	c p. 830
12.	c p. 816	41.	d p. 830
13.	a p. 816	42.	c p. 830
14.	a p. 817	43.	c p. 831
15.	c p. 818	44.	b p. 832
16.	d pp. 814, 818	45.	d p. 832
17.	d p. 819	46.	b p. 832
18.	b p. 819	47.	d p. 833
19.	a p. 820	48.	b p. 834
20.	d p. 820	49.	d p. 835
21.	b p. 821	50.	a p. 836
22.	d p. 822	51.	c p. 839
23.	a p. 822	52.	b p. 839
24.	c p. 822	53.	b p. 840
25.	b p. 823	54.	a p. 840
26.	d p. 824	55.	a pp. 841, 842
27.	d p. 825	56.	a p. 843
28.	b p. 825	57.	b p. 843
29.	a p. 825		

Investigating Psychological Phenomena

DEMONSTRATION OF ROLE PLAYING

Equipment: None
Number of participants: Yourself and one other
Time per participant: Thirty minutes
Time for experimenter: Thirty minutes

As the authors discuss in the text, role playing is one technique used by therapists to educate their patients about various aspects of interpersonal relations. This technique requires at least two people to assume the roles of individuals other that themselves in a particular social situation. In so doing, the hope of the treatment is that the participating individuals will gain some insight about the feelings, emotions, and cognitions of the persons whose roles are being played.

Although the technique sounds simple enough in principle, in actual practice it is a bit risky. As the following quote illustrates, role-playing participants frequently lapse back into their own personalities and have to be reminded about their role-playing activities.

> [The therapist] says "Tom, do you really care for me?" Tom says "I would say to her that I do, but she'd complain." Therapist: "Don't tell me what you *would* do. I'm Jane. Talk to me. Tom, do you really care for me?" Tom (turning away, looking slightly disgusted): "Yes." Therapist (still as Jane): "You don't say it like you mean it." Tom: "Yeah, that's what she says, and I usually . . ." Therapist (interrupting): "You're again telling me *about* what you'd say. I'm Jane. Tom, you don't say it like you mean it." Tom: "It's very hard for me to answer her when she says that." Therapist: "OK, I'm Jane. Tell me how you feel." Tom: "Jane, when you do that it really turns me off. Maybe if you didn't ask me so often I'd be able to say it spontaneously without feeling like a puppet . . . (then, in a tone that indicates he is now talking to the therapist as therapist) Gee, I wonder what would happen if I really said that to her" (Wachtel, 1977, pp. 234–35).

You can try role playing on your own to discover some of its features. Solicit the participation of a fellow student of the opposite sex from your introductory psychology class and set up the following situation.

The two of you are married and have just graduated from college. Each of you has very well-defined career plans, and you have each been skillful and lucky enough to have been offered very attractive first jobs that fit precisely the career lines that you have planned. The problem is that your job offers are in cities 1,000 miles apart. How do you decide what to do?

You should go through two sessions: First, have a discussion about this problem with your partner with each of you playing yourselves. Write down each of your responses on paper. Second, switch roles and try having the discussion again. In each case, put yourselves in the other's situation. Again, write your responses on paper.

After you have finished playing both roles, talk about differences in the conversations that resulted from your playing the male versus the female role. Compare the transcripts of each session. Did this help you gain a different perspective on the problem?

At this point, you might want to try another role-playing exercise in which the two roles are quite different from one another. This will allow you to take two very different perspectives on a scene. Try out the following scene:

One of you should assume the role of an instructor for a course you are both taking (perhaps introductory psychology) while the other plays the role of a student. The issue is that the student has scored poorly on the midterm examination, but feels that at least part of the reason for his or her poor performance is that he or she was graded unfairly by the instructor. In addition, the student was faced with taking four midterm exams within three days, so his or her performance was bound to suffer. Now imagine that the student has come in to talk with the instructor about these issues. The person playing the role of the instructor should really try to assume the personality and attitudes of the real instructor in the course as much as possible. After you have acted out a scene, switch roles. This time, to add some variety, have the student role be one of a very aggressive student who is determined not to leave the instructor's office without a change of grade. Again, after each scene, write down your impressions so that you can later discuss and evaluate them.

Having finished this scenario, think about some of the following questions: Was it more difficult to assume the role of the instructor or student? Was it difficult to stay in character without lapses? What insights have you gained about instructor-student relationships? Would this be a useful exercise for students and instructors to try in general? How was this role-playing exercise different from the first one?

Reference

Wachtel, P. L. 1979. *Psychoanalysis and behavior therapy: Toward an integration.* New York: Basic Books.

APPENDIX 1

Methods of Scientific Research

Learning Objectives

1. What can one learn by understanding the methods of scientific research?

WHY SCIENCE?

2. What differentiates psychology from other fields of inquiry that are also concerned with the mind and with behavior?
3. What is the scientific method, and what are some of its basic principles?
4. Describe the steps in testing a hypothesis and drawing conclusions about it.

DESIGNING A PERSUASIVE EXPERIMENT

5. What is an experiment, and what are its essential features?

Formulating a testable hypothesis
6. Describe the critical features that a hypothesis must have in order to be testable.

The need for systematic data collection
7. Be able to describe the problems that are encountered in relying on anecdotes to test hypotheses.
8. What is the file-drawer problem, and how does it limit conclusions one can draw about hypotheses?
9. Describe the dangers in relying on memory as a source of data about a hypothesis.

Specifying the dependent variable
10. Be able to differentiate between a dependent and an independent variable.
11. When is interrater reliability an important issue?

Using a control group
12. What makes a control group an important part of an experiment?
13. Describe how a control group should be treated as part of an experiment. How should it be matched to the experimental group?
14. Demand characteristics are an important feature of some experimental situations, and must be avoided. What are they, and how does a double-blind procedure avoid them?

Confounds
15. Define a confound and describe how it can be avoided.

An overview of an experiment's design
16. Summarize the various safeguards that go into designing an effective experiment.

Evaluating evidence outside of the laboratory
17. The logic of the experimental method applies well outside of the laboratory. Describe how, and give several examples.

OBSERVATIONAL STUDIES

18. When are observational studies, rather than experimental studies, demanded?

Correlational studies
19. Describe what defines a correlational study. How is this similar to an experiment?
20. Be able to describe cases where cause and effect is difficult to determine from correlational data. How can one make inferences about cause and effect from these data?
21. Describe the third-variable problem and how it is related to causality.
22. How do experimental studies differ from correlational studies in being able to assign causation? What are the critical features of experiments that make this possible?

Studies of single participants
23. What role do single-case studies play in psychological work? How can one insure that such studies are done rigorously? What needs to be safeguarded here?

THE IMPORTANCE OF MULTIPLE METHODS

24. Describe some of the data-collection methods used by psychologists. How are these methods used in connection with one another to investigate some phenomenon?

GENERALIZING FROM RESEARCH

25. What is external validity, and what factors influence it?

Selecting the participants
26. Understand what a biased sample is and how it can affect the generalization of results.

27. How does stratified sampling help in permitting us to generalize results?

28. Understand that it is important to have a proper sampling of responses or behaviors to permit proper generalization.

External validity

29. What are some of the factors that affect external validity? When are these factors more or less influential?

RESEARCH ETHICS

30. Describe some of the protections that humans and other animals should be afforded during the course of a research protocol.

31. What is informed consent? Describe some cases in which it is difficult to obtain informed consent and not interfere with the course of a research protocol.

32. Understand that the nature of ethical research depends on the standards of the society in which it is conducted.

Programmed Exercises

WHY SCIENCE?

1. A testable _____ is one that allows a scientist to make specific predictions about results in some particular situation.

   hypothesis

2. Psychologists are constantly in a quest to _____ a hypothesis because it is not possible to prove that a hypothesis is correct, only that it is incorrect.

   disconfirm

3. One can't prove a hypothesis correct, but one can _____ a hypothesis, providing supporting evidence that it is not false.

   confirm

DESIGNING A PERSUASIVE EXPERIMENT

4. A study in which a scientist manipulates some factor to assess its effect is called a(n) _____.

   experiment

5. _____ evidence is evidence that has been informally collected.

   Anecdotal

6. The _____-_____ problem refers to the tendency for unsuccessful experiments not to be reported whereas successful experiments are reported.

   file-drawer

7. People are subject to the _____ bias in which they are more likely to recall events that are consistent with their beliefs.

   confirmation

8. There are two variables in an experiment: The _____ variable is what is manipulated by the experimenter, and the _____ variable is what is measured as an outcome.

   independent
   dependent

9. Some measures are not completely stable and thus they must be measured by several observers; in cases such as this, it is important to have high _____ reliability to ensure that the multiple observers are in good agreement with one another.

   interrater

10. The simplest experimental design has two groups of participants: One is given the manipulation that is of interest in the experiment; the other is not given this manipulation. The former is called the _____ group and the latter the _____ group.

    experimental, control

11. Sometimes a manipulation has an effect only because participants expect it to have an effect; this is called a _____ effect, and is of particular concern in testing out the effectiveness of new drug therapies.

    placebo

12. If an experiment has subtle cues that lead participants to believe that one response is expected or more desired than another, this is called a(n) _____ characteristic.

    demand

13. A very effective way to eliminate any subtle expectations about the outcome of an experiment on the participants is to use a(n) _____-_____ design, in which neither the participants nor the experimenter knows which group is the control and which is the experimental.

    double-blind

14. Sometimes there is more than one variable that might have influenced an outcome in an experiment. In addition to the independent variable, there may be one or more _____ variables that might not have been controlled.

    confounding

15. _____ validity refers to an experiment measuring what it is supposed to be measuring; _____ validity refers to an experimental manipulation being a valid indicator of some real-world property that is of concern.

    Internal
    external

OBSERVATIONAL STUDIES

16. One type of observational study depends on measuring the _____ between two variables, or the amount of relation between them.

correlation

17. In principle, one cannot attribute cause and effect to a pair of variables that show a _____ between one another.

correlation

18. One of the reasons that it is difficult to assign causation from correlational evidence is the _____-_____ problem, in which two outcomes are both caused by a common variable.

third-variable

19. One of the reasons that one can draw cause and effect inferences from experimental studies rather than correlational studies is that experiments often involve the _____ assignment of participants to each condition.

random

20. _____ studies are important sources of data when the data from a single individual are critical to answering some question; this is often the case when one is studying some pathology, such as brain damage.

Case

THE IMPORTANCE OF MULTIPLE METHODS

21. Various measures are of value to psychologists. They rely on _____-_____ data, in which a participant provides information on his or her own internal state; measures of _____, such as accuracy or response time; and _____ measures of the physical state of the organism.

self-report
behavior
biological

GENERALIZING FROM RESEARCH

22. Although experiments are always conducted on a sample of participants, the real interest is in the _____ from which this sample is selected.

population

23. A _____ sample is one that is not representative of the group that is of interest.

biased

24. A _____ sample is one that is selected haphazardly from the population of interest so that any person has the same chance of being selected as any other person.

random

25. A _____ sample is one that is selected so that different subgroups within the population are represented in the final sample.

stratified

RESEARCH ETHICS

26. Participants in an experiment must give their _____ consent prior to their participation.

informed

27. One of the critical issues in conducting experiments on humans is that people's _____ must be protected by ensuring that the participants' identity is not revealed to others.

confidentiality

28. Occasionally it is necessary during the course of an experiment to deceive participants about the true purpose of the experiment; that is, they are intentionally _____ about the goal of the experiment.

misinformed

29. One of the hallmarks of a well-conducted experiment is a full _____ of participants at the end of the experiment so that they understand the purpose of the experiment.

debriefing

Self Test

1. Why should we, as members of the general public, be interested in how experiments are designed and what constitutes a well-conducted experiment?
   a. We all constantly draw conclusions about behavior in everyday life from evidence we observe.
   b. We all need to evaluate the conclusions that others draw about some event based on evidence that they claim is relevant.
   c. Experimental methods can be applied to solving everyday problems, such as diagnosing a fault in a computer program that is not working.
   d. all of the above

2. The study of the mind and behavior is the province of many disciplines, such as theology, philosophy, and many of the humanities. What makes psychology different from these other disciplines is that it uses:
   a. observations
   b. anecdotes
   c. the scientific method
   d. tight logic about its inferences
   e. all of the above

3. When you are testing a hypothesis:
   a. it is possible only to show that it is false, not to prove that it is true
   b. people are often lured into tests that will confirm the hypothesis rather than ones that will disconfirm it

c. you need to provide sufficient detail about the test so that others can replicate the result; otherwise, it is possible that your test had some idiosyncrasy that made it come out the way it did
d. all of the above
e. a and b, but not c

4. Which of the following is the most testable hypothesis?
   a. It takes five years of effort before one can write a truly good novel.
   b. This car is not working because the carburetor is clogged.
   c. Caffeine makes one more tuned in to the environment.
   d. Apples are a better fruit than pears.
   e. A vacation at the beach is more satisfying than one at the mountains.

5. A critical and identifying feature of an experiment compared to an observational study is that it:
   a. has two variables
   b. has a dependent variable
   c. records correlations between variables
   d. records observations about behavior
   e. all of the above
   f. none of the above

6. There are a number of problems in interpreting evidence and making judgments about cause and effect. Among these is that:
   a. sometimes evidence is in the form of anecdotes that are not systematic enough to be representative
   b. sometimes we have access to only some of the evidence that is relevant because the rest has not been made public (the file-drawer problem)
   c. sometimes evidence is in the form of correlations that are not sufficient to permit cause-and-effect inferences
   d. sometimes evidence comes from experiments that are not sufficient to permit cause-and-effect inferences
   e. all of the above
   f. a and b only
   g. a, b, and c only
   h. a, b, and d only

7. Consider the following experiment: An investigator tests whether people can tell the difference between sugar and an artificial sweetener in a cola drink. She does this by asking participants to drink a sip of cola and then tell her whether it contained sugar or the artificial sweetener. In this experiment:
   a. the participants' judgments are the independent variable
   b. the participants' judgments are the dependent variable
   c. whether the cola contained sugar or the artificial sweetener is the independent variable
   d. whether the cola contained sugar or the artificial sweetener is the dependent variable
   e. a and d
   f. b and c

8. Consider the following experiment: An investigator tests whether performance in a speeded task depends on time of day and age. He tests older or younger participants either in the morning or in the afternoon, and he records their response time to a light when it is flashed. In this experiment:
   a. time of day is a dependent variable
   b. response time is a dependent variable
   c. age is a dependent variable

d. all of the above
e. none of the above

9. In the experiment described in Question 8:
   a. time of day is an independent variable
   b. response time is an independent variable
   c. age is an independent variable
   d. all of the above
   e. a and b, but not c
   f. a and c, but not b
   g. b and c, but not a
   h. none of the above

10. A drug company has developed a drug to alleviate shyness. To test this drug, they select two groups of participants. One is given the drug during the first month of the experiment and then a sugar pill that tastes the same as the drug during the second month. The second group is given the sugar pill during the first month and then the drug during the second month. Shyness is assessed by having a panel of observers make judgments about a set of videotapes that are taken of each participant during 10 social situations. The observers rate the participants on each occasion for their shyness. In this experiment:
    a. Group 1 is the control group
    b. Group 2 is the control group
    c. Group 1 is the experimental group
    d. Group 2 is the experimental group
    e. both groups serve as control and experimental groups at different times

11. In the experiment of Question 10, the drug company must take pains to be sure that:
    a. there is internal validity to the observers' ratings
    b. there is external validity to the observers' ratings
    c. there is interrater reliability to the observers' ratings
    d. there is complete and total agreement among the observers' ratings

12. In the experiment of Question 10, if there is a placebo effect:
    a. the sugar pill will be more effective than the drug
    b. the sugar pill will be as effective as the drug
    c. the sugar pill will be less effective than the drug
    d. any of the above

13. In the experiment of Question 10, the drug company must be careful to conduct the experiment so that:
    a. the participants are blind to the purpose of the experiment
    b. the raters are blind to who has taken the drug and who the sugar pill
    c. the company itself is never told who took the drug and who the sugar pill during the first or second month
    d. all of the above
    e. a and b, but not c
    f. b and c, but not a

14. In the experiment of Question 10, if the participants knew that the purpose of the experiment was to test a drug for its effects on shyness, they might be influenced by:
    a. double-blind procedures
    b. demand characteristics
    c. anecdotal evidence
    d. confounds

15. In the experiment of Question 10, suppose that during the first month Group 1 was paid for its participation but during the second month it was not, and vice versa for Group 2. This would constitute a:
    a. double-blind procedure
    b. demand characteristic
    c. anecdotal piece of evidence
    d. confound

16. You read in the newspaper that taking garlic pills will prevent cancer and heart disease. The paper reports interviews with 50 individuals, all of whom have taken garlic pills and all of whom appear to be completely healthy. What you need to properly assess the quality of this evidence is:
    a. the ages of the interviewees
    b. the number of garlic pills that each has taken
    c. the frequency with which the interviewees have taken the garlic pills
    d. interviews with a group of people who have not taken garlic pills and whose health has been assessed

17. Some time ago, it was reported that left-handers die at a younger age than right-handers. This fact allows the inference that:
    a. left-handedness leads to an early death
    b. right-handedness leads to a later death
    c. handedness and age of death are correlated
    d. handedness and age are causally related to one another

18. Children of overweight parents are, on average, more overweight than children of normal weight parents. This fact allows one to conclude that:
    a. weight is determined by heredity
    b. weight is determined by environmental factors governed by parents
    c. overweight parents and children are both exposed to a common factor that induces overeating
    d. none of the above

19. You read in the newspaper that a study of 50 individuals who committed suicide shows that the majority had a history of treatment for depression in the year prior to their death. This allows you to conclude that:
    a. depression causes suicide
    b. suicide is preceded by depression
    c. suicide and depression are correlated
    d. the factors that lead to depression also lead to suicide

20. In the example of Question 19, suppose that further on the newspaper article states that most of the suicide victims who had a history of depression also had large financial disasters in the year prior to their death. This might be an indicator that the relation between suicide and depression is a result of:
    a. placebo effects
    b. the third-variable problem
    c. a correlation between suicide and money problems on the one hand and depression and money problems on the other hand
    d. all of the above
    e. a and b, but not c
    f. b and c, but not a

21. One way to find out how money problems, depression, and suicide are related would be to select a group of 50 depressed patients who have no money problems and another group of 50 depressed patients who do have money problems. Both groups could then be tracked over a period of time to see whether one or the other shows suicidal tendencies. This would constitute:
    a. a correlational design
    b. an observational study
    c. an experimental study
    d. interrater reliability

22. Another way to study how money problems, depression, and suicide are related would be to study a single patient who was depressed and had money problems. One could then track this patient in detail and see whether he or she developed suicidal tendencies. This technique makes use of:
    a. a case study
    b. a correlational design
    c. an experimental study
    d. a single-case experiment

23. To study depression, one could use:
    a. self-reports of depression
    b. measures of behaviors that are related to depression, such as eating behavior
    c. measures of hormones that might be related to depression
    d. all of the above

24. If you select a number of participants for a study of how often they eat out at fast-food restaurants, and you make your selection so that you have equal representation of people from each of 5 income levels, this constitutes a:
    a. random sample
    b. stratified sample
    c. biased sample
    d. population

25. Proper ethics demands that an experiment include:
    a. informed consent
    b. proper debriefing
    c. an opportunity for participants to cease their participation when they want
    d. deception
    e. all of the above
    f. more than one of the above

Answer Key for Self Test

1.	d p. A3	
2.	c p A3	
3.	d pp. A4, A5	
4.	b p. A4	
5.	f p. A5	
6.	g pp. A6, A7	
7.	f p. A8	
8.	b p. A8	
9.	f p. A8	
10.	e p. A8	
11.	c, p. A8	
12.	d p. A9	
13.	d pp. A9, A10	
14.	b p. A9	
15.	d p. A10	
16.	d pp. A9, A10	
17.	c p. A13	
18.	d p. A14	
19.	c p. A15	
20.	f pp. A14, A15	
21.	c pp, A15, A16	
22.	a p. A16	
23.	d p. A17	
24.	b p. A20	
25.	f p. A22	

Investigating Psychological Phenomena

CONFIRMING HYPOTHESES

Equipment: Paper and pen
Number of participants: One adult
Time per participant: Fifteen minutes
Time for experimenter: Thirty minutes

The scientific method is a very powerful tool for making inferences about cause and effect in the world. Its power is amply illustrated by the huge developments in our knowledge of various fields in the sciences. Use of the scientific method takes training, however. It is not necessarily natural for all of us to think scientifically as we evaluate evidence, test hypotheses, and try to learn the truth about events in the world. This is nicely illustrated when one observes the tendency for people to seek out evidence that confirms a hypothesis they are considering. As you have seen in this chapter, obtaining confirming evidence is of value in evaluating a hypothesis, but it is not as valuable as obtaining disconfirming evidence. The critical observation here is that one can prove that a hypothesis is wrong or invalid, but one cannot prove that it is correct or valid. The problem in proving a hypothesis correct is that there may always be some piece of disconfirming evidence that has not yet been considered and would prove it wrong. However, once a hypothesis is proven wrong, no amount of confirming evidence can make it right. Once wrong, it is wrong. People do not naturally think this way, however, as the discussion of the confirmation bias in Chapter 8 and this appendix makes clear.

The confirmation bias in reasoning is quite easy to illustrate by replicating an experiment that was described in Chapter 8. The technique is to have a participant guess what rule you have in mind that generates a string of numbers. You conduct the test by starting the participant off with a string of numbers that you tell him or her conforms to the rule. The participant is then given ten opportunities to give you a string of numbers and to ask you whether the given string conforms to the rule. You answer "Yes" or "No," but you provide no additional information. After the participant has given you the ten strings, he or she must then articulate what the rule is. Select a participant, and give the following specific instructions·

The purpose of this experiment is to have you figure out a rule that I have in mind that governs the order of numbers in a string of numbers. I have a fixed rule in mind, and your task is to guess it. How do you do that? We'll begin by my giving you a string of numbers that conforms to the rule. The string is:

2, 4, 6, 8, 10

Now, your job is to figure out the rule that I have in mind. You get to tell me ten strings of numbers. For each one you tell me, I'll tell you whether it conforms to the rule or not, but I'll tell you nothing else. After you have given me a string and I have responded, we'll do it again and again until you have exhausted your ten strings. At that point, you'll have to guess what the rule is.

Any questions?"

The rule you will use to govern your judgments about each of the strings you are given is that the numbers have to be in ascending order. That is the only constraint. So, for example, all the following strings conform to the rule:

1, 2, 3, 4
6, 143, 299, 1136
1, 10, 100
2, 118
1, 3, 5, 7, 9

And none of the following conforms to the rule:

10, 8, 6, 4, 2
1, 2, 3, 5, 4
3, 3, 3, 3

Each time the participant gives you a string, write it down. After the tenth string, ask the participant what he or she thinks the rule is, and then give complete feedback to the participant on what the rule actually is. Be sure to get the participant's introspections of what he or she had in mind for every string that the participant generated. This will give you valuable information about the nature of the reasoning that the participant was using in generating the strings.

The data of greatest interest in this experiment are the particular strings that your participant provides to you. If the participant is making best use of the scientific method, he or she should give you strings that disconfirm some hypothesis that the participant has in mind about the rule. However, what you're very likely to find once you debrief the participant is that the strings generated are ones that confirm some hypothesis under consideration, rather than ones that attempt to disconfirm some hypothesis. In other words, the participant is very likely hoping to get a positive answer from you about each string that he or she suggests instead of a negative answer. Of course, a positive answer doesn't give the participant critically valuable information. For example, suppose the participant asked you about the following three strings:

4, 6, 8, 10
12, 14, 16
20, 22, 24, 26

You would reply positively to each of these strings, and the participant might infer from this that the rule is "increasing by 2s." This is a common problem in confirmatory reasoning: You accumulate positive evidence that doesn't limit the space of possibilities in a valuable way. You get drawn into a hypothesis by the accumulating evidence without considering alternative hypotheses. Also, of course, the participant could go on interminably with examples of this sort, and you would answer positively each time, but the participant would be getting no closer to the truth with these examples (the truth being the rule that strings just have to increase in magnitude).

The phenomenon illustrated by this exercise is one to which scientists have to constantly be alert. They must guard against confirmatory reasoning in favor of seeking disconfirming evidence. Apparently, it is not natural for people to do this, but scientists and lay people alike must make a conscious effort to do so, or they will be lured into confirming beliefs about the world that will often turn out to be false in the end.

Statistics: The Description, Organization, and Interpretation of Data

Learning Objectives

1. What is the topic of statistics about? Why are statistical tests needed in psychological research?

DESCRIBING THE DATA

2. What is scaling? Why is it important to understand the types of number scales?

Categorical and ordinal scales
3. Understand what categorical and ordinal scales are. Be able to describe the arithmetic operations permitted and not permitted with each. Give examples of these scales.

Interval scales
4. What is the important feature of an interval scale? Give examples.

Ratio scales
5. What defines a ratio scale? What are some examples of ratio scales?
6. How do interval and ratio scales differ? What arithmetic operation is permitted with ratio scales?

ORGANIZING THE DATA

The frequency distribution
7. How is a frequency distribution created from the raw scores in an experiment? To get practice in constructing a frequency distribution, plot one for the following heights (in inches) of males in a small class: 72, 72, 68, 66, 74, 73, 69, 69, 70, 67, 66, 73, 72.

Measures of central tendency
8. What is a measure of central tendency and why is it useful? Describe the three measures of central tendency that are commonly used. Calculate these three quantities for the scores given above.
9. What does it mean for a distribution to be skewed or symmetrical?

Measures of variability
10. Describe what the range of a group of scores is, and describe why the range has limited utility. What is the range for the scores given in Question 7 above?
11. What is the variance of a set of scores? Why is it a useful measure of variability? Calculate the variance and standard deviation of the scores given above.

Converting scores to compare them
12. How are percentile ranks calculated, and how do they permit comparison of scores obtained from different distributions?
13. What is a z-score? Why is it useful for comparing scores from two distributions?
14. How are z-scores and percentile ranks similar?

The normal distribution
15. What are the characteristics of a normal distribution?
16. Be able to convert a z-score into a rank for a variable that has a normal distribution.
17. Understand the principle that can explain when a variable will be distributed normally. To do this you should roughly understand how a repeated two-alternative event will approximate a normal distribution.

DESCRIBING THE RELATION BETWEEN TWO VARIABLES: CORRELATION

Positive and negative correlation
18. What is the meaning of positive and negative correlation?
19. How is a scatter plot constructed? What does it show? What does a line-of-best-fit have to do with a scatter plot?

The correlation coefficient
20. Understand what various values of r mean.
21. How is a correlation coefficient computed? Do you understand the logic of this computation?

Interpreting and misinterpreting correlations
22. Give examples of cases for which a correlation cannot be interpreted in terms of one variable causing changes in another. What is the danger in interpreting correlations in terms of cause-effect?

INTERPRETING THE DATA

Accounting for variability

23. What does it mean to account for variance?
24. Understand how variance is accounted for in actual experiments, such as the examples given in the text.
25. How does one account for variance in correlational data?

Hypothesis testing

26. Describe the procedure by which you could determine whether a particular test score does or does not belong to a distribution of scores.
27. What are null and alternative hypotheses? How do critical ratios allow us to rule out one of these hypotheses?
28. What trade-off is involved in the decision about where to set the cut-off for the critical ratio?
29. Be able to describe how hypotheses about differences between means can be tested using a critical ratio.

30. What is the relationship between a sample mean and a population mean?
31. What is a standard error, and what role does it play in testing hypotheses about sample means?
32. Be sure to follow the statistical analysis of the imagery experiment presented in the text.
33. Explain what it means to be reasonably confident that the mean of the population will fall within a specified interval.

Some implications of statistical inference

34. Explain how statistical conclusions are probabilistic. How does this affect these conclusions both about population means, and about individuals?
35. Based on your knowledge of how to compute a critical ratio, describe how sample size affects a statistical conclusion. When may statistical and psychological significance differ?

Programmed Exercises

1. The collection, organization, and interpretation of numerical data comprise the topic of _____.   statistics

DESCRIBING THE DATA

2. When all subjects in a group perform differently, or when the same subject performs differently on different occasions, we say that the data contain _____.   variability

3. Differences among subjects _____ groups and _____ groups are the two sources of variability that are analyzed by statistical methods.   between, within

4. The assignment of numbers to events is called _____.   scaling

5. The type of _____ that numbers represent is defined by which arithmetic operations are permitted on those numbers.   scale

6. The assignment of students in a school to the first, second, or third of three kindergartens would involve the use of a(n) _____ scale.   categorical (nominal)

7. If you ask someone to rank order four cola drinks from most to least preferred, you would be using a(n) _____ scale.   ordinal

8. The Fahrenheit scale of temperature is a(n) _____ scale as indicated by the fact that the difference between 30° and 35° equals the difference between 75° and 80°.   interval

9. The scale of length in feet is a(n) _____ scale; thus, we can say that a board of four feet is twice as long as a board of two feet.   ratio

ORGANIZING THE DATA

10. A _____ _____ of birthweight could be represented by a _____, a graph of the numbers of people in a sample who are born at various weights in the range to be studied.   frequency distribution, histogram

11. There are three major measures of central tendency, the _____, _____, and _____.   mean, median mode

12. The distribution of reaction times in an experiment is likely to be _____, since there will be none below 0, many short ones, and fewer and fewer long ones.   skewed

13. The distribution of heights of males is _____ because there are just as many males with heights above the mean as there are males with heights below the mean.   symmetrical

14. The _____ is a measure of variation that is defined as the difference between the highest and lowest scores.   range

15. The _____ is a measure of variation that takes account of each score's deviation from the mean. Its square root is called the _____ _____.

variance
standard deviation

16. The _____ _____ of a score is the percentage of scores that lie below it.

percentile rank

17. A _____-_____ expresses scores in terms of units of standard deviations from a mean.

z-score (standard score)

18. The heights of females in a population form a _____ _____, one in which there are equal frequencies of heights on both sides of the mean.

normal distribution

DESCRIBING THE RELATION BETWEEN TWO VARIABLES: CORRELATION

19. If two dependent variables are related to one another, they are said to be _____.

correlated

20. If we ranked the top 10 runners in the world so that the top runner was ranked 1 and the 10th runner was ranked 10, and if we based these ranks on time to run the 1500 meter race, there would by definition be a _____ correlation between rank and time.

positive

21. On the average, the faster one can complete each item on an aptitude test, the higher one's score, assuming that one doesn't sacrifice accuracy. There is thus a _____ correlation between time per item and test score.

negative

22. Plotting two dependent variables, one on the abscissa and one on the ordinate, yields a graph that shows the relationship between the variables. This is called a _____ _____.

scatter plot

23. A line fit to the points of the graph described in Question 22 is called a _____-_____-_____-_____.

line-of-best-fit

24. A _____ _____ of −1 indicates that there is a perfect _____ correlation between two variables.

correlation coefficient, negative

INTERPRETING THE DATA

25. We say that we have _____ variance when we can attribute some of the variability in a set of scores to a particular factor.

explained (accounted for)

26. Squaring a correlation coefficient yields a proportion of _____ that is explained.

variance

27. The _____ _____ of a test statistic is usually set at 2 so that the probability of choosing the alternative hypothesis when the null hypothesis is, in fact, correct is quite small (one chance in twenty).

critical ratio

28. The standard deviation of a distribution of sample means is called the _____ _____.

standard error

29. The _____ _____ is the range within which we can be fairly confident the actual population mean will fall.

confidence interval

30. There are two important characteristics of statistical conclusions: They are affected by sample _____, and they are _____.

size, probabilistic

Self Test

1. If there are 100 questions on a test, with each question worth one point, then the set of scores from 0 to 100 constitutes:
   a. a nominal scale
   b. an ordinal scale
   c. an interval scale
   d. a ratio scale

2. Suppose you have three children and measure their heights: 49, 47, and 40 inches. These measurements constitute:
   a. a nominal scale
   b. an ordinal scale
   c. an interval scale
   d. a ratio scale

3. If you assert that a jar has twice as much orange juice as another jar, you are making an implicit assertion about:
   a. a categorical scale
   b. an ordinal scale
   c. an interval scale
   d. a ratio scale

4. There are ten digits on a touch-tone phone. If we compare two phone numbers, say 784-5183 and 982-2161, we must use which of the following scales to make that comparison?
   a. nominal scale
   b. ordinal scale
   c. interval scale
   d. ratio scale

5. The results of an examination are graphed so that each score is listed in order on the abscissa, and the number of students receiving that score is plotted on the ordinate. Such a graph:
   a. is a frequency distribution
   b. is a histogram of the scores
   c. is not a scattergram
   d. could be a normal distribution
   e. all of the above

6. Suppose the graph in Question 5 turned out to look like the graph below. From this we could conclude that:

   a. the mean is greater than the median
   b. the mode is 50
   c. the variance is 0
   d. the test was statistically significant
   e. none of the above

7. Suppose the graph in Question 5 turned out to look like the graph that follows. From this we could conclude that:

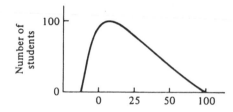

   a. the distribution is normal
   b. the median is lower than the mean
   c. the students with a score of 75 are in the 75th percentile
   d. the mode is 100
   e. none of the above

8. For the following five scores, 1, 2, 3, 4, 5:
   a. the median is 3
   b. the mean is 3
   c. the variance is 2
   d. all of the above
   e. a and b but not c

9. Variability is to central tendency as variance is to:
   a. correlation
   b. z-score
   c. mean
   d. standard deviation

10. All of the following could be measures of variation in a set of scores except:
   a. mean-median
   b. highest score-lowest score
   c. sum of (each score-mean)^2
   d. average of highest two scores-average of lowest two scores

11. Consider two examinations: On one, the mean is 50, the standard deviation is 5, and your score is 65. On the other, the mean is 50, the standard deviation is 2, and your score is 60. Which of the following is true?
   a. Your percentile rank is higher on the second test.
   b. Your z-score is higher on the second test.
   c. You can meaningfully compare your z-scores on the two tests.
   d. You cannot meaningfully compare your raw scores on the two tests.
   e. All of the above.

12. If a set of scores on an exam has a mean of 75 and a standard deviation of 10, then:
   a. the distribution must be normal
   b. the distribution must be symmetric
   c. a score of 50 corresponds to a z-score of –2.5
   d. a z-score of 1.0 equals a test score of 75

13. If SAT scores have a mean of 500 and a standard deviation of 100, and if IQ scores have a mean of 100 and a standard deviation of 15, then with an SAT score of 650 and an IQ score of 115:
   a. the z-score for IQ will be higher than the z-score for SAT
   b. the percentile score for IQ will be higher than the percentile score for SAT
   c. both of the above
   d. the percentile score for IQ will be 84
   e. the scores on the two tests will not be comparable since the tests differ

14. If we found a correlation coefficient of –.88 between reaction time and performance on a test of motor skill, we could conclude that:
   a. a high score on the test of motor skill predicts a fast reaction time
   b. a high score on the test of motor skill predicts a slow reaction time
   c. motor skill causes people to have faster reaction times
   d. reaction time and motor skill are largely unrelated

15. In the scatter plot shown below:

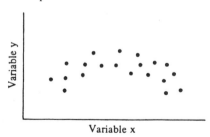

   a. there is no relationship between x and y
   b. the correlation coefficient is statistically significant
   c. the correlation coefficient is close to 0
   d. variable x is the independent variable

16. If a line-of-best-fit for a scatter plot were flat, then:
   a. the correlation would be 1
   b. the correlation would be 0
   c. the correlation would not be significant
   d. we know nothing about the correlation until we calculate it

17. Which of the following correlation coefficients shows the strongest inverse relationship between variables x and y?
    a. .82
    b. −.74
    c. 0
    d. −1.14

18. If the correlation between a parent's and his children's scores on a test of motor skills were .70, then we would know that:
    a. 70 percent of the variability of the children's score is accounted for by the parent's scores
    b. 70 percent of the variability of the parent's score is accounted for by the children's scores
    c. children's motor skills are caused by the skills of their parents
    d. none of the above

19. An experiment is performed to determine whether eating breakfast improves one's test performance. Two groups are given tests, one group after eating a good breakfast, one after no breakfast. Consider the following hypothesis: Eating breakfast has no effect on test performance. This hypothesis:
    a. can be evaluated only probabilistically
    b. is called the "alternative" hypothesis
    c. cannot be evaluated in this experiment
    d. is assessed by examining within-subject variability

20. In the experiment of Question 19 which of the following would be necessary in order for us to believe that eating breakfast enhances test performance?
    a. The sample must be normal.
    b. The sample must be statistically significant.
    c. The between-subject variance must be larger than the within-subject variance.
    d. All of the above.
    e. none of the above

21. Suppose you were to discover a hospital in which there were eight new births each day, and you wished to test the hypothesis that this hospital had more births per day than the average hospital of its size. To do this we would need to know:
    a. the correlations among births at all the hospitals in question
    b. the mean, standard deviation, and number of hospitals in the comparison group
    c. only the standard error of the births in the comparison group
    d. none of the above

22. Two hospitals report eight births per day average with a standard deviation of ten births. For hospital A, this average was computed over 25 days; for hospital B, it was computed over 400 days. The standard errors of births in these hospitals:
    a. are equal
    b. are 2 in hospital A and .5 in hospital B
    c. are not comparable because of the difference in number of days
    d. none of the above

23. If a sample mean is 20, its standard deviation is 30, and the number of participants in the sample is 9, then:
    a. you can be fairly confident that the sample is normal
    b. a participant with a score of 25 is in the fifth percentile
    c. a score of 17 would be equal to a z-score of 1
    d. you can be fairly sure that the population from which this sample was drawn has a mean greater than 0

24. Suppose you're trying to predict whether a Republican or Democratic candidate will win a particular senatorial race. You conduct a poll of the relevant voters and discover that 53% would vote for the Republican and 47% for the Democrat. Who do you think will win?
    a. You can be reasonably confident that the Republican will win.
    b. You can be reasonably confident that the Democrat will win.
    c. Given the polling data, it's not clear who will win.
    d. There isn't enough information to make a prediction one way or the other.

Answer Key for Self Test

1.	d p. B3	13.	d p. B10
2.	d p. B3	14.	a p. B13
3.	d p. B3	15.	c p. B12
4.	a p. B2	16.	b p. B12
5.	e p. B4	17.	b p. B13
6.	e pp. B5–B8, B19	18.	d pp. B13, B14, B15
7.	b p. B5	19.	a p. B23
8.	d p. B5	20.	c p. B20
9.	c pp. B6–B8	21.	b pp. B19, B20, B21
10.	a pp. B6–B8	22.	b p. B21
11.	e pp. B8, B9, B10	23.	d p. B22
12.	c pp. B8, B9	24.	d pp. B23, B24

Investigating Psychological Phenomena

APPLYING STATISTICAL CONCEPTS

This exercise provides an opportunity for you to apply some of the statistical concepts described in the text. Reconsider the experiment described in the text in which participants are tested for recall performance on lists of twenty words with and without instructions to form images. Imagine that twenty participants had been run in this experiment—the ten described in the test plus ten others. The data of all these participants are presented in Table 1 below. In the first column are the recall scores with imagery instructions; the second column contains recall scores when no imagery instructions were provided; the third column is the difference between the first two, the amount of improvement. Finally, the fourth column contains the results of a test of imagery ability that was given to each of the participants in this hypothetical experiment (scores on this test could range from 0 to 40). Using the data in this table, perform the following tabulations and analyses.

TABLE 1

Participant	Score with imagery	Score without imagery	Improvement	Test of imagery ability
Alphonse	20	5	15	30
Betsy	24	9	15	26
Cheryl	20	5	15	27
Davis	18	9	9	21
Earl	22	6	16	33
Fred	19	11	8	26
Germaine	20	8	12	32
Hortense	19	11	8	38
Imogeñe	17	7	10	30
Jerry	21	9	12	27
Kerry	17	8	9	29
Linda	20	16	4	24
Moe	20	10	10	26
Nicolas	16	12	4	22
Orry	24	7	17	36
Penelope	22	9	13	32
Quarton	25	21	4	23
Ronald	21	14	7	26
Steven	19	12	7	24
Terry	23	13	10	28

1. Create frequency histograms for the recall data on the two unlabeled sets of axes below. The left graph is for the recall scores with imagery instructions, and the right is for recall scores without imagery instructions. Note that you must decide what specific values to place on each axis for each graph.

Frequency histograms

2. Calculate the mean, median, and mode of each of the distributions whose scores you have plotted above.
3. Calculate the range and standard deviation of each of these distributions.
4. Analyze the improvement scores to test the hypothesis that imagery instructions lead to better recall performance than no imagery instructions. To do this, you must compute a critical ratio that evaluates the sample mean of the improvement scores against the population mean for the null hypothesis (no improvement). Is this critical ratio larger than 2.0? If so, how do we interpret the improvement scores?

5. Examine the relationship between the improvement scores and performance on the test of imagery ability in two ways. First, create a scatter plot on the axes presented below. Second, compute a correlation coefficient between these sets of scores. Is there a relation between the variables? How would you interpret this relation psychologically?

Now that you have completed your analyses, you should turn to the next page to examine the correct answers and compare them to your own answers.

Answers to Statistical Exercise

1.

2. Imagery instructions
   Mean = 20.35
   Median = 20
   Mode = 20
   No imagery instructions
   Mean = 10.10
   Median = 9
   Mode = 9

3. Imagery instructions
   Range = 9
   Standard deviation = 2.46
   No imagery instructions
   Range = 16
   Standard deviation = 3.89

4. Critical ratio =

   $$\frac{\text{sample mean} - \text{population mean by null hypothesis}}{\text{standard error of the mean}}$$

   standard error of the mean

   $$= \frac{\text{standard deviation}}{\sqrt{N}}$$

   $$= \frac{4.05}{\sqrt{20}}$$

   $$= .91$$

   $$\text{critical ratio} = \frac{10.25 - 0}{.91}$$

   $$= 11.26$$

This critical ratio is much larger than 2.0; therefore, we may conclude that there is a statistically significant improvement in recall scores comparing no imagery to imagery instructions.

5. Scatter plot

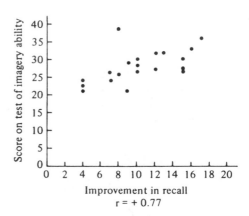

The correlation coefficient, r, is + 0.77.

Both the scatter plot and the correlation coefficient indicate that there is substantial relationship between the variables. We might propose the following hypothesis to account for this relationship. Participants with a better imagery ability are better able to form mental images in the memory task, and thus perform better. Our hypothesis must remain tentative, however, since we are not permitted to draw cause-effect conclusions from correlational data.

APPENDIX 3

Report Sheets

On the following pages you will find the report sheets for several of the experiments in the preceding chapters. If your instructor wants to collect the data for these experiments, use these report sheets. You can cut them out and hand them in to your instructor.

Chapter 3

REPORT SHEET—HEART RATE

Data from three participants (A, B, and C)

Instruction and time	A	B	C
"Begin and Relax"			
00:00–0:30			
0:45–1:15			
"Increase physical activity"			
1:30–2:00			
2:15–2:45			
"Relax"			
3:00–3:30			
3:45–4:15			
"Increase mental activity"			
4:30–5:00			
5:15–5:45			
"Relax"			
6:00–6:30			
6:45–7:15			

List for each participant the basic situation that they imagined in the "increase" minutes.

	Physical	Mental
A	_____	_____
B	_____	_____
C	_____	_____

Chapter 2

REPORT SHEET—NERVE IMPULSE

Practice Trial 1 ankle = Time in seconds*

Part I Trial 1 ankle = _____

Trial 2 ankle = _____

Trial 3 ankle = _____

Trial 4 ankle = _____

Trial 5 ankle = _____

Part II Trial 1 upper arm = _____

Trial 2 upper arm = _____

Trial 3 upper arm = _____

Trial 4 upper arm = _____

Trial 5 upper arm = _____

Test

Part III Trial 1 ankle time = _____

$\div\ 25$ = _____ (a)

Trial 2 upper arm time = _____

$\div\ 25$ = _____ (b)

Trial 3 upper arm time = _____

$\div\ 25$ = _____ (c)

Trial 4 ankle time = _____

$\div\ 25$ = _____ (d)

$\dfrac{a + d}{2}$ = _____ (average ankle time)

$\dfrac{b + c}{2}$ = _____ (average upper arm time)

Average ankle time – average upper arm time = _____

(difference 1)

(1) Distance of ankle to base of neck

(for third tallest person) = _____

(2) Distance of upper arm to base of neck

(for third tallest person) = _____

Distance 1 – distance 2 = _____ (difference 2)

$\dfrac{\text{difference 2}}{\text{difference 1}}$ = (speed of nerve impulse)

*Record time accurate to .1 second.

Chapter 4

REPORT SHEET—LEARNED TASTE AVERSIONS

Number of participants questioned _____

Number of participants with aversions _____

Number of participants who confirm Garcia's notions _____

Summarize the results from all of your participants below. You decide which questions are relevant to each feature of learned taste aversion, and summarize your results with respect to each of the features listed below.

BELONGINGNESS Relevant questions (Nos.)

_____

_____

_____

ONE-TRIAL LEARNING Relevant questions (Nos.)

_____

_____

_____

LONG CS-US INTERVAL Relevant questions (Nos.)

_____

_____

_____

NOVELTY EFFECT Relevant questions (Nos.)

_____

_____

_____

"IRRATIONALITY" Relevant questions (Nos.)

_____

_____

_____

OTHER INTERESTING RESULTS

_____

_____

_____

Chapter 4

REPORT SHEET—MAZE LEARNING

Trial	Time	Number of of errors
1	_____	_____
2	_____	_____
3	_____	_____
4	_____	_____
5	_____	_____

(using paper with cut-out hole)

Chapter 5

REPORT SHEET—MEASURING BRIGHTNESS CONTRAST

Background values:	1	3	4	5	7	10
Matching value 1:	_____	_____	_____	_____	_____	_____
Matching value 2:	_____	_____	_____	_____	_____	_____
Matching value 3:	_____	_____	_____	_____	_____	_____
Total matching value:	_____	_____	_____	_____	_____	_____
Average matching value:	_____	_____	_____	_____	_____	_____

Chapter 7

REPORT SHEET—IMAGERY INSTRUCTIONS

Answer sheet for List 1

1. _____
2. _____
3. _____
4. _____
5. _____
6. _____
7. _____
8. _____
9. _____
10. _____
11. _____
12. _____
13. _____
14. _____
15. _____
16. _____
17. _____
18. _____
19. _____
20. _____

Answer sheet for List 2

1. _____
2. _____
3. _____
4. _____
5. _____
6. _____
7. _____
8. _____
9. _____
10. _____
11. _____
12. _____
13. _____
14. _____
15. _____
16. _____
17. _____
18. _____
19. _____
20. _____

Chapter 9

REPORT SHEET—IMPLICIT LEARNING

1. _____   9. _____   17. _____
2. _____   10. _____   18. _____
3. _____   11. _____   19. _____
4. _____   12. _____   20. _____
5. _____   13. _____   21. _____
6. _____   14. _____   22. _____
7. _____   15. _____   23. _____
8. _____   16. _____   24. _____

Participant's statement of rule: _____

_____

_____

_____

_____

_____

_____

_____

_____

Number of correct responses out of 24: _____

Chapter 10

REPORT SHEET—PERSONAL SPACE

One person elevator	Number of cases with participants in predicted place (7 or 9)	_____/15
Two person elevator	Number of cases with participants in predicted place (7 or 9)	_____/15
Two person elevator	Number of cases with participants in noncontiguous squares	_____/15

Chapter 8

REPORT SHEET—THE STROOP EFFECT

Experiment 1

Color patch list

List 1 _____ sec. _____ errors

List 3 _____ sec. _____ errors

List 5 _____ sec. _____ errors

List 7 _____ sec. _____ errors

List 9 _____ sec. _____ errors

Average = _____ sec.

Total errors = _____

Letter string list

List 2 _____ sec. _____ errors

List 4 _____ sec. _____ errors

List 6 _____ sec. _____ errors

List 8 _____ sec. _____ errors

List 10 _____ sec. _____ errors

Average = _____ sec.

Total errors = _____

Experiment 2

Neutral words

List 1 _____ sec. _____ errors

List 3 _____ sec. _____ errors

List 5 _____ sec. _____ errors

List 7 _____ sec. _____ errors

List 9 _____ sec. _____ errors

Average = _____ sec.

Total errors = _____

Color words

List 2 _____ sec. _____ errors

List 4 _____ sec. _____ errors

List 6 _____ sec. _____ errors

List 8 _____ sec. _____ errors

List 10 _____ sec. _____ errors

Average = _____ sec.

Total errors = _____

Experiment 3

Neutral words

List 1 _____ sec. _____ errors

List 3 _____ sec. _____ errors

List 5 _____ sec. _____ errors

List 7 _____ sec. _____ errors

List 9 _____ sec. _____ errors

Average = _____ sec.

Total errors = _____

Color referent words

List 2 _____ sec. _____ errors

List 4 _____ sec. _____ errors

List 6 _____ sec. _____ errors

List 8 _____ sec. _____ errors

List 10 _____ sec. _____ errors

Average = _____ sec.

Total errors = _____

Chapter 11

REPORT SHEET—IMPRESSIONS

Percent of participants checking favorable adjective at left

	Asch's data		Your data	
	Group A	Group B	Group A	Group B
Adjective pair	(24 students)	(34 students)	(__ students)	(__ students)
generous	24	10		
wise	18	17		
happy	32	5		
good-natured	18	0		
humorous	52	21		
sociable	56	27		
popular	35	14		
reliable	84	91		
good-looking	74	35		
serious	97	100		
restrained	64	9		
honest	80	79		

Chapter 13

REPORT SHEET—CONSERVATION OF NUMBER

1. More blue _____
   More red _____
   Both equal _____
2. More blue _____
   More red _____
   Both equal _____
3. More blue _____
   More red _____
   Both equal _____
4. More blue _____
   More red _____
   Both equal _____

5. More blue _____
   More red _____
   Both equal _____
6. More blue _____
   More red _____
   Both equal _____
7. More blue _____
   More red _____
   Both equal _____
8. More blue _____
   More red _____
   Both equal _____

Chapter 18

REPORT SHEET—DEPRESSION

Self-rating of mood now (enter number) _____

Self-rating of mood over last twelve months (enter number) _____

Number of negative events recalled _____

Number of positive events recalled _____

Negative minus positive events _____

Negative plus positive events _____

Chapter 14

REPORT SHEET—SEX DIFFERENCES

	Your data* (combined with classmates' data)			
	Males		Females	
Item	#	%	#	%
1. Killing cockroach	_____	_____	_____	_____
2. Queen Anne's lace (correct answer: flower)	_____	_____	_____	_____
3. Using word "shit" (fewer than 5 times)	_____	_____	_____	_____
4. Sew clothes	_____	_____	_____	_____
5. Intercourse only after spiritual love	_____	_____	_____	_____
6. Nude in locker room	_____	_____	_____	_____
7. Crying frequently (very often, often, or only with good reason)	_____	_____	_____	_____
8. Feel like smashing things	_____	_____	_____	_____
9. Chest measurement	_____	_____	_____	_____
10. Change tire	_____	_____	_____	_____
11. Playing radio	_____	_____	_____	_____
12. Prefer dominance in relationship	_____	_____	_____	_____
13. Overweight	_____	_____	_____	_____
14. Washing hair when depressed	_____	_____	_____	_____
15. Sleep in nude	_____	_____	_____	_____
16. Closest parent (mother)	_____	_____	_____	_____
17. Keep room neat	_____	_____	_____	_____

*Tabulate your results below in the following way. For the "yes" or "no" questions (e.g., Item 1), add up the number of participants who answered "yes." Then calculate what percentage answered "Yes." For the "true" or "false" questions (e.g., Item 8), record those who answered "True." For other items (e.g., Item 2), add up the number of participants whose answers are the same as those indicated in parentheses under "Item" (e.g., Item 2—flower).

List the femaleness scores of all of your participants:

Males: _____ _____ _____ _____ _____ _____ _____ _____ _____ _____

_____ _____ _____ _____ _____ _____ _____ _____ _____ _____

Females: _____ _____ _____ _____ _____ _____ _____ _____ _____ _____

_____ _____ _____ _____ _____ _____ _____ _____ _____ _____

Copyrights and Acknowledgments

Grateful acknowledgment is made to: F. Garb, A. Stunkard, and the *American Journal of Psychiatry* to adapt from Garb and Stunkard, "Taste aversions in man," *American Journal of Psychiatry* 131 (1974):1204–1207; W. Epstein, I. Rock, and the *American Journal of Psychology* to adapt from Epstein, W., and Rock, I., "Perceptual set as an artifact of recency," *American Journal of Psychology* 73 (1960):214–228; J. R. Stroop and the *Journal of Experimental Psychology* to adapt from J. R. Stroop, "Studies in interference in serial verbal reactions," *Journal of Experimental Psychology* 18 (1935): 643–662; A. S. Reber and the *Journal of Verbal Learning and Verbal Behavior* to adapt from A. S. Reber, "Implicit learning of artificial grammars," *Journal of Verbal Learning and Verbal Behavior* 6 (1967):858–863; S. E. Asch and the *Journal of Abnormal and Social Psychology* to adapt from S. E. Asch, "Forming impressions of personality," *Journal of Abnormal and Social Psychology* 41 (1946):258–290.

Illustrations

Page 2 Bugelski, B. R., and Alampay, D. A., "The role of frequency in developing perceptual sets," *Canadian Journal of Psychology* 15 (1961): 205–211. Adapted by permission of the Canadian Psychological Association.

Page 12 *bottom* and page 34 Keeton, W. T., *Biological science*, 4th edition. New York: W. W. Norton & Company, Inc., 1986. Copyright © 1986, 1980, 1979, 1972, 1967 by W. W. Norton & Company, Inc.

Page 20 Hodgkin, A. L., and Huxley, A. F. "Action potentials recorded from inside nerve fibers," *Nature* 144 (1939):710–711. Adapted by permission.

Page 32 Harlow, H. F., "Learning and satiation of response in intrinsically motivated complex puzzle performance in monkeys," *Journal of Comparative and Physiological Psychology* 43 (1950):289–294.

Page 41 Reproduced by permission of the publishers from Köhler, W., *The mentality of apes*, London, England: Routledge & Kegan Paul Ltd., 1976.

Page 42 *bottom* Pavlov, I. P., *Lectures on conditioned reflexes*, vol. 1. New York: International Publishers, Co., Inc. 1928. Adapted by permission of International Publishers Co., Inc.

Page 44 From Spooner, A., and Kellogg, W. N., "The backward conditioning curve," *American Journal of Psychology* 60 (1947): 321–334. Copyright © 1947 by The University of Illinois Press. Reprinted by permission of the publisher.

Page 74 From James J. Gibson, *The perception of the visible world*. Boston, Mass.: Houghton Mifflin Co., 1950.

Page 75 Photograph by William Vandivert. From *Scientific American*, April 1960. Reprinted with permission of William Vandivert and *Scientific American*.

Pages 76 and 78 Boring, E. G., "A new ambiguous figure," *American Journal of Psychology* 42 (1930): 444–445; and Leeper, R. W., "A study of a neglected portion of the field of learning: The development of sensory organization," *Journal of Genetic Psychology* 46 (1935):41–75.

Page 123 Reprinted from "Reproductive behaviors," by Etkin, E., in *Social behavior and organization among vertebrates* by Etkin, W., by permission of The University of Chicago Press. Copyright 1964 by The University of Chicago.

Page 136 Festinger, L., and Carlsmith, J. M., "Cognitive consequences of forced compliance," *Journal of Abnormal and Social Psychology* 58 (1959):203–210. Copyright 1959 by the American Psychological Association. Reprinted by permission.

Page 164 Nilsson, Lennart, *Behold man*. Boston: Little, Brown, and Company, 1974.

Page 174 Copyright © Hallmark Cards, Inc., used with permission.